BOARDWALK
of DREAMS

BOARDWALK of DREAMS

ATLANTIC CITY
AND THE FATE
OF URBAN AMERICA

BRYANT SIMON

OXFORD
UNIVERSITY PRESS

OXFORD
UNIVERSITY PRESS

Oxford University Press, Inc., publishes works that further
Oxford University's objective of excellence
in research, scholarship, and education.

Oxford   New York
Auckland   Cape Town   Dar es Salaam   Hong Kong   Karachi
Kuala Lumpur   Madrid   Melbourne   Mexico City   Nairobi
New Delhi   Shanghai   Taipei   Toronto

With offices in
Argentina   Austria   Brazil   Chile   Czech Republic   France   Greece
Guatemala   Hungary   Italy   Japan   Poland   Portugal   Singapore
South Korea   Switzerland   Thailand   Turkey   Ukraine   Vietnam

Published by Oxford University Press, Inc.
198 Madison Avenue, New York, New York 10016

www.oup.com

First issued as an Oxford University Press paperback, 2006

Oxford is a registered trademark of Oxford University Press

Library of Congress Cataloging-in-Publication Data
Simon, Bryant.
Boardwalk of dreams : Atlantic City and the fate of urban America / Bryant Simon.
p. cm.
Includes bibliographical references and index.
ISBN-13 978-0-19-516753-5; 978-0-19-530809-9 (pbk.)
ISBN 0-19-516753-8; 0-19-530809-3 (pbk.)
1. Atlantic City (N.J.)—History. 2. Atlantic City (N.J.)—Social conditions.
3. City and town life—New Jersey—Atlantic City—History.
4. Middle class—New Jersey—Atlantic City—History.
5. Atlantic City (N.J.)—Biography. 6. Simon, Bryant.   I. Title.
F144.A8S57   2004
974.9'85—dc22   2004041479

1 3 5 7 9 8 6 4 2

Printed in the United States of America
on acid-free paper

For Annie, Benjamin, and Eli

PREFACE

I didn't grow up in Atlantic City. Born in Pittsburgh, I went to school in Vineland, a city of 50,000 people in the middle of the sandy flatlands of South Jersey with diagonal parking downtown for local farmers' trucks. My family didn't spend their summers in Atlantic City either. But we did occasionally make the thirty-five-mile drive to the shore. When I was twelve, my parents took me to Gordon Alley's in downtown Atlantic City to buy my charcoal-gray Pierre Cardin bar mitzvah suit. In junior high, I went to the Boardwalk a couple of times and rode on rickety bumper cars and ate slices of greasy pizza. After the gambling referendum passed in 1976, my high school math teacher demonstrated the principles of permutations to my class by showing us how to determine the odds at the craps tables. But mostly I stayed away from Atlantic City. Everyone said it was dangerous; the Boardwalk wasn't as busy as Wildwood or Ocean City, and I couldn't get into the casinos to put my newfound knowledge of dice to use, so why go, I thought.

After I went to college, Atlantic City started to become more of a focal point in my life. Several high school friends went to work in the casinos, while I started to spend my summers working in Cape May. Sometimes when the bars closed there, we would drive up the New Jersey Parkway to Atlantic City to listen to casino lounge acts. When the Trieners or Sam Butera played, we went up earlier in the night and stayed longer. My parents took me to see Sammy Davis, Jr., and Willie Nelson in the bigger casinos' show rooms, and every once in a while we headed to a casino buffet to stuff ourselves on Alaskan king crab legs and prime rib.

Then two things happened that brought Atlantic City closer to the center of my life. My family moved its business—Just Four Wheels, a car and truck rental center—to Absecon, a small town outside of Atlantic City. Whenever I stopped by the store, as we called it, my father and brother would send me to pick up customers at the casinos or drop them off at nearby houses and apartments. Late one night during my freshman year of college, my father took me to repossess a car in one of the city's more depleted neighborhoods. Then, in the mid-1980s, my family bought a duplex four blocks from the beach in Ventnor, a shore town just south of Atlantic City.

About then, I also quit smoking, a habit I had picked up working in Cape May restaurants. Trying to clear my lungs, I got up early each morning to ride my bike on the Boardwalk. In many ways, this study of Atlantic City started on those bike rides.

My brother would always say to me, as we headed north from Ventnor to Atlantic City, "Look at the ocean, isn't it great?" "Yes," I would say, but it was the buildings, the Convention Hall, the outlines of the Warner Theater, and Garden and Central piers—the remnants of the past—that caught my eye. But I was watching the present as well. I always slowed down when I saw Celestine Tate Harrington in front of Bally's Park Place Casino. Unable to move her arms or legs, Harrington lay on a gurney and played "Amazing Grace" on an electric organ with the tip of her tongue. I stared at those guys I saw many mornings on the Boardwalk, their suit jackets wrinkled and their hair matted and sandy, screaming into pay phones, "Yeah, that's right. I lost everything, everything! Now come and fucking get me . . . please."

Farther north on the Boardwalk, past the last casino, was another scene that captivated me. Growing up in South Jersey, I had always wanted a house right on the beach, and there, beyond the hotels and piers, was a huge chunk of abandoned beachfront property and beyond that block after block with more holes than houses. Years later, I would learn that this was Pauline's Prairie, an urban renewal site that took its name from the former head of the local housing authority. But on those first rides down the Boardwalk, I just couldn't believe my eyes. How could there be empty spaces right on the beach? How did a city with a convention hall as big as several city blocks end up with a hole as big as ten city blocks? I don't know why these questions fascinated me so much, but they were what got me started asking about Atlantic City.

People told me about the hole and about urban renewal, but they also told me about dressing up in spit-shined loafers and flowered bonnets to go to palace-sized movie theaters. I heard about Jewish numbers runners and about mob hits. I learned about the amusement piers with roller coasters and diving horses and about Louis Armstrong and Louis Prima, the Beatles and Frank Sinatra performing around town.

After my family bought the Ventnor duplex, I took a summer job making sandwiches at Lou's, a vast subterranean deli near the Ventnor–Atlantic City dividing line. Between filling orders for grilled knockwurst and corned beef sandwiches, I heard more Atlantic City stories. The older white people who came into the restaurant got dreamy when they talked about Atlantic City. All of their stories ended with lines like, "You should have seen it back then." Over and over again, I heard about how much fun the Boardwalk was, how classy everything was, how dressed up everybody was, how beautiful and melodious the big bands and singers sounded, and how there was no crime back then, not like now. "Not like now"—that was another common refrain. These people made Atlantic City seem like Disneyland, even better really. Atlantic City sounded to me like a scene from one of those great Frank Sinatra songs: lush, smoky, urbane, cool, and fun. Sometimes I wished I could have spent one night in this now-lost world.

But I heard another side of the story that summer as well. I worked at Lou's with an African American man in his fifties or sixties, who told me about his Atlantic City. He told me about coming from the wrong side of the tracks in Southside, Virginia, about seeing the Boardwalk for the first time and deciding that he was never going back to the South. He told me about earning more money than he had ever seen by making chocolate milkshakes and banana splits for white couples out on dates. He talked about not being allowed to eat where he worked and about not being able to go to some beaches in town. And he told me about seeing Miles Davis play a breakfast show, starting at 6:00 A.M., in front of an all-black audience at a local nightclub.

So this is where I started, with stories, snippets, and snapshots. I had in my head pictures of white couples in formal wear posing in front of nightclub tables littered with empty highball glasses and overflowing ashtrays; postcards of the Boardwalk skyline; images of inexplicable urban decay; sketches of northern-style segregation; and my own memories of driving around and hanging out in the casinos, local bars, and restaurants.

Over the next ten years, I kept coming back to Atlantic City to visit my family, and I kept collecting stories. I also started clipping articles from newspapers and magazines. I picked up a few local histories, but still all I had were fragments, not a narrative that would take me from Sinatra to the hole in the city to the casinos. But I didn't, then, have time to figure out how to connect the dots. I had started graduate school and a dissertation on southern labor history. When this project was behind me, I began to go through the cardboard box in the corner of my office, which was filled with Atlantic City stuff: phone numbers of people my father and brother thought could help me, brochures, pictures, vintage postcards bought at flea markets, and photocopies of dissertations and book chapters. Over the last five years, this box has grown into a wall of boxes and many megabytes of computer notes, as I have tried to make sense of the city's past as a glittery show place, urban tragedy, and casino mecca.

This book is an attempt to finally connect the dots with a clear narrative thread. It tries to explain Atlantic City's history. Like all local histories, it looks beyond this specific place to explore the nation's urban past, the relationship between race and the American Dream, and the tensions between middle-class notions of public space and people's desires for exclusion. But this book is neither a nostalgic coming home nor the observations of a native son. Nor is it a vendetta, my revenge against a place that wronged me in my youth—Atlantic City didn't do this. This is, rather, an account written from up-close—with the help of a lot of locals—by an outsider, someone who has never lived, even for a summer, in Atlantic City proper. Maybe this distance, mixed as it is with an enduring fascination and affection for this place, explains why this is not an uplifting story or a tearful description of the demise of a once-great city. Rather, this is an account of a less-than-perfect place and its role in American culture. And it is, of course, in the end, *my* story of Atlantic City, culled from the stories of thousands of others who walked on the Boardwalk and the city's other Monopoly-familiar streets over the last hundred or so years.

Once again, I chalked up more debts while writing this book than any honest man can pay. The New Jersey Historical Society and the University of Georgia History Department provided financial support. In Atlantic City and the surrounding areas, hundreds of people invited me into their homes, joined me for lunch, and talked to me over the phone and e-mail. Julie Senack and the staff at the Atlantic City Free Public Library opened their arms and their vast collections to me. Local collectors, scholars, and historians Sid Trusty, Tony Kutschera, Allen "Boo" Pergament, and Vicki Gold Levi shared with me their vast materials, memories, and expertise, even if they disagreed, sometimes quite strongly, with my analysis. Over the years, each helped me with fact checking, telling me where things were and where they weren't.

My story of Atlantic City has changed a lot over time. Along the way, friends and colleagues have helped with timely suggestions and pointed critiques. Early in my research and writing, I gave a paper to a faculty seminar at the University of Georgia where Chana Kai Lee, Laura Mason, and Eve Troutt Powell warned me about loving the Frank Sinatra style of the city and the sound of my own words too much. Others from UGA—Monica Chojnacka, Jim Cobb, Josh Cole, Ed Larson, Reinaldo Roman, Susan Rosenbaum, Claudio Saunt, Steve Soper, and Paul Sutter—have listened, read drafts, and pointed me in new directions. At two different junctures, Eugene Moehring and Hal Rothman helped me to rethink my ideas about the gambling city. Marc Stein reminded me to keep reading the historiography and to keep looking for new sources. And my friend—and Tom Joad follower—Bill Deverell heard many first drafts over the phone and usually told me in his gentle way to go back to the drawing board. Jane Dailey and Glenda Gilmore, my co-editors and comrades, checked in on me regularly while Thomas LeBien and Doug Flamming let me talk their ears off at different points as I tried to map out the book's structure. Padmini Jambulapati was a wonderful research assistant, not just because she knew all about libraries, but also because she cared about Atlantic City and its buildings. Toward the end of the project, Matt Lassiter, Max Page, and Sarah Igo provided thoughtful and smart readings of the manuscript. Along the way, José Alvarez, Peter Coclanis, Jeff Cowie, Debbie Doyle, John Dutton, Michael Goldberg, Howard Green, Jim Green, Dave Gutierrez, Lee Gutkind, Beth Hale, Mark Huddle, Steve Kantrowitz, Nancy MacLean, Ichiro Miyata, Pat Morton, David Nasaw, Tom Sugrue, Moshe Sluhovsky, Jonathan Van Meter, and Laura Wexler shared their time and ideas with me. Audiences at the Hagley Museum, Johns Hopkins University, Rutgers University, the University of North Carolina, the University of Texas, Western Carolina University, and University of Pennsylvania asked me hard questions that sharpened the book's arguments. Finally, thanks to Susan Ferber: she gets my vote for the best and most patient editor in the whole wide world. On a snowy March day in New York, she spent five hours with me sitting on rather uncomfortable chairs in a little Japanese restaurant talking about revisions and drawing diagrams of the book's structure. Even after that long afternoon, she retained her enthusiasm for the project.

Jacquelyn Dowd Hall remains a remarkable friend and advisor and an endless source of inspiration. Michael Kwass and Laura Mason, meanwhile, show me all the time how a neighborhood can and should work. Friends, neighbors, research assistants, fans of the Drive-By Truckers, and my kids' best friends, Anne Marshall and Jim Giesen, contributed to this book in more ways than I can count. While she lives a few hours away, Libby McRae is never far and always teaching me about everyday decency and unquestioning friendship. Knowing her and her family is a constant wonder and just plain fun. And my friends Jeffrey Lutzner, Jessica DeGroot, John Shanley, Rachel Shanley, Michael Kline, and Margo Borten are still there.

I have to thank a place as well. I wrote most of this book at the coffee shop around the corner from my house, Jittery Joe's in Five Points. The staff let me sit there for hours on end nursing my coffee, taking up a table for four, and reading all of the stray newspapers. Sometimes they would even play Springsteen for me when I got stuck.

My family surely stood this test of time and energy. My dad and mom, Bob and Susan Simon; my brother and his family, Brad, Sharon, Rebecca, and Max Simon; and my in-laws, Maria and Tom Reardon, embraced this project, just as they embraced me. And then, there is my family in the blue house—Ann Marie Reardon and Benjamin and Eli Simon. They just take my breath away, put a lump in my throat, and make me wonder how I ever got so damn lucky.

CONTENTS

BOARDWALK
of DREAMS

Introduction

Jordan Sayles did not want to go back to his home state of North Carolina, so after graduating from Howard University in the 1930s, he headed for Atlantic City. The New Jersey resort was as familiar as it was different. Reminding him of his southern roots, the movie houses and beaches, restaurants and bars were all segregated. But in contrast to the breadlines snaking through places like Raleigh and Charlotte, the shore town was booming. Hundreds of thousands of people crammed onto the Boardwalk and the beach every weekend. That translated into thousands of jobs. While there were few suitable positions for African American college graduates, there were plenty of opportunities for black men to serve white tourists. Sayles took what was available and started busing tables at the dreamy Moorish-looking Marlborough-Blenheim Hotel. He didn't get paid much there, so to make ends meet, Sayles took a second job, pushing well-dressed white couples down the Boardwalk on one of the city's 4,000 steel-wheeled, white wicker, two- and three-passenger rolling chairs. He kept pushing for the next thirty-five years through much of Atlantic City's reign as the "Queen of Resorts" and the "nation's playground."

Not long after retiring, Jordan Sayles sat down to talk with Cynthia Ringe, a local oral historian. By then it was 1978, the casinos were about to open, and the city was long past its heyday. Every morning, it seemed, the local newspaper ran a story about the planned implosion of one of the city's signature Jazz Age hotels, like the Marlborough-Blenheim. Other accounts told of business closings, foreclosures, and fearless rats taking over abandoned buildings. Just before Sayles taped his recollections, the Federal Bureau of Investigation released its yearly

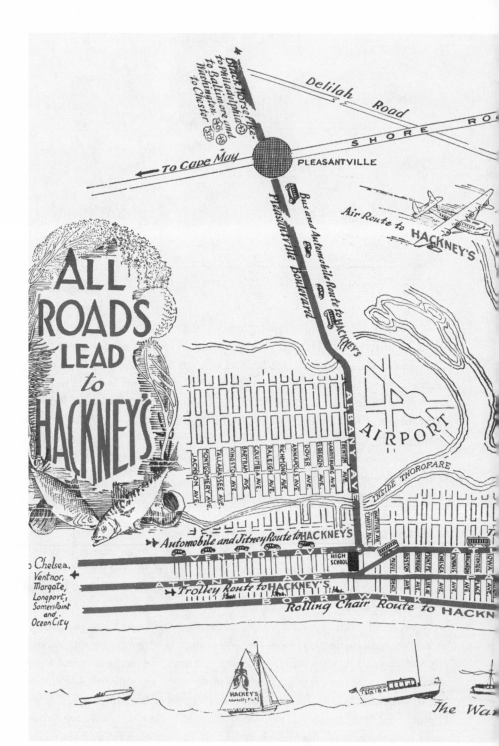

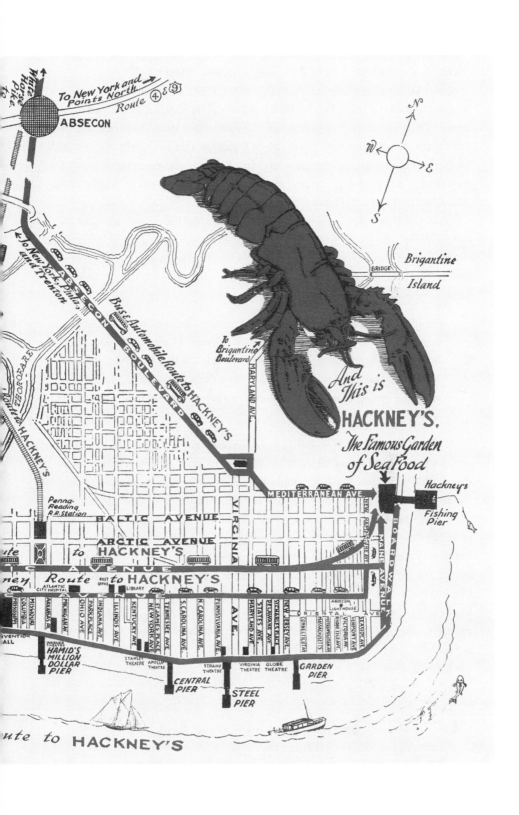

crime statistics. Atlantic City stood near the very top of the federal agency's list of the nation's worst spots for murders, burglaries, and muggings.

Toward the end of the interview, Ringe asked Jordan Sayles why he thought his adopted hometown had fallen on such hard times. He spoke of crime and unsafe streets. Then he told Ringe, "What killed Atlantic City was when they took the pushin' off [the Boardwalk]." Certainly, as Sayles goes on to explain, the removal of the rolling chairs cost hundreds of African American men their jobs and a chance at a decent living. But the oversized strollers were never simply about added incomes and convenient transportation.[1]

Better than the beach, the Boardwalk, the hotels, and the amusement piers, the rolling chairs—those rickshaw-like, wicker baskets on wheels pushed by African American men—captured what the city in its busiest days as a mass resort was all about. Ellie, a hard-boiled, yet still decent, ex-prostitute in a 1978 novel set in Atlantic City, commented:

> People need a place where they can pretend to be something else. They want to believe that if they pretend hard enough, whatever they want to happen will happen. One of my clients used to say that the key to this city was not the beach or the Boardwalk, but in the rolling chairs. You could ride on a rolling chair and dream that you were the kind of person who deserved the rich life.[2]

Atlantic City, like all mass resorts, manufactured and sold an easily consumed and widely shared fantasy.[3] As a setup to the fantasy, city leaders posted confidence builders all over town that made visitors feel safe and secure. Making smart use of ushers and police, bright lights and dress codes, local officials provided white tourists—who made up the overwhelming majority of rolling-chair riders and Boardwalk strollers—with endless chances to act not as they normally did, but as they wanted to be. That's why people came, and still come, to places like Atlantic City. Walking along the Boardwalk, people pretended, noted one of Atlantic City's keenest observers, historian and writer Charles Funnell, "to be better than they were."[4] During the years before the resort slid into decline, the rolling chairs, as Sayles, Ellie, and Funnell understood, represented the city's most accessible and visually arresting fantasy. This is where visitors let down their guards and acted out their dreams.

MAP—HACKNEY'S MAP, *overleaf*
The massive seafood restaurant gave these maps to patrons in the 1940s. Allen "Boo" Pergament Collection (Private Library), Margate, New Jersey.

Once white women and men climbed aboard one of these "temples of content-ment," they caught what the son of a Jewish paint store clerk from Baltimore called "wicker affluence." "Rolling along on flower[ed] cushions, feet up on the lit-tle metal rest, . . . viewing the world without lifting a muscle," this lower middle-class teenager felt an "ineffable superiority" rise in him. On the chair, he was no longer the son of an overworked, insecure, and bitter father. His wealthy uncle, staying at the swank Shelburne Hotel, no longer made him feel self-con-scious about his clothes, his home address, or the jam-packed room without a toi-let or shower that his family rented a couple of blocks from the beach. For this one "bewitching" moment, as a black man pushed him down the Boardwalk, he was on top of the world.[5] He was a rich man, someone rich enough to afford to pay someone else to carry him from place to place. He was someone to be seen, someone comfortable looking at—even looking down at—others. On the rolling chair, he was transformed into a king, a big man, a real American. Atlantic City's ability to stage this public performance of racial dominance, conspicuous con-sumption, class leveling, and social climbing turned the resort into one of the sin-gle most popular tourist destinations in America between 1915 and 1965.

With its middle-class crowds and busy Boardwalk, Atlantic City was Disney-land a generation or so before there was a Disneyland. But the city was more than just a harbinger of what was to come. It was, like Disneyland, a place built on a grand deception. Atlantic City was both real and fake, a big city and a small town, a world of soaring skyscrapers and ocean breezes.[6] From the very start, it was con-ceived as a make-believe place. But this deceit wasn't disguised. No one mistook Atlantic City for his hometown. This knowledge, this participation in such an easy-to-see masquerade, liberated many. With buildings that looked like churches and sand castles on one side and the windswept beaches on the other, tourists felt comfortable acting richer, sillier, sexier, and friendlier than they did in their day-to-day lives. As long as they felt safe and protected, the middle-class millions came to town to participate in this thrilling illusion and fantasy.

"The Jersey coast," wrote travel writer Harrison Rhodes in 1915, "is the most popular part of the American seashore, the most characteristic, the most demo-cratic, the most intensely American."[7] In its red-hot intensity, Atlantic City acted like America on steroids. Along the Boardwalk, the nation's and its citizens' best and worst features were exaggerated and bloated. Teddy Roosevelt once said: "A man would not be a good American citizen if he did not know of Atlantic City." Yet the America that shone so brightly in Atlantic City, like Roosevelt's own poli-tics cast a mean and contradictory shadow.[8]

Atlantic City, like Disneyland, appealed to middle-class Americans and people who wanted to enter the middle class. Because of its location within easy striking distance of Baltimore, Philadelphia, New York, and all of the medium-sized, industrial cities in between and the timing of its reign as the Queen of Resorts, the New Jersey beach town attracted a distinct segment of the middle class. People on their way up made their way to Atlantic City in the first half of the twentieth century. These were men and women for whom, as David Halberstam suggests, the American Dream was about exercising "personal freedom not in social or political terms, but rather in the economic ones."[9] They were people, like the older characters in Philip Roth's masterful novel set in New Jersey, *American Pastoral,* "in love" with their "own good luck" of having landed in the United States.[10] One-time outsiders, these children of immigrant ditch diggers and steel workers felt they had made it in America and into the middle class, and they showed off their newfound inclusion in this national community based on comfort, conformity, and consumption—even more than on citizenship—by coming to Atlantic City.[11]

In August 1921, only a month before the very first Miss America Pageant, California senator Hiram Johnson and his wife caught a glimpse of these newly minted middle-class families on parade. Trying to escape the sullen heat of summer in Washington, D.C., they checked into the Ritz Carlton Hotel, where they had "everything possible for our convenience and comfort." The Boardwalk, however, offered "a vastly different" experience. Crowds filled the walkway to the bursting point. Yet it was the makeup of the throng more than its size that bothered the lawmaker. "On Labor Day," he wrote, "it was estimated that 350,000 people were in Atlantic City. If this estimate was correct, I am perfectly certain that 249,000 of them were the chosen people. Everywhere, and in everything, the Israelite predominates." He even found a few Jews in the Ritz lobby and dining room, but he explained, "They are the sort that we know, the rich, assertive, self-sufficient." Farther down the Boardwalk, he ran into other Jews: "the short, swarthy men, the squatty, dumpy women, and the innumerable daughters, at an early age bursting into overblown maturity." In these parts of Atlantic City, the senator felt like "a stranger almost in a strange land."[12]

But it was not just well-dressed and swarthy Jews who made up the Boardwalk crowds. There were Greeks and Irish, Italians and Slovaks, even a few Protestants on the promenade as well. Atlantic City drew its visitors from ethnic neighborhoods and crabgrass frontiers, from places populated by people who had, often just recently, made enough money to take a few days off from work, buy some dress-up clothes, and pay to have someone cook for them and push them around in rolling chairs. Johnson's strangers were really the newest recruits to the nation's burgeoning middle class.[13]

Behind the Boardwalk and the beach, a town, and then a small city, grew in Atlantic City to meet the needs and desires of the women and men who served the tourists. Physically, Atlantic City looked like one of those places that today's new urbanists, with their fondness for yesterday's lost city, are busy trying to recreate. It had a bustling downtown, neighborhoods with sidewalks and corner stores, houses with front stoops and garages in the back, and affordable public transportation tying this urban world together.

By the 1970s, the rolling chairs, as Sayles pointed out, were gone, and the city's traditional neighborhoods were crumbling. Atlantic City business and political leaders had by this time lost their ability to manufacture the safe fantasy of racial ascendancy and easy social mobility—a fantasy that had depended on a large supply of underpaid African American workers and control over access to the Boardwalk, downtown stores, movie houses, the beach, and all other public places.[14] Once things changed, the neatly dressed families who had for years spent their summer vacations at the colossal Boardwalk hotels and in cramped neighborhood rooming houses bolted town to consume new fantasies in Disneyland—the fantasy there was of long-lost, safe public spaces—and Las Vegas, where the fantasy sold on the strip was of indulgence and chance.

Eventually, the crowds came back to Atlantic City, or at least to one of the twelve casinos that today tower over the Boardwalk and the salt marshes a couple of miles away. Yet despite providing 43,924 jobs (almost 15,000 more jobs than Atlantic City's total population), $6 billion in investment (more than the total investment in New Jersey's four other major cities combined over the last quarter century), and even more in taxes (the casinos have paid $5.5 billion to the state and currently contribute 80 percent of the city's total property taxes), the gaming industry has not saved Atlantic City. In many ways, the city as a place to live is now worse than ever.[15] Although 35 million people visit the Boardwalk and the casinos each year, the city's main street is all but dead and the neighborhoods are in critical condition. There is no place in the gaming city to see a movie or buy a computer. Until 1996, there wasn't even a supermarket. Metal detectors, steel bars, and a small team of security officers now protect the Thriftway, which sits downtown behind a suburban-style parking lot.[16]

The story of Atlantic City's life, near-death, and recent reincarnation is the story I will tell in this book. This could be a tragic, nostalgia-filled tale of the breakdown of a glorious city and of its reemergence as a gilded gambling capital. But as the rolling-chair ride suggests, that perspective would celebrate, at least implicitly, segregation and *Gone with the Wind*–style race relations. There is, therefore, another story to tell; this one is about Atlantic City and the making of the nation's urban spaces. The main characters in this narrative are the tourist entrepreneurs—the pier owners, hotel architects, casino managers, and rolling-chair operators—and the white middle-class millions they tried to lure to town.

When mass culture and mass resorts catch on with their target audience, it is, as historian of the middle class Loren Baritz points out, "an obviously useful clue about what is on the people's mind."[17] Atlantic City functioned like all mass resorts—indeed, all products of mass culture—do. It prospered as long as it soothed the anxieties and stirred the desires of its audience. When it didn't, it struggled to survive.

Dressed in their mink coats and sharply pleated linen pants, white middle-class women and men flooded into town from the 1910s to the 1960s. After that, they abandoned the city. Why? What did the Boardwalk millions get in Atlantic City (and on the rolling chairs) before 1965? Why couldn't Atlantic City keep giving them what they wanted after that? What can we learn about these people—these Americans—from this disappearing act, this white flight of tourists and then residents? Just as important, why did some of them and their children come back to the gaming city? The answers to these questions tell us much about our cities and the nation and about how the vast middle class imagined and practiced democracy on a day-to-day basis.

The white middle-class millions of the much-revered "greatest generation" and beyond were people who equated making it in America with climbing up the economic ladder. At the same time, they were people who thrilled at being pushed down the Boardwalk by African American men. They were people who valued exclusion ahead of inclusion, status before equality, and walled-off public spaces over truly open ones. Few, it seems, had an expansive notion of democratic space. Although they might have objected to legal, southern-style segregation, when it came to public spaces—their public spaces—they demanded exclusion. Most, in fact, saw the democracy of the streets as finite. With only a fixed amount of space to go around, they clung to what they had. Rather than share the social and cultural benefits of democracy with others, they hoarded as much as they could, and that included the wonders of the Boardwalk and the street life of their neighborhoods. Purged of nostalgia, the story of Atlantic City's glory days is, then, a story about the possibilities and limits of American democracy. And the city's present follows a similar pattern. Exclusion, updated and tailored to fit the shifting desires of the middle class, remains crucial to the casino city. Understanding this resort and its history, therefore, means seeing how millions of individual decisions about inclusion and exclusion, which together trace the outlines of the collective consciousness of the middle class, shaped and continue to shape urban America and its public spaces.

Moving chronologically from World War I to the present, *Boardwalk of Dreams* will explore how middle-class notions of space, race, and democracy sustained

Atlantic City's boom times, fueled its sharp decline, and have molded its awkward comeback as a casino town over the last twenty-five years. The first three chapters look at how the city worked and functioned as a place to live and visit and how the public was constituted during most of the early years (1915–1960), when African American men pushed well-dressed couples up and down the Boardwalk. This section moves through space rather than time. It starts on the Boardwalk with pictures of the elaborate built environment on one side and the natural world on the other. After that, the narrative tours the city's once-vibrant entertainment zones and back lots, including the "black and tan" nightclubs, gay bars, and sex shows. From there, it goes on a drive through several of the city's racially and ethnically defined neighborhoods. Next, chapters 4 through 7 examine from different angles the desegregation of public spaces downtown and on the Boardwalk and the years of painful decline that followed (1955–1978). Along the way, this volume looks at how middle-class couples and families, city planners, tourism officials, investment bankers, gay vacationers, hippies, and African American and Puerto Rican residents came to terms with and talked about the city's fall from the top of the list of the nation's favorite tourist spots. Finally, the book probes the jarring juxtaposition of Atlantic City's present (from 1978 on) with its millions of yearly visitors and hulking neon-decorated casino towers and its scarred urban landscape and impoverished public realm within shouting distance of the gaming palaces.

On the surface, the plot line for *Boardwalk of Dreams* may seem obvious. For much of the first half of the last century, as Jordan Sayles pushed people down the Boardwalk, Atlantic City reigned as the Queen of Resorts and the "nation's playground." It hosted tens of millions of people each year. Its hotels were the largest in the world, and it was home to the world's longest boardwalk, the only one spelled with a capital *B*. It was where the Miss America Pageant and saltwater taffy were invented. It was where Jerry Lewis and Dean Martin first got together and where other members of the Rat Pack honed their acts before heading to Las Vegas. And it is from the streets of Atlantic City, finally, that the board game Monopoly took its property names.

By the late 1960s, Atlantic City had earned a new sort of renown. The city had become a poster child for urban blight and decay. Journalists dubbed it the "Bronx by the Bay" and compared it to bombed-out Dresden and war-torn Beirut. By the decade's end, comedians had folded the city's downfall into their stand-up routines. "This town really swings," one performer quipped in 1970. "Every Friday night we shop till 10 at the supermarket." When someone asked him what had happened to all the action, the comedian cracked, "Are you kidding? Listen, the typical couple visiting Atlantic City these days is a very, very old lady . . . and her mother."[18] A few months later, a local police officer sneered: "This town has had it. All you got on the Boardwalk are old folks, niggers, and hippies."[19]

With the local economy at rock bottom, casino gambling came to town, bringing back the crowds and even the Rat Pack to the Boardwalk. In the middle of the 1990s, more people visited Atlantic City each year than any other place in the United States—more than Disneyland or Dollywood or even Las Vegas. But the couples and families, senior citizens and college students who come to town now don't stay for a week or a month, and they don't parade up and down the Boardwalk in their flashiest clothes like people did in the old days. They arrive by bus or car, pull into a parking garage, gamble, and escape—usually six hours later, or sooner if their money runs out. So despite all the money changing hands on the Boardwalk—the casinos have won $67.9 billion since the first one opened in May 1978—Atlantic City now represents one of the country's starkest versions of the tale of two cities.[20] Within a few short blocks of Donald Trump's gaudy and gilded showplace, the Taj Mahal, are some of the loneliest, most desolate streets in all of America.[21]

At first glance, this would seem like the typical "declension" narrative that dominates urban studies.[22] It looks like, and is, a story of urban decay, white flight, the rise of the suburbs, and the use of quick fixes, like gambling, to solve deep and vexing economic and social problems. But by focusing on the white middle class and its ideas about urban space, the Atlantic City story contains a twist. There is, it turns out, a strong thread of continuity running through Atlantic City's apparent roller-coaster history.

When Atlantic City reigned as the nation's playground, it was, to quote the new urbanist barnstormer James Howard Kunstler, "one of [the] nation's great public spaces."[23] Its busiest days coincided with an earlier era when middle-class women and men spent evenings chatting with neighbors and passersby on their front porches and nights out on the town dancing, drinking, and watching movies. During these days, people consumed their leisure in front of huge crowds of strangers, not at home in front of wide screen televisions or at some bland suburban multiplex. Across the country, the desire for the public consumption of leisure turned the public entertainment industry into big business. Whole sections of cities, like New York's Times Square and Atlanta's Five Points, developed and thrived on serving the public what it desired *in public*, in front of crowds of strangers. Atlantic City was like these places, but fundamentally different. Anticipating Las Vegas and the transformation of urban areas from manufacturing centers to playgrounds, it was the first city in the country built from scratch and devoted entirely to the production and public consumption of entertainment.[24]

CROWDED BOARDWALK, 1920S
Probably from the Easter Day Parade, this photograph shows just how many well-dressed people crammed onto the Boardwalk on a busy weekend (Atlantic City Free Public Library, Heston Room, Atlantic City, New Jersey).

Contemporary commentators from Andres Duany to Ray Suarez to Michael Sorkin lament the decline of the "public" sphere in America.[25] Too many of us, they complain, have fled the old neighborhood's front stoops and downtown's bright nights for the dull predictability of suburban backyards and featureless malls. Along the way, we have, we are told, tossed aside the vital day-to-day interactions of the street that oil our democracy. According to these new urbanist thinkers, buildings, design, and planning made this older world work. Their answer to today's problems, then, is to return to the past, to the lost city of sidewalks and window-shopping, corner stores and showy movie theaters. Atlantic City had all of these elements of urban life. But in Atlantic City, the public spaces of the past—the world of the Boardwalk, the rolling chair, downtown department stores, and tight-knit neighborhoods—was never about democracy; it was about exclusion. Moving up required stepping over others. Yet the idea of social mobility provided exclusion with a cloak of democracy. Atlantic City boosters constantly talked about their town as a place where the rich rubbed elbows with the middling and poor, creating a melting pot of united Americans. During Atlantic City's much revered heyday from World War I to the middle of the 1960s, the resort was, however, in the words of an Athens, Georgia, native who grew up in the Boardwalk's shadow, a "Jim Crow town for sure."[26] As Jordan Sayles quickly learned, African American tourists were kept off the Boardwalk, away from all but one beach area, and confined to the crow's nests of the movie theaters. Local practices, at the same time, confined black residents to a virtually all-black, overcrowded, and underserviced neighborhood away from the Boardwalk. Then the world changed.

The civil rights movement made Atlantic City's street corners and hotel lobbies, taverns and movie houses open to just about anyone and thus more democratic. In fact, the Boardwalk, the nightclubs, and the city neighborhoods behind them became too democratic for most middle-class Americans. Worried that public space was now unmanageable and out of control, the accountants and clerks who had in the past spent their summers in town opted for self-containment. They went into hiding in segregated suburbs, malls, movie theaters, amusement parks, and outdoor worlds. Fears of criminals, rioters, and militants drove the last few middle-class white people left downtown out of these dense urban spaces in the late 1960s. In their leisure time and in their neighborhoods, these families on the run didn't ask for explicit performances of racial deference and superiority any more; they didn't fantasize about being pushed down the Boardwalk by happy African American servants. They showed off their middle-class status in other ways, including by abandoning the city. When it came to organizing their new worlds away from the cities, they wanted to seal people of color off in their own spaces, as far away from them as possible. But they wanted to do this without calling attention to the new way of carving up public space. So they tolerated a handful of well-behaved Others on their streets and at their malls. That way, they could say to themselves and anyone who asked that the sorting of people along race and class lines was natural; it just happened that they lived in virtually all-white neighborhoods, sent their kids to virtually all-white schools, and vacationed in virtually all-white theme parks.

At the same time, civil rights battles and postwar prosperity lifted many, although not all, African Americans out of poverty. Like the European immigrants and others who climbed the economic ladder before them, they brought their hopes and dreams to Atlantic City. They came to swim in the ocean, spin around on the rides, and listen to the singers and horn players. They came to act rich, eat fancy meals, and escape the grind of their day-to-day lives. With African Americans on the Boardwalk, and even in the rolling chairs, many white salesmen, plumbers, pencil manufacturers, and homemakers bypassed Atlantic City in favor of newer, cleaner, more exclusive resorts. As the white tourists stayed away, fancy Boardwalk jewelry stores turned into hot dog stands; expensive auction houses became sleazy jam joints; and downtown movie theaters were torn down and replaced by parking lots. As the city became more honky-tonk than classy, black tourists started to stay away as well. By the 1970s, locals quipped that you could roll a bowling ball down the Boardwalk in the middle of the summer without hitting anyone. Others joked, "Would the last person out of town please turn off the lights?"

Over the last couple of decades, the middle class has trickled back into Atlantic City. But they haven't returned to neighborhood taverns or downtown clothing stores. They have gone to the casinos, highly regulated and heavily policed places that are set off from the city. The irony is that these guarded and gated places are in many ways more integrated than the exclusive city of the past.

Race was Atlantic City's primary and most important form of exclusion, but movie theater ushers and Boardwalk policemen made sure that others—those not properly dressed or too loud or too crude—were kept away as well.[27] Creating the public's entertainment during most of the twentieth century, therefore, required keeping undesirables and the poor at a distance—although not entirely out of sight, since someone had to push the rolling chairs. When city leaders couldn't contain the Other in Jim Crow roles and separate neighborhoods, the middle-class millions left the city behind, segregating themselves in the suburbs and suburban-style resorts.

Atlantic City's halcyon days and hard times highlight two key moments, not just in the city's past, but also in the nation's urban past. The classic period of the busy, fashionable Boardwalk points to the widespread appeal of racialized versions of the American Dream during the last century when an essentially segregated Atlantic City stood as the nation's most popular middle-class resort and just about every major performer in the country from Bob Hope to Sammy Davis, Jr., to Bing Crosby got his start in blackface. The city's demise, meanwhile, underscores the awesome scope of the urban crisis and mass exodus to the suburbs of the 1960s and 1970s. No urban place, not even a beach town, was left untouched by the fears and anxieties of this riotous moment and great American moving frenzy.

Charting these two time periods and what they represent means investigating the changing strategies of tourist entrepreneurs and the shifting tastes of middle-class vacationers, the collapse of main street and the downtown public entertainment industry, and the emergence of the mall and the appeal of mall-like places as models for urban renewal. Atlantic City's past brings to light, moreover, changing patterns of government and private investment that together funneled money away from the cities and toward the suburbs. But none of this has wiped away the central importance of continuity to this story. Access to public space was, in the eyes of middle-class America, never supposed to be inclusive. Only through exclusion could the public take shape. Most middling women and men imagined this public space as bringing together like-minded, racially and economically similar strangers. Once Atlantic City, and other cities, couldn't legally exclude, the people from the middle left. But they came back when Disney and the Donald—Trump, that is—came to town, highlighting a third moment in the nation's urban history.[28]

Exclusion remains the key to the Disneyesque rebirth of urban tourism at the Jersey shore and across the country in the last quarter century. Atlantic City's demise—situated as it was between two moments of exclusion—coincides not just with the desegregation of the city's public spaces, but also with the opening of Disneyland in Anaheim, California, in 1955. Within a decade, Disneyland had replaced Atlantic City as the nation's most popular middle-class resort. Disney achieved this preeminent position through control—through the use of gates, high ticket prices, carefully designed advertising strategies, security officers, grooming codes for employees, and its ex-urban location beyond the city and the reach of public transportation. Behind its thick fortress walls, Disney created a public sphere, much like the Boardwalk, the shopping mall, and later the casino, based on the economically viable principles of exclusion mixed with the illusion of equal access and democracy. Disneyland, in fact, copied from, learned from, and updated Atlantic City by creating an exclusive public space made to fit the changing ideas of the postwar, post–civil rights era. In this new urban world, the middle class didn't show off in public. Unlike their parents riding proudly down the Boardwalk in Jordan Sayles's rolling chair, they didn't use their leisure time to make public performances out of racial and class privileges. Instead, they tried to cover up and deny the significance of their race and class advantages.[29]

Once the neon gaming halls landed on the Boardwalk, the copying went in the other direction. In the past, Disney had borrowed from Atlantic City, but beginning in 1978, the city's tourist entrepreneurs took from the theme park. With the coming of the slot machines and green felt tables, local leaders essentially turned the city over to casino executives, letting them serve as urban planners. Like their counterparts in charge of remaking beleaguered urban areas across the country, Harrah's and Trump executives borrowed heavily from Disney's scripts and designs. Through rigorous control over the crowd, elaborate surveillance, and defensive architectural codes, Atlantic City's gaming directors manufactured a new kind of public realm built around the containment of the urban—read: unsafe—

world and the fantasy of getting something for nothing, and throwing everyday norms of behavior out the window. The numbers speak for themselves. Twice the population of metropolitan New York comes to Atlantic City each year, and they wager almost enough money to fund the nation's space program. Obviously, the casino managers are doing something right, at least when it comes to drawing free-spending crowds to town, even if they have failed to bring back much life to the city's downtown and traditional neighborhoods.

Paul Goldberger, Kenneth Jackson, Robert Putnam, Robert Goodman, and other current commentators and scholars complain that the entire world is a mall, or even worse a casino, and that we are all sadly bowling alone.[30] Several of these scholars suggest that we are the buildings around us; windows and lobbies, sidewalks and doors make us who we are. In the past, according to these narratives, we lived in a world filled with more authentic and meaningful spaces, more inspiring architecture, and better urban design. As a result of this built environment, urban life back then was more democratic. Now the critics of our Disneyesque cities proclaim: public space is dead! Yet this lament, usually without intending to, romanticizes the past. Again, based on the Atlantic City story, the much-revered public experiences of going downtown or hanging out on the front stoop was just as unreal, just as exclusionary, and just as contrived as the Disneyland public experience of today. The public space of the past is largely a myth, an illusion. The public in America has always been segregated and walled off. What has changed is the way segregation is produced and the size, dimension, and height of the walls surrounding its protected places. What hasn't changed is the fact that only when there are clearly marked walls does the great middle-class public take shape. Attitudes about space, therefore, not space itself, defined and continue to define our cities. This rather relentless continuity holds the key to understanding Atlantic City's jazzy past, its bitter demise, and its vexing present as a money-making casino town without much town left.

A few years ago, a Web site called Atlantic City Memory Lane was started. Almost every day, yesterday's visitors to and residents of the city write in and recount their memories of bygone days on the streets, beach, and Boardwalk. One contributor, Nick Geiger, recalled "walking down the boardwalk, or Atlantic Ave. during the holidays, and just knowing almost everyone." A Las Vegas man who grew up in Atlantic City chimed in with sweet reminiscences of the "sounds of delivery trucks in the morning."[31] Others tell of first kisses, chance meetings with Frank Sinatra, shaking hands with Mr. Peanut on the Boardwalk, and buying cool Nutty Buddies on hot beach days from Singing Sam the Ice Cream Man. The home page, at first, featured a 1950s photograph of a white couple riding in a rolling chair. Someone, however, had airbrushed out the pusher. That's not where the erasures end, however. On-line correspondents regularly talk about why their city went into decline. They point to cheap airfares and air conditioning, bad press coverage and the spread of television. But they do not talk about their own actions, their own retreats from the city. When it comes to the Boardwalk of today, they see only misty visions of a gold-hewed yesterday. The perfection of those dress-up nights fifty and sixty years ago makes clear the shortcomings of the casino city. "We use[d] to have such fun down there," writes a Bristol, Pennsylvania, man who loved the diving horse. "I only wished that my own son could have had the fun times there that I did. But now it[']s all casinos and so different. He goes and likes it, but to me it[']s just not the same. Those are my wonderful memories of AC."[32]

This erasure of the meanness of the past and the walling off of public space is not that different from what goes on in current urban studies and urban planning. While there are innumerable books on the decline of American cities and the need for neotraditional designs to save them, they are frequently nostalgic, if only in subtle ways, for an urban past that we all too often forget was defined and shaped by exclusion. Keeping some people out because of how they looked or acted was not just an unfortunate aspect of these places; it was what made them public places to begin with. *Boardwalk of Dreams* challenges this thinking. The Atlantic City story told here makes clear that the solutions to our urban ills must be found in the future, not the past, and that the remedies we come up with must confront the taint of exclusion at the very core of middle-class notions of democracy and public space.

1

Staging Utopia on the Boardwalk

In 1920, Bruce Bliven, a writer for the *New Republic*, came to Atlantic City. The visit changed his understanding of the nation. "When Americans dream of that perfect society which is some day to be," he asked, "what form does their imagining take?" He answered, "Atlantic City, New Jersey . . . obviously." The resort, he insisted, served as a testament to the "sturdy middle-class millions." It was a fantasy of their ideal world. "If you would know the best that the American bourgeoisie has thus far been able to dream," Bliven insisted, "then, come to Atlantic City and behold." After just ten minutes on the Boardwalk mingling with the crowd of "well-dressed, good-looking" people, he crowned Atlantic City "the American Utopia."

Something of a Menckenesque elitist, Bliven held his tongue in his cheek as he made this declaration. He joked that none of the city's newsstands carried the *New Republic*. When he asked a bookstore clerk for a couple of well-known nonfiction titles, he was told, "We don't keep none of them. . . . They ain't no call for 'em." He did find plenty of "Filthy Stories, Undressed Stories, Naughty Tales and the like" on the shelves of the city's four bookstores. These, he guessed, must be what utopians wanted when they were on vacation. They weren't what he wanted to read, but he didn't doubt for a moment the merchants' wisdom. Atlantic City, he surmised, was a place that thrived on giving the "public"—that is, the "American bourgeoisie"—"What . . . [It] Wants."

From before World War I to after World War II, the glory days of Atlantic City and of urban America in general, the Boardwalk reigned as a middle-class "American Utopia," because as Bliven learned, it gave salesmen from Baltimore and plant managers from Reading what they wanted. What they wanted was a safe and comfortable place where there was no poverty and where they could show off by imitating the rich. Visitors looked to spend money only, as Bliven observed, "where it shows." Everyone, he noticed, dressed in "new and smart" clothes and devoured meals with a "fearful variety of dishes." "We Utopians," Bliven announced, "overeat enormously." Following multicourse dinners served with silver utensils on white linen tablecloths by doting tuxedoed waiters, some utopians strolled down the Boardwalk. The most committed utopians, however, hired Jordan Sayles or another black man to push them toward no particular destination in a rolling chair. "Though Atlantic City is technically a health resort . . . some of us," Bliven explained, "ride in wheeled chairs, but we do so as a sensuous experiment, not from infirmity. Indeed, we sit erect with such an air of almost belligerent health as to prove to every observer that we ride merely because we have the dollar."[1]

The showing off didn't end with the visitors. Atlantic City's set designers—architects, interior decorators, store owners, and amusement pier operators—constructed an over-the-top, fantastic backdrop for the Boardwalk. Buildings sparkled and glowed. Some looked like dreamy castles, others like futuristic skyscrapers. Business and political leaders also made sure everyone knew their parts. Through gentle urging, legal sanction, and official force, they tried to get everyone in the right place, saying the right lines, so that middle-class visitors could pretend to be whom they wanted to be while in town.

With its large audiences, detailed backdrop, and well-coached players, Atlantic City provided middle-class visitors with a stage for acting out their American Dreams of upward mobility.[2] In these dramas, visitors cast themselves as romantic figures in the last scenes in back-breaking journeys that took them from working-class tenements and immigrant ghettos into the national mainstream. A few days off, expensive clothes, fancy food, and a ride in a rolling chair were their just rewards for months, maybe even years, of hard work and playing by the rules. Everyone else on the Boardwalk was participating in the same sort of showing off. Cast members, then, were also audience members. They performed stories of success, while watching others do the same. It was all very reassuring, and the scale of the performances underlined the perfection of the American Dream. Making the city even more appealing was the fact that it gave the new middle-class millions endless chances to buy things, often useless things, in public, in front of a teeming and fluid throng of harmless strangers. Atlantic City was, then, not just a showy consumer's paradise, but it represented the crowd's ideal of the perfect urban, public space.

Like all utopias, this one along the Jersey shore brought together individuals with commonly held beliefs and turned them, if only for a moment, into a community. Manufacturing community in America has always meant pulling some people together, while excluding others. This paradox lay at the heart of Puritan New England and revolutionary Virginia—and Atlantic City.

Performing middle-class success by acting rich, which was exactly what people did in Atlantic City and on the rolling chairs, entailed more than parading along the Boardwalk buying expensive trinkets and boxes of saltwater taffy. To show that they had made it into the middle class, the Boardwalk millions kept the poor and, more important, African Americans away from the hotels, restaurants, and nightly parades, but not off the stage. They cast African Americans in servile positions, and they did this in the same way that they performed their acts of consumption: in public, in full view. African Americans' very public poverty and marked difference accented the Boardwalk players' equally public performances of success and inclusion. Again, there was nothing discreet or subtle about the race and class exclusion on the Boardwalk. It was in full view, and it was another way of showing off.

All of this spending and consuming, pushing and pulling, climbing and sliding, in turn, produced the fantasy of leveling up—Atlantic City's most important product. Leveling up featured the two-way, public spectacle of acting rich, while holding others down. Both things had to happen for the fantasy to work. The ability of Atlantic City's tourist merchants to produce middle-class dreams of democratic ascent alongside racial and class exclusion was the reason that tens of millions of Americans flocked to the Jersey resort in the middle of the twentieth century.

THE BOARDWALK

The history of the rolling chair and the Boardwalk stretches back almost to the beginning of Atlantic City. Before the railroads came, handfuls of Indian families and a few white farmers lived among the duck ponds, briar thickets, and swamps of Absecon Island.[3] But then a businessman, noting that Cape May attracted 100,000 visitors a year, looked at a map and recognized that the northern tip of this skinny barrier island was the closest point between the beach and Philadelphia. In 1854, Jonathan Pitney and Richard B. Osborne, a doctor and an engineer, bought a chunk of land near the ocean, lined up investors, and laid down a ribbon of track from Camden, New Jersey—directly across the Delaware River from Philadelphia—to the shore. A tourist boom began immediately. Well-heeled families in search of an easy escape from the blistering heat and stifling humidity of summer in the city started to come to town for cool breezes and fresh salt air. After the Civil War, another railroad opened between Philadelphia and Atlantic City. Competition cut the cost of the trip, making the beach town more accessible to the most skilled workers and the ever-expanding urban middle class. In 1873, nearly a half million people made the fifty-five-mile trip from Philadelphia to Atlantic City.

As the tourism industry took off, a town grew up behind the beach. Along the carefully plotted streets named after the states and oceans, there was a telegraph office, a railroad terminal, and a handful of wooden hotels that looked like oversized barns with dormers and porches. Then came theaters and drugstores, churches and schools, and more hotels and residents.[4] Italians from South Jersey, Irish from the mill districts of Kenningston, Quakers from the Philadelphia suburbs, and Germans from Trenton built homes around the businesses and the beach and stayed year 'round. African Americans from Virginia, North Carolina, South Carolina, and Georgia in search of work and the freer air of the North joined them and were among the city's earliest residents. Hotel and business owners hired black women and men to wash clothes, carry bags, clean dishes, and hammer railroad ties. By 1880, thirty years after its founding, Atlantic City boasted a permanent population of 5,477, a quarter of whom were African American. Over the next twenty years, the city and its black population doubled. By this time, Atlantic City had the largest proportion of African American residents of any urban area in New Jersey.[5]

To the hoteliers and railroad operators, more tourists (and, to a lesser extent, more locals, black and white) meant more business, but more people also meant more sand. Sand of course got everywhere. Soon it covered hotel lobbies and railroad coach seats. In 1870, Jacob Keim, the owner of a Boardwalk hotel, and Alexander Boardman, a railroad conductor, got an idea. They suggested laying wood planks over the sand for people to walk on. With $5,000 from municipal authorities, the two men oversaw the construction of the first boardwalk. Eight feet wide, it stretched for a mile and was an instant hit. When a storm wiped away the first boardwalk, city leaders built a second, a third, and then a fourth wooden walkway along the sea. Pounded by winds and waves, none of these lasted. Finally, on the fifth try, in 1896, engineers, using steel and concrete reinforcements, constructed a more permanent structure. As wide as a two-lane highway in places, the new four-mile strip of six-inch-wide wood planks set by 1916 in a herringbone pattern quickly emerged as the city's signature attraction, its Fifth Avenue, its Champs d'Elysee, its front door, its equator, and, just like in the game of Monopoly, its most valuable real estate. City boosters, always prone to hyperbole, promoted the promenade as "the eighth wonder of the world," the only boardwalk anywhere that deserved to be spelled with a capital *B*.[6]

Throughout this initial boom, nature anchored the city's promotional campaign. One brochure asked, "When you go to your physician and tell him your brain is full of cobwebs, or your liver is misbehaving itself what does he say in nine cases out of ten? 'Take a sea voyage, if you can spare the time.' " Philadelphia physicians traded these kinds of testimonials for free trips to the beach. One doctor swore that Atlantic City possessed "three of the greatest health giving elements known to science—sunshine, ozone, and recreation." The town's first resident doctor claimed that Atlantic City's ozone- and oxygen-laden air could cure everything from asthma and digestive disorders to diabetes and even insanity. The salt water, too, was said to be medicinal.[7]

But boosters didn't stop there. They urged not only the sick to come. Echoing contemporary thinking about nature and urban environments, one of Atlantic City's founders boasted that the resort offered the "perfect refuge from the debilitating atmosphere of the growing cities." "There's robust health awaiting you at Atlantic City," another city leader crowed, "but you have to come for a while."[8] Families from Philadelphia and beyond did come and usually they stayed for a while, a week, a month, or even the entire summer. Beginning in the 1920s, each year, Dorothy Webber's family took a train from Cincinnati to Atlantic City. Coming to town, her father told her, "wasn't a luxury—it was a necessity. He believed the ocean and the beach and all was very good for your health. It was all nice and relaxing, anyway."[9]

William Hayday owned an Atlantic Avenue hardware store in 1887. But he was looking to capitalize even more on the city's emerging tourist boom. He saw an opportunity to make some additional money on the Boardwalk. That summer, he bought several baby strollers from Henry Shill, a Philadelphia chair manufacturer, to rent to tourists. He quickly learned, however, that the town attracted more people seeking "robust health" than it did toddlers. During Hayday's first season on the Boardwalk, visitors repeatedly asked him for, what they called at the time, invalid chairs. The next year, he purchased a bunch of single-passenger wheelchairs from Shill and brought them to the shore.

The city's health promotion campaign worked, and the Boardwalk crowds grew. In these early years, thousands of sick and ailing women and men headed to town. Eager to breathe the city's famed "ozone laden air," they walked along the Boardwalk or rented iron-tired wheelchairs to get from hotel to hotel. Noticing Hayday's growing orders, Shill himself decided to get into the rental game and hauled a trainload of his own chairs to town in the 1890s. At this point, neither Hayday nor Shill provided their customers with pushers. Usually nurses or companions guided the chairs down the Boardwalk.[10]

Nearly forty years after Hayday first began renting chairs on the Boardwalk, Arthur Conan Doyle, Sherlock Holmes's creator, visited Atlantic City. By this time, the rolling-chair business had changed.[11] Seeing all of the "huge invalid chairs" on the Boardwalk, the writer at first thought he had stumbled onto some sort of bizarre town populated only by "convalescents." Conan Doyle soon discovered that the chairs were not just for "invalids." As early as 1892, another reporter noted that the rolling chairs had become a "fad" and that "healthy people as well as sick people [were] affecting the custom." As the rides got more popular, Shill and Hayday redesigned them to suit their new purposes. They transformed the single-passenger wheelchairs into white wicker baskets that could hold two or three adults and looked more like crosses between rickshaws and chariots than sensible hospital gear. Shill and Hayday now also provided the pushers, almost always African American men dressed in suit jackets and working for tips. Without retelling this history, Conan Doyle noted that the rolling chair had become "one of the favorite amusements in Atlantic City." Like the thousands of people around him, he came to the shore "for a much needed rest" and "fun" and found it "with . . . [a] daily swim" and "rides up and down the Boardwalk in the double-bath chairs, propelled by one-negro-human machines."[12]

By the 1920s, the rolling chairs thundered down the Boardwalk "like a distant herd of galloping horses" in two separate, unbroken lines, one going north and one going south.[13] On either side of these two strips of "baskets on wheels," there were people, masses of people. "It's like a million going this way," one man said of the Boardwalk, "and a million going the other way."[14] "In fifteen minutes," another visitor gasped, "you long for the comparative ease of rush hour on the Brooklyn Bridge."[15] Atlantic City was no longer principally a health resort or a place for a quiet retreat. With all of those rolling chairs and people, it was now a showy and noisy urban stage for race and class role playing. Sensing, and in many ways anticipating, these shifts, hotel architects and tourist entrepreneurs remade the city's built environment to reflect the shifting profile and desires of its clientele.

THE BACKDROP

A travel writer using the pseudonym George Birmingham joined the Boardwalk crush in 1914. He almost didn't make it to town. Toward the end of an extended trip that took him from Dublin to Chicago, he stopped over in New York City. Wanting to see an authentic American "holiday resort," he told his friends there that he planned to go to Atlantic City. "You won't enjoy *that* place," these "well-instructed people" told him. But Birmingham did enjoy Atlantic City.

The Boardwalk's western skyline captivated Birmingham. Staring at the lights, spires, and domes decorating Atlantic City's hotels, Birmingham wondered about the architects who designed these structures. He wanted to know how they came up with such wild and whimsical ideas. He imagined that before they sat down to sketch their blueprints they spent two weeks on the Boardwalk staying up late, riding on the rolling chairs, eating "crab dressed in various ways," and drinking countless "gin rickeys." After fourteen days of this, Birmingham thought that the architects' "dreams" must have become "imprinted on [their] memories," allowing them to "draw plans of hotels suitable for Atlantic City." Out of this trancelike state came buildings, he judged, more fantastic than stately. Birmingham didn't even try to describe them. They were structures, he wrote, "which anyone would declare to be impossible if he did not see [them] in actual existence."[16]

Philadelphia architect William Price had built three of the buildings that stopped Birmingham in his tracks. Fifteen years before the travel writer came to town, Atlantic City businessman Josiah White hired Price to design a hotel for him at the corner of the Boardwalk and Ohio Avenue. Completed in 1902, Price's long, narrow, rust-colored, four-story, stone, brick, and wood structure with a slate-shingled roof captured in many ways the refined simplicity and elegance of Queen Anne–style architecture and of Atlantic City's early mission. At a glance, the Marlborough Hotel—named after an English duke—looked like an inflated but still courtly country manor where wealthy nobles might go on retreat. Despite its size—the building filled almost half a city block—there was something shy, even demure, about the Marlborough. Its entrance and most of its ornamentation turned away from the beach toward its manicured lawns. Boardwalk crowds saw only a series of discreet sundecks and graceful bay windows.[17]

In 1906, White once again called on Price. He wanted him to add an annex to the Marlborough. The Quaker hotelier gave the architect two clear instructions. Following a series of sensational and well-publicized fires in East Coast resort hotels, he told Price to make sure that the new hotel was "fireproof." He also instructed him to design a building that reflected the style of Atlantic City in 1906, not classical Greece or Renaissance Italy or Edwardian England. Price followed at least one of the directives. Experimenting with a new and untested form of reinforced concrete developed by New Jersey native Thomas Edison, Price created a structure as immune to fire as any at the time. In terms of style, he went a step further. His building anticipated the future of resort architecture more than it reflected the times.

Not long after finishing the Blenheim, as the Marlborough's annex came to be called, Price published an essay on "modern architecture." Architects, he argued, should, on one level, act as "preachers," but "most primarily," he said, they should be "interpreters of the public mind and public feeling and public habits." Toward the end of the article, he talked specifically about his latest project, the Blenheim. Many fellow architects, Price acknowledged, didn't like the building, but he thought they didn't understand what he was trying to do. The Blenheim stood as an "expression of the purpose . . . of the place where it was built: that . . . is[,] an expression of the purpose of the gay and sumptuous life . . . of the people that go to Atlantic City."[18] With the expanding middle class looking to show off in mind, Price built a hotel using an architectural vocabulary that seemed to shout, just like the flashy couples in Jordan Sayles's rolling chair, "I've made it and I'm here."

One visitor said that the Blenheim's exterior "glued" his feet to the Boardwalk.[19] Cream colored and fifteen stories high, it looked at first glance slightly out of place standing next to the Boardwalk's stout tan and beige buildings. Nonetheless, the hotel quickly became the city's most familiar postcard image. With its playful collection of domes and minarets, long looping curves and roller coaster–like swoops, rectangular and arched windows, the Blenheim was hard to miss, and harder to forget. More than any other Boardwalk building, Price's masterpiece created an exotic, fairytale-like backdrop of luxury and extravagance for passing pedestrians and rolling-chair riders.

On the outside, Price made explicit reference to the hotel's setting, decorating the building with detailed sculptures of sea horses, seashells, crabs, and seaweed mixed with gold naval crests and geometric patterns of Mediterranean blue tiles. But the building at the same time evoked another faraway place. Visitors nicknamed the hotel "Baghdad by the Sea."[20] Two decorative towers, which looked like crosses between the Washington Monument and steamship chimneys, fronted the building. Hovering over the pillars was a tremendous eight-story, gold-tinted, spire-topped, Byzantine-looking domed rotunda flanked on either side by tall, open-air cupolas. The Blenheim was, one rather ahistoric observer recently proclaimed, "the original Taj Mahal in Atlantic City."[21]

Speaking in an orientalist vocabulary, the building, like all themed buildings, told an easily recognizable story. Schooled by nickelodeon films and pulp fiction serialized in the back pages of newspapers, visitors easily read the Blenheim's visual clues. Curves and minarets, domes and spires translated into the "East" and the Orient, with their connotations of unbridled passion, sensual pleasure, and wild adventure. Using these familiar quotations, Price turned the Blenheim from a hotel into a public destination, a place that told visitors that they were in a different, extravagant, and sumptuous place, just the kind of place middle-class tourists with a little money to spend thought they deserved to be while on vacation.[22]

Before the start of World War I, Daniel White, Josiah White's cousin and the owner of a wood-framed hotel a few blocks south of the Blenheim called the Traymore, contacted Price. He asked the architect to turn his property into "the signature building of the resort." Price jumped at the chance. Completed by the start of the 1915 summer season, the new Traymore was more restrained than its Moorish neighbor. One critic praised the building's "sobriety." Yet it could only be described as sober when compared to the Blenheim. Price's third Atlantic City creation was massive, the biggest structure on the beach. From end to end, the 600-room, seventeen-story concrete Traymore took up half of a city block. Several tall columns climbed to a trio of large, wide domes and bracketed the building's central block. Vertical lines shot up from everywhere, accenting the Traymore's and the Boardwalk's profuse urbanity. Two smaller wings flanked the main space. Each section, as Price's biographer explains, "celebrate[d] concrete's inherent plasticity." But it also fit its beachfront setting. In many ways, the Traymore with tan face and multiple layers looked like a giant chiseled sandcastle.[23]

Price's Marlborough-Blenheim and Traymore hotels stuck out on the Boardwalk. They were taller and wider than the buildings around them, but in the late 1920s, they were not entirely unique. On either side of each of them stood other examples of Atlantic City's "architecture of fantasy."[24] Some city leaders called the Boardwalk America's Main Street. But that wasn't quite the point of the place. This part of Atlantic City didn't look like other towns. With no function other than to entertain, Boardwalk buildings eschewed repetition and exhibited few clear patterns, little symmetry, and even less stylistic relationship to each other. Yet their dramatic fronts told visitors that they were someplace different and special. Anticipating Disney's Epcot, the gaudy structures offered visitors a quick, cartoon tour of world architecture. The Blenheim copied its design from Istanbul's St. Sophia. The Dennis mimicked a French chateau; the Chalfonte-Haddon Hall looked like a temple-topped tower with an English Renaissance design; and the Claridge, the last of the city's great hotels of this era, resembled the Empire State Building. Mixing classical and modern styles, the Boardwalk towers created an "outward eclecticism" and, more important, a clear architectural break from the blandness and repetition of everyday life in industrial America.

Architects and business owners accented their Atlantic City buildings with lights. At night, the Boardwalk burst, in one man's words, "into a carnival of flame."[25] Atlantic City, wrote one of its many poets, was

> where the nights are later
> and the lights are brighter.[26]

Coming from every direction, the artificial lights changed the color and texture of the night sky. A neat line of tall streetlamps, resembling a row of carefully planted pine trees, lit the Boardwalk's beach side. Across the way, the tall buildings beamed. Lavishly lit marquees that looked like jewels atop kings' crowns hung above every theater entrance. As the sun set, restaurant owners plugged in flash-

MARLBOROUGH-BLENHEIM HOTEL
Even in the 1970s, William Price's turn-of-the-century wonderland retained its
grace and whimsy (Temple University Libraries, Urban Archives, Philadelphia,
Pennsylvania).

ing signs that beckoned patrons to come in and sit down. Many buildings near the
Boardwalk decked out their sides and rooftops with electric billboards. Going
a step further, Brighton Park, in front of the Claridge Hotel, had a towering
water fountain with thirty different colored lamps that threw off a wild and ever-
changing array of pinks, greens, and yellows.[27]

The city's showiest "urban jewelry" beamed from the amusement piers.[28] Dangling a quarter of a mile out into the dark ocean, Steel Pier—the largest and most
famous of the city's piers—was draped with thousands of electric lights and
dozens of large signs and billboards. Every three minutes, Boardwalk strollers
stopped to watch four "electrified" thoroughbreds race around the Seagram
sign—relocated from Times Square—atop Million Dollar Pier. From there, they
could see the Schmidt's sign over Mammy's Restaurant, home of "delicious waffles" and "chicken in a basket," on Steeplechase Pier. Until the mid-1930s, this
pier—the self-proclaimed "happy place"—also boasted the largest sign in the
world. Towering over its merry-go-round, ferris wheel, and wacky slides stood a
Chesterfield cigarette sign made of 27,000 individual light bulbs.[29]

All the lights gave the city a pop-art feel along with a bright sheen that could be
seen for miles. Up close, the glow turned night into day, creating yet another illu-

sion. The lights also seemed to block out vice. Some believed that crime could not exist under such brilliant scrutiny. In the end, the Boardwalk's dazzling lights, like the Blenheim's loud exterior, created an appeal similar to that of other twentieth-century vertical cities that was, according to urban scholar Witold Rybczynski, "vivid and visceral."[30]

Like their big city counterparts, Atlantic City business leaders constructed every novel, luxurious, extravagant inch of the Boardwalk's built environment to tickle, as one observer cracked, "silver out of the jingling pockets of the throng."[31] On his trip to the city in 1914, travel writer George Birmingham—the same man who marveled at the Boardwalk's architectural wonders—caught the "holiday spirit of the place which gets a hold on visitors." All year long, Birmingham noted, "commonplace people" spend their money with a "carefully calculated useful-ness." But in the shadows of Moorish turrets and twinkling advertisements for cigarettes, these same steady, middle-class women and men let their guard and their discipline down. On the Boardwalk, Birmingham concluded, "Our souls revolt against spending money on things which are really good to us." He was not immune. On his first trip down the promenade, he stopped to listen to a fast-talking hawker. He couldn't imagine when he would ever need a magical potato cutter, but that didn't stop him from buying not just one, but two, of the flimsy utensils. "Such," he determined, "is the strange effect of places like Atlantic City on people who are in other places sane enough."[32]

But it wasn't just the buildings and lights that gave the Boardwalk its fantasy, urban free-spending feel. Even after the city ceased being primarily a health re-sort, nature remained a central attraction. By day, people sunbathed, swam, built dripping sandcastles, and paraded up and down the shore. And nature loomed in other ways. To the west of the Boardwalk stood the modern, vertical city, to the east, the unchanging sea. The Atlantic Ocean, as city historian Charles Funnell ar-gued, purified and legitimized pleasure along the Jersey shore. Certain of the es-sential goodness and virtue of nature as embodied in the sea, middle-class visitors justified their Atlantic City trips. They could tell themselves that they were going to the world's playground for the wholesomeness of the ocean. Assured that at least one part of the resort offered natural, and thus morally decent, benefits, they could then turn to the edgier parts of the city without too much guilt.[33]

Atlantic City's power and allure stemmed, perhaps even more, from the mar-velous tension between nature and urbanity played out every moment on the Boardwalk. "The Boardwalk," wrote a Philadelphia journalist, "provides a combi-nation of nature to the east and civilization (no matter how bizarre or banal) to the west that is quite suitable for relaxation." Was this, he asked, a "poor compro-mise? . . . I think not." Most Atlantic City visitors, he knew, thought that "[n]ature in large doses can be overwhelming. She is at her best when she catches you with your guard down."[34]

Architect Robert Venturi, coauthor of the path-breaking book *Learning from Las Vegas*, grew up in Philadelphia and spent his summer days in Atlantic City. The juxtaposition between the city and nature captivated him as well. When, he explained in a 1982 interview:

> you come to analyze the combination of the ocean, the beach, the Board-walk, and the great hotels, you realize that the dramatic quality came be-cause you had on one side the vast space of the ocean—purely a natural phenomenon, always the same, never touched—and on the other side you had this highly artificial, very urban, constantly changing space.

"The drama of one side," he added, "with one thing and the other side with the other was simply amazing."[35]

The interiors of Boardwalk buildings extended the illusion of wealth and fantasy created by their exteriors and the nearby ocean. In 1969, a Phoenix food writer walked through the lobbies of the Shelburne, Chalfonte-Haddon Hall, and the Marlborough-Blenheim. Even with the city outside decaying from neglect, these spaces remained impressive. "They are so big the lobbies have lobbies," she wrote, marveling at the array of padded cornices, flowered chintzes, and high-carved ceilings.[36] Thirty years earlier, the lobby of the Ritz Carlton Hotel had left the son of a middling Baltimore clerk, whose family couldn't afford to stay there, dizzy with awe. Chamber orchestras played Bach—just about the classiest thing he could imagine—in the background. The carpet felt so thick and lush to him that he worried about leaving ugly footprints with each step, and there were so many ferns and potted trees that he imagined he was in Africa.[37]

Throughout the middle decades of the twentieth century, "nattily dressed" couples walked arm in arm through the Marlborough-Blenheim lobby, which was filled with Chippendale chairs, overstuffed sofas, Oriental rugs, chandeliers the size of truck tires, bubbling fountains, and enormous marble fireplaces. On their way upstairs or to the solarium, they passed walls decorated with murals of English country life and moldings of sea creatures. They went by a florist's stand with orchids in the window, a perfume shop, and a French hair salon. After walking under the domed rotunda in the center of the room, the guests breezed by the hotel library, which was filled with leather-bound volumes of Shakespeare, and then by the writing room furnished with large teak desks. Pool tables with webbed pockets filled the next room. From there, they went down a long, sun-drenched corridor to the dining room, where, as one guest described it, "the chandelier floats in glittering orbit and soft lights rim the base of the vaulted ceiling, suited waiters and crisp tablecloths form a sea of white."[38]

During the city's heyday, these busy hotel lobbies, and to a lesser extent the dining rooms, functioned not as safe havens in a heartless urban world, but rather as extensions of the Boardwalk. They were, in other words, public—yet still rigidly segregated—spaces. It didn't matter if they stayed in the crummiest boardinghouse in town, any white woman or man in their Boardwalk clothes could sit down on lobby chairs, have a drink, or meet a friend. This equal access gave Atlantic City its all-important democratic cloak.

In the lobbies, just like on the Boardwalk, streams of energy and activity converged. Even though he was afraid to step on the plush carpet, the lobby of the Ritz thrilled a Baltimore teenager. "Someone," he observed, "was being paged. Someone was wanted on the telephone. A bellhop moved across the carpet, a small silvery tray extended in his hand." Filled with men in "white suits" and women "in dresses the colors of summer rainbows," the lobby, to this teenager, smelled of the "scent of money" and the "overpowering fragrance of luxury." Loretta Bessler of Philadelphia said of the Blenheim, "All those big ceilings on the inside made you feel like you were in Hollywood." "I loved the Marlborough lobby," wrote Louis Hertz, a long-time Atlantic City visitor, "where I could walk and feel like a rich man's son."[39] Strolling through the ground floors of the Blenheim, the Ritz, or any of the other Boardwalk hotels gave these visitors a taste of how, they imagined, wealthy families lived every day. Even more, these spaces transformed visitors. As contemporary architectural critic Paul Goldberger explains, a great hotel lobby gives people the impression that they are "cosmopolitan, sophisticated, dignified, attractive, busy, daring, or rich."[40]

On the Boardwalk's northern and southern edges, just outside the shadows of the palace-like hotels, there were ordinary pizza parlors, hot dog stands, and tiny storefronts with fortune-tellers. But the stores and shops between the colossal hotels added to the Boardwalk's fantasy backdrop. Scattered amid the saltwater taffy stores, lemonade stands, Chinese restaurants, and Jewish delis were an array of specialty shops and upscale boutiques. Most sold things and styles people couldn't get or wouldn't think of buying at home. One man believed that there were more fur shops on the Boardwalk than on any other street in America. At the Needlecraft, attendants served women finger sandwiches, tea, and cocktails and brought them designer clothes to try on in private suites. Walking south from the Blenheim just after World War II, Boardwalk strollers passed Kane Furs, Au Louvre Children's Clothing, Arthur Leonard's Men's Limited Fashions, Maison Mae's and Yamron's jewelry shops, and Ella Packer Perfumes.[41]

In this section of the Boardwalk, each block had at least one linen shop and one souvenir stand. Before leaving town, most visitors combed the aisles of the Virginia Souvenir Shop or Jack's Souvenir Shop. They bought plates, vases, ashtrays, purses, notebooks, moccasins, and handkerchief boxes—all inscribed "Atlantic City." As they picked out their knickknacks and cheap suede and leather items, most purchased a few postcards. Later, sitting in their hotel lobbies or on their guesthouse porches, they scribbled a line or two about the weather, the Boardwalk, and the beach before dropping the cards in the mail.[42] What, after all, was the point of traveling to the Jersey shore and spending all that money if you couldn't show off to your friends and family back home about the trip?

After combing through souvenir store bins, vacationers usually headed to a nearby linen shop. Rachel's Linens, Bon Marche, Ambassador Kerchief, and Grande Maison Blanche sold Belgian silks, Italian scarves, and hand-made French ties.[43] But what these stores really sold was an image of class and elegance. Without a doubt, most Boardwalk visitors saw themselves as loyal patriots, even fervent American nationalists. That didn't stop them from almost slavishly imitating the fashions of Europe, at least those that they could get their hands on. To them, European style stood for fashion and good taste. Owning a Belgian handkerchief or eating a dish with a French name transformed them, they believed, into refined and tasteful women and men.[44]

Steel Pier was more boisterous than the linen shops and more like Coney Island than the Hamptons. Its interior matched its flashy exterior and created yet another Boardwalk fantasyscape. The pier did have among its many attractions a few places that offered the extravagance and luxury on display at the linen shops and in the hotel lobbies. The Marine Ballroom featured velvet curtains and a radiant gold-domed ceiling. At night, well-dressed couples—sometimes as many as 3,500 of them—crammed into the room to dance. But what visitors really got at the pier was the chance to see and do something different every moment without feeling cheap or ordinary.

Calling itself "a vacation in itself," "a wonder of the modern world," and the "Showplace of the Nation," Steel Pier resembled other amusement parks that were springing up across the country in the early years of the twentieth century. For one reasonably low price, pier patrons got, in the words of cultural historian Russel Nye, "an alternative to daily life."[45] Going there, one visitor remembered, was "like going to the circus, the theater, and the movies all in one day."[46] Steel Pier impresario Frank Gravatt and his successor, George Hamid, Sr., made the pier into a world of constant stimulation. From front to back, the clatter and cacophony of strange lights and noises flashed and rang. Visitors remember running through the gates in the morning and heading to a printed schedule, and from there, they would carefully plan their day so they wouldn't miss anything. Starting in the morning and ending at night, the pier ran three movies, vaudeville productions, a children's show of the "stars of tomorrow," and, until 1945, minstrel performances. Where Steel Pier met the Boardwalk, General Motors operated a pavilion, displaying the company's latest makes and models. Salesmen roamed the showroom telling shoppers about turbo-charged engines, double-barrel carburetors, and the scientific wonder of air brakes.[47]

"From 1920 through the '50s," writes one observer, "everyone who was anyone played Steel Pier." Guy Lombardo, Benny Goodman, Jimmy Dorsey, Rudy Valle, Mae West, the Three Stooges, Abbott and Costello, Louis Armstrong, Gene Krupa, Duke Ellington, Dinah Shore, and Perry Como all performed there. Someone once quipped, "[B]ig bands weren't big until they [played] Steel Pier."[48] Making it on the pier could be exhausting. Early in his career, Frank Sinatra appeared in the Marine Ballroom with the Harry James Orchestra. Afternoon rains and the crooner's growing popularity swelled the crowds, forcing Sinatra to do eleven shows in a single day. The singer woke up the next morning with a sore throat and had to cancel a scheduled appearance at the Michigan State Fair.[49]

Along with big-name shows and first-run films, Steel Pier presented an endless stream of gimmicks and gags. Gravatt and Hamid booked wild animal acts, trained seals, boxing cats and kangaroos, incubator babies (an attraction first displayed at Coney Island's Luna Park), a human cannon ball, and the High Diving Hawaiians. Alvin "Shipwreck" Kelly once spent forty-nine days and one hour—a world record—sitting on top of a pole on the pier. Patrons could also experience the "thrill of a lifetime" in the Marine Diving Bell. More like a ball than a bell, the blue and white steel contraption with narrow ten-inch windows lowered a dozen people at a time fifty feet into the sea. In 1949, a North Jersey couple got married underwater in the thing. An usher, who guided guests on and off the ride, remembered that people saw "some bass feeding around the pilings, or weakfish, bluefish, dog sharks [and] some stingrays." Mostly, he recalled, the bell offered little more than a dark and dull view of the Jersey shore's greenish-brown water. "People would get disappointed," the usher admitted, but he added, "The ride up usually took care of things." If that didn't do the trick, the Diving Bell also had a speakerphone, which allowed people to call up to their friends on the deck.[50]

The diving horse, however, remained Steel Pier's biggest attraction. Four to six times a day, as many as five thousand people packed into the bleachers of the Marine Stadium. To start things off, a young woman in circus sequins climbed up a steep, narrow ramp, which looked like a roller coaster incline. Just as she reached the top a trainer gave a large horse a swat, and off it went, racing up the slope, its steel shoes smacking against the wooden planks. The woman quickly mounted the horse when it reached the platform forty feet above the Boardwalk. "The crowd," wrote one fan of the spectacle, "hold[s] its breath." Then the woman and the horse dove. "It's like flying," the observer explained, "the horse and the rider suspended in silent air . . . dropping." A loud crashing sound followed as the duo hit the surface of a twelve-foot-deep pool of water. The impact cost one diver her eyesight, but she kept performing the trick, and the people kept coming to see this novelty act.[51]

Steel Pier's interior places created yet another illusion. Like other amusement parks, sections functioned as an extension of an outdoor picnic. Early in the twentieth century, Boardwalk vendors and restaurant owners persuaded city leaders to pass a statute making it illegal for the piers to sell food. Side-stepping the law, Gravatt built and Hamid maintained a picnic deck on the pier's second floor, encouraging patrons to bring packed lunches. Even today, visitors recall leaving sacks of ham-and-cheese sandwiches wrapped in wax paper hanging from hooks over the covered wooden tables and then rushing off to a movie or a show. The lunches, these people are quick to add, were always there when they got back.[52]

"Wholesome entertainment for the whole family" was what a Steel Pier brochure promised to deliver.[53] The outdoor picnic, along with educational exhibits like the Parade of Presidents, infused the pier with a dose of middle-class wholesomeness. Wax figures of Lincoln and Truman and packed lunches said that despite its tricks and Coney Island gimmicks, Steel Pier remained a safe place. Like the rest of the Boardwalk, it was a place where the ordinary rules of behavior might be modified, but they were never completely abandoned.

THE SCRIPT

Atlantic City, with its "sweep of colour . . . , riot of sound and chaos of movement," its ribbons of rolling chairs, towering hotels, noisy amusement piers, and armies of people, was a mass resort.[54] Like Coney Island to the north, it was a place that counted its visitors after 1920 in the hundreds of thousands each weekend and by the millions each year. In 1939, more than 16 million women and men—a number surpassing the combined populations of Philadelphia and New York—made the trip to Atlantic City.[55] People flooded onto the northern tip of Absecon Island for the same reasons they went to Coney Island and, later, to Disneyland and Las Vegas. They came because Atlantic City offered them something they couldn't get at home, something different and a little daring, but nothing too perilous or dangerous. To dress in furs and sequins at home was, for most, to risk ridicule. But on the Boardwalk, pretending to be rich was a virtual requirement, the ticket for admission. Indeed, tourism officials constructed and contrived the promenade and its themed backdrop to encourage people to pretend and playact.

Atlantic City was all about the pleasure and fantasy of participating in the democracy of the imagined well-to-do, if only for a long weekend, and as long as it could stage these moments, it would remain a mass resort.

Like Coney Island, families came to the New Jersey resort to soar on the roller coasters, spin on the Tilt-a-Whirl, and escape the day-to-day grind of work and family. But in a class sense, Atlantic City was, until the 1960s, a step up from Coney Island.[56] Boardwalk visitors dressed better and stayed longer. Bruce Bliven, the *New Republic* reporter who in 1920 tagged Atlantic City the "American Utopia," visited Coney Island a year later. Amid what sounded to him like ceaseless and dissonant clatter, he spotted only the "battered souls . . . [of] industrial civilization." Luna Park revelers stood out to him because of their Otherness. "Coney," Bliven remarked, "is one more place from which the native Yankee stock has retreated before the fierce tide of the south[ern] European and Oriental." Several months earlier in Atlantic City, he had spotted no Jews or Balkan refugees. It wasn't that they weren't there. As Senator Hiram Johnson made clear, recent immigrants and their families filled the Boardwalk. But it wasn't the crowd's ethnic roots that stuck out to Bliven; it was instead its sharp attire and steady comportment. He saw only white Americans on the Boardwalk. Just by going to Atlantic City and putting on their Boardwalk clothes, people who might be considered ugly outsiders in Coney Island became respectable middle-class Americans in New Jersey.[57]

Unlike Coney Island, the Atlantic City Boardwalk, true to its middle-class nature, was never intended to be a place of "vulgar exuberance" where vacationers could shed their inhibitions.[58] The Boardwalk was, instead, a place where public decorum mattered above all else. Guests were expected to dress properly and behave correctly. The children of cigar makers, ditch diggers, and garment workers came to Atlantic City to announce to everyone who was there and to everyone back home, who were sure to get a postcard, that they had made it out of the working class and into the middle class. A trip to Atlantic City was, then, a public performance of personal success. On the Boardwalk, the middle-class multitudes cast themselves as successful, free-spending Americans and acted out their parts by creating a public realm built around continuous shows of middle-class respectability and conspicuous spending. In participating in these slightly forced, slightly canned performances of well-mannered purchasing, they defined themselves as better than the Coney Island crowds, the rolling-chair pushers, and everyone else who couldn't come to Atlantic City.

The Boardwalk differed not just from Coney Island. By the start of World War II, Las Vegas, while not yet "the first city of the twenty-first century," was already a significant mass resort. In the 1940s and even more in the 1950s, women and men who went to church on Sundays and to Parents-Teachers Association meetings on Wednesdays in Ventura, California, and Davenport, Iowa, took a plane ride to the desert to, as historian Hal Rothman observes, "cut loose, to disappear, and publicly entertain their demons." They came to Vegas to escape for a couple of nights the cultural conventions of middle-class America at midcentury.[59] But the same people, or at least their East Coast cousins, came to the Boardwalk for different reasons. They came to the Jersey shore to make a claim of respectability. They came to the Boardwalk to show off their hard-won middle-class status by acting like classy men and women. They came to celebrate the American Dream of inclusion and social mobility.

Visitors constantly talked about the Boardwalk as a marvelously democratic place. No matter where they slept in town, at a swank beachfront hotel or a wooden rooming house on a back alley, on the Boardwalk everyone was equal. Factory owners rubbed elbows with carpenters, blue-eyed Germans mixed with olive-skinned Italians, and Irish walked next to Jews. As long as they acted with grace and decorum, everyone—everyone, that is, who could pass for white—was welcome. Unlike Las Vegas, then, families came to Atlantic City not to fade into the background, but to see and be seen, to show off that they had made it in America and that they had enough money to skip a few days of work, buy new shoes and matching handbags, and pay someone to push them down the Boardwalk.

Many of the families who came to Atlantic City from the 1920s to the 1950s hailed from the Little Italys and Little Warsaws of what Ray Suarez has called the "original urban giants"—New York, Philadelphia, Baltimore, and Pittsburgh.[60] Others came from smaller, gritty, industrial cities like Newark, Camden, Trenton, Bridgeport, Allentown, and Reading. Still others who came had only recently left the old neighborhoods for the Bronx, Queens, West Philadelphia, or some other blue-collar or middlebrow suburb. Whatever their financial or ethnic differences, the people who came to Atlantic City were people for whom the city was still relevant. Some still worked there. Most still shopped there and went to baseball games there. Even more, they still had a romance and fascination with urban spaces and city nights, a romance and fascination that their children would abandon.

For these Baltimore and Bronx families, the Boardwalk represented an urban dream. "It was not a place for introspection," travel writer James Huneker commented in 1915. "It was urban, it was jittery." But this metropolis by the sea seemed at the same time to purge the city—the everyday city—of urban ills. "Wealth fairly envelops you," Huneker continued. "There is apparently no such thing as poverty or sickness in existence."[61] There was no soot or hulking factories, no racing cars or barreling buses pushing pedestrians off the sidewalks; there were only bikes and slow-moving rolling chairs. With its tall Boardwalk buildings, the city had a shimmering skyline. But the scale of the hotels was not overwhelming or intimidating. The air was crisp and clean. And nature, that mystical and cleansing force, was right there on the other side of the Boardwalk. When the wind blew, it smelled of fresh salt water, not noxious gases. Even more important, visitors saw Atlantic City as a place where civil and well-behaved strangers filled the streets from early in the morning to late at night. The mob became the good-natured crowd. That transformation turned Atlantic City into a place of constant motion and activity, variety and spontaneity. It was a place of bright lights, the latest gadgets, and the right mix of fancy cafes and hot dog stands, elegant linen shops and tacky souvenir stores. As the stage for this electric blend of urban commerce and lights, the Boardwalk stood as a site where a lot—but little that was bad—could happen.

Like all middle-class fantasy spaces, the Boardwalk had to offer visitors "riskless risks" in order to bring them out of their homes and into the public sphere. For this public realm to take shape, guests had to feel like they were getting something different and novel. But before they threw themselves into this world of difference, they first had to feel comfortable sitting next to strangers on the rides and in hotel lobbies. They had to know that the people around them were like them and that they would regulate their conduct and curb their emotions and desires.[62] Once they felt confident that they were in a community of like-minded, similar women and men, all of the other fantasies—the knowing deceptions—were possible. On the roller coaster and the Tilt-a-Whirl, people who never saw each other before touched as they willingly shared the ruse of danger. Riders zoomed to the edge of disaster, and then at the last stomach-sinking moment, they were snatched back to safety. Then, they did it all over again. No one bought a ticket thinking they would be hurt, but they let themselves be fooled.

The Boardwalk encouraged people to abandon other conventions of daily life as well. Visitors wore shirts and ties exploding with pinks and purples, hauled around stuffed animals the size of small children, and ate exotic foods from France and China. Normally reserved couples walked hand in hand, sneaking kisses here and there. Total strangers met and struck up conversations. Though ordinary behavior might be modified, it was never a free-for-all. In the end, in order for the Boardwalk to operate as a place of riskless risk, it had to appear safe.[63] Inspectors had to check the rides and garbage men had to empty the trash-cans every night. Uniformed ushers and doormen had to patrol the theaters and hotels. Even more important, city officials had to keep undesirables—criminals, the poor, and those marked as Other—contained and under wraps.

City managers posted confidence builders all along the Boardwalk to reassure white visitors. Normally tight-fisted local politicians spent money like drunken conventioneers on Boardwalk lamps and lights. They invested in this overheated wattage to convince tourists that Atlantic City nights had been purged of all threatening forces.[64] Offering visitors further comfort, as the sun set each evening, the police department dispatched battalions of beat cops to keep watch over the Boardwalk. Hotels and theaters placed bellhops and porters dressed like Buckingham Palace guards at their front doors to raise the comfort level of patrons and to keep out unwelcome intruders.

Adding to the sense of public order, city leaders passed in 1907 the Mackintosh Law, which made it illegal for anyone "to bathe in the ocean or to appear on the beach front . . . in a bathing suit which does not reach at least four inches above the knee." Another measure made it illegal for anyone to walk on the Boardwalk in a bathing suit not covered by a "robe or cloak reaching from shoulders to below the knees." Violators faced a penalty of $200 or ninety days in jail.[65] Beachgoers, apparently, enforced the laws themselves. "The other day at Atlantic City," claimed a travel writer in 1915, half jokingly, "the crowd upon the beach mobbed and nearly killed a woman the skirt of whose pretty bathing-suit was, they considered, slashed too high."[66]

Unofficial dress codes strengthened the city's official policies. During the day, tourists and locals, explains a lifelong area resident, made sure they were "neatly dressed, but not 'dressed up.'" For a visit to Steel Pier, this woman remembers putting on "sandals and a summer cotton dress." At night, everyone—and everyone will tell you this—"dressed up."[67] They didn't wear their Sunday best; Atlantic City was a Saturday night kind of town. The Boardwalk was like "going to a ball," one woman remembers with a toothy smile and a big laugh. Another compared nighttime to a "fashion show." "We dressed up like we were going out formal," this woman told an interviewer in 1978. "Sputz, that's what we called it. You know, really all duded out. Sputz!" On weekend nights, Herman Silverman wore a white jacket, his wife a blue satin evening gown with rhinestone-studded shoes and a matching belt.[68] All around them people paraded up and down the Boardwalk in their swankiest clothes. Men dressed in boxy, double-breasted blazers and pleated white linen pants. They accessorized with monogrammed cufflinks, silk ties, and felt hats. Women wore cashmere sweaters with mink collars over silk blouses and, atop their freshly done hair, lacy bonnets or hats decorated with flowers. The dress code did more than turn the Boardwalk into a nightly, roving fashion show; it marked the promenade as a formal and exclusive place. Those who couldn't afford the right clothes were clearly unwelcome and could expect to be stared at and made to feel uncomfortable.

Fearful that a slip in public decorum would let the wrong people onto the Boardwalk, city leaders constantly tried to regulate behavior along the "eighth wonder of the world." In 1945, the Chamber of Commerce urged local officials to do something about "indecent clothing."[69] A year later, "a man from Wall Street" with "the interest of Atlantic City at heart" told a South Jersey newspaper that "people here in New York are referring to Atlantic City as being dirtier than Coney Island." Clearly worried about more than overflowing trashcans and stray hot dog wrappers, he counseled resort leaders to launch a "clean up campaign" and "see that bathers do not cross the Boardwalk in bathing suits."[70] Six years later, city commissioners authorized the formation of a "beauty squad." Officials expected the ten-member unit to "shoo bathers away from the walk and watch out for other violations of police rules and regulations."[71]

Along with getting rid of uncovered bathers, city leaders wanted the beauty squad to keep "an eye on the rolling chair pushers."[72] If visitors felt threatened at this crucial point of interracial contact, they might, local officials feared, stay away; with this in mind, city leaders tried to control the behavior of African American pushers. A few years before the beauty squad formed, hotel operators called on municipal representatives to make "pushers wear badges, dress better, and be subject to discipline if they insult passengers, drink on the job, or demand exorbitant tips."[73] Another group suggested in 1950 that chair pushers wear uniforms "and at the very least be neatly dressed."[74]

White city leaders tried to govern—even narrate—every black-white encounter in the city, not just those on the rolling chairs. Throughout most of the twentieth century, segregation prevailed in Atlantic City. Boardwalk hotel and Inlet guesthouse owners refused to rent to African Americans. When four dark-skinned women showed up at the Brighton Hotel in 1948 with reservations, they were told that there was a mistake and that there was no room for them. But the clerk did volunteer to find them a room in the black section of town.[75] Before the 1920s, African Americans could swim on many city beaches. But after that, hoteliers started to complain that they lost "hundreds of thousands of dollars" because whites "positively will not stand rubbing elbows with colored bathers." The Traymore's owners informed the mayor that "friends ridiculed them for coming to Atlantic City" where "colored people were all over the beach." In response, city leaders decided to try to corral African Americans onto a single beachfront.[76] About the same time, movie houses introduced their own rules of segregation. The manager of the Strand Theater on the Boardwalk told an interviewer in the 1930s that if it were up to him, "Negroes would sit anywhere they like." But the movies were a business, he said, adding that "95% of the Theater goers . . . are whites." "They object," he observed, "to close association with Negroes, especially the transient tourists that come in the summer." So the Strand manager reported that he found "it expedient for the 5% Negroes to be put on the left hand side."[77]

After the 1920s, African Americans could gain full access to the Boardwalk's middle-class utopia only if they could pass as white. "Did I ever tell you," one man, who usually identified himself as African American, asked a friend, in the 1950s, "about the time I passed for Greek in Atlantic City? . . . Man, I was the King of the Boardwalk. I had a tailored suit, suede shoes, and a diamond ring set in solid gold. All the women knew me as Jimmy Williams, the Greek Adonis."[78] Those not willing or not light-skinned enough to pass must have felt on the Boardwalk like James Baldwin once did in a Swiss village. "Whenever I passed," he wrote in a 1940 essay, "a wind passed with me—of astonishment, curiosity, amusement, and outrage."[79]

Sometimes African Americans got more than just cold stares if they broke the city's unwritten Jim Crow rules. Police in the 1930s "forcibly eject[ed]" black families from any beach other than the black beach, known then as Chicken Bone Beach, located between Mississippi and Missouri avenues. Throughout most of the 1920s, the city's black beach had been at Indiana Avenue, but when the Claridge Hotel opened there toward the end of the decade, the owners complained and managed to have African American sunbathers moved a few blocks south to the space in front of Convention Hall and behind a sandstone wall. Blacks were at the same time barred from the best seats in the movie houses, restaurants, and nightclubs. No Boardwalk store would allow African Americans to try on clothes no matter how much money they had. While the police might leave well-dressed black couples on vacation alone on the Boardwalk, they would harass city residents who tried to join the roving fashion show. They didn't want them to think they had free access to this public space. White bar owners regularly threw black men out of their establishments or charged as much for a shot and a beer as a lobster dinner would have cost down the street. Steel Pier's owners, sponsors of minstrel shows until the mid-1940s, sold tickets to African Americans, but they would not let them dance at night to the big bands in the ornate ballroom.[80]

Tourism officials patrolled white behavior along the color line as well. Terri McNichol started taking French classes during her freshman year in high school in 1962. That spring, she came to Atlantic City with her dance company to perform in Tony Grant's children's revue on Steel Pier. As she waited to check into a Boardwalk hotel, she practiced French with a classmate. An African American bellhop overheard them and called out, "Merci." The teenagers smiled and started to talk with the man. Later, an adult chaperone knocked on McNichol's door.

"You will have to go home," she announced. "Why?" Terri asked. It was the hotel, the dance teacher explained, reporting that the managers were uncomfortable with the way Terri and her friend had talked with the black man. The conversation apparently sent the wrong message.[81]

With interracial contact tightly controlled and regulated, white strangers felt free to press up against each other on the rides and sit in the dark next to each other at the movies. When they did meet black women and men on the Boardwalk, like on the rolling chairs, in restaurants, or at the shoeshine stand, they met them in heavily scripted settings staged to fill them with reassuring feelings of safety and superiority.

While police, merchants, and Steel Pier managers tried to keep African Americans from enjoying the Boardwalk, black people as workers remained visible. Lugging bags, clearing dishes, and pushing rolling chairs, they played central roles in the city's tourist narrative. Indeed, the inclusion of African Americans in the story was central to the fantasy for sale in Atlantic City, a fantasy like the minstrel show, built around stock Jim Crow characters. Local businesspeople hired local blacks to do jobs that had them, as Robin D. G. Kelley has observed, squeezing "nickels and dimes from white men who longed for a mythic plantation past where darkeys liked to serve."[82]

Middle-class white people—people who during the rest of the year generally did not have servants—came to Atlantic City to rise above the masses and to show that they were not ordinary. To many, taking the next step on the American economic ladder meant having black people wait on them. In this public production of race making, whites, particularly the children of women and men from Gdansk, Palermo, and Budapest, made claims to whiteness, giving up their status as immigrants and becoming full-fledged Americans. This made Atlantic City, then, a crucial site of race and nation making.

Atlantic City's busiest days in the middle decades of the twentieth century coincided with, maybe even foreshadowed, a marked shift in ideas about American democracy and the proper path to assimilation. Throughout the nineteenth and early twentieth centuries, national leaders isolated European immigrants on the social margins. Only through near-complete assimilation could Germans, Poles, Russians, Italians, and Romanians gain full acceptance in America. But beginning with the New Deal and culminating in the broad-based effort to win World War II, many Americans seemed to embrace a more pluralistic, yet still racially determined, notion of the nation. Focusing on common suffering and sacrifice, this new melting-pot model stressed, for those of European descent, equality over difference. Immigrants no longer had to drop their linguistic, religious, culinary, and cultural traditions to join the national community.[83] They only had to have enough money to engage in a few moments of conspicuous consumption and, in so doing, act with middle-class restraint and decorum. Passing as white, eating fancy meals, and dressing up in public transformed them into Americans.

Glenn Miller's hugely popular swing band, a regular act on Steel Pier, epitomized this new America. The trombone-playing leader, as historian Lewis Erenberg has pointed out, "consciously sought to build an all-American team that fused the ethnic big city and the Protestant heartland." Jewish, Catholic, Protestant, and Christian Scientist jazz musicians and singers dressed in crisply tailored suits and played in his band, but Miller barred black musicians from his star-making ensemble. Wartime films created another idealized, white, seemingly inclusive version of America. In these movies, Connecticut Yankees, Poles from the Chicago stockyards, Jews and Italians from the Bronx, farmers from Georgia's Tobacco Road, and Irish from Boston crouched together in foxholes, creating visual images of a nation based on shared commitment, cultural pluralism, and—implicitly—on exclusion.[84]

"I should say," the always sharp-eyed Alexis de Tocqueville predicted long before the midpoint of the twentieth century, "that the abolition of slavery in the South will, in the common course of things, increase white repugnance for blacks."[85] Something similar happened as the New Deal era and the wartime melting pot heated up. Immigrants' embrace of America seemed to intensify their prejudice against African Americans. Americanization was, for them, largely about the slippage between race and class; becoming an American meant becoming white and middle class. Turning themselves into Americans entailed a simultaneous process of making sure that African Americans, other nonwhites, and, to a lesser extent, the undisciplined poor could not be assimilated into the American mainstream. In cultural terms, this process meant excluding the Others from playing swing, riding roller coasters, getting cast as war heroes, and gaining full access to luxurious hotels and movie palaces, while still keeping them in view.

Atlantic City did just that. It included everyone who passed as white and middle class and no one who looked not so white or not so respectable. The Boardwalk served as a platform for this exclusive form of nation building as white people—in particular, immigrants on their way out of the working class—acted out stories of making it in America against a backdrop of contrived blackness.

The rolling chair presented the Atlantic City and, indeed, national drama of race and class making in its most striking form. Each trip began long before the actual ride down the Boardwalk. Days, weeks, maybe even months before they got to Atlantic City, white families started to look for the right clothes, checking department store sales and tailoring older garments. On the night of the ride, they took their time getting dressed. Their hotel and boardinghouse rooms reeked of powder and perfume. Looking like they were ready for a flashy formal, the family walked onto the Boardwalk. The father threw up his hand and hailed a rolling chair. An African American man pulled up, said hello, asked where to, and after the family had climbed aboard, maneuvered the clunky, three-wheeled vehicle through the crowds into one of the long straight lanes of wicker chairs running down the Boardwalk.

On the front cover of the sheet music for the song "On the Boardwalk," there is a drawing of a white couple riding in a rolling chair. The broad-shouldered white man in the picture exudes confidence, even arrogance. He is not smiling, nor is he frowning. He sits erect, wearing a sleek, tailored suit, a stiff high-collared shirt, a neat tie, and bright, spit-shined shoes. He has a hat on his head and a thin, machine-rolled cigarette in his hand. Across his lap rests an elegant walking stick. Sitting next to him is a woman, probably his wife. She is dressed in a long, frilly, light-colored dress with a fresh flower pinned to her chest. Another flower—this one quite large—sticks out above her narrow-brimmed straw hat. Her long, slim fingers hold a frilly parasol. With a calm, contented smile on her face, she is looking around, maybe to see who is looking at her. Behind the well-dressed couple is an African American man, who is pushing them down the Boardwalk. He is wearing a loose-fitting dark jacket, white shirt, floppy bow tie, and light-colored pants with the legs rolled up, not hemmed. On his head, the artist placed an oversized porter's hat, on his feet are well-worn lace-up shoes. His face pulls the caricature together. The pusher's eyes are blank, wide-eyed, almost childlike. They hide nothing; there is no hint of pain or suffering. And of course, he is smiling, not a full-toothed, laughing grin, just a closed-mouth, cheerful greeting. Clearly, this black man is happy bowing for tips, pushing white people down the Boardwalk.[86]

The rolling chair in drawings was an illusion, but so too was a real ride on a rolling chair. The illusion began with the pusher. In this fantasy, Jordan Sayles and other African Americans enjoyed serving white people. The pushers did not suffer, like they did in real life, from "nervous fatigue, ruptures, tuberculosis," and "boardwalk feet." Every day, these men tasted the bitterness of having escaped the South only to find themselves waiting on a new group of white people.[87] In the riders' illusion, they deserved, even earned, the deference they received from these smiling servants. It was their just reward for hard work, for getting ahead, for making it in America. Once in the chair, the famed "wicker affluence" swept over them. For this one bewitching moment, the passengers made themselves into central characters in a dreamland of wealth, splendor, and urban grace. They were the nation's leading citizens, living embodiments of America's promise of redemption through discipline, hard work, and following the rules and of the nation's equally important tradition of exclusivity. The Atlantic City Boardwalk gave these striving members of the midcentury's middle class exactly what they wanted, and that's why it was their utopia.

2

The
Midway

ocal law made it illegal for rolling-chair pushers to leave the Boardwalk. But no one really paid attention to the statute. Late at night, with the kids in bed, Jordan Sayles took white couples over to the Paradise Club, only a short walk from the Marlborough-Blenheim Hotel and Steel Pier.[1] None of Atlantic City's dozens of clubs and nightspots were more than five blocks from the Boardwalk. But somehow the distance seemed greater. Going from the Boardwalk to the smoky showrooms was like moving from one city to another, from a world of staged decorum and respectability to a world of carefully managed and choreographed exoticism and danger. The trip took tourists from places to see and be seen to places designed for gazing at others and taking on new roles. The Chamber of Commerce and the Visitors Bureau did not boast as loudly about this side of the city as they did about the lobby of the Ritz Carlton Hotel and the diving horses, but during the city's heyday they also used the public, yet still exclusive, world of the clubs and exotic sideshows to lure tourists to town and keep them coming back.

The Paradise Club on North Illinois Avenue, where Sayles took white couples before World War II, was not much to look at from the outside. It was a plain building with a simple neon sign hanging over the door. But inside, past the thick-necked bouncer, another world existed. During the 1930s, Count Basie's Orchestra regularly performed at the Paradise. Basie said that playing there was "a gas." Before his hard-swinging, hard-living band took the stage, black vocalists entertained the crowd with risqué vaudeville tunes, and black comedians in overalls and straw hats told raunchy jokes. Then the half-dozen, dark-skinned, full-bodied Sextuplet Dancers, dressed in top hats, short black shorts, and tuxedo vests a size

45

or two too small, took the stage. The house band picked up the beat. The women wiggled and shook. The crowd smoked their Chesterfields, drank their seven-and-sevens, and howled with delight. On other nights, the Paradise floor show featured a trio of African American drummers dressed like the natives in a *Tarzan* movie playing behind light-skinned female dancers decked out in boas and feathered bikinis.

Count Basie, Jimmie Lunceford, Lucky Millinder, and the other musicians who played the Paradise knew that they were sometimes sideshows. White tourists came primarily to watch the black women do their shake dances, not to listen to music. Drummer Chris Columbo joked that after watching the Sextuplets or the Colored Revue, "they [the audience] just weren't ready to sit down and listen to a concert."[2]

With its raucous nightclubs and Boardwalk linen shops, hip-thrusting African American dancers and upright, uniformed ushers, Atlantic City resembled the World's Columbian Exposition. Staged in Chicago in 1893 to mark the 400th anniversary of Columbus's landing in the "new world," this carefully plotted world's fair divided its attractions into two distinct, separate, and racially marked spheres: the White City and the Midway. "The White City," writes cultural historian Gail Bederman, "depicted the millennial advance of white civilization, while the Midway . . . presented the undeveloped barbarism of uncivilized, dark races." An artificial city within a real city—rapidly industrializing Chicago—the White City spoke in highbrow tones through a series of classical architectural quotations. Its perfectly symmetrical buildings and deliberately right-angled streets announced that this was an urban utopia of order and rationality, a place of refinement at the very pinnacle of the Darwinian hierarchy. The Midway, of course, evoked another place. Haphazard and confusing, its twisting streets took visitors through seemingly disorganized Persian, Turkish, and Egyptian villages. Strange music wafted through the air. Women in skimpy outfits danced and sang. Eroticism and a hint of criminality ruled this place.[3]

While Atlantic City lacked the strict and coherent divide of the Victorian era Columbian Exposition, it nonetheless functioned throughout the twentieth century as though it were, to paraphrase Lewis Mumford, "a World's Fair in continuous operation."[4] Like the Chicago fairgrounds, Atlantic City had a perfect White City—the Boardwalk, the hotels, and the theaters—and a funky Midway of nightclubs, street corners, and backrooms. The dressed-up world of the Boardwalk was, like the White City, an artificial city within a city. Against the ocean backdrop, order, decorum, and middle-class respectability spiced with a bit of frivolity ruled. So perfect was the Boardwalk that many agreed with *New Republic* reporter Bruce Bliven and considered it a magical, utopian wonderland. At night, in the

◥THE SEXTUPLET DANCERS
These women shook and shimmied at the Paradise Club in the 1940s (Atlantic City Free Public Library, Heston Room, Atlantic City, New Jersey).

clubs behind the Boardwalk, both literally and figuratively, a different regime reigned. Under the gray veil of cigarette smoke, with drums beating and highball glasses clicking, "soft primitivism," "managed eroticism," and stylized danger took over.[5] Clubs, like the Paradise Club, created a raucous and bawdy world that stretched, without rupturing, racial boundaries in the city. Other Midway sites, illegal casinos and racy drag shows, extended class and sexual borders. But all of the acts at the same time still highlighted exclusion and difference.

For most of the social climbers walking on the Boardwalk, doing a little slumming on the side in the glitzy nightclubs and at risqué shows represented another just reward for hard work. The excesses of these places, like the colossal hotels, underscored the presumed perfection of middle-class values. But for others, the city's Midway extended the range of the town's playacting possibilities. Away from home and the reproachful eyes of their peers, these visitors tried on different personas, sometimes even different sexual and racial identities. The Midway offered an escape, too, from the orderly, decorous, and formal performances of the Boardwalk. Here visitors could imagine themselves as hipper, as more daring and adventurous people. Some Atlantic City visitors, then, came to town for the Midway. They went through the motions of a ride down the Boardwalk on a rolling chair or a dressy, five-course hotel dinner and then headed to the edge of town, to slip their own skin, if only for a night, and become someone else.

Just about every American city contained a White City and a Midway, a respectable entertainment zone and a red-light district, sparkling movie palaces and dark nightclubs. What made Atlantic City different from Philadelphia and Reading and even Las Vegas was the close proximity and relative safety of the two sites. The Paradise Club and the Club Harlem, the city's leading black-and-tan spots, that is, clubs where black performers entertained white audiences, stood only a few blocks from the dreamscape of the Marlborough-Blenheim Hotel. Cross-dressing drag queens strutted across the stage of Louisa Mack's Entertainer's Club, only a football field or two away from Yamron's, a swank Boardwalk jewelry shop.

Even more important, Atlantic City offered Midway visitors a safe cover. Back home in Harrisburg or Newark, people associated Atlantic City with the Boardwalk, splendid hotels, and glittery amusement piers. When a lumber store clerk told his boss he was going to Atlantic City for the weekend, the employer didn't raise an eyebrow. Once the clerk got to town, he could parade up and down the Boardwalk in a pressed suit and white shirt in the evening and then, after midnight, dive into the clubs, moving from middle-class respectability to middle-class thrills in a matter of minutes. To him and millions like him, this was the best of both worlds. Easy access to the White City and the Midway was a key factor in making Atlantic City the world's playground, the most popular resort in mid–twentieth-century America. And the Harrisburg clerk and the Newark foreman knew without thinking about it that these two worlds were really not as far apart as they appeared at first glance.

GOING OUT

Location on the Midway generally dictated how tourists and businesspeople used the spaces. The Boardwalk featured its own primitive, sensual attractions. Before the 1960s, most middle-class, East Coast families could only go as far as Atlantic City for their vacations. With them in mind, leisure merchants brought distant lands and distant people to the Jersey shore.[6] Beginning in the 1920s, Steel Pier featured an "authentic" Hawaiian village. Throughout the day, "real" Hawaiians came out of their thatch-roofed huts to entertain the crowds. Dark-skinned men in flowery shirts played bouncy island tunes, while dark-skinned women in bikini tops and grass skirts shimmied and swayed in a version of the hula dance performed only on the mainland. Parents gawked and mumbled to their children, "Look, there's a real native."[7]

Other Boardwalk attractions offered the same illusion of foreignness. As early as 1891, four "Japanese" goods dealers and a Turkish importer operated along the promenade. "The 'connoisseur,' " promised the local travel bureau in 1907, "would be mightily attracted by the 'rarest importations' from Armenia and Syria, China and Japan, Canada and Mexico, Egypt and London." Foreignness prevailed in entertainment as well. During the summers, the Garden Pier orchestra performed "Turkish Patrol" and "The Wizard of the Nile." The "Egyptian tent" at South Carolina Avenue and the Boardwalk featured snake handlers and mummies, while the nearby Japanese Tea Garden presented "a delightful patch of Orientalism" and a "Japanese Fairyland on a Mammoth Scale." Not far away, under a billboard-sized red and gold picture of a Chinese dragon, Million Dollar Pier offered tourists rides on the Orient Express.[8]

"You want to go native?" asked advertisers for the Chalfonte-Haddon Hotel. For those who did, the hotel offered three "exhilarating" off-season weekend parties—that's the only time the conservative hoteliers would let the Midway onto their properties—Caribbean Carnivals, Frivolities Francaises, and the Hawaiian South Seas Party.[9] On the front of one brochure beckoning visitors to the shore in January, February, and March, company representatives placed a pair of "calypso" dancers. A shirtless, dark-skinned man with his hair teased up toward the sky and a string of teeth and bones hanging around his neck appears next to an athletic-looking black woman in a low-cut dress with long slits up each side. Both figures are moving their hips, asking the reader to turn the page. Inside, there is another picture of people of color. Under the caption "Jungle Club," the hotel promises, "Lithe native dancers, direct from the islands, lend their authentic exciting and exotic rhythms to the festivities." Singer "Calypso Joe," the brochure brags, is the "real thing straight from Trinidad," "constantly improvising, creating witty lyrics and outlandish rhymes. He's occasionally risqué and always amusing." A cartoon figure of Calypso Joe says:

> Dey got de steel band and de native girl,
> De transported zombies dat will make your head whirl;
> Who wants to go to Cuba when the party's in Atlantic City
> I'm headed for dat party wit me bongos on me knee.[10]

Calypso Joe and other blackface characters were familiar figures on the Midway, and not just as rolling-chair pushers. Throughout the early years of Atlantic City's reign as the Queen of Resorts, minstrelsy was the most popular and ubiquitous form of entertainment across urban America. On the Boardwalk, both Steel Pier and Million Dollar Pier presented minstrel shows well into the 1940s.[11] Even later, into the postwar era, members of the local fire department and the Elks

Club "corked up" for their annual fundraisers.[12] At these shows, "colored comedians" and "black-faced singers" told mythic tales of the Old South, conjuring up familiar images of shiftless plantation hands and nurturing mammies. Every performance included a couple of songs of yearning for the "protective hand" of the "dear ole massa." When the minstrel tales shifted to the North, they poked fun at the uppity city slicker and the clumsy country bumpkin. Through it all, white audiences grinned and clapped.[13]

Once a year on the weekend after Labor Day, the Miss America Pageant turned white women into actors on the Boardwalk Midway. Begun in 1921 as a ploy to extend the summer season, the beauty contest quickly became both a local and national tradition projecting its own contradictory images of femininity and heterosexuality. Like other local and national traditions, this one was limited to whites only well into the postwar period. Eventually, as part of the fanfare, contestants paraded down the runway in high heels and bathing suits. Perhaps there was nothing as "primitive" about this show as there was about the hula dances or Calypso Joe's routine, but there was something mildly erotic and maybe even pornographic about the pageant. The competition put women on display, welcoming viewers to undress the participants with their eyes and their fantasies. While organizers placed the contestants on a huge, faraway stage, keeping leering eyes at a safe distance and upholding the essential respectability of white, middle-class women, they still turned the teenagers—and that is how old many of them were—into sexual objects and tourist attractions. When they came to protest on the Boardwalk in 1968, feminists noted this Midway connection and complained, "Miss America and *Playboy*'s centerfolds are sisters over the skin. To win approval, we must be both sexy and wholesome, . . . demure yet titillatingly bitchy."[14]

Set a few blocks back from the beach, the nightclubs displayed the same primitivism as the Boardwalk's Midway attractions. Like Steel Pier and Chalfonte-Haddon Hall, they featured "authentic" persons of color dressed in exotic outfits and positioned in erotic poses. The 500 Club, for instance, employed the Tokyo Coats, a dance group made up of Asian-looking women. Mer-Lyn, the "Oriental Songstress," regularly sang at the club in the postwar era. Another bar booked an act called the House of Flowers, promising the audience a "Caribbean Fantasy." Several clubs, especially after World War II, hired "genuine" Cuban dancers and "real" Latin bands.

The soft primitivism of the clubs was, however, wrapped in a rawer, bawdier, and more sexually explicit package. The women wore fewer clothes and edged closer to the crowd than did the performers on the Boardwalk's Midway. The music curved and snaked more seductively around the beat. And the rules continued to change the farther people went from the Boardwalk. Standards of behavior were relaxed. It was, then, at these venues that tourists got the chance for playacting of a different sort from their Boardwalk performances.

The most popular form of the "primitive" in Atlantic City, and across the country, during the middle of the twentieth century came in a parcel marked "authentic blackness." That was what Jordan Sayles's passengers went looking for at the Paradise Club and nearby at the bars and nightspots located around the intersection of Kentucky and Arctic avenues. Just three blocks from the Boardwalk, Ky. at the Curb, as locals called the area around that corner, was a world away from the lobby of the Ritz Carlton or the front porch of a South Inlet guesthouse. By day, Jordan Sayles and other black people, and pretty much only black people, lived in the houses and apartments around the area's clubs and eateries. But at night, white couples traveled to the Northside, the name used to designate the city's African American neighborhood. The entertainment at many area bars was, according to drummer and band leader Chris Columbo, "90 percent black," but "the trade was 90 percent white." Jordan Sayles noticed the same pattern. "Here's the way the town was," he explained. "You didn't find Negroes going anyplace, because they knew they were not wanted, and they didn't want to be embarrassed, so they didn't go. But you found more white people coming over there than you found black people coming over here. I guess people are curious."[15]

Atlantic City wasn't the only place where white people acted on their curiosity. Tracing the same steps as New Yorkers who headed uptown to Harlem in the 1920s, white visitors to Atlantic City over the next several decades went slumming at Ky. at the Curb. At home in Wilmington and Trenton, white clerks, salesmen, store owners, and dentists lived, for the most part, carefully segregated lives. On the Boardwalk, they recreated a fantasy version of segregation, one that kept black people in view and at their beck and call, but at a safe distance. Yet at night, on vacation out on the Midway, they felt a little braver than normal. They went on tour to see, feel, smell, and maybe even touch primitive blackness up close. They went to the Timbuktu, Wonder Gardens, and the Club Harlem to hear black men belt out jazz riffs and to watch black women shake their bodies and to Sapp's, Jerry's Ribs, and Wash's Restaurant to eat southern "soul" food, plates piled high with crispy fried chicken, smoky tender ribs, and fat wedges of sweet potato pie.[16]

Of course, segregation still prevailed on the Northside; club owners just drew the color line in different ways to allow white tourists to edge closer to what they imagined to be authentic blackness. The white and black men who ran the jazz joints and food stands at Ky. at the Curb made sure of one other thing. While thrilling and titillating white visitors, offering them a taste of life on the other side of the racial divide, they also reassured the slummers that they were welcome on the Northside, that they were safe there, that black performers did not resent them or the racial order, and that there was an easy way back to Atlantic City's White City.

When most white tourists went slumming in Atlantic City, they went to the Club Harlem. Opened in the mid-1930s, the Kentucky Avenue nightspot was Atlantic City's version of New York City's famed Cotton Club, a place the songwriter Harold Arlen once called "the hangout for the Mink Set, escaping Park Avenue for the earthier realities of Harlem."[17] For white tourists, the experience of going to the Club Harlem began even before they got inside the building. It started with the ride—perhaps in Jordan Sayles's rolling chair—from the Boardwalk. Patrons had to cross Atlantic Avenue, the city's dividing line between white and black. Almost as soon as Atlantic City's Mink Set went over to the other side, they saw the club's tall neon sign sticking out over the sidewalk. Announcing to white tourists that they had arrived in a "black" space, the word *Harlem*, spelled out in bold, block letters, ran diagonally down the center of the marquee with *Club* printed on one side in smaller, swirling letters. On the other side was the silhouette of a dark-skinned woman, wearing a bikini top and beating an African-looking drum. At the bottom of the sign, club owners advertised what many guests came to see at the nightspot. Neon lights spelled out the name of the club's dancers, the Sepia Revue.[18]

The shows at the Club Harlem, choreographed for many years by the legendary producer Larry "Good Deal" Steele, followed the same script as the shows staged at the nearby Paradise Club and at New York nightspots, like the Cotton Club. The performances had, as singer Lena Horne recalled, "a naked quality that was supposed to make a civilized audience lose its inhibitions."[19] Comedians dressed like clowns, plantation hands, and frumpy old ladies told dirty jokes to start things off. Then came the house band. Mimicking Duke Ellington's famed Jungle Band, the trios and quartets played hot, loud, brassy jazz. The drummers banged, tapped, and rapped cymbals, tom-toms, and bells. The bass players thumped thick, hypnotic lines. Over the beat, the trumpeters, trombonists, and sax men spit out "dirty solos" filled with "insinuating" notes "winding curvaceously up" and punctuated by weird muted sounds produced by derby hats and toilet plungers.[20]

Next came even more outrageous warm-up acts. During the summer of 1946, the Club Harlem featured the Three Chocolateers, Leonardo and Zollo, "Cuban ritual dancers," and the Numb Nymb. On other nights, the crowd might get what satirist and critic George S. Schuyler called a "corpulent shouter of mammy songs with a gin-roughened voice." Then the headliner appeared. Just about every famous African American singer or entertainer did a stint at the Club Harlem. Over the years, Billy Daniels, Cab Calloway, Jackie "Moms" Mabley, the Will Mastin

Trio, Redd Foxx, Slappy White, Billy Ekstine, Peg Leg Bates, Sarah Vaughn, and, later, Jackie Wilson, Al Green, Gladys Knight and the Pips, James Brown, and Sam Cooke all danced and sang in the club's main room.[21]

At the center of every Club Harlem show was the high-energy gyrations of the Sepia Revue backed by the "red hot" house band. Twelve coffee-skinned women dressed in black high heels, skimpy, sequined dresses, long boas, and feathered headgear strutted across the stage. They started with a mix of tap and soft shoe. With each step they danced, the beat quickened. Like the hula dancers, the women shook their bodies and thrust their hips; they wiggled and quivered. The beat got faster still. They shimmied and quaked. Sweat dripped from their nearly naked bodies, and the white crowd howled and stared.

Over at the Paradise Club, white audiences in the 1940s screamed for Dorycee Bradley, described by a *New York Amsterdam News* reporter as a "torrid hip tosser." When a bandleader sang "Take It All Off," one observer wrote, Bradley "artfully obeyed . . . until only a G-string remains." Not far away at the Paddock International Bar, crowds watched Joe Gregory. Dressed in a black-and-white-checked zoot suit with a bright bow tie, this "hep cat" tap danced as he belted out songs like "I Ain't Got Nobody."[22]

By the time Gregory, Bradley, and the Sepia Dancers left the stage and the last funky note sounded, the first rays of daylight were peeking over the ocean. A few patrons wandered off to the back rooms behind the clubs to shoot a game of pool against a local hustler or put a few dollars down on a horse running later that day. Most drained the whiskey from their highball glasses, stubbed out their cigarettes, and shuffled outside to a line of rolling chairs, which were waiting to take them back to their hotels and rooming houses. For most, the trip to the other side was over.[23]

Back across Atlantic Avenue, on the "white" side of town, the 500 Club offered white tourists another set of thrills. Located within the shadows of the city's massive Convention Hall on South Missouri Avenue, the Five, as regulars called the place, operated out of a building next to the Garibaldi Social Hall where, writes journalist Jonathan Van Meter, Italian immigrants played "card games like steemezza, briscolo, scopa, and pinochle."[24] From the outside, the club looked a little out of place in ornate, over-the-top Atlantic City. The original builder had arranged the pale yellow bricks in front in an austere, modernist pattern.

Above a recessed doorway, the 500 Club had a three-sided marquee, with black and white block lettering spelling out the name of the place. Standing underneath the sign in the 1940s and 1950s was Roy "Slim" Gaines, the club's giant of a doorman, outfitted in a tiny black bow tie, stretched-out uniform, and bright red porter's cap. Some said the African American man was seven feet, seven inches tall and could dunk a basketball without jumping. Inside, patrons walked through a roomy bar area decorated with zebra-striped wallpaper. The twisting jet-black bar curled back and forth in several directions. Booths upholstered with more black and white fabric lined the walls. Toward the back of the room, there was a fake waterfall framed by ultraviolet lights and exotic-looking plastic plants. Past this bar was another smaller bar and show room, and beyond that, the Vermilion Room. Big enough after a handful of renovations for a thousand people, the main room contained a stage at one end, booths along the walls, and dozens of long, thin cocktail tables down the middle. Stiff white linens covered every table, on top of which each had a full liquor set-up of ice, tonic, bitters, lemons, and limes. Burgundy velvet wallpaper with white speckles gave the room a dark, formal, almost gothic feel. The service was as ornate as the setting. Waitresses and busboys filled the room, lavishing attention on customers, who were dressed like they were going to a black-tie affair, with new forks for each course, fresh drinks, and lots of "yes sirs" and "yes ma'ams."[25]

On Five's stage, the biggest stars of the day—Sophie Tucker ("The Last of the Red Hot Mamas"), Patti Page, Liberace, Martha Raye, Donald O'Connor, and Louis Prima—performed. In 1946, Dean Martin and Jerry Lewis teamed up for the first time at the 500 Club. The king of the Rat Pack, Frank Sinatra, played the club a few times each year in the 1950s. As the decade came to a close, he was such a regular that when the marquee read, "He's Back," everyone in town knew it meant Sinatra. Usually the Five booked only white acts for its white audiences, but once African American crossover performers like Nat King Cole and Sammy Davis, Jr., proved that they could fill a large hall, they got a chance to play on the Missouri Avenue stage.[26]

Most people came to the 500 Club for the music, the drinks, and yet another chance to play the part of an urban sophisticate. For others, the biggest attraction was the club's host, proprietor, and owner, Paul "Skinny" D'Amato. Everyone remembers Skinny as suave, charming, charismatic, and a really sharp dresser. He showed up for his first date with his future wife wearing, writes his biographer, "a yellow, brown, and white plaid shirt and matching yellow pants."[27] But people didn't line up in front of the 500 Club just because of Skinny's bright smile and flashy wardrobe. They came because of his cool, unflappable demeanor and magnetic Damon Runyon personality. Tall and handsome, with twinkling, even devilish, brown eyes, D'Amato oozed a detached urban cool. He crossed a room with such ease and grace that he seemed to float more than walk. A committed night owl, Skinny rarely rose before noon. With a cigarette in one hand and a cup of coffee in the other, he spoke his own hipster slang, calling his male customers "daddy-o" and "man." Admirers remember him always saying the right thing, the funny thing, the disarming thing. With Skinny at the helm—he took over the club during World War II—the Five became a hangout for all kinds of people and a mandatory tourist destination.

Knowing that ordinary people flock to places just to be in the same room as celebrities, D'Amato courted the rich and famous. He didn't just hire stars to play in his club; he ate with them, drank with them, and joked with them. Skinny made sure everyone knew about his famous friends. Every night, the emcee began the show by announcing who was in the audience. It didn't matter how modest a person's fame was; if she appeared in a movie or a Boardwalk show or a radio soap opera, the spotlight shone on her. And you couldn't talk to D'Amato for more than a few minutes before he told you about his buddies Joe DiMaggio and Frank Sinatra. But Skinny didn't talk about all of his associates.[28]

Mystery surrounded Skinny D'Amato. No one knew everything there was to know about him. Some people probably knew that he was a card shark and that he started in the gambling business as a teenager. A few others must have known that Skinny had a police record and that sometime in the 1930s he did a short prison stint for "white slavery." By the 1940s, no one said much about this crime. Yet rumors still swirled around him. Some said he worked for Camden mob boss Marco Reginelli and later for Angelo Bruno when he took over Atlantic City's underworld. FBI agents reported that Skinny knew Chicago gangster Sam Giancana as well as Joseph Kennedy, the patriarch of the nation's most powerful political family. (One story—probably false—circulated that D'Amato carried money to West Virginia in 1960 to help seal John F. Kennedy's presidential nomination.) Whether Skinny was a made man no one knew for sure, but everyone knew that mobsters and their associates sat at the best tables and got the royal treatment at the Five and that some made men, like Bruno, loved Skinny like a brother.[29] That's one of the reasons that dressed-up middle-class couples went to the Missouri Avenue nightspot, to get close to the mob and its disdain for the law and the mundane rules of everyday life. It was a kind of slumming back across the color line. With its aura of lawlessness, the 500 Club offered visitors a way to make light of middle-class values without shedding these same principles.

The 500 Club's back room added to the mystery of the place. Behind the room in which Sinatra played stood a blank door and a doorman. The right word or a nod from Skinny opened the door. Then the guest was in one of the largest of Atlantic City's dozen or so illegal casinos. Blackjack tables, craps tables, and roulette wheels were spread across the room. Yet gambling at the 500 Club was apparently not like gambling in postwar Las Vegas, or even present-day Atlantic City. At Skinny's place, the thrill, it seems, came not from winning, but from doing something illegal and a little dangerous. Apparently, few people expected to win. In twenty years, a local man, Herman Silverman, never put together a winning streak of any kind at the club, but he kept putting on his tuxedo and playing cards there, and he kept laughing about losing.[30]

Eight blocks south of Skinny D'Amato's 500 Club, on New York Avenue and still on the white side of the Atlantic Avenue divide, existed another of the city's Midway attractions. Mobsters were around this site also, but that's not what made it a dangerous place. Sex made it dangerous. A few years after the start of Prohibition, Louisa Mack opened the Entertainer's Club, the city's first gay-tolerant bar. From its earliest days as a resort, Atlantic City's climate of relative sexual freedom, a by-product of the exoticism of the beach, attracted men and women, although mostly men, who, away from employers, families, and the hometown police, took advantage of their relative anonymity to engage in homosexual behavior.

Before the Entertainer's Club opened, men searching for other men identified themselves to each other on the beach and the Boardwalk through their clothing.[31] As early as 1896, just a couple of decades after the construction of the resort's first hotel, a journalist spotted some men wearing brightly colored silk garters—a kind of marker of same-sex desire—with their black bathing suits. In 1925, a *New York Times* reporter found "cunning-looking men wearing trick pants, pale purple hose, tan shoes with two-inch soles and lavender neckties" on the Boardwalk.[32]

Like many of the nation's first urban gay bars, Louise Mack's club was situated on a hard-to-find street, away from middle-class residential areas and business centers.[33] Located behind New York Avenue on Westminster Avenue—nicknamed "Snake Alley" because the narrow, one-block-long street slithered from right to left—the bar stood among a few inexpensive rooming houses and a handful of modest private homes just off the beach. Up the street from Louisa's, where New York Avenue met Pacific Avenue, there were a couple of smoky bars, some apparently owned by mobsters and their friends. Prostitutes worked nearby street corners. Although South New York Avenue ran right up to the Boardwalk and was within a few blocks of Steel Pier and the Dennis Hotel, the block's cultural distance from the resort's mainstream limited the amount of social and actual policing in the area. This, in turn, provided a cover—a thin cover, to be sure—for gay men.

Understanding the sexual politics of the day, Louise Mack provided her customers with another layer of camouflage by making her club as invisible as possible. Even after Prohibition ended, she did not advertise or put up a sign. Just a bare light bulb hung over the door to let customers know they were in the right place. "It didn't look like a bar. It looked like a house, painted yellow with green trim," one man recalls of the Entertainer's Club. "If you didn't know it was there, you'd never see it." Enough men, however, found the bar to keep it in business for more than fifty years.[34]

"Oh, Miss Mack," one regular remembers, "she loved the gay boys." As men walked into her club, she slapped their backsides.[35] But Mack, decorated with bright orchids woven into her hair and running down over her chest to the floor, did more than greet customers with friendly pats. She looked over each one and tried to spot malicious pretenders and undercover police. She also wanted to make sure that her club exuded a certain sense of style, even class. The Entertainer's Club, like other places in the city, enforced a strict nighttime dress code. For men, jackets were required after six o'clock. One man laughingly recalled, "You had to wear suits. I remember standing outside, sweltering in the summer, waiting to get in."[36] Hoping to keep the police at bay and add another layer of anonymity to the place, Mack made sure the sidewalks got cleaned every night and the building painted every year. On Sunday morning, Mack put on a dress, marched off to church, and sat in the very front pew. Inside the bar, she kept her customers' bodies from touching. She forbade dancing and kissing in the club.[37] These sanctions, she thought, provided her with plausible deniability; that is, if asked, she could say she ran a fancy nightclub and didn't care who came, so long as they dressed up and behaved. But she couldn't keep the police away all the time. Officers occasionally raided the club, and in the 1950s, the city closed down Mack's bar for 190 days.[38]

Fearful of arrest and exposure, some gay men probably stayed away from the Entertainer's Club and New York Avenue, meeting instead at private house parties.[39] Others continued to hook up on the Boardwalk, on the beach, and even at the bar at the Brighton Hotel. Beginning in the 1930s, still other men interested in meeting men went to the flashy drag shows or "pansy acts" staged at ostensibly straight bars like Atlantic City's own Cotton Club and at the Pansy Club. The shows caused alarm in some quarters. Worried that the "spread" of drag shows would generate "adverse advertising," the city's mayor banned the acts in 1933. But these "minstrel shows of gender bending," as Gary Giddins calls them, continued.[40]

Same-sex thrills were not the only sexual fantasies available along the Midway. The beach was (and is) a place where people wore less clothing than usual. With half-covered bodies on display all day, an erotic charge filled the shore air. Atlantic City, like beach towns everywhere, had a lustier feel than everyday places. Teenagers prowled the spaces above and below the Boardwalk, while honeymooners came to town to begin their marriages. Vacationers could, if they wanted to, go sexually slumming at the Paddock International to see Zorita and her eight-foot "Arabian blue snake" or to the Nomad to watch the performances of "Donna

Darnell—That Tantalizing Texas Tornado—The Torrid Tycoon of Zam" and a "Bevy of 'Bare-Entities' Beauties in the Racy, Riotous, and Risqué." Across the city, smaller taverns and bars staged "g-string" performances and striptease shows.[41]

Along the way to these nightspots, visitors could not help but run into prostitutes on street corners and in hotel lobbies and club bars. Conventioneers no doubt made up the bulk of the city's commercial sex trade customers. Beginning in 1929, when the marble and limestone, Romanesque Convention Hall, a building big enough to fit a flying helicopter, opened on the Boardwalk ten blocks north of New York Avenue, Atlantic City hosted some of the nation's largest business and professional meetings. Each year, thousands of doctors, teachers, and plumbers on expense accounts flocked to the city and to the Midway in particular. Some slipped away from their hotels and rooming houses in search of sex. Near the public restroom on the Boardwalk at the end of New York Avenue, men, some with painted cheeks, turned tricks.[42] Along Pacific and Illinois avenues, white women walked the streets. Black women sold their bodies to white men on Chalfonte Alley, and other prostitutes operated out of bordellos on North Mississippi, Michigan, and Delaware avenues. Atlantic City's most expensive call girls, meanwhile, hovered around the zebra-striped bar at Skinny D'Amato's 500 Club.[43]

MIDWAY POLITICS

The muckraker Lincoln Steffens once described municipal government in Philadelphia as "corrupt and contented."[44] During the twentieth century, Atlantic City was probably even more corrupt and even more contented. According to one municipal official, city business and political leaders created a sturdy, and not really hidden, infrastructure to provide visitors with easy access to the Midway treats of "booze, broads, and gambling."[45] Prostitutes worked the streets, bars, and hotel lobbies without fear of arrest. So did brothel owners, bookies, and horse room operators. (The horse rooms were prototypes for legalized off-track betting. Operators took wagers on races around the country, while patrons listened to the results live over the telephone.) By one estimate, in 1951, 300 bookies and 200 numbers runners "openly" plied their trade in the city.[46] Earlier, Prohibition did little to stem the flow of beer, whiskey, and Brighton Punch, the fruity concoction served at the Boardwalk hotel of the same name, in Atlantic City. Blue laws, which limited the days of the week and times of day that alcohol could be sold and which were adopted once Congress scrapped the Eighteenth Amendment, applied to other New Jersey towns but not to the nation's playground. Bartenders poured drinks twenty-four hours a day, seven days a week. As more than one visitor noted, before 1960, Atlantic City was a "wide open" town.[47]

Atlantic City's political establishment made sure that the city remained wide

A BETTING PARLOR

The men are gathered here in the 1930s to wager on horse races up and down the East Coast. Note the policeman on the right-hand side. He seems to be participating in the proceedings more than disrupting them (Atlantic City Free Public Library, Heston Room, Atlantic City, New Jersey).

open. Starting with the hotel owner-turned-political kingpin Louis Kuehnle in the 1900s, continuing through the early and middle decades of the twentieth century with the dapper, free-spending, mob-friendly Enoch "Nucky" Johnson, and ending with the bland but still efficient reign of Francis Sherman "Hap" Farley from 1941 to 1971, this succession of powerful political chiefs ran the town and especially the Midway. Each wielded power from a different position. Kuehnle served several terms on the city commission. Johnson never held elected office but oversaw things from his post as county treasurer. Farley used his state senate seat as a base of authority. No matter what they did for their day jobs, over the years, these Republican bosses built a system of one-party rule backed by graft, patronage, intimidation, and electoral muscle that rivaled any political machine in the country, including Chicago's Daley machine and Memphis's Crump machine.[48]

Everything had a price in Atlantic City, and the machine always got its cut. To make sure visitors got all the "booze, broads, and gambling" they wanted, the bosses made a pact with the racketeers. The vice operators could sell whiskey and sex, put on high-stakes poker games, and run numbers as long as they paid protection money. If they didn't pay, they didn't get a license or a building permit. If they continued to hold out against the machine, they got arrested, or maybe beaten up. Those who did make their payments on time could expect the police to look the other way and even to tip them off if outside investigators were headed to town. For their troubles, the police, of course, got their cut of the action and they, in turn, paid the machine. They also protected the machine. "In Atlantic City," a reporter discovered in the 1940s, "if a New York or Chicago racketeer set up a casino or bordello, the local lads merely complained to the police vice squad, which drove the interlopers out of town."[49] Every once in a while a crusading police officer came along with the idea of cleaning up the city. Maybe he arrested a prostitute working at the 500 Club bar or busted a cigar-store owner who ran numbers on the side. But this lawman didn't get a pat on the back from the sergeant at the station. More often, he got demoted or fired.[50]

The machine used the money generated from the rackets to stay in power, keep the Midway wide open, and make sure the graft kept coming their way. Local politicians, in turn, practiced their own brand of trickle-down economics. Money from the rackets went to pay the doctor bills of elderly widows, purchase winter coats for poor kids, and deliver coal to laid-off waiters and bellhops. If a constituent had a problem, she went to her ward captain, and he solved things. He might get a driving-while-intoxicated arrest expunged from the record, see that a street got cleaned right after a parade, or shoo a building inspector away from a property that didn't quite live up to code. Exceedingly cautious and anxious to quell any kind of dissent, the machine made sure that every part of the city and every ethnic group got a bit of representation. In a practice started by Nucky Johnson, the bosses put forward each election cycle a balanced ticket for the city council made up of a Jew, an Irishman, an Italian, a Protestant, and even a Democrat, or a Farleycrat as they were later called. African Americans, who loyally voted Republican in Atlantic City—it was the only game in town—didn't get a place in the city government until the 1960s, but before then they did get a few of the spoils, including money for promoting black tourism and positions in the post office and police department.

The most loyal party supporters got city jobs, with no-show positions going to the truly dedicated. Every stenographer and dispatcher owed his or her job to the machine. They knew, in turn, that each job had a price. They knew that they had to buy $10 worth of tickets to the Republican party's Christmas dinner, take out a $20 advertisement in the program for the lifeguards' season-ending dance, or contribute $15 to the campaign of the party's nominee for county sheriff. If they didn't pay up, they didn't work. And they surely knew that at election time, they had to turn out the vote. Simple majorities were not good enough for the machine. When in the mid-1960s, a Philadelphia philanthropist offered Atlantic City his billion-dollar art collection, Hap Farley turned it down, saying, "No votes in it for me."[51]

Leaving nothing to chance, machine candidates regularly won 60, 70, or 80 percent of the vote. Such decisive majorities translated into significant political leverage. Buttoned-down Republicans from Bergen and Salem counties might have turned their noses up at the city's vice business, but they liked having a dependable chunk of votes coming in from the southern half of the state in every election. In exchange, these state political officials usually kept investigators out of Atlantic City. The same majority provided the basis for Hap Farley's power in Trenton and even Washington, D.C. Guaranteed reelection by the machine, the state senator, known by insiders as the "king of special interest legislation," accumulated tremendous power through the spoils of seniority. With these treasured political commodities in his back pocket, he brokered deals for Atlantic City—new highways, special tax breaks and revenues, and piles of federal subsidies.[52] He never, it seems, forgot the source of his power—it all started on the Midway and with the money that came from "booze, broads, and gambling." The other side of the Boardwalk greased the wheels of the machine, and the machine, in turn, kept the Midway and Atlantic City in the business of selling middle-class tourists and conventioneers naughty pleasures, racialized fantasies, and a chance to be someone else.

MAKING SENSE OF THE MIDWAY

During the middle of the twentieth century, white middle-class families, the people who fueled Atlantic City's economy, had a strong desire for the exotic, for the unusual, and for foreignness. Many decorated their basement recreation rooms with bamboo wet bars, three-dimensional murals of Hawaiian beaches, and fluffy black and orange leopard-skin pillows. Upstairs in their living rooms, they displayed ivory elephants from India and bright replicas of African masks. Outside, tiki lamps lit their barbecue pits.[53] On the other side of the Boardwalk in Atlantic City, they tried to move a little closer to what they imagined—or were told—were the real and exotic worlds of the African jungle, Hawaii, the Caribbean, the mob, and Harlem. That's what the Midway sold—the illusion of authentic tastes of difference, danger, and sex.

Like a ride on a rolling chair, a trip to the Midway was, of course, not what it seemed. The hulas hardly resembled traditional dances. African American musicians didn't only play gimmicky jungle music. The actors in drag shows were made-up; they were acts in a performance. While the physical distance between the Boardwalk and the clubs was real enough, the cultural distance was an illusion. When Jordan Sayles, the rolling-chair pusher, delivered white couples to the Paradise Club, he took them from one scripted tourist space to another. And the narratives told in these spaces were remarkably similar. Both told stories about race, class, and gender, and both, in the end, underlined, rather than challenged, prevailing social hierarchies.

Campy pansy acts and drag shows drew in men and women because of their bawdy undertones and explicit homoeroticism. But they affirmed difference as well. The over-the-top femininity of the acts highlighted the normativity of patriarchy and heterosexual masculinity. At the 500 Club, the undercurrent of the illicit emphasized the apparent lawfulness of everyday middle-class life.

Whiteness, not blackness, was the central theme of Club Harlem shows and the minstrel acts on Steel Pier. Jungle music, jungle dances, and jungle costumes accented the differences between white people and people of color. The sounds, movements, and dress of the performers highlighted primitiveness—a primitiveness that many white men and women found to be alluring. Maybe these encounters did, as some have suggested, humanize black people for some white people, but in the end, they provided a larger number of whites with, as Ralph Ellison once pointed out, "a more secure place (if only symbolically) in American society."[54] By underlining the natural, primitive, and sensual nature of blackness, the performances highlighted—to white audiences—the inherent superiority of whiteness. In an unspoken Darwinian drama, whites, the story went, could not regress to the primitive, so they had to go to the Midway to watch uncivilized Others in order to experience the sensation.

Yet the Midway served, on yet another level, as an implicit critique of the mainstream cultural lives of most Atlantic City visitors. On and off the Boardwalk, salesmen, hospital workers, and housewives came to the shore to get things—the beach and ocean, the Boardwalk stage, and hot nighttime thrills— they couldn't get at home. White tourists couldn't watch women shake their bodies like water at home; they couldn't hear the tom-tom beat of jungle music; and they couldn't or wouldn't let themselves feel the pleasures of homoeroticism. But in Atlantic City, women and men could indulge their desires. Of course, they participated in the transgressive world of the Midway usually as voyeurs; this was a place for seeing and for gawking at Others.

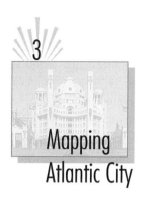

3

Mapping
Atlantic City

When a reporter asked a long-time city cab driver to show him the "real" Atlantic City, the hack quickly drew the journalist a map. "The blacks," he stated, "they couldn't cross Atlantic Avenue" after dark. "You had," he continued, "your Jewish homes and hotels from Maine to Massachusetts from Atlantic to the Boardwalk. The Irish were in the Inlet from Maine Avenue all the way down to New Jersey Avenue, north to the bay. You had an Irish bunch between Georgia and Florida." Without taking a breath, he added, "Italians lived from Missouri Avenue up to Texas Avenue on the north side of the bay." Seen through the cabby's eyes, Atlantic City looked like the map of the Balkans, and this residential map got traced over the city's already Balkanized tourist world. Jews lived here, the Irish lived there, and African Americans lived over there—that was the way it was, he said, before the city's fall from grace.

Locals understood the city's residential geography in the same way. Knowing where someone lived or where they stayed on vacation revealed everything, or so most people thought, there was to know about that person. It said how much they made, where they came from, and what their racial and ethnic identity was. Like in most American places, geography—which side of the tracks or the freeway you lived on—was not an abstract notion. Place meant everything. Every corner, every bar, every lunch counter, and certainly every neighborhood in Atlantic City had meaning and suggested who could live there and who was not welcome.

In many ways, the neighborhoods, especially the white ones, were gated communities before there were gated communities. The walls around these places became the lines on the map of the city. On this grid, a person's ethnic and racial background could be determined from his street address. Up close, however, each neighborhood looked rather similar. From downtown to Little Italy to the African American "ghetto," the streets and homes, churches and stores exhibited a traditional urban form. The design nurtured feelings of community, just not a unified citywide community. The Atlantic City of the past had many communities and many public spaces, each closed off from the other—and that was the point.[1]

URBAN FORM

In books, articles, and university lectures, James Howard Kunstler laments the passing of the old neighborhoods of the old cities. Now he wants to bring them back and, with them, the imagined communities of yesterday. "Everybody agreed," Kunstler writes with confidence:

> that buildings on Main Street ought to be more than one story tall, that corner groceries were good to have in residential neighborhoods, that streets ought to intersect with other streets to facilitate movement, that sidewalks were necessary, and that orderly rows of trees planted along them made the sidewalks much more pleasant, that rooftops should be pitched to shed rain and snow, that doors should be conspicuous so you could easily find the entrance to a building, [and] that windows should be vertical to dignify a house.

In these traditional neighborhoods, grocery stores, newsstands, cigar shops, and taverns ringed every intersection. Cars were a luxury, not a necessity. "You walk to a store," Kunstler writes, "enjoying the felicities of the street as you go—and you are able to see other people." Along the way, he says, mocking today's suburban enclaves, "you may even have a conversation with a stranger." This, he concludes, "is called *meeting people*, the quintessential urban pleasure."[2]

Atlantic City, Kunstler asserts in another context, was "a true city."[3] Beyond the Boardwalk and the twinkling lights of the amusement piers, Atlantic City resembled other American turn-of-the-century industrial cities. Like them, it developed over time into a thick grid of intersecting commercial thoroughfares, smaller side streets, and back alleys. On Pacific Avenue, one block east of the beach, there were government buildings, sandstone churches, dentists' offices, the YMCA, Knights of Columbus Hall, and Carnegie Library. One more block up from the Boardwalk was Atlantic Avenue where the trolley, until 1955, ran down the middle of the street.

This was downtown. Theaters and department stores, swank shops and nice restaurants lined Atlantic Avenue between Arkansas and North Carolina avenues. Although it lacked the Boardwalk's total fantasy feel, the busy street remained well into the postwar period a place worth dressing up for. Store clerks wore jackets or skirts, striped ties or nylons. Men tipped their hats to passing ladies, and the side-

▰ATLANTIC AVENUE
Atlantic City's main street busy with traffic and people in the 1940s (Atlantic
City Free Public Library, Heston Room, Atlantic City, New Jersey).

walks echoed with the "click-click" of high heels.[4] Gracefully ornamented three-,
five-, and seven-story buildings of brick, stone, and terra cotta housed downtown's stores and movie houses. Tall, gleaming signs rose to the sky, and elegant
awnings covered the sidewalks. At street level, a long row of stores with large glass
windows ran from block to block, and the retail temples and specialty shops
arranged their wares in ever-changing, holiday- and season-themed window displays.

More than architecture and design made downtown a special place. For locals
and families from nearby shore towns and inland farm communities, Atlantic
Avenue set the beat for the rhythms of their lives. This was, to paraphrase a big-
city newspaper columnist, where children first saw Santa Claus riding down the
street on a float at the annual Christmas parade, where fathers took their sons to
buy gray flannel suits for bar mitzvahs and confirmations, where teenagers went
on their first dates and purchased penny loafers and prom outfits, where mothers
came with their daughters for white-gloved lunches of tomato soup and tuna
on toast before heading off to try on wedding dresses, where young couples
bought furniture for their first homes, and where expectant mothers picked out

maternity clothes, then baby clothes, and, finally, introduced their own children to Santa Claus.[5]

Atlantic Avenue was a classy place, a special place, a fun place, and a romantic place; it was also the city's most important social boundary. Everyone from locals to Midway revelers called the street the "great divide."[6] This, they knew, was where Atlantic City's color line was drawn. Everyone understood that whites generally lived to the east of the busy street, while blacks lived to the west, although when locals mapped the city, they rotated the compass, calling the white sections around the 500 Club and Louisa Mack's Entertainer's Club the Southside, and the black areas near Club Harlem the Northside.

Most of Atlantic City's racially exclusive neighborhoods developed within walking distance of Atlantic Avenue and of jobs at hotels, restaurants, bakeries, and small factories that made machine tools and saltwater taffy. The homes, roughly 75 percent of them built before 1939, copied the traditional form of the city's main street.[7] Along the streets named after the states, which flowed away from the Boardwalk—most cross streets were named after oceans—families lived in two- and three-bedroom houses, in cramped walk-ups above stores, and in four-, six-, eight-, and ten-unit apartment buildings packed together so tightly that neighbors could visit through their windows without raising their voices and could tell without trying what the family next door was having for dinner. Sidewalks ran next to the streets. Thin, tight driveways clung to the buildings' sides. The garages were usually tucked in the back away from the street. Few homes had front lawns and the ones that did were the size of tiny postage stamps just big enough for holiday displays, birdbaths, and a couple of pink flamingos. And just about every house had a front porch or a three- or four-step stoop that acted like a porch.

Above all, the front porches gave residential Atlantic City its feel, its tone, and its publicness. Prior to the 1950s, few families had televisions and none had air conditioning. Parents spent evenings in front of their homes talking, while children played hopscotch on the sidewalks and stickball in the streets. "You didn't need a car," one former resident, now living in the suburbs, remembered of his childhood neighborhood near the beach. "If you had a car," he added, "you used it to visit someone, not to commute to work." Most people—white people, that is— went downtown fairly often, but they didn't have to. Each neighborhood acted like a city within the city. In these "virtually self-sufficient" commercial areas, a man on his way to work in the morning could, as E. B. White observed of the urban landscape of the twentieth century, complete a myriad of tasks within shouting range of his front door. He could buy a pack of cigarettes, a newspaper, and a chance at the daily number, drop off shirts for dry cleaning and a pair of shoes for repair, order paint for a room he planned to fix up, and tell the butcher that his wife was coming by to pick up a roast. Eight hours later, on the way home from his job, he could, still within shouting distance of his front stoop, stop for a beer and some pretzel rods, pick up light bulbs and salted peanuts, and double check the time of his Elks meeting that night. Throughout the day, his family walked the same streets. His wife wheeled her shopping cart to the bakery for fresh bread and butter cookies, then to the delicatessen for some bologna, and finally to the corner store for clothes pins, kitchen sponges, and a dozen eggs. Their children walked to school and then to the playground, stopping by the corner store for an ice cream sandwich or a bag of penny candy.[8]

On the way to the store, work, school, or jitney—the city's distinctive thirteen-passenger buses, which looked like airport transportation vans and took people downtown and along the avenues—neighbors met neighbors sitting in front of their houses, going to church, the bar, or waiting in line at the butcher shop. And they did this day after day, year after year. Before the mid-1950s, most Atlantic City neighborhoods were stable places. Sisters and cousins lived next door to each other or only a couple of blocks away. Families stayed in the same houses for decades. Everybody exchanged nods, hellos, hugs, and, sometimes, snarls and groans. Whether they liked each other or not, neighbors recognized each other and their children. One man who grew up in a two-bedroom apartment on New Hampshire Avenue remembers, "If I was five blocks away and said 'damn,' my mother knew about it before I got home."[9] A Northside resident recalled, "[Y]ou had a lot of parents."[10] And parents, particularly moms, were, it seems, always around, keeping a watch over things from their kitchen windows and front steps. Down the block, the druggist, the deli man, and the owner of the corner store policed their turf, looking out for young kids and the elderly, scolding rowdy teens, and staring down outsiders. With these "eyes of the street"—to borrow Jane Jacobs's famous phrase—watching over and policing their neighborhoods, people in Atlantic City before the 1960s left their doors unlocked and felt safe going out at night.[11]

Atlantic City's traditional urban form and front porch culture clearly nurtured a sense of community. People looked out for and even disciplined one another. But in Atlantic City, this meant caring only about people like you. Outsiders were regarded with suspicion and wariness. Contradicting James Howard Kunstler's new urbanist creed, the sense of community fostered by the town's front porch culture did not break down the walls dividing different ethnic and racial groups. Rather, the residents of Atlantic City's neighborhoods—the North and South Inlet, Ducktown, the Northside and Westside, Venice Park and Bungalow Park, Chelsea and Chelsea Heights—viewed the lines on the city map as a way to define themselves, as a badge of belonging, which created a sense of place, a certainty of who they were and where they stood in the world.[12]

SOME NEIGHBORHOODS

The Northside

"Negroes," the cabby-turned-tour guide told the *Atlantic City Press* reporter in 1987, "lived above Atlantic Avenue." This was not always the case. Atlantic City, like most northern cities, did not begin as a segregated place. Before the turn of the twentieth century, African Americans, who arrived in a steady stream from Virginia, North Carolina, Pennsylvania, and other parts of New Jersey as soon as the railroad connected the shore to Philadelphia, lived close to where they worked and close to white people.[13] They lived in hotel servants' quarters and beachfront boardinghouses. They attended nearby schools with white children, and they worshiped in nearby churches with white followers of the same faith.

Jim Crow arrived in Atlantic City about the same time that he came to Mississippi, Alabama, and Georgia. He appeared along the shore, however, in less formal garb. Rarely did he wear a judge's robe, but still he had the power to draw thick lines across the map of the city. In 1893, a *Philadelphia Inquirer* writer asked, "What are we doing to do with our colored population?" Atlantic City, he grumbled, "has never before seemed so overrun with the dark skinned race. . . . [B]oth the boardwalk and Atlantic Avenue fairly swarm with them during bathing hours like the fruit in a huckle-berry pudding."[14] Jim Crow's answer to this writer's racial fears was to divide blacks and whites. After 1900, white students in Atlantic City went to white elementary schools while black students attended black elementary schools. Just to make sure they knew who was whom at the polling station, local officials started to mark ballets *W* for white, *C* for colored.[15]

Not surprisingly, the same Jim Crow system of formal and informal rules that prevailed along the Boardwalk, in the schools, and at the polling stations determined where people lived. By 1905, Atlantic City had its own African American "ghetto." Carefully drawn red lines on real estate maps confined black residents to a boot-shaped area called the Northside. Starting at the great divide, Atlantic Avenue, the neighborhood stretched west to the bay and Absecon Boulevard. Arkansas Avenue marked its southern boundary, Connecticut Avenue the northern terminus. Street names solidified the racial borders, changing depending on the area's racial makeup. Starting at the beach, whites lived on Grammercy Avenue. But when the east-west street hit Connecticut Avenue and the Northside, it turned into Arctic Avenue. The same thing happened with Melrose and Mediterranean avenues. Whites lived on Melrose, blacks on Mediterranean. Madison Avenue changed its name to Baltic as it crossed through the Northside, and then became Fairmont as it moved west of Arkansas Avenue and sliced through an all-white section of town. The naming patterns reflected Jim Crow's effectiveness.[16] By 1905, African Americans made up a quarter of the city's population. Yet only 3.3 percent of black residents lived outside the Northside. Ten years later, according to one historian, less than 1 percent of the city's African American families had a white neighbor.[17]

Just about everything else in the city was divided between north and south, black and white. "There were always two YMCAs," one woman recalled, "always two of everything!"[18] The Chamber of Commerce looked after the comings and goings on the Southside, while the Board of Trade, a group of black professionals and business leaders, managed dealings north of the great divide. The city had two musicians' unions, two Elks clubs, two Republican and two Democratic political clubs, and two old-age homes.[19] Poor, elderly whites found housing on the Southside, while city leaders chipped in every year to pay some of the expenses for the Old Folks Colored Home on Adriatic Avenue.[20] In the 1920s, when the city built a new high school—the city's only integrated educational facility—the architects put a pool in the basement. But it never opened. Fearful of interracial contact, educational officials covered it up. Afterward, the high school's all-white swim team worked out at a Boardwalk hotel, while African American Boy Scouts drove to Philadelphia to learn how to tread water and do the backstroke.[21] One jitney driver motored around town with a sign in his bus saying, "This front seat is for colored people and dogs."[22] Even holy days were divided along racial lines. Most years, more than a quarter of a million people crammed onto the Boardwalk to watch the floats and children in spring clothes pass by on Easter Sunday. Barred from taking part in the procession, African Americans started their own Easter parade down Arctic Avenue in the 1940s.[23]

Jim Crow divided people not just on Easter but every Sunday morning. Virtually every city neighborhood had a Roman Catholic church, including the Northside. "When the number of Black Episcopalians began to increase," recounts the history of a local African American congregation, "all the churches—which were situated on the Southside, became somewhat alarmed." New Jersey Episcopalians answered the threat of integration by funding the construction of St. Augustine's on Arctic Avenue. Knowing how some white people felt about sharing a pew with a black person, members of the financially strapped Northside house of worship called on the "White churchmen of New Jersey" in 1924 to show "their appreciation for the Colored brethren who are saving them from a 'problem' by freeing this Colored church of debt."[24]

While Jim Crow divided people, denying blacks equal access to lunch counters, hotels, and jobs, it also created opportunities. Almost as soon as the red lines appeared on the city map, businesses catering to African Americans opened on the Northside. By 1920, Arctic Avenue emerged as the city's black Atlantic Avenue. Stretching from east to west from Arkansas Avenue to Virginia Avenue, Arctic Avenue featured a continuous line of stores, meeting halls, rooming houses, and churches. Many African American businesses along the street provided services that whites balked at supplying for blacks. They ran barbershops and beauty salons, restaurants and guesthouses, funeral parlors and insurance companies. Next to these establishments were newsstands, furniture marts, radio repair shops, and luncheonettes. Many of the owners, especially the African American ones, lived above the shops. (Whites, particularly Jews, owned the furniture and clothing stores on the street, but they tended to live on the other side of Atlantic Avenue.)[25]

The Liberty Hotel, Perry's Bar and Restaurant, and Mrs. Gertrude Moss's Guesthouse stood down the street and around the corner from Northside shoe stores and lunch counters. These places catered to African American visitors from cities and towns from Richmond to Newark and Cleveland to Brooklyn.[26] Barred from the Boardwalk showplaces and plainer Southside lodgings, black tourists stayed in black-owned wood-framed boardinghouses and small hotels. When the black Elks, the Inter-City Bridge Club, or the AME (African Methodist Episcopal) Youth Congress came to town for their national or regional conventions, meeting at the black YMCA or veterans building, these Jim Crow accommodations and the restaurants next to them burst at the seams. As late as 1964, when the Democratic National Convention brought Fannie Lou Hamer and other members of the insurgent Mississippi Freedom Democratic party to town, they could not find "decent accommodations," so they ended up hot and sticky in the un–air-conditioned, run-down Gem Hotel.[27]

For decades, black tourism remained important enough to white city leaders that the Farley political machine funneled money each year to the Board of Trade. This Northside chamber of commerce used the funds to advertise in black newspapers and travel to black churches and community centers up and down the East Coast pointing out the benefits of a trip to Atlantic City. They especially tried to get African Americans to visit during the off-season, when any business was good business. "Come to Atlantic City for the perfect honeymoon or vacation," a Board of Trade advertisement read. The group's adherence to Jim Crow was key; it promoted the wonders of golf, horseback riding, clubbing, and dining in a segregated city.[28]

Most Northside families and tourists lived and stayed within easy walking distance of Arctic Avenue. At night, local residents and tourists mingled, shopping

"JOIN NAACP NOW"
Looking down Arctic Avenue, the heart of the Northside, in the 1940s, this image captures the rhythms and politics of this place (Atlantic City Free Public Library, Heston Room, Atlantic City, New Jersey).

for shoes, picking up some groceries, eating plates of greens and barbecued chicken, checking on the daily number, and relaxing over a shot and a beer. The street life on Arctic Avenue was as vibrant and alive as the scene along Atlantic Avenue.[29]

The Alan Theater's distinct, red, V-shaped marquee hung over the corner of Kentucky and Arctic avenues. A white man, a Mr. Greenberg, built the theater in 1937 for, in his words, "purely business reasons, and not for charity or to help or hinder race problems." One local leader opposed Greenberg's ownership saying, "[N]o white man should come over on the Northside and put up a moving picture house. It would be all right if the show was owned by Negroes." But African Americans patronized the completely fireproof, automatically cooled and heated, 900-seat theater because tickets were cheap, and they didn't have to deal with the humiliation of segregation, at least not directly. Through the 1940s and 1950s, the Alan featured Hollywood films, like Jane Russell in *Underwear*, alongside Sidney Poitier movies and other pictures centering on African American characters.[30]

Around the corner from the Alan, on Kentucky Avenue, stood the famed Club Harlem, where for much of the evening blacks entertained whites. Jackie "Moms" Mabley regularly appeared at the venue. Decked out in her trademark floppy hat, a flower-print dress that fit like a bag, and raggedy house slippers, Mabley told "dirty old lady" jokes. Older men bore the brunt of her humor and ribald sexuality. "An old man," she would say, "couldn't do nothin' but bring me a message from a young man." Sometimes Mabley would step across the street and perform at Grace's Little Belmont. There, in front of a more black than white audience, Mabley mixed political commentary with her old lady lines. She talked about being black in a white-controlled world, of advising presidents on civil rights, and of a black man killed only minutes after marrying a white woman.[31]

Once the Boardwalk dining rooms were scrubbed and the rolling chairs stowed away for the night, black men and women headed back to the Northside. Some, still wired with adrenaline, stopped off at either the Paradise Club or the Club Harlem for one of their "breakfast shows," usually on Sunday mornings. Black singers, saxophonists, and bass players, who had already performed two or three sets earlier in the night at the city's hotels and clubs, began to play again around 6:00 a.m. With most whites safely back across Atlantic Avenue, the music changed, the whole vibe changed. The tuxedos came off. Swing became bop. Jungle music turned into daring improvisation. Around 9:00 AM, the jazz musicians wandered off, and the bars finally closed for a few hours. By then, the shops on Arctic Avenue had started to open, and another part of the neighborhood came to life.[32]

Jim Crow and raw racism, the same conditions that guaranteed the Alan and other Arctic Avenue businesses a steady clientele, shaped residential life on the Northside as well. Segregation confined all African Americans, northern-born and southern-born, rich and poor, skilled and semiskilled, to the physical ghetto above Atlantic Avenue. Doctors lived a few doors down from bellhops. Innkeepers set up shop around the corner from rolling-chair pushers. Penned in by the red lines drawn around the Northside, African Americans had limited housing options. "The fact is," commented a local journalist in the last days of segregation, "that the Negro even though his economic status may rise, is limited largely to this Northside ghetto while the white has the rest of the Island in which to find housing."[33]

As a result, black families often paid twice as much as white families for rental properties, but usually got half as much for their money. Hard-working Northside residents lived in frame houses with drooping porches and windows pitched at awkward angles. Others rented unpainted shacks on unpaved alleys. Still others crowded into tiny uninsulated apartments where they froze in the winter and baked in the summer. The lucky ones occupied sturdy but narrow row houses on streets where garbage men rarely visited. Pierre Hollingsworth, a 1949 graduate of Atlantic City High School and later president of the local NAACP (National Association for the Advancement of Colored People), grew up at 354½ North Connecticut Avenue in a basement apartment. "Every time it rained," he recalled, "we had to go upstairs because the rain would come in and flood everything." He studied by candlelight or a kerosene lamp because the apartment didn't have electricity. The building didn't have hot running water either. Still, doormen and chambermaids, store owners and clerks lined up to rent dingy and dirty places like the Hollingsworths' apartment. They had no place else to go.[34]

Throughout the city's heyday, African Americans on the Northside faced a persistent housing crunch. Between 1920 and 1950, the city's black population doubled as the Great Migration brought sons and daughters of the south to Atlantic City. A small, tidy, middle-class enclave took shape in a neighborhood on the edge of the Northside, called the Westside. Yet for the most part, private developers steered clear of the streets near Arctic Avenue, and banks balked at extending credit to investors who wanted to spend money between the red lines on real estate maps. With the New Deal, the federal government intervened, spending large sums on public housing for the first time in the nation's history. Some of this Washington money eventually made it to Atlantic City, but it came bundled in a Jim Crow package. Fearful of alienating the Democratic party's southern wing, the Roosevelt administration proved unwilling to tackle residential segregation and allowed local racial customs to dictate who lived in which public housing projects. In 1937, the same year the Alan Theater started to show movies on Arctic Avenue, the completely segregated, 200-unit, federally funded Stanley Holmes housing project opened on Adriatic Avenue. These well-designed, modern apartments marked an improvement for those fortunate enough to live in them, but the modestly sized development did little to alleviate the Northside's pressing housing shortage.[35]

Even though many Northside houses leaned a little to the right or the left, the wooden shacks still had front porches. Just like in the city's other neighborhoods, life in cramped, un–air-conditioned apartments pushed people onto their stoops. Ministers and mail carriers, students and Boardwalk sweepers, waiters and rolling-chair pushers walked to work, to the grocery store, and to church. Public life—people out on the streets who knew each other—created a sense of vitality and urban density on the Northside.

Northside residents, like those in Chicago's "lost city" who were studied by sociologist Alan Ehrenhalt, "went out of their way to make their lives more public" by going to church socials, attending community meetings, and joining clubs and organizations.[36] During a rather ordinary June week in 1955, Northside women and men attended a children's play at Jethro Memorial Presbyterian Church. They went to see a production of *The Promised One* at Asbury Methodist Church or listened to Rudolph Lewis and the Lewis Specials perform a gospel show at the Sardis Tabernacle. A few showed up for a meeting to elect new officers of the Northside Business and Professional Women's Association. Others gathered at Carl Coke's house on North Illinois Avenue for the Just Friends Vacation Club.[37] Ten years later, just as the city started its downward slide, federal investigators found more than eighty different clubs still holding regular meetings on the Northside. Women and men belonged to the Benevolent and Protective Order of Elks, Prince Hall Masons, American Legion, American Legion Auxiliary, Veterans of Foreign Wars, Iota Chapter of the Phi Delta Kappa Sorority, Ambassador Social Club, Les Gendarmes, Gentlemen of Sports, Algonquin Civic and Social Club, and four separate chapters of the PTA.[38]

Southside residents rarely paid attention to the Northside, except maybe to see who was playing the midnight show at Club Harlem. Road crews and street sweepers rarely went above Atlantic Avenue. The city commissioner of parks and recreation had little reason to go there either. The area had no parks, no pool, and only a couple of poorly maintained municipal baseball fields.[39] But in the late 1950s, as the city first started to lose its edge with middle-class tourists, white city leaders began focusing on the area.

After World War II, most Atlantic City visitors arrived in town by car. The White Horse Pike, the connector between Philadelphia and the shore, dropped families off on Absecon Boulevard, a four-lane road that cut through the Northside. Before tourists saw the beach and the Boardwalk, they saw crumbling shacks and black workers. This was not the way the members of the Chamber of Commerce and the Visitors Bureau wanted the city's tourist narrative to open. "We often wonder," one city representative wrote, "what kind of impression our guests receive when they arrive by motor-car and have to drive to their hotels through blighted areas."[40]

Taking a page from Baltimore's playbook, city leaders decided that they better clean up the ghetto. Just after World War II, the Maryland city had begun to tackle blight by eliminating it. With this model in mind, Atlantic City leaders launched a program of destroying homes and apartments along Absecon Boulevard to give the city a grander, whiter entrance. What they didn't take into account was where the people who lived in the ghetto and the thousands of African Americans who kept coming to the city in the postwar era would go after parts of the Northside were cleared away and how these movements would rewrite the city's map.[41]

Ducktown

Christopher Columbus greeted guests to Ducktown. His ascent over the neighborhood took twenty-one years and countless bake sales and pasta dinners. When the larger-than-life white marble statue of the Italian explorer atop an eight-foot podium finally went up in 1958, 4,000 people were there, waving American and Italian flags, cheering politicians, and praying with the parish priest. The statue was more than just a greeting card; it was a stamp, a signature of the Italian presence in Atlantic City.

Christopher Columbus stood in a park on Arkansas Avenue, right where Baltic Avenue turned into Fairmont Avenue, marking another divide in the city's racial geography. Going from north to south, Ducktown stretched from the statue to California Avenue. On the east-west axis, it went from the beach across Atlantic Avenue to the bay. Many of the area's earliest residents apparently trapped ducks along the bay, so in the nineteenth century, locals started to call this wedge of houses and small side streets "Ducktown." By 1920, it had become a designation for Atlantic City's Little Italy. When people spoke of Ducktown, they marked the area, as they did the Northside, as a racially, religiously, and ethnically distinct space. Again in Atlantic City, identity created geography and geography created identity.

In the 1880s, the Siracuas and the Ruffas, "two prominent Sicilian families," so the story goes, settled near the duck farms on the bay. Around this time, African Americans still waited on diners at most Boardwalk hotels. Angry about low pay and poor conditions, these black workers went on strike in 1906. The hotel owners crushed the protest and afterwards refused to hire black waiters altogether. Desperate for new sources of "white" labor, employers urged the Siracuas and the Ruffas to bring their families and friends to Absecon Island.[42] Soon cousins and uncles from Sicily arrived and settled on North Mississippi, Georgia, and Florida avenues. "Almost overnight," writes one observer, "Ducktown became an Italian neighborhood." In 1903, the Catholic church established St. Michael's on North Georgia Avenue. Within a decade, the church became the community's focal point, where neighbors went to mass, attended school, and marked christenings, communions, confirmations, marriages, and deaths.[43]

Surrounding St. Michael's Church lay yet another city within the city. Locals could find three bakeries selling warm, crusty loaves of Italian bread. Next door were fruit stands and fish markets. Nearby grocery stores sold milk and eggs, roasted peppers and imported Parmesan cheese. Around the corner, sandwich makers built long Italian hoagies made out of lettuce, tomatoes, onions, provolone, Genoa salami, cappicola, prosciutto, and hot red peppers. Neighborhood tailors and barbers played scratchy opera records and decorated their walls with pictures of the pope and Frank Sinatra. Ducktown restaurants served big bowls of gnocchi with garlicky marinara sauce and stubby glasses of homemade wine. Above the eateries and stores were social clubs like the Knights of Columbus and the Al-Ki Club where men who spoke only Italian played nickel and dime games of hearts. Teenagers hung out at a Mississippi Avenue pool hall or checked out the double bill at the Surf Theater—Ducktown's movie house—on Atlantic Avenue.[44]

Every August, to mark the Feast of the Assumption, St. Michael's hosted the Wedding of the Sea. Loosely copying a fifteenth-century Venetian tradition, local residents walked to the sea, where they watched the mayor toss a wedding band into the ocean to symbolize "the union . . . [and] the love between God and his people." On the way to the beach, women pinned dollar bills, the occasional five or ten, or a rare twenty, to a statue of Mary, her arms outstretched, on wheels.[45]

The streets that the virgin rolled through had the look of a working-class neighborhood that had seen better days but was still a long way from its worst days. Most of the houses were neat two- and three-story detached and semidetached row houses. Almost all of them had front stoops, porches, wood-carved front doors, and wide welcome mats. Flower boxes filled with gardenias and herbs hung from side windows. Stone Madonnas centered the small patches of lawn. Women scrubbed the sidewalks every night. Men fixed cracked windows as soon as they broke, and the city picked up the trash every week. Tucked behind Ducktown's main streets, the ones named for the states, there were narrow alleys, like Italy Terrace, where on hot summer nights neighbors pinned sheets together to make a tent. Protected from the heat, residents played cards and drank red wine.[46]

Across Atlantic Avenue, although still in Ducktown, there were more row houses with front porches and more delis making Italian hoagies. But the landscape changed somewhat. Ten- and twenty-room guesthouses stood next to single-family homes. Even the row houses were different. Most had small apartments in the back or finished basements below that the owners rented in the summer or stayed in themselves to free up more room for boarders. Between Memorial Day and Labor Day, thousands of blue- and white-collar Italian families from South Philly spent their week or two at the shore in Ducktown. Usually they stayed at the same place with the same family every year. After a day on the beach and a bowl of pasta at Fedelli's, they sat on the porch talking, blending right in with the neighborhood.[47]

Like the Northside, Ducktown's traditional urban form—tightly packed houses, sidewalks, and corner stores—encouraged daily interactions. "This neighborhood is like a family," Grace Patroni of South Bellevue Avenue told a reporter in 1978. "We're mostly Italian, we're close-knit and we help each other. Like a family."[48] Wheeling her shopping cart to Brigadell's Pharmacy and Bongiovani's Grocery, Patroni bumped into friends, neighbors, and acquaintances. And she saw them again at mass at St. Michael's Church. Back on her block, she swept the sidewalk in front of her house after dinner, talking to passing tourists and keeping an eye on her neighbors' children. An accordionist entertained everyone with show tunes. Her husband gathered with the men a few doors down to sip grappa, talk sports and politics, and joke about who had the neatest house, the biggest furnace, and the best garden.[49]

No doubt a sweet, "those were the days" kind of nostalgia permeated Grace Patroni's view of Ducktown. Filtered from her recollections are the feuds, spying, gossip, adulterous affairs, and petty jealousies that go along with life in any tight-knit, closely packed community. Nonetheless, the area's front stoop social life and corner store commerce did help to make Ducktown residents feel safe. Families left bikes, beach chairs, and fishing equipment on their porches overnight, and they always found them right where they left them the next morning, largely because someone was watching. A bartender reflected in 1978, "I can remember you could leave your front door open . . . not just in the day, but all night." Another woman added, "[N]o one locked their doors. Everyone looked out for each other. Nothing bad happened."[50] This sense of safety and security, however imagined, nurtured the public realm. Ducktown was, like the Northside, a place where life was lived in public, on the streets, in the bars, in the clubhouses, and in the churches. But the idea of the public in Ducktown was never inclusive.

Ducktown residents studied their streets. They noted every new face and shift in the daily flow of commerce and people. Strangers could expect to be eyeballed until they were out of sight. African Americans were, of course, the easiest outsiders to spot between Arkansas and California avenues. Although a few Japanese families rented apartments in the area, virtually no black families lived within Ducktown's boundaries before the 1960s. Most blacks never went near the area. On their way home, most African American high schoolers walked out of their way rather than cut through Ducktown. If a black man who didn't know the city's social geography wandered into a tavern on Mississippi or Georgia avenue, the bartender quickly changed his prices. A glass of beer that cost locals fifty cents suddenly went for $5. Actions like these were what wrote the map of Atlantic City; they traced and retraced the lines between communities and people tens of thousands of times each day.[51]

South Inlet

Long before the South Inlet became a place to escape from, it was a place to live in.[52] Born just as World War II ended, Connie Turton Degrassi spent her childhood in the beachfront neighborhood. "What a wonderful place to grow up," she exclaimed on the "Atlantic City Memory Lane" Web site in 2000. She called Jack Kemp, who ran the candy store at Massachusetts and Oriental avenues, a "patient and kind man." There was, she warmly added, a bar on every corner where it was "safe for kids to go in and order a Coke and chips."[53] Jennette Patterson Adams lived down the street from Degrassi. She too remembers the South Inlet as a "great place to grow up." She could see the beach from her bedroom window. "For good-ness sakes," she cooed, "you could get a cup of soda (from about 50 or more choices) for a nickel" at the Sodamat, a Boardwalk store that dispensed carbon-ated drinks, as if by magic—or modern science—out of a machine on the wall. All of the big parades, the Miss America, Easter Day, Elks, and Shriners parades, began in the South Inlet right near her house. And there were, Adams remembers, Saturday matinees at the movie houses and summer days on Steel Pier.[54]

Many locals called the part of the city where Degrassi and Adams grew up the "Uptown" area. Like the sections in other urban communities that went by the same name, the neighborhood that stretched from Virginia Avenue to Rhode Island Avenue and from the Boardwalk to Atlantic Avenue was once seen as a "fashionable residential area, evok[ing] elegance, gentility, and sophistication."[55] The city's very first hotel, the United States Hotel, built in 1853, was located in South Inlet but burned to the ground a decade later. Over the next thirty years, wealthy Philadelphians erected in the area, especially on States Avenue, sprawling beach homes with wide porches and back bedrooms for servants. Nearby on the Boardwalk stood the stately, 450-room "aristocrat of Kosher hotels," the Breakers.

When the first notes of the Jazz Age sounded, the center of fashionable tourism moved south from the Uptown area toward Park Place and the Marlborough-Blenheim, Traymore, and Ritz Carlton. The rich moved their summer homes even farther south to Chelsea, another city neighborhood, and to Ventnor and Mar-gate, small beachfront towns below the city but still on Absecon Island. As they did, the character of the Uptown section changed. It started to look less like New-port or some other tony resort area and more like a typical residential neighbor-hood in a typical industrial city in New Jersey. With its tidy houses and narrow streets, the area felt like Camden or Paterson or Newark, except for one thing; it was right next to the beach and the Boardwalk. The South Inlet or the Uptown area was, by this time, a place of duplexes and apartment buildings, family-owned hotels and wooden boardinghouses, fishing piers and stickball games. On the Boardwalk, there were no linen shops or jewelry stores. Hot dog stands, lemonade booths, noisy arcades, and, of course, the Sodamat faced the ocean in these parts.

Around New Jersey and New Hampshire avenues, short, densely packed blocks filled the South Inlet. Along these streets stood an eclectic mix of wood and brick houses, many with ornamental moldings over the windows and roomy front porches and all built right next to the street on tiny lots. Closer to the Boardwalk, the houses were wider and taller. By the 1920s, however, the owners had transformed many of these oversized, one-time summer get-aways for the rich into reasonably priced guesthouses for middle-class and blue-collar families. "People," one local explains, "would come back to their same rooming houses year after year and have their same rooms. They would have community kitchens and in these kitchens would be your refrigerator, with your name on it, and your stove, and there would be your table, and that's where you would cook your breakfast, lunch and dinner."[56] The guests, like those who vacationed in Ducktown, got to know the neighborhood and felt a part of it. Next to the broad guesthouses and stout single-family homes and duplexes were small apartment buildings, the kind with two or three stories and two or three apartments on each floor.

Just like in other parts of the city, there was a store on every corner selling milk, aspirin, and candy bars. Across the street was the tavern where the familiar bartender poured shots of whiskey and glasses of beer. Along the avenues running parallel to the Boardwalk, the South Inlet had its own commercial centers. A few Kosher butchers and fish markets dotted Oriental Avenue. On Pacific Avenue, there were churches and synagogues, delis serving corned beef sandwiches as thick as copies of *War and Peace*, and Chinese restaurants dishing out steaming plates of chicken chow mein. One more block up on Atlantic Avenue, there were bigger and more specialized stores selling furniture, children's clothes, and engraved invitations for christenings and weddings. Inlet families and guests walked to the ocean and the amusement piers, to the dry cleaners and tailor, to the greasy spoon and Irish pub, and to catch a ride on the trolley or jitney to go to a downtown department store or movie theater.[57]

Like everywhere else in the city, a South Inlet address revealed important social facts. Unlike Ducktown, no single ethnic group dominated the South Inlet. Home to Jewish, Irish, and Italian families, the area was, recalled long-time resident Paul Carr, "a melting pot." Over the years, he added with a hint of pride, it earned "a reputation as a tough neighborhood." Most South Inlet families stood somewhere on the rungs between blue collar and white collar on the occupational ladder. This was a neighborhood of police officers, fire fighters, clerks, accountants, plumbers, and shop owners. It was a place where the houses didn't come with deep closets and men didn't own thirty shirts, just, in Carr's words, "a couple [of] pairs of pants, and some work clothes, some dress shirts, and some casual shirts." Above all, it was marked on the city's map as a white neighborhood.[58]

Operating much like it did in Ducktown and on the Northside, the South

Inlet's front porch culture of hanging out and walking to the store created a feeling of belonging and community, which in turned nurtured feelings of safety and security. "At that time," former state bantamweight champion Teddy Leonard recalled in 1978, "there was no such thing as muggings and hoodlum[s], and hippies." No one had air conditioners, he pointed out, "so 2, 3, 4 in the morning [my mom] would sit outside on a bench or chair and eat an ice cream cone and drink a bottle of soda and relax and cool off . . . and nobody molested her. Nobody thought of anything like mugging anybody or molesting people, and everybody was happy." In the morning, as he remembers the daily flow of activity, neighbors "got up and [when] they saw each other, they'd say, 'Good morning, how are you? Can we do anything for you?'" "Today," he lamented, "you can't even walk the street." Unlike the world he grew up in, as soon as it gets dark "you see the business places close up at 4 or 5 o'clock. People are off the street." He concluded, "Today people live with fear, with double locks on their doors, afraid to open their door, afraid to go outside. Years ago we opened the doors. Up in that Inlet section, that's terrible today, we used to keep our doors open and go in and out without any trouble. But you can't do it today."[59]

Marven Gardens

In the 1970s, writer John McPhee, inspired by the game of Monopoly, went searching for Marvin Gardens. On his first scouting expedition through the city, he spotted a woman in blue sneakers and red socks. He asked her if she knew how to get to Marvin Gardens. "I sure don't know," she told him. "I've heard of it somewhere, but I just can't say where." Next he turned to a clerk at the Claridge Hotel. "Is it a floral shop?" the attendant wondered aloud. "Never heard of it," a cab driver told him. McPhee found a postman sitting over a shot and a beer at the Plantation Bar at 9:15 in the morning. Despite the drinks, surely he would know how to get to Marvin Gardens. But the postal worker had no idea how to get there either.[60]

Forty years earlier, when Charles Darrow, then an out-of-work radiator repairman, sat down at his kitchen table in the Germantown section of Philadelphia to sketch out what would become the game of Monopoly, he found himself at the end of the night one name short of a full board. He scribbled the name Marvin Gardens in the blank slot next to the other yellow properties and shut out the lights.[61]

As McPhee searched for Marvin Gardens, he walked the streets of Atlantic City. Everywhere he looked he saw "the ghetto": "a white Ford station wagon stripped to the chassis" on Tennessee Avenue, "pawnshops, convalescent homes, and the Paradise Soul Saving Station . . . on Virginia Avenue," "people . . . on porches, six deep, at nine on a Monday morning" on North Carolina Avenue, and abandoned brick houses with "a thousand broken windows" along Mediterranean and Baltic avenues.[62]

Eventually, McPhee did find Marvin Gardens. It is, he learned, the one property on the Monopoly board not in Atlantic City. Instead, it is a few miles south of town. Not only was Marvin Gardens not in the city, it was, McPhee discovered, a remarkably different kind of place. Built in the 1920s, this "secluded . . . suburb within a suburb," as the author called it, looked, with its slant and tile roofed Tudor, Mission, and Spanish style houses on curvy, tree-lined streets, like a wealthy southern California neighborhood. But the essayist found the layout of the area even more remarkable than its West Coast ambiance. All the houses faced each other, giving the area, McPhee wrote, the feel of a "planned compound."[63]

McPhee met a Marvin Gardens resident on his visit there. Immediately, the man started to talk about property values, how many bedrooms he had, and how much his house was worth. "We're heavily policed," he told the writer. "We don't take any chances." McPhee drove away knowing that he had found "a citadel and sanctuary of the middle class."[64]

No one, not even his editor, corrected McPhee about the name of this place. Marvin Gardens wasn't just the only property Darrow put on the Monopoly board not in Atlantic City, he spelled it wrong and so did McPhee. This "compound"—McPhee uses the word twice in his tight one-paragraph description of the area—was really named Marven Gardens, because of its downbeach location right between Margate and Ventnor. Even if he did get the name wrong, McPhee must have known that he had discovered the fate of Atlantic City along the inward-looking streets of suburban Marven Gardens.

THE TURN INWARD TO SEGREGATION

Nostalgia runs like a mighty river through Ducktown and South Inlet residents' memories. They are not alone. People who grew up in other parts of the city mourned and continue to mourn a lost past. Women and men from Chelsea, Chelsea Heights, the North Inlet, Venice Park, and other neighborhoods on the city's map talk tenderly of the good old days, friendly grocers and tavern owners who knew your name, safe streets, unlocked doors and windows without bars, after-supper socials on the sidewalks, and knowing that someone was always there looking out for you and your family. Among some African Americans, there is even nostalgia for the Northside. Some speak fondly of the lost days of segregation when black-owned businesses thrived and the black middle class lived next door to the black working class.[65]

The memories of yesterday's Atlantic City neighborhoods blur images of the political bosses, Nucky Johnson and then Hap Farley, who ran the city as a private enterprise from the 1930s to the 1970s. The memories brush away the poverty and cramped quarters. They blot out the petty gossips and malicious liars, the tyrannical priests and rabbis, the crippling effects of homophobia, racism, and sexism, and the neighborhoods' insistence on conformity. They erase from the map the gates, walls, and local patrols that divided blacks and whites and kept the city segregated. Some Northside residents, in the meantime, edit from their views the fact that white families—sometimes mean and greedy ones—owned many of the shops where black people spent their money.[66] But for all that it hides, nostalgia still does point to the passing of the most crucial aspect of neighborhood life in Atlantic City.

Beginning in the 1960s, Atlantic City stopped being a place where people lived their lives on the streets and on their porches. Many families retreated inside behind lace curtains, barred windows, and double-locked doors, and then out to the suburbs. Forgoing sidewalks, parks, corner stores, and movie houses, they looked inward, and in so doing, they exchanged the close quarters and intense daily interactions of the neighborhood for the more controlled, easily protected, yet less stimulating life of private homes in segregated, middle-class sanctuaries like Marven Gardens.[67]

As the long-time residents abandoned the sidewalks and front porches, new groups rewrote the city's map. Puerto Ricans replaced white ethnics in the South Inlet; African Americans settled in Ducktown; gay men took over New York Avenue; and just about anyone who could fled the Northside. The city's geography was different, but a resident's presumed ethnic and racial history could still be read in her street address. By then, however, most people read this map from out of town or through rolled-up car windows.

4

The Last Picture Shows

Throughout the 1930s, Herb Frost's parents scraped together a few hundred dollars each year and took the family to Atlantic City for a week or two every summer.[1] In those days, they stayed at a place like the Hotel Majestic, a stout wooden boardinghouse in the South Inlet with un–air-conditioned rooms, toilets at the end of the hall, and rocking chairs on the front porch. The hotel, like the others in this area, which one writer called "Warsaw-on-the-Sea," served only kosher food.[2] Frost hated the way the place smelled. Not just the dining room, but the small bedrooms and cramped lobby, even the sidewalks, reeked of boiled cabbage and chicken fat. But to Frost the smells were worth it, because the Hotel Majestic sat only half of a block from the Boardwalk.

To Frost, the Boardwalk was a magic kingdom, the greatest place anywhere. He never thought of entering this world in anything but his best clothes, a jacket and a tie. You didn't, Frost now says, want to be mistaken for a poor person. They were the only ones on the Boardwalk in sneakers. Just to make sure everyone knew he had class, Frost wore a cabana jacket over his swimsuit during the day and a pressed sports coat when he headed out at night.

Sometimes on those nights when he was dressed up, Frost hired a rolling-chair pusher. "That," he says, "was the thing to do." He had a cousin who wouldn't ride in one of the wicker baskets, but Frost dismissed him as "communist or something."[3] After a short trip to nowhere on the Boardwalk, Frost liked to window-shop and people watch. He stopped in front of Yamron's to admire the gold necklaces and Swiss watches. From there, he walked to Higgins confectionery to pick up a box of cherries drenched in dark chocolate. If he had a date, he took her dancing at the ballroom at the end of Steel Pier.

On his Boardwalk nights out in public, Frost never passed up a chance to see the robot man. Outfitted in a silver metallic suit, the performer mimicked the stiff, rigid movements of a new age machine. People followed him down the Boardwalk like he was the Pied Piper. "Before you knew it," Frost chuckles, "he had 150 people behind him." He would lead his flock into an auction house and then slip behind a curtain. Before the crowd could leave, the auctioneer told the room full of people that the robot would be back shortly, but while they waited, he wanted to tell them about a terrific deal he had on diamonds. The auctioneer wasted no time as he sprayed the room with words:

> We sell some of the finest diamonds from estates and private individuals like yourselves. You all know about diamonds, how good an investment they are. When the people fled Nazi Germany they couldn't take their money. All they could take was diamonds. And [when] the banks failed during the Depression and the stock market crashed, what was still worth every cent? Diamonds.[4]

Not wanting to miss anything, Frost inched to the edge of his seat, but he never bought any of the auctioneer's priceless diamonds. "That," he laughs, "was for tourists."

When Frost got back from World War II, he married Rachel from down the street. They continued to go to Atlantic City. Even though they are Jewish, Herb and Rachel never missed the Easter Day parade. Early in the morning, Rachel put on a new pastel-colored suit, a flowered bonnet, and white gloves. She tried to sit still in the car, so her clothes wouldn't wrinkle. One year, the sixty-mile drive from Philadelphia to the shore took almost four hours. A million people, it seemed, crammed onto the Boardwalk to watch the floats and the streams of children in patent leather shoes and lacy dresses. When Rachel recently learned that African Americans held their own Easter Day parade on Arctic Avenue, she was flabbergasted. "We didn't see blacks on the Boardwalk," she admitted. "It was all very segregated."

Around the time that local businesswoman Sara Washington inaugurated the Arctic Avenue Easter Day parade, the Frosts checked out of the Hotel Majestic. Climbing the postwar economic ladder, they "moved up," as Frost put it, to the Breakers Hotel. Just down the street from the "Borscht Belt" boardinghouses where they used to stay, this ten-story hotel served food that earned a rabbi's stamp of approval, but still had French-sounding names. The Breakers even served asparagus, which at the time was the most exotic thing Frost could imagine. The Breakers had bathrooms right in the rooms and a lobby the size of four apartments back home.

By 1952, the Frosts had climbed even higher up the Atlantic City social ladder. They started staying at the Traymore, a hotel like many along the Boardwalk that had shut its doors to Jews before 1945, but now welcomed all white customers with enough money to pay for a room and three meals a day. Not only did William Price's famous building feature fancier foods and shops than the Breakers, it had, much to Frost's wonder, an indoor pool, the first Frost had ever seen. "We really had arrived," Rachel now says with a smile.

A few years later, the Frosts, still riding the wave of postwar prosperity, bought their very own summer home in Chelsea. "Wealthy Philadelphia Jews—manufacturers, etc.," lived in the houses next to Herb and Rachel. When the last school bell rang in Philadelphia in June, Rachel and the kids headed to the beach. Herb came down on Thursday nights or Friday afternoons every weekend until Labor Day. The best thing, he remembers, was walking. Once he parked the car, it didn't move until he had to go back to work on Monday. Jewish bakeries, fancy Italian restaurants, the movies, and the Boardwalk were all just a few safe blocks away. During those days, Rachel now says, "[W]e lived in a world of grace." Fifty years later, she still misses the "safety on the streets" and the "kind of people that used to come to Atlantic City."

Rachel and Herb agree that by the mid-1960s Atlantic City started to change. Long-haired hippies, Rachel says, made the Boardwalk look shabby, grubby, and low-down. Nodding his head in agreement, Frost maintains that "the tone of the Boardwalk," a phrase you hear over and over in Atlantic City, changed. Looking back, Frost thinks the relocation of Yamron's—the pricey jewelry store where he used to window-shop—to Naples, Florida, symbolized the Boardwalk's sharp decline.

But above all, the Frosts point to crime as the reason that they started to avoid the Boardwalk. "It was dangerous," Rachel now says, referring to the 1960s and 1970s. One of her relatives, she recalls, lived in Ventnor at the time, right on the Boardwalk, but he wouldn't dare go on the promenade walking at night. Frost told a story about a family friend who had her pocketbook cut off her arm by a daring bandit. Then, crime hit them directly. One night, Frost was walking on the Boardwalk with a few friends when suddenly a group of black teenagers approached. The young men didn't rob the older men, which was Frost's first fear. Instead, they walked up to the white men and blew cigar smoke right into their stunned faces. Then they disappeared as swiftly as they had first appeared.

After that, the Frosts went into retreat from the Boardwalk, from the delis and bakeries, and from Atlantic City. They didn't want to leave, they loved going out in Atlantic City, but they couldn't take the new crowd, the crime, and the uncertainty of city streets. They went in search of a new kind of exclusion.

THE BEST SEAT IN THE HOUSE

Before fleeing, the Frosts liked to do in Atlantic City what most middle-class Americans liked to do during their time off—go to the movies. Atlantic City's final years as the Queen of Resorts coincided with what a number of scholars have dubbed "the golden age of American cinema." From the middle of the 1930s to the early 1950s, 90 million Americans—the nation's population at the time hovered between 123 and 150 million—went to the movies each week and spent more money on movies than on any other recreational activity. Across the country, theater tickets alone accounted for 80 percent of all spectator amusement expenditures.[5]

Each year hundreds of thousands of people went to the movies in Atlantic City. The city had almost one theater seat for every year-round adult resident. With all these movie houses, the resort offered the Frosts and others a range of entertainment choices. They could go to the Astor, a small neighborhood theater on Atlantic and New Jersey Avenues, or to the even smaller Ventnor and Margate theaters located down beach. Downtown, between Blatt's Department Store, Kensington Furniture, Miller's Fine Men's Clothing, and the other main street shops, there were a handful of bigger, dressier theaters. On Saturday nights and other special occasions, the Frosts went to the movies at one of the palatial Boardwalk theaters. A block north of Atlantic Avenue stood the Alan, but there was little chance that the Frosts would go to this Northside theater.

Well into the postwar period, the Warner stood as the brightest, showiest, and most regal picture house in Atlantic City. On those Saturday nights that the Frosts went to the huge theater near the corner of the Boardwalk and Arkansas Avenue, they put on their opera clothes: she in her mink stole and he in his razor-creased linen pants. The evening began with a walk down the Boardwalk. The Frosts would never have driven the twenty blocks to the movies and missed the magic of a summer night. Walking north from Chelsea, they crossed Albany Avenue, passing a line of rolling chairs with their backs turned to the ocean. In those days, some families showed off by renting chairs for the entire summer. But they didn't go anywhere in the wicker baskets. Every night, they got dressed up and climbed aboard the stationary chairs to see and to be seen by couples like the Frosts on their way to the movies and other places. After Rachel and Herb passed the firmly fixed rolling chairs, they walked past the massive Convention Hall, where the *Ice Capades* performed all summer long. Then they hit traffic as pedestrians and rolling chairs—the ones in motion—bottlenecked near the front of the 4,000-seat Warner Theater.

Standing across from the massive movie hall, it was hard to know where to look first. The theater's gold-plated doors stood at eye-level on the Boardwalk. Sticking out above the entrance loomed the copper and plate glass marquee. Shaped at the top like a jeweled crown, the sign glowed so brightly that on cool nights men and women huddled under it to get warm. Perpendicular to the marquee stood another gleaming sign. This one spelled out the name of the theater in huge block letters and towered forty feet above the Boardwalk almost like a church steeple. Behind the lights, the Warner showcased an eclectic mix of architectural forms. Four classic-looking columns rising up to a series of Byzantine minarets framed the structure. In between, the designers placed a series of stained-glass windows that recalled a grand Renaissance church. At the top, there was a Roman statue encased in a spire-topped enclosure. On the day the Warner opened in 1929, a movie executive told a crowd of more than 6,000 people, "There is no place more fitting for a theater of this type than Atlantic City because it is the playground of the world and its patrons will appreciate it."[6]

Maneuvering through the crowd, the Frosts took their place in the line stretching from the Warner's box office two blocks down the Boardwalk. Standing next to other dapper white couples, they let the anticipation of the place, the lights, and the evening build up inside of them. Before the Warner and the other movie houses could deliver on their promises of fantasy, they had to create a sense of trust. Without trust, there was no mass audience, and without a mass audience, the movie palaces could not exist. The movies had to build an even stronger sense of trust than the city's other public, yet still exclusive, places, since they had to assure audience members that they would be safe sitting in the dark next to strangers. To manufacture this sort of trust, movie house owners constructed a network of confidence builders in and around their showplaces.[7]

Ushers played a key role in the trust-building process. Early in the twentieth century, picture house attendants did little more than take tickets and quiet unruly patrons. But as screening rooms turned into movie palaces, theater owners made ushers into cast members. Managers held auditions for the roles. Usually only tall, handsome, white male college and high school students got the parts. From there, they were sent to wardrobe to be fitted. Typically, ushers dressed in red jackets with yellow epaulets, creased black pants, and white gloves, making them look like crosses between soldiers from Napoleon's army and Johnny from Philip Morris advertisements. Next, they had to learn their lines, so that, according to a trade journal, they could make a "steam fitter feel like the owner of 10,000 slaves."[8] Ushers were not permitted to put themselves on the same level as customers. Managers instructed them to speak sparingly and in hushed voices and to address patrons as "sir" and "madam," never "mister" or "girl." Armed with their flashlights, the battalion of uniformed ushers served as the theater companies' in-house security and surveillance forces. They were everywhere. They took tickets and looked over the crowds. They marched through the lobbies and paraded up and down the aisles shushing teenagers, keeping sexual contact on the safe plane of hand holding and the occasional kiss, and handling "degenerates, intoxicated persons . . . [and] morons" with swift vigilance. But the policing—even in its most hawkish forms—was as symbolic as it was real. The ushers' uniforms, flashlights, and patrol duties told customers that theaters like the Warner were places of exclusivity and aggressively enforced middle-class decorum.[9]

The crowds, moreover, reassured themselves. Once again, dress mattered. Persian sheared-lamb coats and monogrammed tie clips were more than personal statements of making it in America. They marked the movie house as a place filled with members of the respectable middle class. So as the Frosts stood in line waiting to buy a ticket or in the lobby waiting for the program to begin, they looked around and saw people dressed just like them. Assured that the crowd consisted of the right kind of women and men, they felt comfortable taking the next step of going into the dark. The crowd also reassured itself in one other way—it appeared to be all white.

As on the Boardwalk, however, African Americans were never completely absent from Atlantic City theaters. They scrubbed the floors, scraped gum off seat bottoms, and polished bathroom fixtures. They appeared on screen as well. Playing overweight mammies and happy servants, they stuffed their faces with watermelon, sewed ball gowns, and served white bosses fancy dinners on silver trays, always with a smile. The Boardwalk itself became the stage for one of these reassuring Jim Crow performances in the 1944 film *Atlantic City*. In this light melodrama about an overly ambitious businessman reformed by love and marriage, African American rolling-chair pushers fill in the backdrop of every scene. As they dig in, launching hundreds of pounds of steel wheels and human flesh, they never grimace or strain. Like characters out of *Gone with the Wind* and *Casablanca*, they grin, nod, and happily answer to "George." When they do speak, they mumble "yes, sir" and "thank you, sir" as kindly white men toss tips at their feet.[10]

The Frosts probably watched scenes like these on screen without saying anything, and they probably didn't talk about race or segregation as they waited in front of the Warner. But exclusion defined their night out at the movies, like it did an evening on the Boardwalk, in the hotel lobbies and restaurants, and in the clubs. The Warner's owners offered the illusion of opulence only to women and men who passed as white. Ushers greeted African American patrons with cold stares, steering those who didn't walk away to the back of the movie house and up a set of steep metal stairs to the crow's nest at the top of the balcony.

In the mid-1930s, African Americans in Atlantic City campaigned to end Jim

Crow seating in the movie houses. But theater owners beat back the challenge, and the movies remained for blacks a site of reckoning and confrontation with segregation.[11] Jazz drummer and long-time city resident Chris Columbo recalled that in every theater in town:

> [I]f you were Black and walked into it, you had to sit on the left-hand side of the theater. And if you made the mistake of walking down the center aisle and sat on the right-hand side? A little fourteen-year-old girl would come and flash a flashlight in your face and tell you what side you had to sit on. You had to go to the back door, climb five or six flights of steps and when you sat in the balcony you looked down between your knees at the show on the stage. You couldn't sit on the ground floor. You could be the principal of the school, you could be in the police department. But if you were black . . .[12]

Columbo never finished this last sentence. He didn't need to. He knew and everyone else knew that the Warner and the city's other theaters, with the exception of the Alan, welcomed only whites through their baroque front doors into their luxurious interiors.

LUXURY AT A MIDDLE-CLASS PRICE

Although a ticket for a show at the Warner wasn't cheap, it wasn't prohibitively expensive either. Continuing an Atlantic City tradition, the picture show offered white moviegoers a "luxury experience at a middle-class price."[13] Inside, in the 1940s and 1950s, the theater still looked like a palace, a place of overdramatized elegance.[14] After buying tickets, patrons like the Frosts in their Saturday finery walked down a long hallway with a vaulted ceiling that recalled an English manor. From there, they funneled into the lobby. A pianist sat in front of a baby grand playing sweet melodies. Chandeliers threw gentle streams of light onto Oriental rugs and antique sofas. The marble sinks and gold ashtrays in the restrooms and parlors glistened and smelled fresh and clean. And the main auditorium with its balconies, retractable orchestra pit, red velvet seats, and sparkling ceiling drew oohs and ahs from the crowds. When the last star dimmed and the low hum of the pipe organ faded, the screen started to glow, first with a newsreel, then with trailers, and finally, the featured attraction. Films at the Warner were part of the show, but never the whole show.[15]

Although they lacked the Warner's jaw-dropping opulence, the other Boardwalk movie houses, like the Stanley, the Strand, and the Virginia, still offered a luxury experience at a middle-class price well into the postwar era. Customers headed to these theaters for a night out, and they got at these showplaces an evening of live music, vaudeville comedy, movie trailers, and Hollywood's latest releases in a plush setting. The buildings and employees were part of the performance at the Stanley, the Strand, and the Virginia as well. All of them had lavish lounges and sitting rooms, solicitous ushers, and gracious bathroom attendants. Egyptian-themed murals lined the auditorium walls, and crushed red velvet covered the seats.

Catering to locals and tourists, the ten movie houses along Atlantic Avenue stayed open year 'round. And, like the Boardwalk showplaces, they also sold a night's luxurious indulgence at an affordable price, and here too the experience started with exclusion.[16] Up and down Atlantic Avenue, uniformed ushers guided white couples in jackets and dresses to their seats on the main floor of the theater, while they steered African Americans to the left side of the auditorium or to the top of the balcony.

Although less spectacular than the Warner and the Strand, the movie houses on main street shared more in common with the beachfront showplaces than with the cramped, unadorned viewing rooms of today's strip malls. Opened in 1934, the Hollywood Theater, a typical downtown picture show located near the corner of Atlantic and Kentucky avenues, featured heavy, ornamented bronze doors. Inside, it had a barrel-shaped, vaulted ceiling and a mural that depicted *Arabian Nights* stories. All of the lighting fixtures were aluminum with colored, etched-glass shades. The theater, its owners bragged, had a well that pumped what they called "spring air" into the auditorium every seven minutes, clearing away any noxious odors. For added comfort, the Hollywood offered extra-large couch seats "so couples could sit closer together."[17]

Providing a luxury movie experience at a middle-class price made Atlantic City's Boardwalk and Atlantic Avenue theaters anomalies in the last years of the golden age of American cinema. The Great Depression initially devastated the theater business. Between 1930 and 1933, movie houses lost a third of their audiences. By 1936, however, the crowds had come back to watch gangster films and other items on Hollywood's escapist menu. Even though business rebounded, studios and theater owners remained cautious about the future and looked to trim costs. Companies shelved plans to build movie palaces on the scale of the Warner after 1932. In their place, film executives erected smaller, more austere theaters. Most of the new picture houses came without orchestra pits, hanging balconies, atmospheric ceilings, lavish lobbies, or marble-floored bathrooms. Streamlined modernism replaced exuberant eclecticism as the dominant architectural style across the nation. Many theaters, at the same time, got rid of their battalions of ushers, retaining just a few untrained high school students to collect tickets and turn the lights up between shows so customers could seat themselves.[18] Together, the changes stressed the stars on screen and the movie itself over churchlike stained-glass facades and Spanish Baroque interiors. Well after these trends took hold in Philadelphia and Chicago, Atlantic City movie managers clung to the old way of doing things, selling luxury and continuing to make an evening at the movies into a night of fantasy and play acting.

This was the key to Atlantic City's enduring appeal in the postwar years. While Atlantic City was once a trailblazer, a city of many firsts, in the 1950s it represented something of a throwback. In these first days of McDonald's fast food, white-gloved waiters still served extravagant meals on monogrammed, gold-trimmed china. Swing bands still played Benny Goodman tunes. Women still wore dresses and men still wore coats and ties. While segregation broke down in some places in the 1950s, African Americans still sat in the crow's nests in Atlantic City. Outside, black men still shined shoes, and the movies still played in elaborate palaces. While some visitors, especially the children of immigrants and shopkeepers who had graduated to employment in accounting firms and stock brokerage houses, drifted away from the city for more exclusive and more remote resorts, the newest recruits to the American middle class—trade unionists taking annual vacations for the first time as a result of new union contracts and veterans from working-class neighborhoods moving into white-collar jobs as a result of the G.I. Bill—took their places in rooms at the Traymore and the Hotel Majestic. Like couples on the Boardwalk in the 1920s and 1930s, these women and men came to Atlantic City to show off in still largely segregated places that they had made it in America. And they wanted to act out their success stories in the same ways the people before them had—in an exclusive and embellished public space—and they wanted to do it in that place they had heard so much about: Atlantic City.

Along Atlantic Avenue—to look at one of the city's movie-dependent public spheres—patrons of the Hollywood, the Shore, the Beach, the Lyric, and the other picture houses filled the sidewalks well into the Eisenhower era. Families from Millville, a farm town thirty-five miles east, came to downtown Atlantic City to shop for Easter outfits and wedding clothes. After roaming up and down the avenue buying a dress and a handbag, a suit and a tie, they ate dinner out and took in a movie. Couples from Marven Gardens drove to town for a show. Beforehand, they walked arm-in-arm down the sidewalk, which was thick with other women and men also on their way to the movies. After the film, friends met at Kornblau's deli for overstuffed sandwiches of corned beef, cole slaw, and Russian dressing, and couples stopped at the Penn Atlantic Hotel for a slice of New York cheesecake or a plate of Welsh rarebit.[19] Others lingered in the U-shaped, tile-floored alcoves of the furniture showrooms and shoe stores, checking out the window displays.

Trusting that the police, merchants, and ushers would keep "undesirables" at a distance, whites still spent their leisure time on the streets and in the dark with strangers in the postwar years. Well aware of their customers' sense of security, Atlantic Avenue and Boardwalk theater owners regularly scheduled midnight shows. Before the 1960s, being downtown or by the ocean at two o'clock in the morning did not scare white women and men. Filled with "the right kind of people"— Rachel's phrase—the areas around the movies seemed safe and alive. As long as they did, the public entertainment world of going out to the theater, clubs, and restaurants, of strolling and eating, and of playing the parts of rich swells and important persons thrived, but when middle-class perceptions of these urban spaces changed, this world collapsed, and the ornate facades of the movie houses came crumbling down.[20]

THE MOVIE BUSINESS IN ATLANTIC CITY

In the summer of 1956, fifteen theaters with segregated seating for nearly 20,000 customers operated in Atlantic City. Most of the movie houses appealed to a large, white, middle-class audience by playing Hollywood's latest mainstream productions. Steel Pier, for instance, featured three "first run selected motion pictures each day." All of them, the owners assured customers, "are chosen by a special board of review with the purpose of providing the finest entertainment for all members of the family."[21] Adhering to the same booking policy, the Warner, a few blocks from the pier, featured Marilyn Monroe in *Bus Stop* that summer. On July 4, the peak of the season, *The King and I* ran for its fourth consecutive week at the Virginia, while *High Society* with Bing Crosby, Grace Kelly, and Frank Sinatra played at the Apollo, and Paul Newman, Sal Mineo, and Pier Angeli starred in *Somebody Up There Likes Me* at the Strand.[22] Main Street moviegoers had the choice that summer of seeing Tyrone Power and Kim Novak in *The Eddy Duchin Story* at the Beach or Gregory Peck in *Moby Dick* at the Astor a few blocks away. Every Saturday morning, the Hollywood, the Earle, and other Atlantic Avenue theaters presented matinee double bills for children. Around midnight, they ran late shows for couples and night owls.

With crowds still lined up in front of their theaters well into the postwar period, cinema owners continued to pour money into their properties. The Strand and the Embassy installed expensive new air-conditioning systems in the mid-1950s. In 1953, George Hamid, Jr., who after graduating from Princeton University joined his father in running Steel Pier and the family's other enterprises, spent $150,000 on a state-of-the-art Astrolite screen and just as much on a brand-new stereophonic sound system for the mammoth Ocean Theater.[23] Hamid made an even bigger investment in the city's movie business two years later, when he purchased four theaters, the Colonial on Atlantic Avenue and the Strand, the Virginia, and the Warner on the Boardwalk. "The key factor" in this decision, the public amusement entrepreneur told the local paper, was "a rebirth" that he felt was sweeping over Atlantic City.[24]

The next summer turned out to be the high-water mark for Atlantic City's cinema business. Just after the crowds went home in September following the Miss America Pageant, the wrecking ball knocked down the Earle Theater to make way for a parking lot, a development repeated again and again over the next two decades.[25] At the same time, the Warner, the Versailles of Boardwalk movie palaces, began to show signs of wear and tear. Despite his public enthusiasm, from the time he bought the theater Hamid practiced fiscal restraint and a wait-to-see-what-happens attitude. Under an arrangement with the previous owners, he promised to change the theater's name. Rather than buy a whole new marquee, Hamid saved money by transposing a couple of letters, calling the thirty-year-old theater the Warren. When things didn't turn around right away, Hamid moved to cut his losses. He eliminated two-thirds of the theater's seats and started booking live acts like Ricky Nelson, Mel Torme, and Ella Fitzgerald. Once, he had the chance to bring Elvis Presley to the Warren, but certain that no one would pay to hear someone named Elvis sing rock-and-roll songs, he turned down the offer. Searching for other ways to generate earnings, Hamid began to stage Broadway previews at the theater, reviving an Atlantic City tradition that had waned. But this didn't work either. Designed for movies, the Warren turned amplified voices into garbled noise, and patrons complained that they couldn't hear the actors.[26]

By the winter of 1960, the Warren lay vacant, its marquee dark at night. City leaders complained that the building once tagged the Wonder Theater of the World now represented a business-draining eyesore. After months of wrangling about what to do, Hamid applied for a permit to raze the entire structure except for the front facade. "We feel very sad about tearing down this beautiful showplace," Hamid said, "but there is nothing we can do about it. We have tried everything for the past four years, but it wasn't a practical building for a private operation."[27] Several local business leaders considered buying the building, but in the end, they all agreed with Hamid: it was just too expensive to operate. Eventually he sold the aging theater to a bowling alley company.[28]

In the summer of 1963, teen idols Frankie Avalon and Annette Funicello went on the road to promote their new film, *Beach Party*—"It's What Happens When 10,000 Kids Meet on 5,000 Beach Blankets."[29] At a stop in Atlantic City, cameras flashed as the bright-faced stars bowled a few frames to celebrate the opening of the Boardwalk Bowl on the site of the old theater. Apparently no one noticed the irony of film stars marking the destruction of a movie house. Behind the Warner's facade now stood thirty-four fully automated bowling lanes where the legendary professional Snooks Pearlstein and a whole lot of amateurs chased their dreams of a perfect 300 game. But even the bowling alley would not last.[30]

The closing of the Warner was just the beginning. Between 1960 and 1970, the city's movie business lost its mass audience and fantasy feel. Throughout the 1950s, most theaters still hired live bands and teams of ushers and continued to show blockbuster, first-run films. But over the next ten years, the crowds steadily decreased, creating fiscal problems for the Boardwalk and Atlantic Avenue theaters. Providing a luxury experience at a middle-class price required constant upkeep and a steady stream of people going through the turnstiles. Crystal chandeliers and marble sinks needed daily polishing and scrubbing. When gate receipts dropped, the owners cut back on repairs and skimped on improvements. Because of the theaters' showy appearances, the signs of decline were glaring and obvious. Peeling paint and broken air conditioners made a mockery of the movie houses' productions of splendor.

When the Apollo Theater, located on the Boardwalk near New York Avenue, opened in 1934, it exuded the over-the-top lavishness typical of the city's theaters. The owners equipped the 1,700-seat auditorium with a brand-new Western Electric sound system. Even more impressive, they promised patrons perfect 70-degree temperatures year 'round. "There is not the slightest possibility of deviation from this mark," they boasted, "because automatic 'policemen' do nothing else but watch that one point." On the theater's walls, designers installed a fluorescent mural of Apollo standing with Virgil, Plato, Socrates, Homer, Aristotle, Dante, and Shakespeare. When the lights dimmed, the painting took on another life. A yellow moon rose over the luminaries of Western thought, making them look like three-dimensional wax figures. Twenty-five years later, the Apollo gave up pretending to be a grand theater. The cooling system rattled, and Dante needed touching up. In the early 1970s, the movie house changed its name to the Apollo Burlesque Theater. Each night, strippers shared the stage with "baggy pants comics."[31]

Bidding for respectability, the owner of another Atlantic City burlesque theater, the Globe, located toward the northern end of the Boardwalk, told a reporter in 1966 that he was looking to attract a middle-class audience. That's not what he or the owners of the Apollo got. "The upper crust ladies and gentlemen of yesteryear," commented an observer, "would no doubt be appalled to find that the Apollo occupies space near Steel Pier." The owner of an Italian restaurant shook his head when he looked up and saw the Apollo's marquee announcing X-rated films and the Miss Nude International Pageant. To him, this was a clear sign that "the class of people in Atlantic City changed from the 1950s to the 1970s."[32]

By the time the Apollo turned into a burlesque house, Rachel and Herb Frost

THE WARNER THEATER
AND THE BOARDWALK BOWL, 1960S
(Atlantic City Free Public Library, Heston Room, Atlantic City, New Jersey.)

had noticed the changes on the Boardwalk. Each summer when they opened their shore houses for the season, they saw that another small bakery or retail shop had gone out of business. Although the Nikko continued selling imported vases and rugs and Grande Marche still carried imported scarves and doillies, these kinds of posh shops were becoming the exception. Again and again in the late 1960s and early 1970s, Boardwalk jewelry stores and linen shops closed. Lemonade and hot dog stands replaced Chinese restaurants and delis. Stores selling T-shirts featuring Mickey Mouse and Charlie Brown in sexually suggestive positions cropped up on every block. Borrowing a trick from Coney Island barkers, T-shirt store owners blared messages about 99-cent sales and two-for-one specials over loudspeakers all day long.[33] Others hired pushy salesmen who tempted passersby with mind-boggling bargains and incredible deals on precious jewels.

As Herb Frost's robot story makes clear, this was not an entirely new phenome-non. Before he became Johnny Carson's sidekick, Ed McMahon peddled "handy

Morris Metric Slicers" on the Boardwalk, but the salesmen lost their charms as the backdrop behind them grew frayed and tarnished.[34] Tripping over T-shirt displays and hot dog wrappers, a *New York Times* correspondent complained in the early 1970s about the Boardwalk's "crass vulgarity."[35]

It didn't take long for the changes on the Boardwalk to make their way over to Atlantic Avenue and its theaters. One by one in the late 1960s and early 1970s, the movie houses along the city's main street either went out of business or lost their middle-class audiences. The Liberty, which had been the Astor, closed in 1969. Four years later, a discount furniture store bought the Shore and turned it into a parking lot. About the same time, the Center cut back its schedule, opening only for the summer. Then in 1976, the Center and the Capitol went under for good.[36] The handful of downtown movie theaters still operating rotted from neglect. Porcelain toilets and sinks turned an ugly shade of yellow; stuffing oozed out of holes in the red velvet seats; and book-sized chunks of paint dangled from the walls. A few theaters continued to show blockbuster films, like *Patton* and *Love Story*, but others, like the Embassy, started to specialize in slasher flicks, Kung Fu movies, and blackploitation films aimed at increasingly distinct segments of the consumer market like teenagers and younger African Americans.[37] Catering to yet another crowd, other Atlantic Avenue theaters, including the Beach and the Hollywood, began featuring XXX-rated motion pictures running on a loop twenty-four hours a day. Blaze Starr, Louisiana governor Earl K. Long's one-time lover, did a special striptease performance at the Capitol in 1966. By 1969, *The Curious Female* and *Cherry, Harry, and Raquel* played in the same picture houses that had once featured *The Philadelphia Story* and *Singin' in the Rain*.[38]

Most middle-class residents and tourists saw the theaters' new offerings as unmistakable signs of decay. When a local group complained that Atlantic Avenue picture shows no longer offered anything for kids, a couple of cinema owners agreed to revive the tradition of showing Saturday morning matinees. But not many, it seems, came for the Hollywood's screening of *Godzilla vs. the Thing* and *The Time Traveler*, so the once-regal theater and the ones nearby pulled the G-rated films and went back to showing pornographic and B movies from morning to night.[39]

The decay of the downtown movie scene moved in lockstep with the decline of the middle-class public realm along Atlantic Avenue. Nightlife—the backbone of the mass public entertainment industry of the past—depended on a careful balance of exclusion, density, and a sense of safety in order to produce mainstream consumer fantasies. As the theaters shut down and changed their marketing strategies, they took away the lights, sounds, and energy from Atlantic Avenue. With fewer of the right people on the streets, stores and restaurants closed earlier, even on Saturday nights. Then, some shut down altogether. Paralleling what was happening on the Boardwalk, with each passing year in the late 1960s and early 1970s, another venerable Atlantic Avenue shop went out of business or moved out of town. With commerce in retreat, stores stayed vacant for long stretches. When the family-owned Shirt and Tie Shop closed, for example, the building remained unrented for more than a year.[40]

Fewer shops meant even fewer people on the streets, and fewer people meant that neither Atlantic Avenue nor the Boardwalk could stage middle-class fantasies of leveling up in public. At a bare minimum, the spectacle of social climbing required an audience of the right kind of people. Without respectable, well-dressed crowds, Atlantic City lost its ability to host nightly reenactments of the American Dream of upward mobility, and when that happened, the cycle of decline was on a vicious, unrelenting course.

The few middle-class patrons who did come downtown in the late 1960s and early 1970s to see a film hustled back to their cars when it was over and raced home. They no longer lingered to shop or grab a sandwich. Increasingly, shopkeepers were not around either. In the past, many merchants lived above their stores, but as businesses closed and nightlife disappeared, more and more shopkeepers moved to other parts of the city and surrounding areas. Without customers milling around, store owners locked up before dark and left German Shepherds to watch over their merchandise. Window-shoppers had to peer through thick metal gates to see the cabana wear and checkered jackets.[41] As growing numbers of people stayed away from Atlantic Avenue, the street started to look dead and lifeless, but mostly, as the snarling dogs and steel bars made clear, it felt cold and dangerous. The world of going out to the movies—like the rest of the public entertainment industry—depended on a sense of safety. By the late 1960s, Atlantic City could no longer produce the reassuring messages of security and exclusion that middle-class theatergoers demanded.

Crime, of course, was a key factor in eroding trust. But crime was not—and this should not be surprising—new to the city. Throughout the 1930s and 1940s, the local newspaper regularly reported on hotel heists, numbers running, and vice violations. But in the 1960s, crime became more violent, more personal, and more harrowing. Everyone, it seemed, had a story to tell of a mugging, a purse snatching, or a beating. In January 1968, thieves broke into James E. Kunik's Atlantic Avenue men's store three times in three days. In August, robbers clubbed a cigar store clerk over the head with a bat. A few years later, two men walked into the shop owned by David and Samuel Freedman in the late afternoon and forced the brothers, both in their seventies, into a back room. The thieves tied them up with rawhide shoelaces and then took turns pistol whipping them and punching them in the face. After the pummeling, the intruders emptied the cash register and fled on foot into the city.[42] Even the movie houses got caught in the crime wave. One night near midnight in 1971, while *The Organization* starring Sidney Poitier played at the Embassy, a man with a knife forced the manager to open the safe. He got away with $760.[43]

The Boardwalk did not seem much safer than Atlantic Avenue. A "Great Place to Walk" read a headline in the *Philadelphia Inquirer* in 1971, "But Few Realize That Danger Exists." A couple of years earlier, two visitors discovered firsthand the Boardwalk's many risks. Returning from a late night along the Midway, itself in retreat, these men accidentally bumped into a couple of teenagers. A fight broke out, and when it was over the tourists ended up bruised and cut.[44] In 1971, robbers grabbed a Baltimore woman's purse. Her husband fought back, but the thieves beat the couple with a steel pipe and then ran off with the pocketbook.[45] Showing no mercy, criminals even victimized the architects of the city's physical destruction. In 1972, robbers stole $1,200 worth of equipment from the company in charge of the Traymore's demolition.[46]

By the early 1970s, the Queen of Resorts had, according to federal statistics, become a crime capital. The government reported that the city possessed the highest crime rate of any city its size in the entire country.[47] But it was a rash of killings more than these statistics that destroyed the community's once-glorious and massive public entertainment industry. In 1971, two white men, a conventioneer from Easton, Pennsylvania, and an Atlantic Avenue merchant, were murdered in quick succession. Both were taken by surprise and gunned down at close range.[48] Trouble broke out on the Midway as well. A year later, shots rang out at Club Harlem when feuding Philadelphia drug dealers brought their dispute to the shore. One witness described the bloody battle in the dimly lit club as being "just like the OK Corral." When the gunfire stopped, four were dead and twenty-six were wounded.[49]

Convinced by anxious television reports of crime as well as news of riots in Newark and Detroit that urban spaces were by definition dangerous places, fewer and fewer middle-class women and men chanced a visit to Atlantic City in the 1970s. Like downtowns everywhere, Atlantic Avenue became a haunted place of vacant stores and empty windows with fading For Rent signs.[50] On the Boardwalk, there was still some life. The Strand still showed first-run films in its slightly shabby auditorium in the 1970s. Conventions still brought buses and carloads of people to town, but they were rarely those treasured delegates with fat expense accounts.[51] While the mass gatherings of free-spending teamsters and doctors met in Miami Beach and Las Vegas, struggling cosmetologists and blue-collar Shriners in fez hats came to Atlantic City. In the early 1970s, the Eastern General Conference of Charismatic Revival brought 30,000 born-again Christians to the motels, hotels, restaurants, and movie houses of the nation's playground. The president of the Atlantic City Convention Bureau wasn't impressed. "We had the Charismatics on [the] Boardwalk," he scoffed, "buying hot dogs and sleeping five to a room at very low rates."[52]

Standing next to the faithful in line at Boardwalk food stands were women and men wearing those cheap T-shirts for sale along every block of the promenade. Couples in their Saturday-night clothes started to stand out, especially after dark. Many families came just for the day. They drove into town, parked, changed into their bathing suits in public bathrooms, ate ham sandwiches packed at home, and then left before dark. Overnight visitors tended to stay in their motel rooms behind metal doors and extra locks watching TV, rather than risk a chance encounter with disaster or someone unfamiliar. "I don't see as many people on the Boardwalk at night anymore," noted a local commentator in 1972. That was bad news for the movie house owners and others in the public entertainment industry.[53]

FLIGHT

Just about every picture house in town was within walking distance or a short jitney ride of the 300 block of Melrose Avenue. In 1955—near the high point of the city's movie business—white families occupied every house on the street. That same year, a black man, Jacob Downing, and his family moved into a house in the middle of the block. Someone planted a "crude five-foot cross" on Downing's lawn to welcome him to the neighborhood. Others tossed rocks through his windows. Most, however, protested with their feet. By 1961, Downing had only one or two white neighbors. The rest had bolted to the virtually all-white suburbs located on Absecon Island close to Marven Gardens or offshore. The pattern of black settlement and white flight was repeated again and again in the postwar era as African Americans desegregated the city street by street, movie theater by movie theater.[54]

Integration, some have said, was that brief moment between segregation and retreat. That certainly is the Atlantic City story. The picture shows followed Downing's neighbors to the suburbs and away from African Americans. As early as 1950, the Atlantic, the area's first open-air drive-in, started showing films in a field ten miles west of the city, not far from several growing all-white residential developments. With speakers and parking spaces for 900 cars, a playground with swings, a merry-go-round, pony rides, and a bottle-warming service, the new drive-in acted like a one-stop entertainment center for baby boom parents. But even more, it reflected the turn to new kinds of public space taking shape in the face of the breakdown of the older, urban, now not so exclusive, public spaces of the past. Drive-ins operated like safe extensions of the living room. Customers watched films encased in their cars. They didn't have to rub elbows with strangers in the dark if they didn't want to. Private, convenient, and centered on the automobile, the drive-in hinted at the walled-off public entertainment world to come.[55]

When the Atlantic Drive-In first opened, there were few other businesses around. By the time the Warner/Warren became the Boardwalk Bowl ten years later, the area near the drive-in had changed. Nearby stood the new home of Kensington Furniture. For two generations, the Grossmans had sold bedroom sets and love seats from their showroom in the heart of Atlantic City's central business district, close to the Hollywood Theater. But in the late 1950s, looking for more space and parking, and perhaps sensing the changes to come, the family opened a store in the suburbs.

Kensington was one of the first businesses to flee the city.[56] Not long after the furniture showroom left Atlantic Avenue, construction began on the area's first enclosed mall. Located near the Atlantic Drive-In, Sears Town opened in 1967 with more than a half million square feet of retail space, making it the area's largest shopping facility. By 1973, the mall's annual sales had reached $35 million, just about equaling revenues on Atlantic Avenue. Trying to capitalize on that success, Philadelphia-based Steinbach's department store opened a branch at the mall in May 1974. About the same time, developers broke ground on the Cardiff Circle shopping center down the road, adding another 335,000 square feet of shopping space to Atlantic City's suburbs. The new strip malls had no trouble finding tenants, including companies selling entertainment, like carousel rides for kids, pinball machines for teenagers, and movies for adults.[57] Within a few years, a bland, multiscreen movie theater with a huge parking lot opened next to Sears Town. Cheap land, the growing dependence on cars, and government tax breaks for suburban development, support for road and school construction, and low-interest mortgage subsidies made the move out of town more attractive and economically feasible.[58] Businesses needed customers, and Kensington Furniture, Steinberg's, and the cinemas were all chasing white flight to the growing suburbs of Northfield, Linwood, Absecon, and Somers Point.

White flight cut deeply into the city. Between 1940 and 1970, the city's population dropped by 25 percent, from 64,000 to 48,000. Mirroring national trends, white families made up the largest chunk of those who fled. The U.S. Census reports that 22,000 white people left Atlantic City in the thirty years after World War II. The people left behind on the Monopoly streets were mostly older, underemployed, poor, and increasingly African American and Puerto Rican. No one except for a few men selling suits and refrigerators on installment plans, pizza makers, and the managers of a handful of moldy theaters seemed to be chasing after their business.[59]

White residents were not the only people running from Atlantic City. By 1970, long-time tourists had abandoned the Boardwalk, the showy hotels, and the sparkling theaters. Some escaped to quieter shore towns, places like Bethany Beach and Rehoboth in Delaware and Avalon and Sea Isle City in New Jersey. Others took their kids to Colonial Williamsburg or Disneyland or to ride the speedy new roller coasters at Great Adventure or some other place located far from the city and public transportation. Still others journeyed into the "wild," seeking nature in remote locales. By this time, being outdoors in Atlantic City and other urban areas, given rising crime rates and graphic reports of riots, seemed more like a health risk than a healthy choice to white middle-class families. As the tourists fled from the Boardwalk and downtown, tax receipts dropped, pushing up local property taxes and driving more families out of the city.[60] Business and home owners cut back on upkeep, spending only on vital repairs. Some just gave up and tore down their buildings, turning their properties into parking lots. In a strange twist, even as the city declined and its population fell, the demand for parking spaces rose, as more people drove to town rather than walk or ride the jitney. Business leaders insisted that they could lure shoppers back to their stores only by promising to take care of their customers' cars in imitation of the suburbs.[61]

More parking, however, couldn't sustain the city. Beginning in the late 1960s, investors stayed away, and as a result, new construction virtually ceased. The whole city started to look tattered and worn, hardly the kind of place to go to show off making it in America. Things only got worse for the city through the early 1970s. Each year, another grand hotel came crashing down, and another movie house shut its doors. As city theaters faltered, more multiplexes opened in the suburbs. Rising from yellow-striped parking lots, these flat-roofed, steel-beamed barns housing film projectors and popcorn machines were bereft of luxury, whimsy, or fantasy. But style and architectural flair did not seem to matter much to suburbanites any more. Seeing urban spaces as scary, they chose to stay close to home in dull movie theaters rather than chance an encounter with potentially dangerous people of color or the poor in downtown movie palaces. They gave up on older, urban public places and fantasies in exchange for personal safety, and that individual choice, played out over and over again, led to the destruction of the nation's playground.

POSTSCRIPT

Once he had that smoke blown in his face by African American teenagers, Herb Frost gave up on Atlantic City, its Boardwalk, and its over-the-top movie houses.

He and Rachel sold the family's second home in Chelsea and bought a place in Bethany Beach, Delaware. Marketed as a "quiet resort" and "a haven for rest," Bethany, with its bungalow houses, neat picket fences, front porches filled with white wicker furniture, and grass-covered sand dunes, looked like a scene from a Frank Capra movie set at the beach.[62] The Frosts missed the rolling chairs, the clubs, the hotel lobbies, and the playful exteriors of Atlantic City's extravagant buildings, but they cherished the safe streets surrounding their new summer home even more. No one locked their bikes there, and that's what they liked about the place.

Lois Wallen didn't retreat to Delaware, but she did leave the city. For years, her entertainment world had centered on Atlantic City's movie theaters. On most Saturday nights, she and her husband, Marvin, would put on dressy clothes and go to see a film. Afterward, they took a walk before heading home. Even after they moved in the early 1960s to Absecon, a small offshore town with a short two-block main street eight miles east of the Boardwalk, they still drove into Atlantic City on weekends to catch a film and split an oversized deli sandwich and a thick milkshake.

Wallen vividly remembers the last time she and her husband took the drive over the bridge onto the island for a movie. They wanted to see Robert Altman's critically acclaimed 1970 blood-soaked comedy, *M*A*S*H*. It was only playing at a downtown Atlantic City theater. "I remember that night," she now says, "because I was a bit shaken by the atmosphere." The ticket takers and ushers seemed jittery, as if they were waiting for something terrible to happen, like the bloodbath that took place a few years later at Club Harlem. That night, the Wallens encountered a new security regime. As they walked up to the theater, an attendant in jeans and a spotted white shirt poked his head out and looked around suspiciously before he unlocked the door and let them in. As soon as they crossed the threshold, he bolted the door shut behind them. After the film, Wallen recalls, "We hightailed it to our car, locked the door, and immediately left the city." "It was the last time," she says, "we went into Atlantic City at night until the casinos changed the town."[63]

For Lois Wallen, the last picture show had shut down, and just like in Larry McMurtry's beautifully mournful novel, the closing of the theaters marked the end of an era. The public entertainment worlds of the Boardwalk and Atlantic Avenue were dead and so was the city's mass middle-class appeal.

5

Narrating Decline and Erasing Race

irector Bob Rafelson called his 1972 film *The King of Marvin Gardens*, but most scenes were shot in Atlantic City. As the picture begins, the laconic David Staebler wraps up his dreamy late-night AM talk show on a Philadelphia radio station. He walks alone in the dark and desolate city to the trolley and then to the house he shares with his grandfather. Before going to bed at dawn, David learns that his brother Jason has called to tell him: "Get your ass to Atlantic City. Our Kingdom has come." David feigns indifference, even disdain, toward the idea. It is, he tells his grandfather, just another of his grifter brother's cons. Yet later that morning David packs his faded blue suitcase, pulls a shabby brown overcoat over a rumpled black suit, and boards a train to Atlantic City.

A gray winter sky, Jason's forty-something girlfriend, Sally, dressed in a kind of Miss America costume, and a motley five-piece brass band greet David at the station. Sally gives the horn players the signal to start playing. Out of tune and disorganized, they spit out a few notes. Sally and David stand there for a beat or two and then make their way on foot to the Boardwalk. Apologizing, Sally says, "It was supposed to be a whole lot better. Things don't always work out like you plan, right?"

Sally could have been talking about Atlantic City, not just the band and the grand entrance that didn't come off. In many ways, Atlantic City, rather than Sally, Jason, or David, acts as the main character in *The King of Marvin Gardens*.[1] Aching disappointment infuses every shot and every scene. The city's crumbling but still lavish built environment hangs in the backdrop. Clearly, the camera shows that the city used to be a whole lot better.

By the time *The King of Marvin Gardens* opened in theaters, Atlantic City had become almost a parody of the American Dream. From Ducktown to the North-side, the city's neighborhoods, as the film reveals, were now made up of cracked sidewalks, houses desperate for new paint, and storefronts barricaded with steel bars. Along the Boardwalk, Going Out of Business signs stretched across the fronts of once-elegant linen shops; movie marquees advertised films long gone; and an empty lot was all that was left of the Traymore.[2] Yet despite the signs of decay, much of the old city remained. There was still the Marlborough-Blenheim and Steel Pier, a cluster of fancy jewelry stores and saltwater taffy stands, and a number of hotel restaurants serving French foods like chicken cordon bleu and beef bourguignon on gold-trimmed dishes. Boosters still claimed, louder than ever, that the city remained the nation's playground. But as *The King of Marvin Gardens* makes clear, the city with its decaying buildings and tired remnants was a cruel tease.

Along the Boardwalk, the American Dream of upward mobility now seemed more like a sham. Hard work didn't pay off; it created disappointment and empty lots. But that's why for Jason, the dying Atlantic City remained a quintessentially American place. He loves the city because, as he says with a smile, "the hustle is out in the open." His America—a post-Vietnam (almost), post–civil rights move-ment, and post–postwar boom America—was different from the America of the Boardwalk's glory days. His was a nation where get rich quick schemes and decep-tion, not hard work and diligence, reigned. Jason was a dreamer, but his dream was a scam, a scam born in Atlantic City.

When David gets to Atlantic City, Jason sits in jail, charged with possession of stolen property. Then, without explanation, he is out on bail, riding down the empty Boardwalk on a new-fangled electric rolling chair. He picks up David and they check into the Marlborough-Blenheim Hotel, named the Carlton Essex in the film. As they pass through the domed lobby, the camera focuses on elderly men with walkers and empty chairs and couches. On the floor of their room, which is decorated with frilly, yet faded, Victorian lampshades and frayed velvet curtains, they unfurl a map. Jason points to a tiny speck just below the Big Island in Hawaii. That, he says, is the location of the "tropical paradise" that will serve as the site for the "Staebler Brothers' Renaissance." Jason calls this fantasyland "Tikki," and he asks David to help him find investors to finance his American Dream.

David knows his brother is a penniless hustler, but he can't help himself from getting swept up in the dream of Tikki. Although he remains detached, that is just the way he is; he still participates in every phase of the resort's planning. One af-ternoon, Jason and David take a break from their drawings and head over to Cen-tral Pier to catch a ride on the Sky Tower Observation ride. Perched above the city, they gaze down at the wide-open Boardwalk and the bombed-out urban land-scape beyond. "It won't be like this in Tikki," Jason says. "We will have strict con-trol," he insists. "No pokerino. No frozen custard." David agrees. "Anyone litters," he says with a slight smile on his face, "we will deport them." Control, the brothers know, guaranteed a resort's success, and the loss of control over the crowds, dirt, and the city itself, they also know, were the causes of Atlantic City's demise.

TALKING ABOUT DECLINE

Atlantic City locals and faithful visitors have their own theories for the city's de-cline. Depending on whom you ask, they will tell you that the city lost its movie house crowds and its status as the nation's playground in the 1940s or the 1950s or the 1960s. After an attempt at periodization, they will launch into long, usually interesting soliloquies. Their narratives of decay are remarkable for their insight into the complexity of urban problems and for how they link seemingly mundane and unrelated shifts in commerce and technology to changes in people's leisure choices and vacation desires. Yet the explanations are equally remarkable for what they do not say. Observers of Atlantic City's fate stubbornly refuse to discuss in explicit terms the public, control, and exclusivity—the very things that made the city work during its glory days. They are not, however, unique. All across the country, from the late 1960s onward, people framed their discussions of the "urban crisis" in similar ways: talking about some things and editing out other matters.

Repeating what he heard on a visit to the city in the 1990s, South Jersey native and author Gay Talese argued that families, and by this he surely meant white families, stopped coming to Atlantic City in the 1960s because the Boardwalk ho-tels with their Byzantine domes, art deco lobbies, and sweeping verandahs had by then become musty relics. Throughout the 1920s and even during the Depression years of the 1930s, other locals suggest, the owners of the hulking pleasure palaces raked in piles of money.[3] Then came World War II. As the United States prepared for battle, local leaders made a calculated gamble on the city's future. Judging that mobilization would cut into tourism, city officials turned the town over to the U.S. military. This gave Atlantic City business owners the chance to keep making money during the conflict, while also generating favorable publicity about the re-sort's patriotic spirit. But it also meant that single men, on their own and away from home, stayed in rooms occupied in the past by middle-class couples. The soldiers were, to say the least, hard on the hotels. More than a few rooms were trashed when they left. After the war, rather than clean-up, reinvest in, and update their properties, the owners, the story goes, pocketed the profits. It didn't take long for the paint to start peeling off the walls, dust to collect on the chandeliers, and the dining room chairs to creak with each shift of a customer's weight.[4] Beginning in the 1950s, locals whispered among themselves about the shabby state of the city's hotels. After Atlantic City hosted the Democratic National Convention in 1964, so this theory of decline goes, there was no need to talk in hushed voices any more: the secret was out.

Certain that Lyndon Johnson would win his party's nomination in 1964, journalists went in search of other stories. Too many, from the Atlantic City perspective, filed articles about the ragged condition of the city's hotels and their spectacularly greedy owners. "This is the original Bay of Pigs," one reporter joked. Readers in Indianapolis and San Diego learned about hotel switchboards that did not work, room service that took hours to deliver cold meals, and food and drink prices that soared just in time for the convention. A newsman from southern California tugged on the doorknob to his room and it fell off. Later, he reached up to adjust the shower head and it too fell off.[5] The articles made people think, one novelist has written, that every "delegate had been issued a souvenir cockroach."[6] Making matters worse, loyal visitors, the people who had faithfully returned to Atlantic City year after year, tried to book rooms in familiar places during the summer of 1964 only to find themselves shut out of town by the convention. Angry about the rebuff, locals say, many never came back, and one by one, the hotels and boardinghouses went out of business.[7]

With hotel door handles falling off in guests' hands, long-time visitors and new recruits to the growing postwar middle class looked for other vacation spots. Technology, people will tell you, multiplied their choices. Atlantic City had thrived in the railroad era and survived the first decades of the automobile revolution, but the jet age, many believe, created insurmountable problems for the nation's playground. By the early 1960s, the major airlines had slashed prices, making airplane travel affordable to middle- and working-class Americans. Now a family from the blue-collar Philadelphia suburb of Keswick could get to a newer fantasy spot with cleaner hotels and restaurants, like Miami Beach or the Bahamas, in about the same time it took to drive the narrow roads leading to Atlantic City. At the same time, travel merchants introduced package deals, making the cost of a week-long trip to Florida or the Caribbean not much more than going to the Jersey shore. According to this jet theory, a particularly popular one in Atlantic City, "the airplane killed the city," as "the white-collar set" started to seek "its pleasures at a somewhat further remove."[8]

Not only could Eastern and TWA take people far away, but as Charles Funnell suggests, the airlines offered a new way to perform middle-class success. By the mid-1960s, air travel represented the most prestigious, and exclusive, form of transportation. In a striking parallel to the Boardwalk of old, just by climbing aboard a plane, travelers, almost certainly decked out in sport coats and dresses, announced and confirmed their middle-class status.[9]

"It's always been my contention," wrote a Philadelphia journalist in 1971, "that air-conditioning killed Atlantic City." From its earliest days, Atlantic City marketed itself as the "lungs of Philadelphia," as a healthy escape from the grime, soot, and stickiness of summer in the city. "Here at the shore," one man remembered, "you'd get the cool breeze, and you could always take a dip in the ocean." But with window units pumping thousands of BTUs of icy air into newly built suburban homes, the beach's cool breezes were less of a draw than before. Why drive to Atlantic City in a car that probably was not air conditioned, many thought, when you could keep cool right at home? Others must have asked themselves if it was worth making the trip to the shore, when many of the more affordable, older hotels and guesthouses did not have air conditioning.[10]

Along with air conditioning, suburban home owners began to invest in backyard swimming pools. Before the postwar period, only the richest Americans could afford their own pools. During the 1960s, installment plans, falling prices, and the development of the above-ground pool made this luxury item available to a growing number of middle- and working-class families. Like the drive-in, swimming pools at home offered a privatized version of the fantasy city. In the past, some Atlantic City observers will say, families dressed up and went to the Warner Theater to demonstrate that they had made it out of the working class. Once they had a pool, they didn't leave their backyards. Cool water on a hot summer day stood just on the other side of a sliding glass door. With a pool close by, some families felt less compelled to leave home and the security of the suburbs to go to Atlantic City and mix with strangers. Urban race riots and the rise of crime—all broadcast on television—only enhanced the appeal of fenced-in, backyard entertainment.[11]

Then there is the television theory. Simply put, once the nation got plugged in, the streets emptied, as people couldn't pull themselves away from the pale blue glow.[12] Local historian Anthony Kutschera offers an interesting twist on television's role in Atlantic City's decline. Before an RCA console filled the corner of every American living room, he explains, General Electric, Heinz, Dupont, Ford, and General Motors all had elaborate exhibits advertising their latest products on the Boardwalk. They paid dearly for the chance to pitch their wares to the middle-class millions visiting the city. Kutschera estimates that General Motors spent as much as $200,000 a year to lease a showroom at the front of Steel Pier. The Hamids, in turn, used this money to hire fresh acts and to repair their buildings. But the exhibits, Kutschera points out, were more than simply sales come-ons. Like the robot man that Herb Frost liked to follow, they added to the Boardwalk's public life. Every Sunday after church, Kutschera's family went walking down the promenade, going from exhibit to exhibit, checking out GM's latest models, watching the science experiments at Dupont Hall, and seeing if they could get another free peanut butter sandwich and green pickle pin at the Heinz Pier. After television took over—by 1960, 89 percent of American households had a set— advertising executives determined that they could reach more people over the airwaves than on the Boardwalk. Soon after, companies pulled out of Atlantic City and made deals with NBC, CBS, and ABC. After that, Kutschera says, there was less to do on the Boardwalk, and the piers and hotels had less money at their disposal to update their attractions and ballrooms. Once the crowds picked up on this, he explains, they went elsewhere.[13]

Some business leaders and public officials blamed the city's deterioration on the Midway's decline. Before the mid-1960s, the 500 Club, the Club Harlem, and other nightspots brought the biggest names in show business to town. But as the crowds diminished, the clubs no longer had the money pay these stars. Desperate to stay afloat, several bars and clubs remade themselves into "bust-out" joints. In these smoky venues, women, working for the house, hustled men for drinks, usually expensive ones like Long Island Iced Teas and double shots of Crown Royal. The word on these places got out quickly. Locals stayed away; then tourists found out about the scams. That left only the loneliest conventioneers on the barstools.[14]

Sue Pollack had her own theory for the Midway's decline. The lifelong Margate resident and aspiring writer blamed the collapse on Estes Kefauver. The Tennessee senator's Special Committee to Investigate Organized Crime in Interstate Commerce stopped off in Atlantic City in the spring of 1951. Comparing the shore town to notoriously corrupt Miami, one committee member called the resort's political set-up "pretty rotten."[15] Kefauver and the other senators' questions didn't break the machine, but they did, according to Pollack, "in some strange way" destroy the town. Clubs, she explained, had a harder time running their casino businesses, at least out in the open. Cash from roulette wheels and blackjack tables had in the past helped to pay for headlining acts and to keep money flowing during lean times. Without this steady source of revenue, Midway entrepreneurs, like Skinny D'Amato, had to make it on food and drinks. Once the crowds thinned in the 1960s, this got harder and harder. And with less people in their showrooms, places like the 500 Club had to book less well known acts, and then, fewer people showed up at the clubs to drink and eat. Friendships, even in D'Amato's case, didn't help. After the lines in front of his club got shorter, he couldn't afford Frank Sinatra any more, especially now that his buddy drew hefty paychecks from Las Vegas casinos, where they obviously did have gambling.[16]

Fewer people left their homes for the shore in the 1960s, locals will tell you, for yet another reason—more women worked for pay outside the home than had twenty years earlier. When Atlantic City reigned as the Queen of Resorts, many families stayed at the shore for the whole summer, or a month, or a couple of weeks. Life at the beach in those days had its own rhythms. Early on Monday mornings, slightly sunburned fathers gingerly put on their suits and ties and climbed into their cars or boarded the train, heading west to their jobs in the city. Their wives and children remained behind, riding the waves and going to the movies. On Friday nights, the men in suits returned.

Postwar shifts in employment altered the rhythms of summer life. After 1945, an increasing number of married middle-class white women entered the paid labor force.[17] With both parents tethered to jobs and with obligations to make installment payments for new Pontiacs, pools, and bedroom sets, fewer middle-class families could afford to spend the entire summer at the shore. As vacations got shorter, vacancy rates rose at Atlantic City's hotels, motels, and guesthouses. Profits dropped, and then, according to this view, the domino effect, the same one that hit the movie theaters and nightclubs, took over. Property owners had less money to put back into their homes and businesses. Turned off by chipped paint and tarnished silverware, tourists decided to spend their yearly vacations in spiffier towns with gleaming new buildings or at more remote locations away from the crowds.[18]

"There are more cars, TV's, homes, etc., than ever," noted an Atlantic City doctor in 1963, "so to attract the visitors we must give them a clean city, and a clean beach." But providing "clean" outdoor leisure got harder and harder. Throughout the 1960s, Atlantic City visitors complained about fearless seagulls swooping down and snatching food right out of their hands. Swimmers felt plastic bags and tampon applicators, not jellyfish or seaweed, brushing up against their legs. Erosion caused by years of mismanagement and flawed policies swept away huge chunks of the sandy beaches. Spurred on by the emerging environmental movement, Philadelphia and New York journalists began printing stories about fecal counts and bacteria in the waters off Atlantic City. Having read about the polluted Queen of Resorts, a few more people decided to stay home and do their swimming in chlorine-soaked pools.[19]

Nature itself, some insist, delivered further blows to the city. Local collector and historian Allen "Boo" Pergament sat in a third-floor South Inlet apartment in 1944, watching as a hurricane, really a nor'easter, "picked up and lifted whole sections of the Boardwalk like they were matchsticks." When the storm passed, Pergament went out to survey the damage. The wind and waves, he immediately saw, had wrecked dozens of homes and ripped a gaping hole through the Heinz

Pier, leaving the number 5 from the famous "57 Varieties" sign bobbing in the water. Almost sixty years later, Pergament is quick to point out that the landmark never reopened. The tempest also hacked off part of Garden Pier and destroyed the Marine Ballroom at the tip of Steel Pier. The Hamids quickly rebuilt the pier and erected a new gold-domed dance hall. But to Pergament, the remade ballroom didn't have the same feel, and the hurricane, he thinks, accelerated the decline to come.[20] Eighteen years later, an unusual combination of high winds and high tides blew through town. Flood waters filled hotel lobbies, and a runaway barge hacked a hole through the middle of Steel Pier. And then in 1969, a fire broke out, consuming a fifth of "America's showplace." Again, the Hamids rebuilt the pier, but this time, they didn't use any gold.[21]

An even larger shift in ideas about nature and vacations took more visitors away from Atlantic City. During the resort's heyday, men and women, who like Woody Allen, were "two with nature," flocked to the Boardwalk and the beach.[22] They wanted the sun and surf mixed with showers and room service. They drank up the crowds. Summer afternoons on beaches packed with so many people that towels covered every inch of sand and equally crowded nights on the Boardwalk thrilled them. The crowds told the visitors that they were someplace important and special. But to the children of the two-with-nature generation, the same people who had fled the cities for the suburbs, Atlantic City by the 1960s seemed too crowded with cars, people, and Boardwalk hucksters. These people, then, went in search of less built over places and of leisure that they thought was more authentic. A vacation, for them, meant a trip away from dense, noisy urban worlds to a national park, a ski resort, or an out-of-the-way beach town. Some, of course, went even farther into the "wild." Others thought, as Jennifer Price explains, "To appreciate Nature . . . [is] to be a more real person. It is to be a *better* person and the right *sort* of person."[23] Going into nature, some people believed, made them middle class or even better. Wherever these women and men trying to become "one" with nature went, it was far away from the buzz of cars, rolling chairs rumbling over wood planks, horses diving into pools of water, and nighttime throngs. Again, the remarkably contrived and packed Boardwalk, with its tall buildings and bright lights, hardly fit these people's—mostly second-generation middle-class men and women—changing notions of leisure and leisure space.[24]

With tourist profits falling, Atlantic City boosters in the late 1960s and early 1970s tried to regain the city's natural advantages. They lobbied state officials for funds to stop beach erosion and to clean up the shore and the ocean. The Chamber of Commerce launched an Earth Day campaign to bring people back to town. "It's official," the executive committee broadcast. "We can shout it loud. There is no 'measurable regular air pollution' along the Boardwalk."[25] Trumpeting the findings, business leaders urged bikers and runners to use the walkway as a great outdoor health spa. Others proposed enclosing the Boardwalk under a plastic bubble. That way, it too could become like a mall, a perfectly climate-controlled space. But this never happened.[26]

Thousands of business, family, and individual decisions, then, explain why white women and men—the staple of the city's tourist trade—stopped coming to Atlantic City in the 1950s and particularly in the 1960s. Some stayed away because the hotels were not what they used to be, while others remained at home in the suburbs, watching television in their artificially cooled recreation rooms. Still others flew to faraway places, showing off in the process their wealth and good taste. All of these factors surely kept people away from Atlantic City. But there is something missing from all of these theories. They can't completely explain where the moviegoers and other members of the crowd from the old days on the Boardwalk went or exactly when they left.

The fading luster of the hotels, to start with one popular theory, was a symptom rather than the main cause of the city's decline. No doubt, greed propelled some owners to cut corners and cheat customers, although it is worth noting that many hotel companies dumped bucketsful of money into their properties in the twenty years after World War II, the presumed starting point of the city's decline. The Chalfonte-Haddon Hall added a huge new indoor pool in 1959. Over the next few years, the Shelburne installed a new elevator system, the Traymore redecorated its lobby, and the Claridge put in a massive air conditioning system. Clearly some investors remained bullish about the city's prospects.[27] Still, as big-ticket conventions canceled reservations and vacancies rose in the mid-1960s, hotel managers undoubtedly had less to spend on the upkeep of their aging Jazz Age showplaces. Once they fell behind on repairs, it was hard to catch up, and wear and tear became more noticeable. Just like at the movie houses, chipped paint at the great Boardwalk hotels made a mockery of their claims of grandeur and offers of a luxury experience at a middle-class price. But the cracked walls and lobby tables scarred with cigarette burns were, again, by-products of the drop in tourism, not the causes.

To be sure, backyard swimming pools, televisions, air conditioners, jet travel, and a growing thirst for the rugged outdoors took bites out of Atlantic City's tourism business. Yet neither separately nor together can these factors explain where the crowds went. Not everyone was staying at home. While demolition companies began to implode Atlantic City's massive Boardwalk hotels in the late 1960s, the crowds swelled at other Jersey and Delaware shore towns. From this time on, real estate prices and summer rental rates soared at beach towns north and south of Atlantic City, places like Long Beach Island, Avalon, and Bethany

Beach, the quiet, middle-class resort where the Frosts relocated. Each of these spots had a quaint town center, sandy side streets, and places to park bikes with baskets without fear of them being stolen. Clearly then, the people who used to go to Atlantic City and their children were not fleeing the shore entirely, nor did airplane trips and package tours rule out a weekend at the beach or diminish the desire for a beach house. The flight from Atlantic City was, more accurately, part of another flight pattern, the one that swept the white middle class from the cities to the suburbs, from the downtown movie palaces to the drive-ins, and from urban amusement parks to the tightly controlled worlds of Disneyland and its imitators.

THE CHANGING CROWD

The restless son in Bruce Springsteen's song "Independence Day" warns his father:

> [T]here's . . . different people coming down here now and they see
> things in different ways
> And soon everything we've known will just be swept away.[28]

Springsteen's character didn't live in Atlantic City—although the singer grew up fifty miles north of the city along the shore—but he might as well have. Different people *did* converge on the Boardwalk in the 1960s—the most precise moment of the city's decline—and they *did* see things in different ways, and the changes— changes that mirrored the great social battles of the decade—*did* sweep away the past. With different people around, the same middle-class playacting, so popular and liberating during the old days, seemed forced, contrived, and, in the end, not that much fun and certainly not worth the trip to Atlantic City. In 1970, a young policeman, leaning up against the railing in front of the Claridge Hotel, then in receivership, looked around and delivered a blunt assessment of what happened to the city. "This town is going to hell," he snorted. "There's nobody here any more but niggers, queers, and hippies."[29]

Before then, white teenagers filled Atlantic City's public places. Since the World War I era, young adults had crashed into waves by day and roamed the Boardwalk in the evening. Even later at night, some snuck into Midway clubs or drank a few beers under the piers, dodging police flashlights. A few made their way to Chalfonte Alley where black prostitutes sold their bodies to white customers. Sometimes these adolescent shenanigans irritated adults, but for the most part, the young and old walked in comfort together in Atlantic City. Most high-schoolers and college students came to town with their parents or some other adult, an aunt, their grandparents, or a neighbor's family, and most did what their parents did in town—hung out on the beach all day and got dressed up and went out at night to see and be seen.

Before "the dawning of the age of Aquarius," Atlantic City remained a family resort.[30] Culturally, the social world of the young mirrored the world of adults. Teenagers put on their best clothes before heading out to the Boardwalk at night; they rode the rolling chairs if they had some extra money; they went to the movies in pairs; and they tapped their feet to the snappy, but still tame, Latin jazz riffs of the "Rumba King," Xavier Cugat. Even the first stirrings of rock and roll didn't disturb the peace between kids and parents on the Boardwalk. Bowing to market pressure, Steel Pier in the early 1960s booked Ricky Nelson and Paul Anka. While some older women and men might have scratched their heads at the new electric rhythms, they knew that the smiling white boys singing about "puppy love" were really good kids.[31]

By the late 1960s, many parents and kids couldn't agree on music or anything else, and it didn't take long for the decade's culture wars to break out on the Atlantic City Boardwalk. The nation's playground represented much of what the counterculture came to detest about America. From end to end, the Boardwalk stood as a celebration of conspicuous consumption where bigger and newer was always better. Without apology, visitors came to town to show off their newfound American wealth by spending money on useless things. Except along New York Avenue, the city's White City and Midway catered to the desires of middle-class, white, heterosexual couples. Celebrating the mainstream ideal of white femininity, the Convention Hall hosted the Miss America Pageant each year. Away from the runway's bright lights, the city served in countless other ways as a bulwark of traditional gender values. The swinger in the mold of Frank Sinatra was as daring as the city's culture got. Every check in every restaurant went right to the man, no questions asked. Trying to capitalize on its fidelity to heterosexuality, each June, the city threw its doors open to newlyweds. In the early 1970s, on the television show "All in the Family," the nation's most famous cultural conservative, Archie Bunker, wanted to take his wife, Edith, on a second honeymoon. He thought he knew where to go. Atlantic City was, or used to be, his kind of town.[32]

Taking an even bolder stand in the era's culture wars, city leaders in 1966 launched a campaign to "get behind United States troops fighting in Vietnam." Hotel owners provided wounded soldiers with free rooms. Waving a kind of populist flag, Chalfonte-Haddon Hall advertised that it served the fighting men the very same meal—for free—that it had served to President Lyndon Johnson a year earlier, when he came to town to address the American Association of School Administrators.[33]

When the veterans and Archie and Edith got to town, they quickly found that they had to share the city with hippies. Letting their long hair fly like "a freak flag," in David Crosby's words, the Boardwalk representatives of Woodstock Nation dressed in counterculture uniforms of beads, sandals, ripped jeans, tie-dyed T-shirts, and round rose-tinted sunglasses.[34] By day, they stretched out on benches, dozed on the beaches, and bought a slice of pizza and maybe ice cream and waffles, but little more. At night, they usually stayed in one of the motels with broken neon signs that lined Pacific Avenue. Until the postwar era, city leaders, doing the bidding of the powerful Boardwalk hotel lobby, had barred the construction of these low-slung, unadorned, car-friendly accommodations. But in the early 1950s, local officials lifted the ban, and a motel building boom broke out across town, evidence along with the hotel improvements of another important stream of investment.[35] The heyday of the motel, however, proved short-lived. By the middle of the 1960s, vacancy signs flashed on many summer weekends outside of John's Motel, the Rio, and the Lido. Desperate for revenue, the motels started to rent rooms to just about anyone, including cash-strapped teenagers and college students, who, in turn, sometimes crammed as many as a dozen friends into rooms built for a family of four. Local residents grumbled that the teenagers used these places for "sex parties" and "orgies."[36] But just as important, motel overcrowding drove the young people out of their rooms and onto the streets and the beaches. Hippies, it seemed to some locals and tourists, were everywhere, wearing what one observer described as a "look of insensitivity about them as if to say it's just another day in the short unhappy life of whomever he or she might be."[37]

All across America, hippies and squares fought over public spaces. On streets from Cambridge to Austin to Berkeley, Jerry Rubin wannabes turned cultural politics into theater as they staged endless performances of their rejection of the old order. On the Boardwalk, college-aged men paraded around without shirts and college-aged women wore only bikinis, no cover-ups. At night, they might have thrown on T-shirts and jeans, but certainly no jackets or dresses. While older couples still strutted in their opera clothes, young people sat on Boardwalk benches taking long pulls from jugs of cheap red wine and engaging in messy, open-mouthed kisses in full view of everyone. In a language that both Jerry Rubin and Archie Bunker would immediately have picked up on, the clothes and the public groping were one big "fuck you" to the establishment.

Hippies and their cultural cousins, feminists and civil rights activists, delivered their most public rebukes to the city in 1968. Even at this late date, the Miss America Pageant—the only show Richard Nixon allowed his daughter Tricia to stay up and watch on television—remained a celebration of grandeur in Atlantic City. White families came back to town for the event and put on their flashiest clothes. With the Boardwalk packed like the old days, rolling-chair pushers had plenty of customers and maître d's turned away diners. Inside the Convention

Hall, tens of thousands watched in 1968 as Judith Anne Ford of Bellvedere, Illinois, "clasped her hands to her mouth and started to cry" when she learned that she had become the first blonde in ten years to win the Miss America Pageant. Outside, 100 women picketed, singing anti–Miss America songs in three-part harmony, swinging "brassieres in the air like lassos," and chanting, "Atlantic City is a town with class. They raise your morals and judge your ass." Huddled around a "freedom trash can," the protesters threw out girdles, stenography pads, hair curlers, false eyelashes, and copies of *Playboy* and *Ladies Home Journal*. Legend has it that this was the first bra burning in America, although participants have insisted that no bras were actually burned because the local police chief wouldn't let them start a fire on the wooden walkway. It hardly mattered. Just the thought of women setting fire to undergarments of any kind in public came to symbolize to the men and women on the Boardwalk and across mainstream America the women's movement of the 1960s and its rejection of traditional gender roles. Feminist scholar Robin Morgan, who was among a handful of women arrested at the 1968 Boardwalk protest, captured the significance of the moment with a dig at the city, commenting, "It was right here in super tacky Atlantic City that this wave of the [modern] feminist movement was born."[38]

Counterdemonstrators quickly formed and confronted Morgan and the other protesters on the Boardwalk. Wearing a Nixon for President button and carrying a hand-painted sign that read, "There's Only One Thing Wrong with Miss America. She's Beautiful," Terry Meewsen, a former Miss Wisconsin and runner-up to Miss America in 1967, led a pro-pageant contingent. "Why don't you throw yourselves in," one man shouted as the demonstrators tossed those "symbols of the enslavement of women" into the freedom trashcan. Another man yelled, "Go home and wash your bras." Most visitors, however, remained on the sidelines, silently resentful of the intrusions into their trips down the Boardwalk and memory lane.[39]

Speaking for an older generation, a leading psychiatrist told a reporter from *U.S. News and World Report* in 1967 that mentally unstable and arrogant "beatniks and hippies . . . make us . . . uncomfortable."[40] Rachel Frost, the Philadelphia woman who spent her summers in the 1950s and 1960s in Chelsea, couldn't have agreed more. Her husband, she maintained, worked hard and played by the rules. She was proud of him and his accomplishments, and she liked coming to Atlantic City because it provided her family with a place to enjoy their success. She didn't want to be ridiculed for wearing an expensive new jacket or eating a fancy meal. She didn't want to spend her vacation defending hard work or the male-female dance of opening doors and holding chairs, but that's what it felt like with the hippies and feminists around. So, Rachel left her opera clothes in mothballs and her jewelry in a safe deposit box. Why call attention to yourself?

Not only would the hippies laugh, but also the muggers might see her and mark her for robbery. Hippies, she added, made the place look ratty and unkempt, not just because of the way they looked, but because of their sullen disregard for middle-class values and tastes. Atlantic City, Rachel Frost insisted, just wasn't, after 1967 or so, the kind of place to go to feel good about yourself. "Hippies," another man added, sounding the same themes, "are not wanted. They don't spend any money, and they give a drab and depressing picture to the boardwalks."[41]

Burlesque houses and X-rated theaters made the city look even drabber and less middle class. These new entertainment centers marked the public areas around them as male spaces, not family spaces. Unattached men, many of them middle class, went to see the smut shows and pornographic movies. Without their wives and children, they behaved differently and created a different public feel. Families, in turn, stayed away from places where children did not go. In the old days of the Boardwalk, children served as symbols of discipline, markers of a family place where adults would act accordingly. As the crowd of unattached men grew larger in Atlantic City in the 1960s, the crowds of families and children grew smaller.[42]

No group, however, chased away the white crowds in the 1960s like African Americans. Six feet, seven inches tall, Mall Dodson, the city's chief tourism official, saw race, not Lyndon Johnson's certain election or the shabby condition of the hotels, as the key to the 1964 convention's failure to trigger local economic growth. "That August," he said a few months after the Democrats left town, "was a big disappointment." But he didn't blame the convention. "The real reason," he speculated, "was fear of demonstrations by civil rights groups. Atlantic City was designated as the target for demonstrations" (by whom he doesn't say). He continued, "Then there [were] those four riots in New York and New Jersey right before the convention. We received much mail: 'Is it safe to come to Atlantic City?'" The letter writers didn't wait for an answer; they just stayed away.[43]

The roots of the retreat Dodson detected had started years before with the breakdown of segregation. Beginning after World War II, civil rights activists and their followers launched a broad attack against segregation and old man Jim Crow in Atlantic City. For starters, the nation's wartime and postwar prosperity lifted many, though certainly not all, black families out of poverty. Like European immigrants before them, they came from Newark and New York to play on the great Boardwalk and on the Midway. Inspired by the freedom movement and its cultural currents, some of these African American tourists drove past the small black-owned, un–air-conditioned Northside hotels where their parents might have stayed. They wanted to be close to the action on the Boardwalk and the beach. Southside hotel owners at first bristled, but as jet travel and swimming pools slowly started to eat into their profits in the late 1950s and early 1960s, some gave way and rented rooms to African American women and men. As they rewrote their racially exclusive policies, they put even less money back into their properties. Hotel owners, it seems, did not value their new African American customers. They saw them more as symbols of decline than as members of a new, potentially lucrative market.[44]

As the racial makeup of the Boardwalk changed, local activists in the NAACP, the Congress of Racial Equality (CORE), and the Afro-American Unity Movement hammered away at the segregation of the city's public facilities. One by one the walls of separation came crumbling down. According to local legend, in the late 1940s, Sara Washington, the owner of a national beauty supply chain headquartered on Arctic Avenue, went into Hackney's, a famous seafood restaurant on the northern tip of the Boardwalk, and demanded service. After hushed discussions, the owners served her the lobster dinner she ordered. Other African Americans followed Washington into restaurants and clubs. Next came the assault on residential segregation. Beginning in the 1950s, African American doctors, lawyers, fire fighters, municipal workers, and others began moving into formerly all-white areas, especially the North Inlet.[45] To mark the start of the new decade and the new spirit in town, local blacks boycotted the Woolworth's on the Boardwalk in solidarity with sit-in protesters in the South.[46]

Local civil rights leaders targeted, at the same time, the Miss America Pageant. Like the city itself, the competition practiced racial exclusion. When the original organizers of the beauty contest wrote the bylaws for the competition, they barred African American women from participating. After World War II, they scratched this section from the rule book, but still no black woman made it to the finals in the years that followed. African Americans were also barred from the Boardwalk Festival of Floats, where contestants showed off their shoes and gowns. Throughout the early 1960s, the local NAACP pushed to integrate the parade. In 1966, pageant organizers relented, and several integrated floats breezed by the Chalfonte and the Traymore.[47] The next year, local civil rights activist Edgar Harris demanded that city leaders keep the contest out of the municipally owned Convention Hall, complaining, "We should not be calling it the Miss America Pageant because it won't be that until we find some Negroes representing some of these United States."[48] The more militant Afro-American Unity Movement threatened to block the roads leading into town during the pageant if city leaders didn't implement rent control, curb police brutality, clean up the Northside, and name a black principal to a local school.[49] A year later, while feminists protested "the mindless boobie girl symbol" on the Boardwalk, the NAACP, meeting at the Ritz Carlton, a fact that itself was a sign of the changes in town, crowned the first Miss Black America in response to the pageant's resistance to integration.[50]

On another front, local civil rights activists concentrated on gaining equal employment opportunities, so that local black families could enjoy the full fruits of desegregation. With the Nation of Islam gaining new recruits and the black power movement taking shape, many African Americans were no longer willing to work for tips in white-directed Jim Crow narratives. They demanded the chance to do something other than push rolling chairs, shine shoes, and clean toilets. Bowing to pressure, several Atlantic Avenue supermarkets and department stores and a number of Boardwalk hotels and restaurants eventually agreed to hire African Americans to fill new roles, as waiters and clerks. Some, however, resisted. When these holdouts could not find enough white college students to fill their staffs, they recruited pale-faced kids from Ireland and England rather than employ local black teenagers.[51]

Because the movie theaters were so central to the city's racialized fantasyscape, they were one of the last bastions of segregation to fall. Led by Horace Bryant, New Jersey's first African American state-level cabinet officer, local civil rights advocates in the mid-1960s launched a protest campaign against separate seating at the movies. The Atlantic Avenue theaters were the first to change their racial policies and allow African Americans to sit where they wanted. Responding to the shift, some theaters, like the Embassy, soon began showing films like *Superfly, Shaft*, and other blackploitation pictures, aimed at the new audience. Whites, it seems, read the marquees and stayed away. The Boardwalk palaces followed suit soon after.[52] By 1970, African Americans could sit on the right or left side of the Virginia and the Beach, and in the crow's nest or near the orchestra pit at the Strand and the Lyric. Yet black women and men faced a bitter irony at the movie houses. They could sit where they wanted now, but the theaters were far from what they used to be, and within a few years, even the relics would be gone. So went the nation's experiment with integration in public space after public space, city after city.

Atlantic City's white political leaders liked to say that their city easily changed with the times, that the walls of segregation came down without any of the violence or rioting that exploded in other places. In 1966, Mayor Joseph Altman bragged that Atlantic City was the "most integrated city in the country." "Fortunately," Mayor William Somers said in 1969, breathing a sigh of relief, "Atlantic City has avoided much of the chaos and turmoil which has beset other Urban Centers."[53] Somers was right, at least in part. The Queen of Resorts did not see a replay of the bloody battles of Birmingham and Selma or the firestorms of Watts and Detroit. But that didn't mean there wasn't a fight. Blacks and whites repeatedly clashed as they tried to make sense of desegregation.

In the spring of 1966, local NAACP members, claiming to speak for the 36 percent of the city's population that was black, hinted that if change didn't come in a hurry, the city faced another Watts.[54] In May of that year, the civil rights organization led a march down the Boardwalk demanding an end to discrimination "against Negroes in promotions and wages" and carrying signs that read, "Jim Crow Must Go," "Better Jobs for the Negro," and "Don't Buy Where You Can't Work." A reporter covering the protest noticed clusters of white vacationers on hotel balconies and terraces watching the march. Most, he wrote, were simply curious; a few were contemptuous; and a few more were downright hostile. Dressed in her Boardwalk best, a wide-brimmed straw hat and a sleeveless print dress, one sixty-year-old woman yelled insults at the protesters. When that didn't get a rise out of the NAACP supporters, she reached into her bag and brought out a whistle, blowing it at the demonstrators "until a sudden gust of wind blew her hat off and sent her lumbering after it."[55]

A week later, on the busy Memorial Day weekend, the NAACP set up picket lines outside of Captain Starns' and Hackney's on the northern tip of the Boardwalk. Each night, these two sprawling seafood restaurants served thousands of lobster, crab cake, and catch-of-the-day dinners. Black people could cook the food and even eat at these places, but they couldn't carry the trays out of the kitchen and deliver them to the tables. Neither restaurant employed a single African American server in 1966 and that's what the NAACP wanted to change. Apparently, the protests enraged Elwood Royston, a thirty-one-year-old boat builder. On his way home from a bar, he drove his pickup truck into a picket line of thirty people, scattering the black men in jackets and black women in dresses. Then he turned around and raced back through the picket line again. Royston's V-8–powered attack left several people bruised and one man badly injured, but it also galvanized the demonstrators. Within hours, more than 200 people stood outside the eateries, and both companies quickly agreed to hire a few black waitresses right away.[56]

Taking up where the whistle blower and Elwood Royston left off, a few angry whites barked "racial slurs" over a fire station public address system. Someone at City Hall, meanwhile, scrawled the word "nigger" across an African American's application for a municipal post.[57] On the streets, racial conflict burst into the open, even as tourism officials tried to keep it covered up. The men of the Chamber of Commerce and the Visitors Bureau knew that "the right kind of people" didn't want to vacation in the middle of a racial minefield. Nonetheless, throughout the Memorial Day weekend in 1966, fights broke out between black and white teenagers on the Boardwalk. The next year, a dance at Steel Pier turned into a near race riot as black and white teenagers once again squared off. The battle quickly spread to Atlantic Avenue, where moviegoers cringed as they watched a pack of youth fresh from the Boardwalk battles smash a row of storefront windows.[58] Over in Ducktown, the all-white high school fraternity Bones patrolled the streets near their homes. They threw rocks at blacks who dared to cut through their neighborhood and hounded interracial couples who walked past their front stoops.[59] Following the annual end-of-season football game between Atlantic City High School and suburban Holy Spirit High School held at the Convention Hall in 1966 and 1967, more fights between blacks and whites erupted on the Boardwalk.[60] Again, civil rights activists—by then, there were both moderates and militants in the city—threatened that if something wasn't done about poverty and lingering segregation, bloody and damaging riots, on the scale of Detroit and Newark, could break out along the ocean.[61]

Then in 1970, the Embassy theater presented *Halls of Anger*, a film, according to one account, about a "dedicated black English teacher who must face the inherent problems of Black and White integration in a ghetto high school." Director Paul Bogart's film had a happy ending: an after-school reading program brings black and white students together to bridge the racial divide. One of the movie's Atlantic City audiences, however, never saw the uplifting conclusion. Halfway through the film, a fight breaks out between a white female and a black female character. Once the two students started to tussle on screen, something clicked in the musty theater. Without warning, dozens of black teenagers, mostly men, stormed the stage and punched holes in the screen. Another group broke away and rushed the candy counter, while others ripped down frayed velvet curtains. It took a dozen armed police officers to restore order at the theater.[62]

In the years after the Embassy theater outburst, a kind of racial calm settled over Atlantic City. But this easing of tensions did not stem from better conditions or interracial cooperation. African Americans remained stuck in low-paying jobs and weather-beaten housing. Some places in the city remained off-limits to blacks. In most Ducktown bars, a shot and a beer still cost African Americans as much as a lobster dinner. Black families continued to face police brutality and official negligence. One man who lived in a Northside neighborhood for thirty years said he never saw a garbage truck on his street. Hearing this story, a man who lived nearby laughed, saying that his neighbor exaggerated, but not by much.[63] And there was no happy *Halls of Anger* ending along the Boardwalk. Except at a few events sponsored by well-intentioned religious and community groups, Atlantic City blacks and whites did not gather around that table of brotherhood of which Martin Luther King, Jr., spoke in Washington, D.C., in 1963. Yet despite persistent inequities and hostilities, the street battles did cool. Whites stopped trying to run over blacks, and teenagers stopped brawling on the Boardwalk. But it wasn't really a truce. Starting in the mid-1960s, whites had gone into a tactical retreat from the city.

Martin Sherman, the author of the acclaimed play *Bent*, invented a character named Rose, who observed this white flight from Atlantic City. Born into a Russian shtetl, Rose ends up in Poland and somehow survives the decimation of the Warsaw ghetto and the daily brutalities of a concentration camp. From there, she makes it into the arms of one of her liberators, a fresh-faced American Jew named Sonny. He brings his new lover to America, to Atlantic City, where his father runs a beach chair concession in front of one of the Boardwalk hotels. After a rare neurological disease slows Sonny's speech and motion, Rose takes a job running the Majestic, a wood-framed boardinghouse with a wide front porch in the Inlet. Year after year, the same guests stay at the hotel. At night, Rose watches with a detached European amazement as they head off to the Boardwalk decked out in mink coats and frilly hats to ride the rolling chairs past the auctions, the life-sized Mr. Peanut, and the *Ice Capades*, "an ice show," Rose explains, "that spent each summer in Atlantic City and was thought exotic because ice-skating was one of those useless things that only goyim did." But all of a sudden, these "fortunate" Jews, as Rose calls them, are gone. They left, she argues, because "[t]here were now black ghettos surrounding the hotel strip, and since victims of prejudice seem susceptible to the disease themselves, Atlantic City just packed up and moved to Florida."[64]

Philadelphia columnist Bruce Boyle's grandmother joined the exodus to Florida. After her Inlet neighborhood became, in Boyle's words, "blacker and poorer," she ran to St. Petersburg "to play pinochle and talk [with new friends] about places like Atlantic City they had left." Boyle knew that the tourists fled for the same reasons as his grandmother. "It was many years ago," he wrote in 1981, "when technology and racism began to kill this place." Air travel, Boyle explains, repeating that familiar refrain, "made it possible to get to nice warm beaches in exotic places." Television commercials showed Philadelphia families pictures of blue water and white sandy beaches. The ad men, Boyle noted, were "careful to show only white people on these exotic beaches," and the suburban audiences in Upper Darby and Ardmore bought this clever ruse, even when it was used to sell Jamaica. Yet the suburbanites knew all about Atlantic City. "Atlantic City," these one-time visitors to Steel Pier murmured to themselves, "had black people, thousands of them." Even worse, Boyle reported, white Philadelphians thought that Atlantic City blacks "were getting cranky, too." Not many wanted to push the rolling chairs any more, and white customers sensed that the sullen drivers still on the job deliberately took them "over some bumps that could have been avoided."[65]

"Now," wrote a pair of journalists in 1970, "the city has reached the point where the blacks have become too numerous for the comfort of white residents." The overwhelming majority of Atlantic City black tourists, they said, "look like everybody else, with perhaps flashier tastes in slacks and headgear." But it was black teenagers, roaming the Boardwalk wearing "big sunglasses, enormous floppy caps and the 'in' thing this season, a version of a cowboy hat with the brim pulled down, hillbilly style," who really alarmed whites. "These kids," the journalists concluded, "are only trying to be cool but they give white tourists a pretty good case of the creeps."[66]

Long-time Inlet resident Leslie Kammerman was troubled more by nonwhite renters than by visiting black teenagers. He agreed with Bruce Boyle that jets, along with the changing character and behavior of people of color, killed Atlantic City. Like all successful resorts, Atlantic City, he argued, had once been a place of "sweetness and light" where people felt safe, entertained, and sheltered. "So what happened to Atlantic City?" he asked rhetorically. Answering his own question, he began to talk about blockbusting and the Inlet's subsequent transformation. "A different type of nonwhite," "the underprivileged," "the Puerto Rican," "the poor black," he said, began to move into the neighborhood. "They destroyed their own buildings," Kammerman declared. "They almost seem to have a tendency toward their own self-destruction. All one has to do today is look at the Inlet."[67]

Sam Boreman grew up in Atlantic City and describes himself as a "scientific, rational man." After studying the city's decline, he concluded that "[a]ll hell broke loose in 1962." That's when, he says, African Americans from Chicago and Detroit with "no respect for private property . . . infiltrated" the city. The new arrivals didn't come by chance. Someone—Boreman doesn't say who—provided these black families with one-way tickets to Atlantic City. Summer people, he argues, didn't notice the changes at first, but locals quickly grasped what was happening. "A new subculture," he believes, invaded the city and "reduced the ambiance of the area." "Crime increased," he argues, "welfare was exploited, and local residents began to move off shore."[68]

Teddy Leonard agreed with Sam Boreman. The former boxing champion longed for the old days in Atlantic City when "a dollar was worth 100 pennies," and "nobody thought of anything like mugging or molesting people and everybody was happy." He never said anything about African Americans, but he insisted that the city's problems started in the "terrible sections" of the largely African American Northside. "People could live like clean human beings, but they don't. They live like a bunch of animals."[69]

When Leonard, Boreman, and Kammerman saw the city, they saw the past—the past built on exclusion—melting away. On streets once occupied by decent, hard-working, white families who had pulled themselves up out of immigrant ghettos by their bootstraps—this is the way they imagined their families—they saw poor, lazy, ungrateful black (and Puerto Rican) families flaunting the law and acting in ways they considered uncivilized. This erosion of what they saw as timeless values and everyday civility made them resentful, but it scared them even more.[70]

"Crime," Carl Biemiller, the city's publicity director, told the Chamber of Commerce in 1972, represented the resort's "single greatest deterrent" to reviving tourism. Mayor Joseph Bradway concurred, bemoaning how muggings, robberies, and murders "discourage[d] repeat visits."[71] Most people, in fact, talked about the city's decline in terms of crime. In the narrative of flight told by the Frosts, the Philadelphia couple who left Chelsea for Bethany Beach, face-to-face confrontations with criminals, even more than sullen-faced hippies, marked the "tipping point."[72] They left town when the criminals entered their lives, and their friends followed behind them after hearing their stories. The crooks in these accounts wore unmistakably black (and brown) faces. As journalist Buzz Bissinger observes, tales of muggings and break-ins, like the ones told by the Frosts, get embellished until "with each retelling and each added detail, they take on the lore of myth." As the criminals became more brazen and sinister, they also became blacker and more at odds with middle-class white culture.[73] Talking about crime became, as cultural critic Carlo Rotella points out, a kind of shorthand to explain, and simplify, the complicated problems behind urban decline and the transformation of downtown leisure zones from fantasy places to metaphoric jungles, places, according to the Staebler brothers, that were out of control.[74]

The rise in crime in Atlantic City, as local merchants and moviegoers knew, was not entirely an illusion. Beginning in the late 1960s, when work started to disappear, the police department recorded more reports of assaults and thefts than ever before. The numbers were startling. In 1970, 48,000 people lived in Atlantic City. Crime statistics for the same year reported 729 assaults, 358 robberies, 3,168 larcenies, 2,097 breaking-and-entering charges, and 975 auto thefts.[75] Over the course of the next year, six people were murdered. According to the blunt assessment of Angelo Gerbino, the head of the city's Police Identification Bureau, black males between the ages of 14 and 21 committed the vast majority of these crimes. The story, he said, was the same in Camden, Newark, and most of the nation's large cities.[76] Across the country, police officers, sociologists, and commentators issued bulletins and delivered papers on the reasons for the upsurge in lawlessness, particularly, as they saw it, among black men. They listed as causes rising unemployment in the urban core, substandard and overcrowded housing, educational inequities, racist police practices, the breakdown of the black family, the debilitating effects of slavery, and the erosion of public morality.

On the streets of Atlantic City, careful, scholarly discussions hardly mattered. An older Inlet woman, who asked to remain anonymous, knew exactly what led to the rise in crime. It was, she said without hesitating, "the black threat." Nathan Sonkin agreed, if somewhat reluctantly. For much of the 1960s, the optometrist was the lone white member of the Atlantic City NAACP. Three times as the decade came to a close, criminals, presumably black criminals, robbed his Atlantic Avenue office. "I feel," he told an interviewer in 1972, "[that] all crimes are definitely related." The liberal in him said, "They are tied to the poor housing conditions in the city, the drug problem in the city." Then Sonkin shifted gears. Blacks, he argued, caused the sharp rise in crime because of their "lack of respect for the law." He elaborated, "When I started out sixteen years ago, women and children came to me, unafraid. I used to go for walks on the Boardwalk. Now I look behind me every 100 feet, expecting black youths to be there with guns."[77]

Long before New Jersey state troopers institutionalized the practice, Nathan Sonkin engaged in a version of what has come to be called racial profiling. Not all black men were thieves and muggers, the one-time NAACP member would surely have said. But enough African American men committed violent crimes that it made sense to him to avoid all dark-skinned men, especially after nightfall. Not wanting to take any chances, Sonkin, therefore, treated all black men as criminals. He avoided them. When he saw a black teenager dressed in a floppy hat and big sunglasses—or someone who looked that way from a distance—he probably walked to the other side of the street or ducked into a building.

Sonkin was not the only person to deploy racial profiling. Hollywood, Madison Avenue, and presidential candidates cast a whole range of social ills in racial terms. All too often drug dealers, hustlers, and welfare cheats wore a black face. The message was clear. Blacks were to blame for much of what was wrong with the country, for the muggings, murders, riots, lootings, and fires that plagued the nation's cities. On a day-to-day basis, the stereotypes turned just about every working-class African American man into a threat to the social order. The message was prescriptive as well. At home and on vacation, places marked as black were places to be avoided at all costs. Once Atlantic City got on that list of black places, it got taken off the map of white middle-class America.

Some shop owners and salesmen certainly feared physical harm, which they associated with crime, which, of course, they in turn linked to the presence of African Americans. Others worried about what the anthropologist Sherry B. Ornter has called, in her profile of postwar North Jersey, "social pollution." Those who experienced this anxiety believed that any contact with others, particularly African Americans, degraded them and pulled them down to the level of their inferiors. Not wanting to risk contamination, they stayed away from integrated public places.[78]

In the mid-1970s, Giuseppe Bonnucci, a restaurateur in a novel set in Atlantic City, reminisced about the old days before integration and dangerous streets. Closing his eyes, he remembered when the Boardwalk had been "packed with vacationers twelve months a year, so crowded that it resembled a rush-hour subway platform with people seeming to be swept along in waves, rather than by any personal volition." Then the floods of people were narrowed to a stream; after that, they were reduced to "only straggling handfuls."

Yet with remarkable stubbornness, the "straggling handfuls" still came to Atlantic City in the 1970s. Some made the trip for sentimental reasons. This was the place of their first kiss or their first meal with white linens and polished silverware. Others came because they heard about the city on television or saw it in films; they knew its streets from Monopoly games or from watching the Miss America Pageant. Still others, working people in particular, came because they could finally afford the trip. And of course, African Americans came now that they could. But almost all of them, as Bonnucci admitted, were "disappointed with what they found."[79]

Like those who came before them, visitors in the 1970s came to Atlantic City to act out a fantasy. But unfortunately these blue-collar and black families found few engaging fantasies available along the Boardwalk. The city didn't offer a luxury experience at a middle-class price any more. What was left were auction house rip-offs, cheap sex shows, greasy slices of pizza, and tacky souvenirs. Piece by piece, at the same time, the city's wonderfully contrived backdrop was coming down. The beachfront hotels had lost their elegance; the movies houses that were still open were moldering and ugly; and the Midway offered second-rate bands and third-rate comics.

By then, the rolling chairs were gone too. New-fangled motorized rolling chairs, like the one David Staebler rode in, and yellow trams pulled by electric engines had replaced the wicker baskets in the 1970s. By this time, it wasn't just whites in the chairs any more either. "There were scenes that would have surprised visitors a generation ago," wrote a *New York Times* reporter in 1971. "Blacks riding in motorized chairs driven by whites." But even these snapshots of racial inversion were not that common.[80] The "Negro-powered" chairs left Atlantic City because there was little demand for them any more. It wasn't just that there were not enough people with enough money to ride in them. Demand for the rides had never been a matter of simple numbers. During its heyday, the city sold an explicit racial fantasy. The striving middle-class millions came to ride along the Boardwalk with an "air of belligerence" that only came from having Jordan Sayles and other black men serve them. But these older Jim Crow narratives embarrassed many of their children. One woman remembered a relative coming to town and wanting to buy her a rolling-chair ride as a gift. She didn't want to go, but she didn't want to appear rude either, so she agreed to climb aboard the chair. She couldn't wait to get off; it just didn't seem right in the wake of all those stirring speeches from Martin Luther King, Jr., to have a black man pushing her around. Probably a lot of middle-class Americans felt the same way.[81] Few welcomed integration, but they didn't want segregation—at least explicit segregation—any more either. Many wanted, instead, to avoid, erase if they could, African Americans from their lives and from national and local narratives. They did not want to confront people of color or their own racial pasts. They wanted to pretend that race didn't matter, but Atlantic City could not do this. Disneyland, however, could.

ERASING RACE

The day Disneyland opened in July 1955, Atlantic City became the past. The changing of the guard, however, was not immediately apparent. Technical glitches and missed stage directions turned Disneyland's kickoff into a small-scale disaster, though the show would, of course, go on. Even more to the point, Atlantic City still attracted hundreds of thousands of people each summer weekend and millions of people each year during the 1950s and early 1960s. Throughout this period, Gene Krupa and Duke Ellington still packed them in at Steel Pier. Teenagers still bounced around on the Tilt-a-Whirl and zoomed up and down on the roller coasters. Trade unionists still gathered at the hotels and the immense Convention Hall. Sun worshipers still marched to the beach every morning armed with their umbrellas, chairs, buckets and shovels, and tubes of Coppertone. By noon, it looked like all of Philadelphia was there, and as the sun set, an exodus of brown-, pink-, and red-skinned tourists shuffled back to their rooms and houses. Beginning in the mid-1950s, Atlantic City witnessed that promising motel-building boom. Bulldozers plowed down aging guesthouses to make way for low-slung motels with large parking lots, rooms with air conditioning and televisions, and no lobbies, just registration desks and a few uncomfortable chairs. And each year in September, beauty contestants from every state still came to Atlantic City for the Miss America Pageant.

The city seemed to be doing all right when Disneyland opened, but a pair of time-lapse cameras—one pointed at Atlantic City and the other at Disney's properties—would tell different stories. One would show the crowds on the Boardwalk thinning a little each year. They would show fewer men in blue blazers with gold buttons and fewer women in cashmere sweaters with mink collars. The images would show dejected rolling-chair pushers looking for passengers on summer nights and off-season weekends. Close-ups would reveal rust on the amusement pier rides and water stains on the walls of hotel lobbies. Each year, the pictures would show more teenagers in informal clothes and more African American families on the beach and at the movies. But still there would be thick crowds on the Boardwalk every weekend well into the 1960s.

The camera pointed at Disneyland would show streams of Edsel sedans and then Buick station wagons driving to the park. It would capture images of khaki-clad families strolling down Main Street and of long lines waiting for the rides. It would show a cluster of bright yellow bulldozers and backhoes plowing down rows of orange trees to make room for more parking spaces.

The camera would then make a quick cut to a swamp outside of Orlando, Florida. In this frame from 1965, an even bigger bunch of backhoes and cranes would be tearing away at the wetlands, while foremen stared at the plans for another colossal theme park just like the one in California. Six years later, this would, of course, become Disney World. Within a few years, the Caterpillars would be back clearing more land for the Experimental Prototype Community of Tomorrow. Opened in 1982, Epcot was Disney's corporate-sponsored tour of the future and, later, of the countries of the world.

By the time *The King of Marvin Gardens* opened in 1972, the Atlantic City camera would show a hot dog stand replacing a Boardwalk linen store; U-Hauls carrying dining room tables and easy chairs from homes in the Inlet to the suburbs; and weary store owners taping Fire Sale signs across their barred windows. Locals in these scenes would be heard telling jokes about rolling a bowling ball down the Boardwalk without hitting anyone.

Disney succeeded in California and later in Florida by copying, and then updating, the Atlantic City model of carefully choreographed control over the public and the creation of exclusion masquerading as inclusion. As a backdrop to their money-making schemes, the company's famed imaginers created a meticulous, richly embellished, and contrived built environment. Just like on the Boardwalk, nothing in Disneyland was real.[82]

Disneyland's fantasy world centered on Main Street, a less urban, small-townish version of the Boardwalk. The 600-foot-long thoroughfare with fake Victorian buildings and Wild West storefronts represented an ideal of an orderly commercial district. Day and night, pedestrians ambled down the tidy, brightly lit street, which had no speeding cars or noisy delivery trucks. (Underground tunnels allowed Disney managers to restock stores out of view of the patrons.) Main Street ended at the majestic Cinderella's Castle. With its domes and columns, the soaring showplace looked like a European castle except there was nothing weather-beaten about the outside; it was as white as snow, and it stayed that way all the time. The rest of Disneyland radiated like spokes from Cinderella's Castle. Walking only a short distance, visitors could go from one make-believe world to another, from Fantasyland to Frontierland to Adventureland to Tomorrowland.[83]

Control over the crowd, not just the staff and script, remained the most crucial factor in Disney's success. Visitors to the theme park, architectural critic Paul Goldberger observed in 1972, "relax in a way that [they] would never dare to in the parks and squares of [their] hometowns."[84] Designers created this feeling of security through the deployment of updated confidence builders. Before families ever got to the Jungle Cruise or Cinderella's Castle, they faced the park's twenty-foot-high main entrance. The barrier gave Disneyland a fortress effect, announcing in clear architectural terms that the space behind it was sealed off and protected from the outside world, a world where public space was becoming more open and democratic. The gate acted not just as a metaphor but as a literal filter as well. Seeking to produce a "wholesome family" image for the park, uniformed security guards, all of them clean-cut, short-haired men who stood at least six feet tall and weighed more than 200 pounds, scrutinized potential guests as they approached. Well into the 1960s, company policy barred men in sandals or African Americans with Afros from entering Disneyland. In 1967, an employee acknowledged that the firm banished hippies from the Magic Kingdom. "If we allowed people in weird outfits into the park," he explained, "that might cause other patrons to make derogatory remarks, and that could lead to trouble."[85] Billing itself as a family resort, managers, again following the Atlantic City model, encouraged adults to come with children. The presence of children, they felt certain, would discipline adult women and men, discourage coarse barroom antics, and promote decorous behavior.

Once again borrowing from Atlantic City, Disney used other confidence builders to create a "wholesome family" feeling. Company managers originally thought about locating the park near the beach, but Walt Disney scotched the idea, fearing that the oceanfront attracted too many grubby, sleazy, unkempt characters.[86] The firm's founder erected his dreamland instead in ex-urban Anaheim. At the time, the Orange County community stood well beyond the reach of public transportation and the urban poor. Adding another layer of exclusion, Mickey's bosses made sure it cost a lot to get into the park. By setting the admission price high, but not too high, they ensured themselves of an essentially middle-class crowd. Location helped on this front as well. Guests had to have cars to get to Disneyland. The poor, therefore, had no way of finding Main Street. Through its aggressive marketing campaigns, Disney's managers further targeted, historian John Findlay explains, "a particular kind of customer—primarily the family-oriented middle class." The park, Findlay continues, "catered to those who owned televisions, watched movies, subscribed to newspapers, took vacations, and accepted the domestic values of mainstream America."[87]

Working on other fronts to assemble the "right crowd," company officials staged special nights for graduating high school seniors (as opposed to drop-outs) and couples (rather than singles or same-sex groups).[88] Other nights featured country music acts and swing bands (no rock and roll at first). Imposing gates, an emphasis on family entertainment, high admission prices, and special promotions guaranteed that the women, men, and children on Disney's Main Street would be neatly dressed in pressed slacks, knit shirts, and sensible shoes, increasingly the uniform of the postwar middle class.

Inside, Disney officials set up additional layers of confidence builders. Employees —renamed "cast members"—had to dress neatly, comb their hair, clip their nails, and avoid powerful perfumes. There would be no surly attendants, fast-talking hucksters, or freak shows at Disneyland. Barriers in front of popular rides turned long, potentially dangerous lines into twisting yet orderly processions. Rocket-sized engines churned out enough electricity to turn nights into days. With uniformed security guards patrolling the crowds, teenagers thought twice before acting as pranksters in the Magic Kingdom. Watchmen enforced heterosexual conformity as well, stopping adult men from dancing with other adult men and women from dancing with women until the 1970s.[89]

What made Disney's signals even more effective was the firm's muted, but still effective, language of race making. Like Atlantic City, but tamer, the California theme park had Midway-like attractions that spoke about manifest destiny and white supremacy. "Disneyland," Walt Disney insisted at the park's opening, was "dedicated to the ideals, the dreams, and hard facts that have created America."[90] According to Frontierland's "hard facts," Davy Crockett in his coonskin cap tamed the unforgiving terrain of the West for all Americans. The Disney narrative erased from the record Crockett's historic insignificance and brutish personality, the slaughter of the buffalo, the sacking of the environment, and the murderous rampage at Wounded Knee. Disney's Midway included some "hard facts" about blacks and whites as well. An exhibit on the presidency portrayed Abraham Lincoln wrestling over the Civil War, but not over slavery. On the Jungle Cruise, guests embarked on a fantastic safari ride. As they traveled through a place marked "Africa," visitors saw bug-eyed men of color dressed in loincloths clinging to trees, while white explorers in sensible khaki jackets protected the indigenous people from indigenous animals. In Disney's historical narrative, the conquests of the frontier and the jungle marked the spread of European civilization, not the plunder of nonwhite people's possessions.[91]

Unlike the Atlantic City Boardwalk or its Midway, Disney's racial discourse, however, was never explicit. During its glory days, the nation's playground didn't pretend for a moment not to exclude. Tourist entrepreneurs made sure white, and black, guests knew that the beaches, hotels, restaurants, and movie houses were segregated. Clearing paths on the Boardwalk for the rolling chairs and making room for erotic dancers on stage, local officials promised white visitors a full cast of happy African American servants and seductresses while in town. Disney manufactured, on the other hand, exclusion through quieter imagery and codes. The company tried to make it look as though the well-dressed, almost exclusively white crowd just happened to be there without any planning. Yet through an as-siduously plotted combination of location and high prices, advertising and story-telling, tall gates and stern security personnel, park officials warded off the poor, the ragged, and all but a small number of African Americans. Convinced that they were someplace free from crime and criminals, in part because there were so few black men there before the 1970s, patrons walked along Disney's essentially segregated—in both racial and class terms—streets without having to confront the morally troubling implications of separation and the subversion of demo-cratic ideals. Denial—the same denial that shaped Atlantic City's narrative of decline—represented the post–civil rights era's updated and most effective form of racial and class exclusion. Nonwhite, non–middle-class persons were largely written out of the story.

Clean streets, as the Staebler brothers understood, were the last part of the Disney strategy of recreating middle-class public space. The company employed an army of cast members to keep the park spotless. They roamed from one make-believe land to another, whisking away cigarette butts, stray candy and hot dog wrappers, and crumpled napkins. Several times a day, they emptied the trashcans, and each night they pressure-washed the streets. The whole place felt "simonized" to a *New Yorker* writer. "The result," he wrote in 1963, "[is] a transfiguration of the traditionally unruly carnival mob, including ourselves, into a decorous assem-blage that might have been hired from Central Casting."[92] Without knowing it, guests tried to match their behavior to the streets. They assumed the parts of re-spectable, middle-class citizens. At home, they might have left their shirttails out or chucked trash out their car windows, but at Disneyland, they smoothed their clothes and walked their paper cups to the garbage can.

Some say Walt Disney knew American middle-class people better than they knew themselves. Inside and outside the park, he put these insights to work. Above all, he understood before almost anyone else did the deeply racialized, anti-urban impulse sweeping the nation in the postwar period. As the civil rights movement and then urban unrest shook the country's foundations, middle-class

Americans came to see the city as a symbol of disorder, crime, and racial strife. From its tall gates to the futuristic above-ground monorail, from Main Street to the Jungle Cruise, Disneyland set itself apart from the city. With its fortresslike appearance, the theme park looked inward. Inside, Disney created a network of sparkling clean, safe streets that stood in contrast to most guests' perceptions of urban spaces. Using an unspoken yearning for the vanishing small town, the theme park provided a public realm for suburbanites uneasy about living in a world without walkable streets or corner stores.[93] But it also made clear that it wasn't a city and that there was almost no possibility of chance encounters with dangerous people and dangerous influences. Disneyland was, then, a perfectly themed space for a posturban, postsegregated, but certainly not integrated, America.

Atlantic City was, of course, a very different kind of place and, by the middle of the 1960s, an increasingly outdated place. When Gay Talese's father, Frank, an Italian tailor, settled in the United States early in the twentieth century, he settled in Ocean City, New Jersey. "I fell for it," he later said, "because it was ideal for me. I didn't like big cities, like New York, Philadelphia, or Atlantic City."[94] Years later, Atlantic City, even though it had fewer than 50,000 residents in 1970, still felt like a big city, and that quality, once its calling card, was increasingly its problem. Atlantic City seemed just too urban, too chaotic, too dirty, and, in the end, too black and out of control for most middle-class Americans.

6

Rebuilding
the Crowd

In his masterful comedy *Annie Hall*, Woody Allen compares relationships to sharks. Both, he says, must keep moving or die. "What we have on our hands here," he tells his partner in a rocky relationship, "is a dead shark."[1] Resorts are kind of like relationships. People fall in love with places, but those places must keep moving or die.

By the 1960s, many thought of Atlantic City as a dead shark. To get the city moving again, boosters launched frantic, even silly, promotional campaigns to bring middle-class families back to the beach and Boardwalk. They sent "Happy Atlantic City" buses to Reading, Pennsylvania, and advertised hotel deals on Times Square in New York City. Seeking an off-season revenue stream, another group of investors came up with the idea of transforming the city dump into a ski hill with fake snow and a short lift. Others suggested starting a "girl-watching week" on the Boardwalk each year. Another local leader put forth the idea of creating a nude beach. Still others talked about jai alai and offshore oil drilling as remedies to the city's woes. Early in the decade, members of the Chamber of Commerce begged Philadelphia weather forecasters to talk about the skies over Atlantic City as "partly sunny" instead of "partly cloudy."[2]

George Hamid, Sr., his son George Hamid, Jr., and Pauline Hill, three influential players on the local scene, also knew that the city—their city—had to keep moving or die. Each of them tried to stir the place; they poked and prodded and offered a slew of new ideas and initiatives. Most of their suggestions had to do with the public, about how to recreate the crowds and commerce. For their part, the Hamids wanted to rebuild the mass market of the past, while Hill embraced the newer concept of market segmentation.[3] Yet however much their ideas about the public and the right kind of crowd differed, none of them rethought the idea of exclusion. Each looked for ways to move, hide, and rearrange the walls around the public realm. But the walls would always be there; they had to be there, the Hamids and Hill believed, in order to give shape to the crowd and to make sure that it did not turn into a menacing mob or a chaotic assemblage of the "wrong" kind of people.

THE HAMIDS' ANSWER

George Hamid, Sr., billed himself as the "man who worked himself [up] from the bottom to the top."[4] Born in a Lebanese village, the owner of the famed Steel Pier started out performing for food in the streets. Remarkably strong and powerful for his age, Hamid joined his uncle's high-flying circus act when he was only nine years old. Sometimes he anchored human pyramids; other times he flew through the air with the trapeze artists. Buffalo Bill discovered the young Hamid and his uncle in the south of France and brought them to the United States, billing them as "Abou Hamid's Arabs."

Buffalo Bill adopted the young Lebanese performer, keeping him close by, teaching him how to shine his shoes and mix his highballs. Hamid, meanwhile, became a circus sensation. At age thirteen, he won a competition at New York's Madison Square Garden and earned the title of the "World's Greatest Acrobat." On the road from town to town, Hamid sat at the foot of the star, Annie Oakley. Years later, he would tell people that she taught him how to read and write. But all was not well with Buffalo Bill's circus. The ringleader was drowning himself in alcohol, and eventually his illness cost him his business.

After Buffalo Bill folded his tent, Hamid drifted from circus to circus. Then he formed his own show, "Hamid's Oriental Circuses, Wild West, and Far East Show." But Hamid couldn't make it on his own, at least not yet. Tired of the show-business grind, he tried his hand at the oil business. But his Texas ventures came up dry, and he drifted back to what he knew—the circus. Using his contacts, in the 1920s, Hamid started to book tumblers, sword swallowers, and clowns in circuses and other venues across the United States and Canada. By the decade's end, he supplied more than 300 fairs and 35 amusement parks with all kinds of acts. Noting his success, North Carolina officials hired him to run their state fair. But they fired him a couple of years later after discovering that he was drawing a higher salary than the Tar Heel governor. He quickly took a job running the New Jersey state fair. That brought him within striking distance of Atlantic City.[5]

In 1938, Hamid leased Million Dollar Pier. Then in 1945, he bought Steel Pier from its founder, Frank Gravatt. Legend has it that Gravatt thought of Hamid as a cheap carny man and refused to sell him the pier. Hamid apparently fooled Gravatt, purchasing his prized possession through a holding company.[6] Whatever disagreements the two men had, Hamid continued what Gravatt had started, running the pier as a one-stop entertainment bazaar, part downtown, part carnival, and part circus. He knew some people liked the movies more than the diving horse, the boxing cats more than the child stars. But he didn't care. He just wanted as many people to come through the gates as he could cram onto the pier, so he tried to offer something for everyone.

Hamid's Steel Pier seemed, according to one observer, to begin "on the New Jersey shoreline and . . . end somewhere near the coast of Spain."[7] "Nowhere else," a pier brochure bragged, "could you get so much, so good for so little money." "America's Great Amusement Bargain" was how Hamid described his showplace.[8] The pier was in the business of numbers. Giving people a choice of three or four movies, "crack bands," a water circus, goldfish races, and a glimpse of the "stars of tomorrow" for "one low price" required, above all, a mass audience. As long as Atlantic City remained a mass resort, the pier had its crowds. Fifteen thousand women, men, and children flocked to the "Showplace of the Nation" each summer day during the city's glory years. When it rained, this number ballooned to 20,000. In 1939, a few years before Hamid purchased the attraction, almost 40,000 people stuffed themselves onto the pier to see Amos 'n' Andy. Twenty years later, more than 44,000 showed up to watch the fresh-faced teen idol Ricky Nelson. That was the pier's peak. Hamid would later explain, "As tourists stopped coming to Atlantic City, the numbers [for Steel Pier] declined. It got hard to run."[9]

Almost everyone who met Hamid commented on his restless energy. Up early and late to bed, the old tumbler worked like a Depression kid afraid that everything he had could be gone in an instant. By the mid-1960s, this feeling wasn't just an illusion. Things were slipping away from Hamid. The crowds on the pier got smaller and more ragged each summer. While some Boardwalk businesspeople moved to Florida, others decided to get what they could, while they could. Following the model of the jam joints, they gouged summer customers and conventioneers, pocketing the profits and putting little back into their businesses. Hamid, however, tried to revive the pier's, and the city's, tourist trade. Mostly he worked to bring the crowds back to the Boardwalk. But Hamid didn't want just any crowd, he wanted the right crowd.

Hamid talked about the crowd all the time. In 1969, he spoke of the city's need to find "decent people" to fill areas of the city that had "deteriorated into ghettoes." Other times he talked about the necessity of luring middle-class vacationers and "high blue collar types" back to town.[10] What Hamid proposed was the rebuilding of the mass public of the past, the public that had gone to Disneyland.

Hamid never spoke about the racial or class makeup of the "decent" crowd. He didn't have to. Everyone knew what he meant when he talked about "decent" people and middle-class vacationers; they were white people who wore jackets and ties and carried a little extra money in their pockets.

George Hamid, Sr., was hard to miss. By almost any standards, he was handsome. His face was shaped like a slightly rounded rectangle and his eyes looked like jewels, shining bright and clear, twinkling often with a touch of mischief. Tall and broad-shouldered, yet agile and graceful, well into his fifties he looked like he could still anchor a circus pyramid or soar across the big top on a trapeze. But it was his neatness that was his most striking feature. His pants were always creased and his shirts were filled with enough starch to withstand a windstorm and enough bleach to disappear into a white cloud. He always seemed to have just come from the barbershop. His hair was perfect; Byrcream provided whatever discipline repeated cutting and combing could not master. Hamid's mustache was as neat and exact as his hair. Wide and tidy, it stopped just before the corners of his mouth as if to call further attention to its owner's fastidious grooming. Outward appearance clearly mattered to Hamid. Good clothes and neat hair seemed to him to have almost moral qualities.

"Many former visitors," the members of the Atlantic City Women's Chamber of Commerce complained in 1959, "stopped coming to the resort because the tone of the Boardwalk has been lowered."[11] Hamid agreed. In the late 1960s, he railed against "scantily clad strollers," "people walking barefoot," and "men without shirts."[12] Rebuilding the public, Hamid believed, required reestablishing the formal and informal dress codes of the past. He pressed city leaders to enforce local statutes on Boardwalk attire, satisfied no doubt when city commissioners in 1967 passed an ordinance—again—making it illegal for anyone to saunter down the promenade "clad only in a bathing costume."[13] The next year, two dozen prominent local business and political leaders appointed Hamid's son, the handsome Princeton graduate who entered the family business after college, to be the head of a committee charged with upgrading the Boardwalk's tone. Addressing the press, George Hamid, Jr., proclaimed, "[W]e are one of the proudest resorts in the world and we want to maintain our dignity and stature." Along with enforcing dress codes, Hamid said his group would press for regulations on Boardwalk merchants and storefronts. His father echoed his concerns, urging city leaders to outlaw blaring loudspeakers and garish window displays. A better-looking Boardwalk, Hamid believed, would bring "better" people back to the city.[14]

The Hamids also knew that bringing back "decent people" meant doing something about crime, or at least the perception of crime. Certainly, father and son agreed with the president of the Atlantic City Improvement Association, who said in 1958, "The Boardwalk should be the safest street in America."[15] To give it that feel and to reassure visitors, the elder Hamid pressed city leaders over the next decade to install brighter lights and to recruit more police officers. In 1968, the Chamber of Commerce, to which Hamid belonged, predicted that the changes would make "people less fearful of muggings."[16]

The owner of Steel Pier wanted to put one more confidence builder in place. Hamid spearheaded a petition drive calling on local officials to deploy K-9 police dogs on the Boardwalk. Some African American leaders opposed the idea. Civil rights advocate Manolette Nichols told city commissioners that he worried that the K-9s "would be used against the black community for the protection of white people." Alfred Washington, head of the Afro-American Unity Movement, suggested that city leaders investigate the causes of crime instead of unleashing police dogs, adding that he thought there would be "mass hysteria in the black community if police dogs were to be used."[17] Hamid dismissed these objections—objections that revealed the level of racial distrust in the city—as little more than the cantankerous outbursts of professional activists and apologists. But Hamid probably didn't care; he wasn't trying to win over the local black community. Lights and dogs, he trusted, would reestablish control over the public realm, giving the city a chance to win back the well-dressed, white, middle-class crowd.

The Hamids supported political boss, Hap Farley. When the Republican Farley threw his political weight around and persuaded the Democratic party to bring its national convention to the Boardwalk in 1964, the owner of Steel Pier applauded the move. The convention, he thought, like everyone else in town, would showcase the city. The strategy, of course, backfired.[18]

Hamid expected a windfall from the convention. Just to make sure, he dressed the diving horses in LBJ coats and booked Eddie Fisher, Mickey Rooney, and Milton Berle to perform in his show rooms.[19] As it turned out, the horses and entertainers played to mostly empty houses. But it was the piercing press reports that troubled Hamid the most. He knew, as Walt Disney did, that consumers' fantasies depended, in part, on service. Waiters, doormen, and busboys had to put visitors at the center of the tourist narrative, making them feel like kings and queens by indulging their whims and imaginations. Taking a cue from Disney's theme park, where managers turned workers into cast members, Hamid and others from the Chamber of Commerce wanted to make sure, in the convention's wake, that service workers dressed neatly and treated guests as royalty. "Bad impressions," it was argued, "from a discourteous act take long to heal." To help the resort to win back visitors after the convention, Hamid recommended that waiters and clerks take "a short course in courtesy."[20]

Hamid copied from the Disney model in other ways. In 1969, he promised that if Steel Pier received "the support of the merchants and hotel/motel people, we will add attractions like Disney does."[21] When General Motors closed down its Boardwalk showroom in 1968 after thirty some years of displaying cars by the ocean, Hamid put a seaquarium in its place.[22] At the same time, he talked about adding a "big zoological garden" with seventy-five animals, which would combine "entertainment and education" at the back of the pier.[23] The changes marked a shift in Hamid's thinking. In the past, the showman had presented animals as spectacles, as boxing cats and diving horses. But he sensed—quite rightly—a shift in middle-class attitudes by the late 1960s. "Decent people," the kind he was trying to lure to the city, now imagined themselves as the kind of people who cared about seeing fish and animals in natural-seeming habitats.[24]

Next to the aquarium and petting zoo, Hamid planned, around the same time, to build a full-sized ice-skating rink. All three of the pier's new attractions, the circus man believed, would enhance the middle-class feel of his showplace and of the city. Nothing seemed to capture this better than the ice rink. Ice skating still carried with it the kind of absurdity that made it an ideal Atlantic City attraction. What could be more fantastic—and nature defying—than ice skating at the beach in the middle of the summer? Only a truly leisured class deserved such a delicious twist of fate. But clearly ice skating also had a target audience. Hamid must have known that few poor people and few African Americans owned ice skates or would spend their leisure time twirling around ice-skating rinks in the middle of the summer. Hamid never talked in public about the demographic profile of the audience he was trying to bring to town, but, like Walt Disney, he sought to shape his attractions to match the constantly shifting tastes and values of the white middle-class millions, and he tried to segregate without calling attention to the filtering process.

While Hamid tried to make over parts of Steel Pier to reflect the shifting self-perceptions of the postwar middle class, he never went far enough. His new attractions were imitations, but only pale imitations, of the truly new and colossal tourist destinations built, for instance, at San Diego's Sea World and award-winning zoo. In part, Hamid didn't have the room, capital, or corporate backing to build a massive nature-based theme park. But at the same time, the old circus acrobat stubbornly clung to the old crowd, those immigrants and families on their way out of the working class, who had crammed onto the pier every weekend during the interwar years. He knew that much of his business even in the 1960s ran on nostalgia's fumes. Tens of thousands of people still came to Atlantic City and to Steel Pier each year, many to relive a bit of their past. Not wanting to lose a single customer, Hamid continued to feature vaudeville acts, swing bands long after the music disappeared from the Billboard charts, and women on horses plunging four times a day, six times on the weekends, into small pools of water.

Hamid and his son were really tinkerers, not revolutionaries. They did not radically rethink the idea of Atlantic City. They still imagined the resort as a place where people came to act out their entrance into the nation's middle-class mainstream. That's why well into the turbulent 1960s, Hamid Sr. continued to fly the flag, turning his own Horatio Alger story into the central theme of the pier's publicity. His journey from circus rags to Boardwalk riches to father of a Princeton graduate proved, he thought, that the American Dream worked. By coming to the pier, he suggested, visitors paid homage to the nation and the idea of social mobility.

Yet as much as Hamid wanted to bring back the old days of well-dressed crowds as thick as a swarm of teenagers at a Beatles concert, he was smart enough to know that the past could not be completely recreated. Surely he read the reports in the local paper about Atlantic City club meetings in Miami Beach and the opening of the new Disney park in Florida.[25] With many of the old faithful in the Sunshine State, Hamid knew that he and other Atlantic City business leaders had to find new groups of "decent" people to fill out the crowd.

Trying to capitalize on the postwar marriage boom, city officials, beginning in the 1950s, dubbed June "Honeymoon Month." Ten years later, feeling the first pinch of decline and looking to add to the crowd, the Hamids and others redoubled their efforts on this front. For a cut-rate price, honeymooners who came to celebrate their nuptials in the mid-1960s got a room, meals, sightseeing trips, a box of saltwater taffy, a rolling-chair ride, and passes to Steel Pier.[26]

As much as the Hamids liked to watch newlyweds slow-dancing on the pier, they were even more enthusiastic, at least from a business perspective, about Canadians. The women and men from the north represented just the sort of "family tourist trade"—in other words, straight, white couples with kids—the pier owners wanted to see on the Boardwalk. "The Canadians saved us from complete disaster last summer," Hamid declared in 1970. "[T]hey still come with their families and stay . . . for a week or two and spend money all over town."[27] To keep them coming and spending, the one-time circus promoter opened an office in Montreal. The Atlantic City Tourist Board and Chamber of Commerce followed suit, leasing storefronts in several eastern Canadian cities. Each year in late June, just as the honeymooners checked out of the hotels, local leaders hosted Canada Week. They started the festivities off with a "Salute to Canada," followed by the crowning of Miss Canadian Visitor.[28]

Canadians and honeymooners, as important as they were, the Hamids knew, could not save Atlantic City; they could stop the bleeding, but they couldn't heal the wound. There just weren't enough of them coming. To bring back masses of "decent" people, the city had to put up new clearly marked walls and more effective gates to keep the poor, hippies, and large numbers of African Americans out of sight. Here the law acted as both a tool and an impediment. City leaders couldn't in the 1960s revive Jim Crow rule nor bring back police tactics of intimidation. Even if they wanted to bring back the past, the Hamids knew that civil rights activists and civil libertarians wouldn't let them. Still they knew enough about the middle-class public to know that it couldn't take shape without exclusion. But the beach and the Boardwalk were public places, legally at this point open to anyone. Unlike Disney officials, Atlantic City leaders could not relocate beyond the city in order to keep away the wrong people—"roving groups of hoodlums," in one man's words. The Hamids and their politically powerful allies had to try to find ways around legal barriers to recreate their vision of a viable post–civil rights, urban, middle-class public.[29]

The elder Hamid's strong support for dress codes and sanctions against tacky Boardwalk displays represented two ways of keeping the indecent at a distance. But the city, he thought, had to remain on guard on all fronts. The public, he knew, was precarious. Steel Pier's owner once grumbled about "long-haired hippies." When a festival brought Janis Joplin, the Jefferson Airplane, the Byrds, Creedence Clearwater Revival, and Frank Zappa to the Atlantic City Race Track, a dozen miles from the Boardwalk, a week before Woodstock in 1969, Hamid fumed, "[T]hese kids are . . . repulsive," adding that they would come "without leaving twenty cents behind, unless, of course, they buy a hot dog and some pot."[30] Given how he felt about the youth culture, Hamid almost certainly supported measures proposed by friends and allies that were aimed at keeping freak-flag-flying members of the counterculture at bay. Surely, he backed proposals floated by some to curb public consumption of alcohol and to limit the number of people who could stay in hotel and motel rooms.[31] And no doubt he agreed with local residents who called for the closing of the Psychedelic Fun House. A self-described "living theater," the coffeehouse located on North Kentucky Avenue, just on the black side of the city's racial divide, staged *Hair*-like musical revues a couple of times a week. Not long after opening, the Fun House applied for a liquor license. One city commissioner opposed the move, describing the theater as "obscene" and charging that it appealed to "a prurient interest" with its "outrightly lewd and indecent" performances that lacked "redeeming social value" and were "patently offensive because [they are] affronts to contemporary community standards relating to sexual matters." "If I were to approve this license," he continued, "I would in effect, in my opinion, be a participant in a criminal action." Within a couple of weeks, the city commission received two petitions, signed by thirty-four persons, objecting to the Psychedelic Fun House getting a liquor license. It is not clear if Hamid joined these protests, but he undoubtedly wanted to limit blue jeans–wearing, long-haired hippies' access to the city and Boardwalk.[32]

Throughout the late 1960s, Hamid groused about day trippers—"shoobies," in the local parlance. (They earned this name because they supposedly jammed all the stuff they needed for a day at the beach into a shoebox.)[33] Shoobies often came as families, but to Hamid, they were the wrong kind of families. He complained about how they ate on the beach and changed in the public restrooms or in the back seats of their cars. Mostly, however, he groaned that they didn't spend enough money. They drove in for the day, taking up precious parking spaces. Then they trudged to the beach. Around 3:30, just as their skin cooked to a shade of lobster red, they stopped off for a lemonade or an ice cream cone, and they left town before nightfall. Hamid never said it out loud, but clearly he worried that the shoobies with their dripping bathing suits, sand-matted hair, and hot dog tastes gave Atlantic City a rough-hewn, working-class, Coney Island feel.

To discourage day trippers, Hamid pressed for a beach fee. Before this, Atlantic City had not charged visitors to use the beach.[34] Some thought this gave the city a competitive advantage over other beach towns that required people to pay to sunbathe and body surf. But Hamid wanted to bring to town the kind of people who wouldn't think twice about paying a small fee to use the beaches. He thought this would act as a filter. Knowing that shoobies, much like him, kept a close eye on the bottom line, he thought they would take note of the beach fee and take their towels and sack lunches to another shore town, where access to the ocean didn't cost anything.[35]

The Hamids apparently worried even more about the Boardwalk's racial mix. By the late 1960s, segregation was, of course, falling apart in Atlantic City as elsewhere. As it did, those cramped, stuffy, un–air-conditioned Northside rooming houses went out of business as fewer black visitors accepted the crumbs of Jim Crow tourism. Taking advantage of their new choices, African Americans checked into Southside hotels. While the Hamids might not have welcomed the idea of African Americans staying at the Marlborough-Blenheim or the Dennis, they were, it seems, more troubled by black shoobies and bus tour passengers.

Following the desegregation of Atlantic City's public places, African American church and civic groups sponsored frequent bus trips to the Queen of Resorts. "On summer weekends," one journalist noted, "busloads of blacks pour into Atlantic City from Philadelphia, New York, Wilmington, and other cities."[36] Two Philadelphia reporters visited the Boardwalk in 1970 and observed, "[F]ar more than half the people were black." Most, they added, "came down . . . for the day on a bus."[37] Hamid never commented on this new flow of tourism directly.[38] Nonetheless, a reporter who spoke with Hamid while working on a series on Atlantic City's decline for the *Philadelphia Inquirer* wrote, "[B]usinessmen and public officials privately complain that this [the African American bus trips] has been hurting the white tourist trade, driving business to the smaller, quieter, whiter resort communities up and down the South Jersey coast."[39]

Again, Hamid never said anything in public about the buses and the bus riders, but he and his son strongly supported an ordinance raising the charge on buses entering the city on Saturdays, Sundays, and holidays. He pressed city commissioners, moreover, to pass a measure requiring all charter buses to leave town by 11:00 PM. When local African American leaders objected to the recommendations, Hamid exploded, sounding like a man who had finally had enough. "Let's face it," he fumed, "the militant, loud, minority spokesmen" are not against the proposal "for moral purposes." They are against it, he wrote in a letter to the editor of the local newspaper, because the new measures would stop their "fellow travelers" who "loot, steal, and abuse law-abiding citizens." The city, he continued, "should not be exposed to rowdyism whether it is done by long-haired hippies or Negro gangs or Mexicans, Asians, Indians, or whatever." If these groups reigned over the city, Hamid warned, the "beach, Boardwalk, and streets" would never be "safe and decent," and "there will be no tomorrow."[40]

PAULINE HILL'S ANSWER

Pauline Hill was a radical. She wanted to sweep away what George Hamid, Sr., and George Hamid, Jr., wanted to fix. Like many Americans in the postwar era, Hill was devoted to the idea of newness. She believed as an article of faith that new things were better because they were new. And she believed the opposite as well. Older things were worse for the simple reason that they were old. Championing newness, Hill had little nostalgia for the past; and as for its remnants, she wanted them erased. That way, there would be room for the new to shine and generate profits.

Apostles of newness, like Hill, could be found everywhere in America. "New and improved" became Madison Avenue's favorite tagline, selling millions of tubes of toothpaste and tens of thousands of automobiles. But the cult of newness didn't stop with fluoride Crest and turbo-charged Plymouths. The nation's "best and brightest" slammed Vietnam with napalm, machine-gun fire, and aerial bombs in order to build a new society. In a grim moment of revelation, a military officer in Southeast Asia outlined the government's wartime strategy. "It became necessary," he said in the most passive of voices, "to destroy the town in order to save it."[41]

The same philosophy—the idea that destruction would lead to rebirth—drove the nation's policy toward its ailing cities in the postwar era. It was called *urban renewal*. Armed with faith in the new and generous federal funding, local authorities—people like Pauline Hill—unleashed columns of bulldozers to level countless city blocks. All too often, little new or profitable came out of this destruction, but the forces of newness continued their charge unabated.

Pauline Hill hardly looked like a commander for the new order. While she worked to rid the city of obsolescence, she remained in other ways strangely unmodern. She owed her position as head of the Atlantic City Housing Authority and Urban Redevelopment Agency, and the power that went with it, to an aging political machine—the one run by Hap Farley—that spent most of the 1960s fighting the forces of change. She didn't look the part either. Throughout the 1960s and 1970s, Hill dressed like June Cleaver and wore her hair in the dated style of a modified beehive. Even after feminists disrupted the 1968 Miss America Pageant on the Boardwalk by trashing girdles and issues of *Cosmopolitan*, Hill insisted that reporters refer to her as Mrs. Pauline Hill. Yet, despite her dowdy, prim, even matronly, appearance and posture, the college-educated Hill did not back down from men, or women, in public. Supporters and opponents described her variously as tough, feisty, wily, abrasive, insensitive, courageous, and innovative.[42]

Pauline Hill was fifty-three years old in 1963, when she was promoted to the position of executive director of the Atlantic City Housing Authority and Urban Redevelopment Agency. Once in power, she promised that urban renewal would reverse the city's sharp decline, restore its tax base, and jump-start businesses. Of course, she was not alone in seeing a bright future in urban renewal. The Housing Act of 1949, later amended in 1954, allocated federal funds to localities to buy and destroy properties designated as "blighted" and to resell the land at a loss if necessary.[43] Across the United States, urban renewal, which acted in many ways like a government subsidy to private developers, cleared a path of houses and businesses on lands the size of Louisville and Atlanta combined.[44] According to a federal official in charge of the program, "The philosophy of urban renewal recognizes a partnership between public authority and private enterprise." "The concept," he continued, "of a public body taking private property from one owner and selling it to another for private purposes is a radical one." Dramatic, wholesale transformation was what this policymaker was after. "The process of urban renewal," he concluded, "would fail unless large areas could be assembled as a *new* [emphasis added] environment. Only this way can slum areas threatening the financial, social, and economic foundation of American cities be eliminated."[45] Following this lead, financially strapped cities across the country caught "demolition fever" and put urban renewal projects into motion, buying old buildings, tearing them down, and sometimes putting up new ones in their place.[46]

Atlantic City began to experiment with urban renewal in the late 1950s, before Hill took over the housing authority. With a treasure trove of federal dollars, the city purchased several blocks of Northside row houses. Over the next several years, the housing authority tore down the aging buildings and replaced them with a single, flat, unadorned high-rise. Despite federal laws barring segregation in urban renewal projects, no whites lived in the newly built Altman Terrace, named after the city's long-time mayor, Joseph Altman.[47] White families in Atlantic City who occupied subsidized housing still lived in the all-white Pitney Village in all-white Ducktown. With the construction of its first high-rise public housing project, Atlantic City—and here again the city was not unique— launched a new era of residential segregation in a new vertical ghetto.[48]

Next, the housing authority turned its attention to the South Inlet on the city's all-white Southside. By this time, Hill ran the agency. Choosing a white district didn't make her, however, some sort of racial egalitarian. She picked the area, still called by some the Uptown district, because it represented one of the city's most valuable and least commercially developed sections. But she also picked this ten-block rectangle because, it seems, she feared that if she plowed down another African American part of town, the urban renewal refugees would move into a white neighborhood. Even more, she was probably worried about blockbusting real estate agents and shifting property values. African Americans had already de-segregated the North Inlet—the area where crosses burned in the late 1950s— triggering a wave of white flight from the area. Surely the next frontier on the city's racial horizon was the South Inlet. Hill wanted to act before African Americans did. That way, she could create a new and more valuable South Inlet before local blacks remade the area.[49]

Approximately 900 families and 1,600 individuals lived in the area that Hill targeted for destruction. With its front porches and corner stores, local delis and pizza parlors, tidy houses and narrow streets, the area looked like any other white ethnic neighborhood in New Jersey. When Hill came around, the South Inlet hadn't changed that much, although its residents had gotten older since the 1940s. Jewish, Irish, and Italian police officers, fire fighters, clerks, accountants, plumbers, and shop owners still lived in the area next to retired couples and widows reluctant to leave houses paid for long ago.[50]

To Pauline Hill, what stuck out about the South Inlet was not its architecture, street culture, ethnic diversity, or the variety of shops, bars, and restaurants; it was its age and competitive position. She couldn't get past the area's postwar stagnation. As Hill noted, the city's motel-building boom, which started in the early

1950s, took a bite out of the area's guesthouse business.[51] With profits declining, some owners skimped on repairs, always a risk in an area so close to the beach. The smaller houses farther from the ocean remained neat and clean, but most could have used a fresh coat of paint and new gutters. As the buildings started to droop, young people left the neighborhood, especially once they had families of their own. Looking for easy parking and bigger lawns and worried about the collapse of residential segregation, the neighborhood's next generation left the gritty streets of their parents in favor of the pastoral lanes and courts of racially homogeneous downbeach and offshore suburbs. Property values in the area, as a result, inched downward.

Hill was not one for subtlety. Chipped paint and falling prices convinced her in the early 1960s that the South Inlet was "tarnished and decayed."[52] Worse still, she saw the beachfront neighborhood as a "wasteful underutilization of very important land." Swept up in demolition fever, Hill never gave a thought to rehabilitating the neighborhood's houses and businesses. The bulldozer was the only remedy she considered.[53]

Hill once described urban renewal as "good business."[54] Arguing that deterioration affected not just "the lower classes . . . but everyone," she promised that federal dollars would provide a "tremendous opportunity to create a revitalized image of Atlantic City." Speaking to the Exchange Club in her trademark staccato voice, Hill elaborated, saying that "urban renewal is giving . . . [Atlantic City] a second chance."[55] On another occasion, she added that the program was sure to help the city "throw off the dead hand of the past."[56] And in a metaphor Hill repeatedly deployed, she compared urban renewal to essential surgery. "Without necessary surgery, you die, you don't stand still—you either go forward, or you die."[57]

Hill was convinced that the South Inlet hovered on death's doorstep. According to a survey conducted by her office, 67 percent of the area's "buildings are substandard, unsafe, insanitary [sic], dilapidated, obsolescent . . . [and] warrant clearance."[58] For Hill, the key phrase was "obsolescent." To her, this was the real problem. As she went around the city explaining why the housing authority chose the South Inlet for clearance, she stressed the outdated character of the buildings there. "Don't forget," she told a crowd in 1966, "that this is an area of antiquated guesthouses and hotels."[59] "The [U]ptown area," she said on another occasion, "was considered for proposed renewal because it has been deteriorating steadily. Loss of income is reflected in the blight and deteriorating condition of many of the transient residential structures and in the fact [that] mortgage money is not available."[60] "Many have questioned why urban renewal is even needed in the [U]ptown area," she explained on yet another occasion. "After all, they say, the homes, most of them guest houses, are generally well maintained and many businesses in the vicinity have prospered through the years." But by the 1960s, rooming houses, Hill was quick to add, symbolized "another era in the resort." They were, she said, "relics of the past . . . geared . . . to the slower pace of past generations."[61] Modern tourists and modern city dwellers, Hill believed, demanded the conveniences of newly built motels and apartments, roads, and parking areas.

Even area residents were, in Hill's mind, dated and obsolete.[62] Once she complained that the South Inlet community had an intolerably low ratio of schoolchildren to adults; in fact, she said, it was the lowest in the city. "The natural result of an aging section of a city inhabited by an older segment of the population," Hill maintained, "is for both the people and their homes to age together, with the people not realizing how their properties have fallen behind the times in terms of convenience and resale value."[63] People's attachments to their aging properties and misty memories worried Hill. "We must not," she concluded in one of her hundreds of speeches on the Uptown urban renewal project, "be lulled into a false sense of security by familiar surroundings, and we must be wary of sentimentality over blighted areas."[64]

While some Inlet residents bristled at Hill's characterization of their neighborhood as blighted and obsolete, others complained about the prices offered for their buildings. Still others feared that they would not be able to find new places to live. But few, in the end, protested. Unlike what happened in other cities undergoing urban renewal, there was, at first, little resistance to the Inlet's takeover.[65] No one hauled the housing authority to court over the matter. In the press, Hill repeatedly cited the willingness of residents to relocate as evidence of the neighborhood's ragged condition. "Most of the property owners," she reported, "were glad to negotiate and to sell since they were experiencing diminished returns." Years later, Hill insisted, "[Residents] weren't calling me and saying, 'don't put me out.' They were calling and saying, 'When are you going to pay me so I can get out of here?' "[66] Guesthouse owners, Hill added, were especially eager to sell. On one occasion, she did concede that urban renewal would hurt 10 percent of the community. While acknowledging that South Inlet inhabitants would suffer from the "violent impact" of demolition and relocation, Hill nonetheless insisted that it would be worth it because the removal of obsolete homes and businesses would allow "Atlantic City . . . [to] throw off the dead hand of the past."[67]

As the bulldozers plowed down block after block of the Inlet in 1964, 1965, and 1966, running over Capital Furniture, Cheng's Chinese Restaurant, the Hudson Fish Market, and the White Cottage Coffee Shop on Atlantic Avenue and Louis Manuiello's, Ethel Tiefenbrun's, Rubin Balk's, and Mae Kesser's homes on Maryland Avenue, Hill started to sketch out her vision of a "new city within a city."[68]

Hill never mentioned the French architect Charles LeCorbusier or any other modernist planner, but it was clear that their ideas about urban space shaped her own thinking about cities. She planned to replace the Uptown area's mix of brick and wood-framed houses with garden apartments and sleek-looking high-rise condominiums. In place of creaky hotels and aging guesthouses, she imagined a combination of low-slung motels and towering luxury hotels. She planned to rip up several of the neighborhood's narrow streets and many of its slender sidewalks to make room for pedestrian walkways, manicured green spaces, and apartments with security locks. Everything would have a place—a separate and distinct place—in Hill's new age South Inlet, and just about everything would be geared to cars. Residential housing with ample parking below would be located near the beach, stores and a theater with even more parking would be closer to the bay. And a massive supermarket with still more parking would replace the family-run corner stores, butchers, and specialty shops that used to operate in the area. Hill's was a vision of a city turned inward. Walls would mark off its boundaries and set it off from surrounding neighborhoods. Behind this fortress, the buildings, just like those in Marven Gardens, would face each other, not the rest of the city or the ocean.

People would be replaced right along with the buildings. Hill's blueprints made it clear that her new Atlantic City would have no place for most Atlantic City residents. She didn't, for starters, imagine African Americans, by then almost half of the city's population, as part of her new city. As Northside urban renewal projects revealed, Hill's housing authority had already demonstrated its determination to uphold residential segregation. Driving home the point, Hill's sketches of her new city featured only people who looked white. African Americans were not the only group excluded. She also wanted to flush out the blue-collar families, middle managers, and retirees who lived in the South Inlet to make room for wealthy tenants. "You can't build poor cities," Hill told a reporter, because the poor "just vandalize places we build [for] them, and then we have to tear them down again."[69]

Again, Hill was a radical, while Hamid and most others were reformers. Her idea was not so much to build the perfect city, but to erect a perfect suburb in the midst of a crumbling city. While never making this expressly clear, except with her plans, she no longer imagined Atlantic City primarily as a resort. She didn't want to put new attractions—an aquarium or a zoo—on the urban renewal site; her vision was much bolder. She saw the city as a bedroom community to Philadelphia, as a place where middle-class white families could come to flee the racial and social changes happening there and in other urban centers. Again, her new city wouldn't really be a city; it would be a car-centered suburb. The newly funded and soon-to-be-completed Atlantic City Expressway would be the new community's main artery. This four-lane highway linked Atlantic City more directly than ever before to Philadelphia. Now, husbands could commute from Hill's well-protected cocoon at the shore to Center City Philadelphia every day in an hour's time.[70]

Hill's new suburban wonderland never came to pass. In 1967, two years after her agency started tearing down houses and businesses, the housing authority hired the Renewal Development Corporation to build on the cleared land. Within a year, the company backed out of the deal without raising a single structure. Control of the project then passed to Philadelphia's Barco Urban Renewal Corporation. Hopes ran high after Barco finished the Beachgate Condominium Complex in 1971. With its seventy-five "garden apartments" facing inward toward a landscaped courtyard, the development previewed Hill's urban vision. But Barco never completed another building.

Angry about the slow pace of progress and having to look at a hole in the city every day, local politicians began in 1971 to pressure Hill to remove the developer. Hill resisted, maintaining that Barco was not to blame. The problem, she asserted, was financing; no one wanted to invest in cities. What Hill did not say, at least publicly, was that the federal government would surely have provided money to build low-income housing in the area. But low-income families were never part of Hill's master plan.[71] She had not plowed down acres of structures to take care of the poor. So a hole remained in the middle of Atlantic City's beachfront—a Chinese (Great) Wall, in the words of one resident—that chopped the city into two, disrupting aesthetic and commercial flows.[72]

Local residents gasped when they saw the hole in the city. Once they caught their breath, they hurled criticisms at Pauline Hill. The Atlantic City chapter of the Congress of Racial Equality (CORE) complained that while the housing authority had spent millions bailing out white businesses and home owners in the South Inlet, it had neglected poverty-strapped black neighborhoods.[73] Hill paid no attention to the civil rights group's grievances; she didn't even answer its letters. But she did listen to business leaders who attacked her for "creating a desert" in the middle of the city.[74] One man rhymed, "If open spaces don't make you scary, come and visit Pauline's Prairie."[75] The label stuck. Everyone from taxi drivers to newsboys started to call the cleared patch of land in the Inlet Pauline's Prairie. About the same time, bright orange and black bumper stickers popped up on cars, stop signs, and storefronts all over town that read: "Down with Pauline Hill and Build a Better City."[76] Then came the call for Hill's ouster. Business and political leaders charged her with incompetence and malfeasance. One man threatened court action if Hill didn't step down. "If Pauline Hill headed a business," wrote an enraged local college student, "her mistakes would have brought her bankruptcy long ago. If she were an elected official, she would have been voted out of office years ago. However, she is an appointed member of a public agency and so she stays on and on." "Frustrated citizens," he protested, "can do nothing but put up bumper stickers."[77] "It was Pauline Hill's doing," charged a city commissioner. Because of the Uptown demolition program, he said, the city had lost millions in revenues, and as a result, the local government had no choice but to boost tax rates. "I say," the politician concluded, "she has failed miserably."[78]

The Hamids, whose Steel Pier sat on the southern edge of the Chinese Wall, emerged as two of Hill's harshest critics. The old acrobat tore into Hill for "prematurely clearing "taxpaying structures *before* replacements were assured." He argued that the "vast wasteland" she created accounted for a 20 percent drop in tourism. "Where is this going to end?" he asked in 1968. "This is the third year that Atlantic City looks like Berlin after the destruction of World War II."[79]

The owner of a Virginia Avenue hotel just down the street from Steel Pier grumbled in the fall of 1969, "I have no business and my taxes aren't cheaper." During the previous summer, a Canadian family, frightened by the eerie silence of the abandoned area, checked out early. As they climbed into their car, they asked the hotel owner, "How do you live here?"[80]

Increasingly after 1970, people answered the question "how do you live here?" by saying, "I don't any more." Feeling walled off in the Inlet, "[a]nybody who could," one man recalled, "moved out." Another man described it as "a mass exodus from the neighborhood."[81] In addition to the 1,600 or so people officially relocated by the urban renewal project, a survey conducted by the census bureau revealed that the bulldozers had displaced as many as 3,500 more area residents.[82] None of these families or individuals received compensation for their losses. Furniture stores and dress shops followed the people out of the Inlet, and then the synagogues and churches left. "All of the merchants," a local bar owner remembered, "were hoping and believing that the area would be built up." But that didn't happen. With families packing up and leaving, he lamented, "I couldn't stay in business any longer. Until this happened, I had a very fine and lucrative business. People came to my bar from far and near, but finally, they were chased away."[83]

With signs of decay everywhere, many South Inlet families sold their homes at fire-sale prices. Others moved out of the area, but held onto their homes or guesthouses and illegally chopped them up into cheap apartments. Still others just abandoned their properties altogether, letting the city take them rather than pay back taxes. Some tore down their houses and waited for something to happen. As they did, the South Inlet blocks still standing began to resemble the gap-tooth smile of a young child, with a building here, a space there, and a couple of buildings farther up the street. Worse still, urban renewal broke up the bonds of community built through generations of conversations on front porches, chance encounters at corner stores, and going to church and synagogue.

Demolition and the flight that followed took people who knew each other off their front porches and off the streets, robbing the area—like it had already done to Atlantic Avenue—of "the eyes of the street."[84] Once Pauline Hill's bulldozers plowed down those ten city blocks, the people left in the neighborhood started to bolt their doors, clear their porches, and bar their windows. With long-time residents rushing out of the city and those who took their places not yet tied to the neighborhood, everyone, it seems, stayed inside. As people retreated behind closed doors and the local economy slowed down, crime increased. Burglars and vandals found further protection in the area's growing number of vacant lots and empty buildings. About muggings, said one man, "[N]o one even knew the word [before]. That word didn't even exist."[85] Unfortunately, he found out soon enough what it meant.

Helen Klatzkin was standing on Oriental Avenue in March 1974 when a man grabbed her purse and started running. A few days before, another man, or maybe the same man, robbed and beat another woman, who later died in the hospital. Around the same time, Herbert Schafritz of the Jitneymen's Association informed city commissioners that his men feared for their lives when they drove past the urban renewal site farther into the Inlet. "We have a problem," he stated. "[T]he men are getting mugged. One man just had both hands sliced open. Another man was hit in the eye with brass knuckles. Kids are riding bikes and [they] pull up to the jitneys at stoplights and pull out the register. They bombard us with rocks. . . . Something has to be done." "We don't want to stop service in the area," he said, "but . . . " and then his voice trailed off.[86]

On the 400 block of Oriental Avenue, Meyer Bluth of Meyer's Market, a family-owned kosher butcher shop founded in 1927, was fighting his own battles. Before the bulldozers, Bluth's family lived above the shop. On most days, women filled his store, chatting in front of the white refrigerator chests while waiting for their fresh kosher chickens. By the early 1970s, Bluth's customers, noted a journalist, were "afraid to walk the streets—day or night." Actually so was Bluth. He had recently moved out of the neighborhood. On his way home each day—he made sure he left the area by three o'clock in the afternoon—he delivered meat right to his customers' houses. That was the only way he could stay in business. In the fall of 1972, robbers broke into his store. Then local kids began to heave rocks at his windows, just for kicks, it seems, but no one was around to stop them. Trying to protect the shop, Bluth covered his windows and doors with chicken wire, masking tape, cardboard, and plywood. But his defenses weren't strong enough. One determined burglar dug a hole through the wall to get into the building. "I want to stay here but they apparently don't want me," Bluth said, not really knowing who *they* were, except that they weren't like him. Soon after, he closed his shop for good.[87]

Pauline Hill didn't think the attacks on Meyer's Market had anything to do with urban renewal. Testy and defensive, Hill lashed back at critics. She accused them of failing to comprehend urban renewal's intricacies. Worst of all, she said, they were hopelessly backward.[88] Eventually, though, the hole in the city proved to be just too big. Nothing Hill said or did could make it or her detractors go away. Finally, in 1973, after thirty-five years with the housing authority, Hill reluctantly announced her retirement as the agency's executive director.

Over the next few years, a couple of buildings went up on the urban renewal site. In 1975, a bank opened a branch office on Atlantic Avenue, and the next year, the Community Haven Apartments for seniors opened near the beach.[89] Once Hill was gone, living in Margate and serving on that town's local planning board, the housing authority launched an aggressive campaign to find a developer to fill the hole in the city. Shifting gears, they abandoned Hill's idea of transforming the area into a car-friendly suburb and focused instead, as Hamid urged, on luring middle-class tourists back to the beach and Boardwalk. Housing authority officials wrote letters to hotel executives across the United States, Germany, and Japan, telling them about the opportunities available on the urban renewal site. They especially courted Canadian investors. "We are certain," a housing authority official wrote to the manager of the Lord Nelson Hotel in Halifax:

> that you are aware of the heavy Canadian influx enjoyed by the New Jersey seashore communities—and Atlantic City in particular. Needless to say, for you as a hotelman, this exodus of money must be very upsetting. You have probably worked hard and long to cultivate this local business and we are sure that you have looked enviously towards our area.

Why not, he asked, go where the people are going? "We are enclosing," he continued, "a brochure outlining some of the development possibilities of an 80-acre beachfront tract. We hope that you will study this literature to see if a hotel development in this area would be of interest to you."[90]

When no one from Canada, Germany, or Japan jumped at the opportunity to build on Pauline's Prairie, housing officials hit the road, sending representatives to hotel and vacation conferences to wine and dine potential investors in person. At the same time, they tried to entice amusement park companies, like Six Flags and Disney, to the cleared land. When these plans didn't work out, they considered bringing a recreational vehicle park to town.[91] Again, nothing happened. Some

PAULINE'S PRAIRIE

Looking across the barren urban renewal site toward Resorts International Hotel and Casino in 1978 (Atlantic City Free Public Library, Heston Room, Atlantic City, New Jersey).

years later, the authority produced *Atlantic City: Cleared for Take-Off*, an amateurish video with a tired aviation theme that bragged about the city's low tax rates and favorable business conditions. Still there were no takers, and the land sat empty.[92]

AN URBAN POSTSCRIPT

John Edgar Wideman may never have been to Atlantic City, and surely he never spoke with George Hamid or Pauline Hill. But the award-winning author understood why their plans to remake the crowd in Atlantic City failed. They failed because middle-class women and men, white and black, associated the city with fear, a fear, he wrote, of "[b]rute niggers, dope fiends, sadistic pot-bellied cops, [and] hippies."[93]

Growing up in Pittsburgh in the 1940s, Wideman feared city streets, especially at night. But as he reached his teens, he became more daring. By then, the city, as a place and as an idea, dazzled and electrified him, and he walked from end to end of the city without looking over his shoulder or listening for distant footsteps. By 1972, one of Wideman's friends had been assaulted and two of his televisions had been stolen, and as a result, he came full circle when it came to urban space, not just in Pittsburgh, but everywhere. "I am convinced," he wrote, that "the night streets are unsafe. . . . I sleep with a bayonet under my bed." He was not alone. He smelled the foul odor of fear all around him. "White fear in the streets," he detected, "is a fear of blacks. Black fear . . . is a fear of whites." He elaborated, "Whites fear the burly, black brute," while "blacks fear the treacherous white keeper of the keys with his guns and whips." Shocked, even embarrassed, by their fears, whites and blacks, at least those who could afford to do so, stayed away from tall buildings, crowded boulevards, smoky jazz clubs, and downtown movie houses.

That flight was, of course, Atlantic City's chief problem. By 1972, when Wideman confessed his fears, the American city no longer captured the imagination of the middle-class millions. As a place and as an idea, the city had become synonymous with fear. Everywhere there was fear, fear of crime, fear of hooligans, and fear of menacing blacks and vindictive whites. "Some days," Wideman explained, "there's just so much city you can't hide."

That sense of there being too much urban-ness in Atlantic City foiled Hamid's and Hill's plans. No matter how many sea lions they shipped to town or how many blighted buildings they bulldozed, they couldn't hide enough of the city. They couldn't hide from visitors the boarded-up businesses and weed-filled lots, long-haired hippies, black teenagers, bus riders, and shoobies. Hamid and Hill tried to build walls around these places and people, but they couldn't make them high enough to keep the Others out of sight. They couldn't, in other words, cover up enough of the city to wipe away the fears of the crowd, first the white crowd, and then the new black crowd. So they were left with places that appeared empty and abandoned.

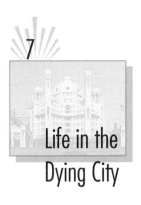

7

Life in the Dying City

Truck rental companies did pretty good business in Atlantic City in the 1970s. White families from Ducktown and Chelsea, Venice Park and the South Inlet pulled the yellow and orange-striped trucks over the sidewalks and up to their front doors. With the help of neighbors, friends, uncles, and cousins, they packed up their sofas, wood-paneled hi-fi consoles, new RCA color television sets, gold-framed mirrors, ping-pong tables, and Little League and Knights of Columbus plaques. Once everything was loaded, they said their last good-byes and pulled away slowly—the wife and kids climbing into the station wagon as the husband guided the moving truck. Creeping through the old neighborhood in first gear, the man—probably a graduate of Atlantic City High School—looked around, wondering if he was doing the right thing by moving his family to Northfield or Somers Point or Egg Harbor Township or whatever suburb he had chosen. But as the beach and Boardwalk got smaller in his rear view mirror and he drove past the old corner store, which was now closed tight, past a pack of teenagers hanging out on a street corner, past the elementary school scarred with graffiti, and past the empty church where he was baptized and married, he nodded his head. This was the right thing to do, he said to himself. Then he laughed, remembering a joke he had heard, maybe it was from the guy at the truck rental company, "If you were looking for signs of economic life in the city, you could hold a mirror to its mouth all day and it wouldn't fog up."[1]

White families were not the only ones renting trucks and leaving town. Beginning in the late 1960s, African Americans joined the evacuation to the suburbs. Marking the change, black churches sent twelve-passenger vans on Sunday mornings to Pleasantville—where most Atlantic City blacks in flight moved—to pick up worshipers and bring them back to the chapels of their youth. Businesses followed their customers. Wash's Inn first opened in 1937 at the corner of Illinois and Arctic avenues in the heart of the Northside. But by 1974, the soul food restaurant, known for its tangy ribs and juicy fried chicken, moved out to Pleasantville.[2]

The black and white urban fugitives of the late 1960s and early 1970s were so wrapped in their own thoughts—thoughts of the life and death of Atlantic City—that they hardly noticed the vans, station wagons, and pick-up trucks crammed with furniture and Saturday night revelers on the other side of the road—going into town.

LIFE IN THE SOUTH INLET

In the winter of 1974, an Atlantic City reporter found Juan Villonieva, his wife, and six children between the ages of six months and eight years old in a second-floor apartment in a brick building on South Massachusetts Avenue. Switching between Spanish and English, the Puerto Rican man told the newsman that he had no heat or hot water. He prayed that the icy winds and snow that sometimes blew through the area would stay away until his landlord fixed the faulty furnace. But he wasn't optimistic about the weather or the landlord.

As he talked, his children huddled on mattresses on the floor under bundles of blankets, fully clothed, three in one room, and two in the other. The infant lay in her parents' room buried under another pile of covers. The refrigerator contained only three half-gallons of milk and a pound of spiced lard. It wasn't in the kitchen because there was no electricity there. Toward the front of the house stood the living room, the Villonievas' only furnished room. The sofa, two chairs, coffee table, matching pair of end tables, and lamp were all that they owned. That's all they had accumulated in their American lives.[3]

The reporter who found Villonieva and his family fighting off the cold explained where they were, but not how they got there. Puerto Rican men and women had lived in Atlantic City since the 1950s, but Villonieva probably came to the United States twenty years later. During the 1970s, more than 20,000 Puerto Ricans traveled to the mainland each year in search of work. These women and men turned out to be America's first airborne migrants. The same inexpensive airfares that took long-time Atlantic City visitors away from the resort brought thousands of Puerto Ricans to the United States and back home again.

Most commuters—as some scholars have dubbed these frequent-flying Puerto Rican migrants—were people running an uphill race against economic changes at home and abroad. Typically, they started out in rural towns in the hill country and in villages near the coastal south, places where roosters still crowed in the morning and chickens wandered down unpaved streets. But by the late 1960s, times were tough for these agricultural communities as coffee, sugar, and tobacco prices collapsed. In response, men like Juan Villonieva left the country for the city. Their timing was terrible. Just as they reached the working-class slums ringing the city of San Juan, jobs were disappearing. Twenty years of government-led industrialization in Puerto Rico was grinding to a halt in the early 1970s. With few options at home, Villonieva probably purchased a $50, one-way ticket to New York.[4]

Villonieva and others like him on that jetliner arrived in the United States with little education and few skills that could translate into decent-paying jobs. Generally, the Puerto Rican middle class stayed put or got white-collar jobs with multinational corporations during these years; it was the poor, the unemployed, and the unskilled who joined the migrant stream north. A majority stayed in New York when they got off the plane, settling in Manhattan's East Harlem (El Barrio), Washington Heights, and the Lower East Side; Brooklyn's Williamsburg and Sunset Park; and the South Bronx. All of these were neighborhoods from which white families had just fled, leaving behind worn-out apartment buildings, sprawling houses chopped into smaller units, and abandoned churches. But not everyone remained in New York City. Thousands of Puerto Ricans contracted themselves out as migrant farm workers picking peaches in South Carolina, apples in Vermont, shade tobacco in Connecticut, and tomatoes, peppers, and eggplant in southern New Jersey.[5]

After a season or two living in converted chicken coops and working from sun-up to sundown in hot fields, some workers had had enough. Many returned home, while others stopped moving from job to job, crop to crop, and put down roots. They coupled up, only sometimes marrying in the legal sense, and started families. Most went where they knew people, including the barrios of New York. But small groups of men and women who neither liked the big city nor picking vegetables on South Jersey farms came to Atlantic City. "This is better than New York," announced Carmen LaBoy from her apartment on Rhode Island Avenue in the 1970s. "In New York the traffic [is] no good for children. Now [here] there is no traffic. Everybody speaks Spanish. In Atlantic City it's good for the Puerto Ricans, but not so good, huh?"[6]

By 1970, according to the U.S. Census Bureau, the 681 Puerto Ricans living in Atlantic City made up 1.5 percent of the city's total population.[7] During the next decade, this number doubled, then nearly doubled again and again. By the time the casinos came, more than 4,000 Puerto Rican men, women, and children made their homes in Atlantic City, and they represented almost a tenth of the city's declining population. Just about all of these families lived in the South Inlet. Like the New York barrios, the area was a neighborhood in transition. Puerto Ricans made their homes in the part of the city just south of Pauline's Prairie, which had recently been abandoned by Irish, Jewish, and Italian families.

Some felt quite comfortable in the South Inlet. The sound of waves beating against the shore, the smell of salt air, and the feel of the cool breezes that rippled through the area reminded them of home. But housing, as Juan Villonieva and his family found out, was one of the "not so good" parts of life in Atlantic City. Almost every Puerto Rican family lived in a rented apartment owned by someone who had fled the area. Absentee landlords put little money into their properties. Official neglect made things even worse. Garbage collectors came to the area with little or no regularity. Local officials repeatedly reassigned "Mickey Mouse cops," police who had, one journalist observed, "misbehaved" in other parts of town, to the neighborhood. Many of the apartments were hacked out of single-family houses. Few had proper wiring. Some landlords simply ran extension cords from room to room, and even from apartment to apartment. According to one report, 75 percent of South Inlet apartments had "severe housing code violations," and a third of the neighborhood's children suffered from lead poisoning. Landlords were rarely, if ever, held accountable. Local housing and health officials treated the area as a kind of rural outpost, rarely, if ever, inspecting properties there.[8] Left to the tender mercies of absentee landlords, Puerto Rican families lived with leaky roofs, clogged pipes, aging furnaces, peeling lead paint, and cat-sized rats.

Olga Perez brought a reporter along to check up on a friend living in a three-story apartment building on Wistar Place, a tiny alley behind Oriental Avenue. "Ick," she said as she climbed the steps, holding her nose against the smell of urine. Then she knocked on a door. "Hola," the thin woman said, and let the visitors in. Perez's friend lived in a single room divided by a curtain into a kitchen and bedroom. Soaked by rainwater coming through the roof, the ceiling sagged a full two feet. Water dripped onto the beds. The moisture gave the cramped apartment, wrote the journalist, a "thick . . . smell . . . that always seems to accompany the presence of rats."[9]

Few Puerto Ricans could afford drier, cleaner, and more spacious apartments. And fewer still could afford to buy their own homes. In 1978, only 11 of Atlantic City's 800 or more Puerto Rican families owned their own homes.[10] Most, like Juan Villonieva and the woman from Wistar Place, lived on top of each other in crumbling buildings in an underserviced part of the city.

Puerto Ricans never made much money in Atlantic City. Most came to town just as the wrecking balls bowled over Boardwalk hotels and the conventioneers with company credit cards moved their meetings to other cities. For the newest arrivals, the economic downturn, what some might call deindustrialization, meant sharp cuts in blue-collar jobs and wages. Yet despite the hard times, most Puerto Ricans found work, albeit at the bottom of the economic ladder. Juan Villonieva and his neighbors made beds, washed dishes, and scrubbed toilets. Some even went back to the fields. During the summer, pick-up trucks with the names of Vineland and Hammonton farms painted on their doors rode through the Inlet at 5:00 a.m., gathering up men, women, and children. They returned them to their rented apartments after a long day of picking blueberries and red peppers just as darkness fell. But work was work. According to a 1970 survey, unemployment in Atlantic City's Puerto Rican community stood at only 1.5 percent. But that work did not provide a shield against poverty. Another study done in the 1970s reported that half of all Puerto Ricans in the city lived below the poverty line. Work might have been work, but it didn't pay much.[11]

Atlantic City's Puerto Rican families lived isolated lives. They were closed off from the rest of the city by geography, urban renewal, language, and poverty. How others saw them isolated them even further. Former South Inlet residents remembered the old neighborhood as a busy and safe place to live. When they took their children on Sunday afternoon rides to look at where they had grown up, they saw broken windows, trash-strewn streets, vacant lots, and rats scurrying in the gutters. The sights left a bitter taste in their mouths. So did reports of muggings and beatings on Oriental Avenue and St. James Place. What they saw and heard made them sad, then mad. Children of the Inlet somehow felt personally violated by the area's decay. More than a few directed their anger at the Puerto Rican families living in their old houses, not at their former neighbors who were now acting as absentee landlords or at city officials who neglected the area or at the raw prejudice that carved new lines onto the map of the city.

Anne Saxe spent most of her life in the South Inlet. She walked to the corner store, the bus stop, and the beach. By the summer of 1972, she told the city commissioners, she was afraid to leave her house after dark, afraid that she would be beaten or robbed. She blamed the rise in crime on her new Puerto Rican neighbors.[12] Another Atlantic City resident compared Puerto Ricans to "animals." Because they sent so much of their money back to the island, he argued, "they weren't spending money fixing up their properties"—properties he forgot that they didn't own. The same man added, "They would burn their own houses if they got mad. They would take the pipes out of the houses they were renting and sell them for scrap."[13] Puerto Ricans, in other words, were the problem and mostly because of their Puerto Rican-ness. "When I came here," Father James Halley, the local priest remarked, "I was astounded at the anti-Hispanic resentment. They were blamed for the demise of Atlantic City. If any group *didn't* do it, it was they. This area was like an old railroad station that had seen too many passengers and these people were the last through."[14]

Faced with this kind of hostility, some Atlantic City Puerto Ricans lashed out. Teenagers, it seems, didn't think twice about dumping trash in empty lots and taunting older residents in Spanish on their way to the store. Walking through the South Inlet in 1972, a white woman spotted a sign declaring, "Kill Gringos."[15] She raced away before finding out anything about the message. If she had stuck around or if she had spoken Spanish, she would have found out that most of her new neighbors were not plotting ethnic warfare or a criminal assault. Instead, they were taking steps to build a community on abandoned lands from the bottom up.

By the time Puerto Ricans moved to the South Inlet, the area had certainly changed, but not entirely. Physically, the houses and apartment buildings retained their traditional urban feel and look. But now it was Puerto Rican families on the stoops and on the streets. It was Puerto Rican men who rose with the sun to troll for weakies and bluefish off the jetties. It was Puerto Rican women who scrubbed the sidewalks in the evenings and Puerto Rican teenagers who played salsa late into the night. A new dance of people, therefore, had replaced the stillness of flight, and with people back on the streets, a new neighborhood—albeit a poor and distressed one—was starting to take shape.

Gil Maldonado was one of those community builders who seem to emerge in every ethnic section of every city. Around the time Anne Saxe left the South Inlet, Maldonado turned an abandoned mom-and-pop corner store—this one on South Rhode Island Avenue—into a busy bodega. Stocking the shelves with cilantro, loaves of crusty white bread, plantains, religious candles, magic potions, and cans of Goya brand black beans and chickpeas, the shopkeeper catered to the tastes and needs of his neighbors. But Maldonado's store was more than just a place to buy familiar products. It was a community center, a place to get news and catch up on events at home and in Atlantic City. Customers hung around the counter gossiping and playing cards. It was also a banking center. Little white slips—IOUs for loans ranging from $5 to $50—stuck out of the cash register. Maldonado extended credit to people in the neighborhood to help them get through economic rough spots and all-too-frequent periods of unemployment. No saint, he surely took bets for the local racketeers on the daily numbers at the same time.[16]

Most of Maldonado's customers were Catholic. They wore gold medals around their necks, built shrines to patron saints in the corners of their rented apartments, and went to mass. Going to mass in the South Inlet meant going to Holy

Spirit Church. For years, Irish and Italian families had filled the pews in this tiny church, which was close enough to the beach that worshippers could hear waves smacking against Garden Pier's wooden supports between prayers. Some of the old congregants welcomed the new parishioners. Others greeted these darker-skinned, Spanish-speaking men and women with cold stares and mean glares. Most just left. Either they followed the parish school to the suburbs or they drove on Sunday mornings to services at St. Michael's or another of the city's Catholic churches. Before long, white flight turned Holy Spirit into a Puerto Rican church.

Father James Halley made the transition smoother. The thirty-something priest came to the church in the early 1970s. With his broad, handsome face and round ruddy cheeks, Halley looked like an Irish parish priest was supposed to look. He spoke with a slight stutter that gave him a kind of gentleness. But the breaks in his speech didn't stop him from learning Spanish. "The Irish priest who spoke Spanish" was how some locals referred to him. Halley's willingness to talk to his congregants in their own language gave them a strong sense of belonging to Holy Spirit. But Halley's idea of what a priest and a church should do added to this sense of identification. Although he never laid out his beliefs in print, Halley clearly adhered to the Catholic tradition of social activism. The church, he believed, had a role to play in parishioners' day-to-day lives. If worshipers sat through mass with their stomachs growling from hunger, the church needed to find them more food; if they lived under leaky roofs, the church needed to patch the holes; and if rats roamed through neighborhood streets, the church needed to clean up the area.

Under Halley's guidance, Holy Spirit became the South Inlet's most important community institution. Congregants gathered there for the Feast of San Juan and to light devotional candles to the Virgin of Mount Carmel. In the same rooms, they set up a trash clean-up drive, English-language classes, and a neighborhood watch program to combat crime. And it was at Holy Spirit or maybe at a nearby self-help center established in 1975 that Atlantic City Puerto Ricans entered the battle over the future of the community, their community.[17]

In 1976, local Puerto Ricans laid out plans for building, with government aid, a "Puerto Rico North" amid the faded apartment buildings and guesthouses of the South Inlet. "We want," one backer said, "to make not only [this] section but the entire city, [become as] it should and could be."[18] Planners pictured something that blended together a stop at a national pavillion at a world's fair with the grittier charms of an urban ethnic neighborhood, like Philadelphia's Italian Market or San Francisco's Chinatown. This idea of a tourist barrio—if you can't go to Puerto Rico, let's bring Puerto Rico and authentic Puerto Ricans to you—evolved in the mid-1970s into an idea of community salvation. Named Villa Santa Rosa after Saint Rose of Lima, the patron saint of the poor, the plans for the neighborhood called for turning a six-block section of the Inlet into a "showcase of Puerto Rican heritage" with "ethnic shops, grocery stores, and restaurants." Boosters imagined sidewalks packed with Latinos from New York, Philadelphia, and everywhere in between rubbing elbows with white women and men in search of a little "Spanish" flavor. At the center of Santa Rosa would be a small mountain range of high-rise housing projects with clean, modern apartments. Local Puerto Ricans would live there, work in the new stores and shops, and, in turn, recirculate their wages back into the community.[19]

The problem with the idea was the lack of investors. Who would be willing to spend money on a Puerto Rican tourist barrio? One can almost hear the cackles coming from the city's white political establishment when they first heard about the idea. Officially local leaders signed off on building Santa Rosa, but they didn't commit any resources to the project, so it never got off the ground. Others criticized, and even ridiculed, the proposal. A Jewish man demanded a kibbutz if Puerto Ricans got their barrio. Local NAACP leaders complained that Santa Rosa would foster, not eliminate, segregation and discrimination.[20] In the face of this opposition, nothing happened. The Inlet just keep rotting, and the Puerto Rican community kept taking shape.

LIFE ON NEW YORK AVENUE

In the late 1960s, the owner of the Fort Pitt bar on South New York Avenue, like most Atlantic City businesspeople, was looking for customers. At the same time, local political boss Hap Farley talked the state legislature into opening Richard Stockton State College in the area. Mixing higher education with countercultural values, the school started as a grand experiment. Students and faculty numbering in the hundreds lived and learned together at the Mayflower Hotel, a Boardwalk building long past its prime. The Fort Pitt targeted students and their teachers as its new market. To get them into his place, the owner featured beer cheap and rock-and-roll bands. But not many came through the doors. Down the street, however, long lines formed in front of Val's bar every night. The place didn't have live music or deals on drinks. What it did have was a reputation for serving gay men and treating them decently. Hoping to lure some of Val's customers his way, the owner of the Fort Pitts hired one of Val's bartenders. A few weeks later, a pair of male go-go dancers bopped and boogied on the bar. The place was jumping. Turning gay brought people into the place and onto the street.[21]

"New York Avenue," wrote a couple of Philadelphia reporters in 1970, "was the gayest street in town . . . [and] probably the liveliest." Twenty-four hours a day, they noted, guys in "tight shirts and deep-cut hip-huggers" moved from "one gay joint to another." "By the early 1970s," a drag queen named Seersucker Suit observed, New York Avenue "reached its peak." "It was alive," she added. "We had parties every night." To her, New York Avenue was like Christopher Street in New York City. "It had an identity, it had vitality, it was the only place in the entire city that was alive." A straight local businessman agrees with Seersucker Suit. "New York Avenue," he now says, was "alive. . . . [I]t was the only excitement that was around."[22]

New York Avenue and Atlantic City's gay scene were not born in the late 1960s with the press-grabbing Stonewall Rebellion. From the resort's earliest days, men interested in other men headed to the beach and Boardwalk. From the 1920s on, drag shows and the discreet men's club, Louise Mack's Entertainer's Club on Snake Alley, were part of the city's Midway attractions. A bar or two near the Convention Hall welcomed gay men as well. But still in those days, the city did not have a clear geographically defined or well-developed gay entertainment zone. That started to take shape during World War II.

Gay men came out "under fire" in Atlantic City during the "good war." With the military using the city's beaches as a D-Day training ground, the massive Convention Hall as an indoor drill field, and the Jazz Age hotels as dorms, hospitals, and recovery centers, soldiers from California to Maine, from gritty industrial towns and grassy streetcar suburbs packed the Boardwalk, movie palaces, restaurants, and clubs.[23] As they did, some members of the armed forces found their way over to the bars on New York and Westminster avenues. In Atlantic City, like elsewhere, mobilization, as Allan Berube has remarked, released some of the pressures that trapped so many "gay people in silence, isolation, and self-contempt." Freed from parental and community surveillance, young men and women, many for the first time, had room to explore their sexuality and erotic desires.[24] Quickly learning local urban sexual geographies, men sexually interested in men and women sexually interested in women wandered over to "combat zones" and "redlight districts." In Atlantic City, men who wanted to meet other men went to the Entertainer's Club and a couple of other New York Avenue bars featuring drag shows. Once this happened, a few other bars on the street welcomed gay men. At the same time, nearby guesthouses began to cater to gay customers. With more gay men around, New York Avenue and the bathroom on the Boardwalk at the end of the street became cruising spots. The development of these homosocial spaces was done by word of mouth; gay-friendly and tolerant spots did not advertise for fear of police or extralegal retribution.[25]

When the soldiers left town and white tourists returned to the Boardwalk after the war, gay life in Atlantic City became more developed and more visible. Postwar prosperity contributed to the growth of New York Avenue. Like most Americans, men interested in finding other men for homosexual encounters saw their incomes rise in the 1940s and 1950s. Again like other Americans, they spent some of their money on weekend trips and new Chevrolets. Cars, in particular, gave gay men increased mobility and freedom; they could get away from home faster and more easily than ever before.[26]

While New York Avenue remained on the city's social fringe throughout the 1950s, it was fast becoming a well-known focal point in an emerging Midatlantic gay resort scene. By then, the area around the street had three or four gay—really, gay tolerant—bars and a number of gay rooming houses. Yet the geography of gay tourism in Atlantic City remained in the immediate postwar era somewhat de-centralized. On summer weekends, gay men congregated on the beach in front of the Claridge Hotel. (They gathered there, several explain with a smile, because of the hotel's phallic-shaped peak.) At night, some men hung out at the bars along New York Avenue or at Louisa's, while others mingled with straight couples at the Madrid Club, Jockey Club, McCrory's Cafe, and the cocktail bar at the Brighton Hotel—all places that tolerated gay men as long as they dressed right and did not act too outrageously or touch each other in public.[27]

Sometime after the war, another bar, Snug Harbor, opened ten miles out of town and away from the local police. Getting there required a car and a pretty good map. The meeting place was east of the city in the piney woods at the end of a dirt road. Quiet during the week and the winter, on summer weekends in the 1940s and 1950s the converted barn turned into a boisterous bar and dance club for gay men visiting Atlantic City.[28]

Despite, or maybe because of, the growing visibility of New York Avenue and other area gay spots, gay tourists and residents did not escape the postwar back-lash against homosexuality. Throughout the 1950s and 1960s, gay men and women across America were harassed and denied the right of free association. As the fear of communism swelled and the ideology of domestic containment spread narrowing definitions of acceptable behavior, gay people found themselves tagged as sexual psychopaths, degenerates, deviants, and even communists. National magazines warned that "Homosexuals Are Dangerous" and "Lesbians Prey on the Weak." Joining the assault on homosexuals, Atlantic City business leaders, politi-cians, and police targeted gay men and gay-tolerant bars for attack.[29]

In 1951, several New York Avenue hotel owners protested the renewal of the liquor licenses of several bars—possibly gay-tolerant bars—on the southern end of the street.[30] Throughout the next decade, local authorities regularly shut down gay clubs. During this same period, many city taverns and grocery stores doubled as illegal lottery outlets; some even scribbled the daily numbers onto wood crates on the sides of their buildings so drivers could find out if they had hit the jackpot without getting out of their cars. Most of these places paid off the right person and remained open. Yet after complaints from religious leaders, Val's, the New

York Avenue gay bar down the street from the Fort Pitt, was closed for twenty-five days in 1953.[31] Three years later, the Social Action Committee of the Ministerial Association of Greater Atlantic City warned that "the homosexual situation [in the city] was 'acute.'" They complained about what they viewed as "a great reluctance to enforce the law" on vice. "Some arrests," they protested, "have been made in this area . . . to try to satisfy the clergy and to fool the public, but no fear has been put into the hearts of the law breakers."[32]

On the streets of Atlantic City in the 1950s and 1960s, individual gay men faced sporadic harassment. Because they never knew when a police officer would strike, most exercised caution in public. "You could not be too flamboyant," a long-time resident recalls.[33] Local business leader John Schultz remembers that the police regularly arrested cross-dressers and drag queens. There was one sergeant who, according to Schultz, "hated faggots." "He would come by Louisa's," Schultz explains, "and try to intimidate people. Louisa would always ask him if he was looking for one of his sons." Two things particularly irked one powerful local judge, Stephen A. D'Amico. He didn't like to hear the word "motherfucker," and he didn't like to see men in dresses. Whenever cases involving either of these offenses came before him, he threw the book at the accused.[34]

Early in the 1950s, the state Division of Alcoholic Beverage Control (ABC) joined the fight against gay bars. Formed at the close of Prohibition, the agency oversaw and regulated businesses serving alcohol. The New Jersey General Assembly explicitly empowered the ABC to close any licensed bar found to be catering to "known criminals, gangsters, . . . prostitutes, female impersonators, or other persons of ill repute." Moving in lockstep with the national postwar antihomosexual panic, liquor investigators began to target gay bars, insisting that "the mere presence of female impersonators in and upon licensed premises presents a definite social problem" and that the "mere thought of such perverts is repugnant to . . . a normal red-blooded man."[35] When the owners of an Asbury Park bar challenged the ABC's contention that homosexuals could be identified simply by observing them, which in turn became the basis for closing bars, a superior court judge upheld the legality of the raids, writing, "It is in the plumage that you recognize the bird."[36]

Not long after launching its statewide campaign against gay bars, the ABC focused on Louise Mack's club. Arguing that "exposure to homosexuals might be harmful to 'some members of the public'" and that "the congregating of homosexuals must be prohibited as a 'threat to the safety and morals of the public,'" the head of the liquor control agency authorized the suspension of Mack's license. One year later, the city closed her bar for a reported 190 days for unspecified reasons. In the early 1960s, undercover ABC agents returned to the Entertainer's

Club. Finding the bar filled with "undesirables," they ordered it closed for 240 days.[37]

Around the same time, the ABC turned its attention to Val's, the New York Avenue gay bar shut down in 1953. By this time, there were four gay bars in the immediate New York Avenue area, a few within a couple of blocks of the street, and another on South Mississippi Avenue next to the Convention Hall.[38] Located in a converted auto repair shop near the corner of New York and Pacific avenues, Val's looked like any other "shot and a beer" joint. It rarely closed and always seemed dark and smoky. The plain, narrow bar was U-shaped with wood stools on all three sides. In the back, there were a few tables that could easily be pushed to the side to make space for a dance floor. Across from the bar stood a shuffle-board machine that sometimes doubled as a stage.

Val's rather ordinary appearance masked its importance to gay Atlantic City. For starters, the bar lacked the formality of the Victorian-looking Entertainer's Club. Even more important, although owned and operated in later years by a straight couple, Val's functioned as a more open, more explicitly gay, and more overtly "out" place. It was, locals said, the first public place in the city where men could dance with each other and touch without being asked to leave.[39]

In 1966, the ABC began its second campaign against Val's. After a series of undercover visits, liquor authority officials concluded that the bar served "apparent homosexuals." When lawyers for Val's and two other New Jersey taverns shut down by the ABC later asked investigators how they determined the sexual orientation of bar patrons, the agents answered with steady confidence. Although one said that the men at Val's and the other clubs were "normally dressed" and showed "very good behavior, . . . they were," he noted, "conversing . . . in a lisping tone of voice, and . . . they used limp-wrist movements to each other." "One man," another agent testified, "would stick his tongue out at another and they would laugh and they would giggle."[40] Yet state officials were most alarmed by Val's tolerance of men dancing with other men. Because it allowed men to swing, shake, and shuffle together, the ABC issued three citations against the bar in 1966 and finally ordered it closed in 1967.

Val's owners and bartenders decided to fight back against the ABC. Almost taunting the liquor authority, Val's management took out newspaper advertisements in 1967 announcing its intention to stay open "all summer long despite rumors to the contrary." In an even bolder move, Val's took the ABC to court. Two other taverns cited for serving homosexuals, one in Newark and the other in Trenton, joined Val's in challenging the liquor board's power to close down bars for no other reason than the presumed presence of gay men and lesbians on licensed premises. The Philadelphia-based Homosexual Law Reform Society

(HLRS), an important early gay rights organization, immediately understood the significance of the case and loaned its financial, tactical, and legal support to the fight. If Val's won, HLRS activists believed, gay men and lesbians in New Jersey would finally gain the right to freely assemble.[41]

Throughout the spring of 1967, the case formally known as *One Eleven Wines and Liquors, Inc. v. Division of Alcoholic Beverage Control* wound its way through the New Jersey courts, eventually ending up before the state supreme court. Surprising many, the justices unanimously ruled that "'well-behaved homosexuals' cannot be forbidden to patronize taverns." Reversing a lower-court's order, they maintained that the ABC "was not justified in suspending or revoking licenses because apparent homosexuals were permitted to congregate at bars." One member of the bench, while agreeing with the decision, cautioned that "although well-behaved homosexuals cannot be forbidden to patronize taverns, they may not engage in any conduct which would be offensive to public decency . . . [such as] . . . (men kissing each other on the lips, etc.)."[42]

In the wake of its courtroom triumph, Val's became a regional symbol of gay resistance to government attacks. Men from all over the East Coast made the pilgrimage to Atlantic City to pay tribute to the bar's stand against state harassment. It hardly mattered when Val's started to charge a cover fee; the lines outside just grew longer. The money, the owners said, went to defray legal costs. Happy to contribute, some threw in more than the minimum. In many ways, the response to Val's victory served as a less dramatic, but still important and revealing, precursor to the fierce resolve to resist harassment that exploded at the Stonewall bar in New York City two years later.[43]

Val's successful challenge of the ABC also marked a key shift in the sexual geography of Atlantic City. After 1967, the whole block, one man observed, "turned." That's when the owner of the Fort Pitt hired male go-go dancers. A few months later, the owner of the bar across the street from the Fort Pitt turned his place into a gay bar. Then a kind of domino effect rolled over South New York Avenue. Within a couple of years, the Saratoga, a one-time country-and-western joint, and the Rendezvous, a former jazz club, became gay bars. At the same time, several more Snake Alley rooming houses turned themselves into inexpensive gay-friendly hotels. "Do you know what happens across the street?" Albert Freeman of 17 South New York Avenue asked city commissioners in 1971. "There are men kissing men and women kissing women," he told them.[44]

A wave of antigay backlash up and down the East Coast added to New York Avenue's growing popularity. Located forty miles south of Atlantic City at the very tip of New Jersey, Cape May, with its gingerbread houses and Coast Guard base, had a reputation in the postwar years as a quiet gay resort. Toward the end of the 1965 summer season, local merchants and city council members held a closed-door meeting to "discuss and discourage the establishment of Cape May as a southern New Jersey Fire Island." (An hour east of Manhattan, Fire Island was widely known as New York City's gayest beach.) To keep gay men out, they passed an ordinance making it illegal for men to wear short bathing suits on the city's beaches. Just to make sure that the decree would be enforced, they voted to provide police officers with rulers and tape measures. That same summer, city officials in nearby Rehoboth Beach, Delaware, tried to discourage homosexuals from "congregat[ing] like bees in a swarm in . . . the area." Several years later, around the time that the New Jersey Supreme Court affirmed the right of homosexuals to freely congregate, the New York State Liquor Commission launched a crackdown on New York City gay bars. As Empire State liquor agents harassed patrons of Gotham gay bars and suspended and revoked the licenses of these establishments, some men and women decided to play things safe and take the three-hour trip to Atlantic City, where, according to a newspaper account, they found a more "permissive atmosphere."[45]

By the time of the Stonewall Rebellion in 1969—a protest triggered by the repressive tactics of New York City police and state ABC representatives—there were eight gay clubs and a number of gay-friendly shops and restaurants on South New York Avenue and the adjoining streets. Looking back, Val's supreme court victory seems to have propelled the growth and centralization of gay space in Atlantic City. Yet the development of New York Avenue was not solely the result of Val's legal triumph or legal crackdowns elsewhere. Other economic and social developments, happening outside of the gay community, were at work here as well. Desegregation, white flight, disinvestment, and an accompanying shift in middle-class perceptions of urban spaces proved to be just as important, if not as obvious, factors in the growth of gay tourism in Atlantic City. But it was emptiness—both literally and figuratively—that really mattered.

"Nobody wanted anything to do with the city," a gay man from Philadelphia says about Atlantic City in the 1970s. "So," he adds, "no one cared if gay men moved into town. . . . Gay people were not welcome in other places, but there was nothing in Atlantic City, so they tolerated the gay community because they had nothing." Emptiness, he believes, created the social space for "outness." Another gay man adds that when "respectable Philadelphians," meaning, of course, straight white Philadelphians, "headed to the family beaches around it, Atlantic City was left to us." New York Avenue, argues another frequent visitor, flourished because its gay patrons "didn't offend anyone—there was no one to offend." As yet another man put it, no one was watching them. Atlantic City's urban decline, he maintains, meant there were fewer hostile heterosexuals around to intimidate gay men and make them feel threatened, unwanted, and self-conscious. Given the homophobia of the times, it was easier, these men believe, to create open and vibrant gay leisure spaces because no one else was there.[46]

These white men's sense of emptiness is revealing. Atlantic City was not actually empty in the early 1970s. Although loaded-down moving trucks pulled out of town each day, tens of thousands of people still lived in the row houses and apartment buildings on the streets that Monopoly made famous. But increasingly most of these people were poor, and many were African American and Puerto Rican. Blue-collar and middle-class white gay men, the people who came to Atlantic City, somehow erased these people from their memories and from the city's urban landscape. Even more important, mainstream investors, bankers, and real estate agents looked at the city through racially skewed lenses. Apparently, to them, the presence of so many poor people and so many people of color meant that the city's homes and businesses had no value. And to them, a city with no value was an empty city.

However, a smaller group of less well connected and established investors— both gay and straight—seized on the opportunities of the apparent emptiness. Taking advantage of sinking property values, businesspeople bought the buildings on New York Avenue and converted them into gay clubs, restaurants, shops, and rooming houses. Emptiness also put a brake on police harassment. Local officials, it seems, did not want to scare off the city's only expanding tourist sector. One other factor might have helped to seal New York Avenue off from the police and other forms of harassment. Rumor had it that several clubs along the street remained in mob hands in the 1970s.[47]

By the mid-1970s, New York Avenue had mushroomed into a full-blown gay scene. City watchers estimated that 3–5,000 mostly, although not exclusively, white gay men and a few white lesbians roamed the streets on summer Saturday nights in the 1970s. From Memorial Day to the Miss America Pageant a week after Labor Day, gay men flooded into town on Thursday nights and stayed until late Sunday afternoon.

New York Avenue's growth depended, in particular, on reasonably priced, even cheap, accommodations nicknamed "fraternities" by gay tourists. As the city's straight tourism sector sagged in the 1960s and 1970s, room rates around town dropped. Inexpensive rooms, in turn, opened up the city to a broad spectrum of middle- and working-class gay tourists. Those who didn't stay the weekend drove down from Philadelphia for the day. "You could nap," one Philadelphia man remembers, "wake up, party, nap, wake up, party until you were ready to go home."

"It was not unusual," he adds, "to close the bars in Philadelphia at 2:00 AM, drive to the shore on one of the small roads, and get there in time to throw beer cans at the [rising] sun."[48]

After those long nights in the 1970s, many revelers dragged themselves out of bed to go to the gay beach located in front of the Claridge Hotel, the same beach that gay men had been going to for years. Getting up early was the only way to get space for a towel. By noon, every inch of sand was taken up with sunbathers and their gear. The beach buzzed with activity. Men wore string bikinis, dresses, gowns, and headpieces. Sometimes couples and friends dined on the beach on tables decorated with linen, crystal, silver, and bouquets of flowers. Even after the town emptied and beach space opened up, gay men kept on going to the gay beach in front of the Claridge. At twilight, everyone headed back to New York Avenue, where the party started all over again.[49]

By the mid-1970s, New York Avenue and the adjoining streets began to resemble a mature business district. The throngs of people led to more investment and eventually to a growing specialization within the market. Although the area never became a full-blown residential area, like San Francisco's Castro district, some gay men and lesbians did rent apartments for the summer above the bars and restaurants lining the street. Still, the city's year-round gay community remained dispersed even as the tourist scene became more concentrated and diverse. Each club and restaurant along New York Avenue catered to a specific segment of the gay leisure market. The Entertainer's Club remained a discreet, rather subdued spot for well-dressed, often older men. Owned by Billy Mott from Birmingham, Alabama, Mama Mott's called itself the "gayest place in town" and served heaping plates of pasta on red-and-white-checked tablecloths under black velvet paintings of men in erotic poses. Frank's X-tra Dry Cafe, located just across Pacific Avenue, featured quarter-pound sandwiches and twenty-five-cent beers twenty-four hours a day. The after-the-beach crowd congregated at the Lark, a couple of doors down from the Boardwalk. Lyle's was the place for "breakfast and gossip," the Front Porch for lunch, and the Puka Lani Lounge for cocktails. Above the Lark stood the Ramrod, a male-only, leather-only, country-and-western bar with a pool table in the back. The Chester, Rendezvous, and Chez Paree featured big dance floors and DJs playing disco music at full bass-thumping volume until the sun came up. Across from the Chez, Dee's Truck Stop served breakfast, subs, and snacks "By Gay People—For Gay People." The Grand Central Resort, a self-proclaimed get-away with "something for everyone" opened toward the end of the 1970s and had a piano bar on one floor and a disco on another. Lesbians and older men, although not the same crowd that hung out at Louise's, went to the Brass Rail, "Home of the Big Mug." Late at night, the Saratoga and Dirty Edna's (the old Fort Pitt) presented drag shows. Dee Dee Lewis would sing, "It Should Have Been Me"; Diane Jones would whisper, "I Can't Stand the Rain"; and Tinsel Garland would cover the Nancy Sinatra hit, "These Boots Are Made for Walking." On Sunday mornings, gay men gathered at the Grand Central Resort to worship at the Metropolitan Community Church.[50]

Sex was a central part of New York Avenue's appeal. The street took off at the moment when growing numbers of gay men believed, as one man put it, "Sex was liberating and more sex was more liberating."[51] New York journalists Jack and Lige celebrated Atlantic City's sexual openness. "If you're tired of piss elegant showy resorts where guys are more concerned with what they're wearing than with the many joys of sodomy," they wrote in *SCREW* magazine, "pack your duds and try a weekend in Atlantic City."[52] Sex was, according to a Philadelphia man, "free and open" in Atlantic City in the 1970s. Yet it wasn't always free. On most days, young men and teenagers congregated near the public bathroom and pavilion on the Boardwalk at the end of the street or leaned against a railing outside of the Lark and the Chez Paree. Throughout the night, men walked off with other men down the Boardwalk or went around the corner in a car. Usually they came back with a $20 bill and a pint of cheap vodka.[53] Someone looking for a trick might wander toward the back of the Ramrod bar. An open door at a Snake Alley guesthouse was often an invitation for sex. "I believe the DeVille had a dark hallway for a while where sex occurred," one man recalls. "I remember specifically," he adds, "seeing a man with a partially open door and going into his room and having sex." Another Atlantic City visitor jokes, "You could leave the bar and turn two tricks on your way home at four in the morning." Hearing this story, another man cracks, "Only two?"[54]

Drugs were another feature of the New York Avenue scene. Locals called the same Boardwalk pavilion where male prostitutes congregated "Acid Hill." Some nights, the "Quaalude Queen" stumbled down New York Avenue passing out the powerful barbiturates. "Ups," "black beauties," "brown and clears," and other kinds of amphetamines were as easy to find on the street as a beer or a gin and tonic. "Sex, drugs, and disco" was how one man remembered New York Avenue.[55]

Before the mid-1970s, straight men and women kept their distance from New York Avenue's packed bars and crowded restaurants. Occasionally Boardwalk strollers stopped to gawk at the street's wild, club-hopping, party-all-night scene. After a few jokes about "fairies" and "faggots" punctuated by limp-wristed hand gestures, they continued their journeys through dusty Boardwalk souvenir shops, broken-down arcades, and tired-looking saltwater taffy stores. In the mid-1970s, however, straight women and men started to trickle over to the street to dance, eat a bowl of pasta at Mama Mott's, buy drugs, or get a dose of the place's fantastic exuberance. Bartender Mike Mann remembers that around this time his straight friends started to pester him to take them dancing at the Chester or the Rendezvous. About the same time, Herb Tapper recalls looking up at the Front Porch restaurant. Seeing the eatery packed with neatly dressed straight couples, he remembers thinking, "[T]his is the end." New York Avenue, he now believes, was a victim of its own success. Once there were straight eyes on the street, staring at the men in tight shirts and hip-hugger pants, the area, Tapper maintains, lost some of its anonymity and with it, some of its vitality, recklessness, and outness.[56]

Although New York Avenue pulsed with life, gay tourism remained virtually invisible to the city's chief financial movers and shakers. Just like they never really backed Villa Santa Rosa, municipal leaders never considered supporting the further growth and development of the local economy's gay business and tourism sector. Instead, the Chamber of Commerce, Hotel and Motel Association, and Visitors Bureau continued to search for other ways to revive the resort, which for them meant recreating a bright utopia for straight, white, middle-class families looking for a weekend of fantasy and fun or, in Pauline Hill's case, remaking the city into a suburb. Despite all the plans for new hotels and Boardwalk attractions, no major bank or developer wanted to invest in Atlantic City during the pre-casino years.

Undeterred local bankers and business leaders continued in the 1970s to look for other ways to boost the city's struggling economy, ignoring the burgeoning gay tourist sector and the city's growing Puerto Rican and black neighborhoods. Instead, like their counterparts in other deindustrialized cities, they looked for ways to bring middle-class families back to town, not to live, but to visit. For city officials in Cleveland and Baltimore this meant building neotraditional baseball stadiums. In Camden, New Jersey, and Bridgeport, Connecticut, two horribly blighted cities, this meant aquariums, and in San Antonio, Texas, and Augusta, Georgia, this meant the construction of riverwalks with the same restaurants and shops found in the malls. Atlantic City leaders thought about all of these ideas, but they could not tear their eyes away from the bright lights of Las Vegas.

8

Disneyland
and the
Devil's Bargain

Everyone was looking for Reese Palley. After New Jersey voters approved the gambling referendum in 1976 on the second go-round, paving the way for casinos in Atlantic City, print journalists and television producers rushed to town. Restaurant owners and gas station attendants told the newspeople to talk to Palley. They said the art dealer was a real character, a local guaranteed to give them "good copy."

Journalists learned that Palley was in his mid-fifties. They found out that his father once owned a jewelry store just off of Atlantic Avenue, he went to local schools, and for a time, he worked in the family business appraising the "priceless" diamonds that tourists purchased at the city's auction houses. During his twenties, Palley left South Jersey to attend the London School of Economics. Degree in hand, the jeweler's son drifted back to town in the late 1950s as the city's lights began to fade somewhat.[1]

Palley's personal fortunes rose in almost inverse proportion to the city's downward slide. Nothing came cheap at his gift shop and art gallery, located on the ground floor of the Marlborough-Blenheim Hotel. Letter openers started at $45 and paperweights, Ceska glassware, Oriental rugs, wall hangings, and, in the words of one travel guide, "the most stunning estate jewelry found anywhere" sold for much, much more.[2] Most people came to see Palley's selection of Edward Boehm's "limited edition porcelain collectibles."[3] The Trenton ceramicist created realistic representations of flowers, ballet dancers, and historical figures, but he was most famous for his birds and animals. Collectors paid tens of thousands of dollars for Boehm's preening chipmunks, prairie chickens, and proud golden eagles, which over time appeared in shows at the Metropolitan Museum of Art,

Buckingham Palace, and the Vatican. Richard Nixon even gave a pair of mute swans worth $50,000 to Chairman Mao on the president's visit to Peking in 1972. Reese Palley's near-national monopoly of the Boehm birds turned the art dealer into the "merchant to the rich" and just about the only person making money in Atlantic City in the days before the casinos landed on the Boardwalk.

Background information like this was just the start of the Reese Palley stories. Locals recalled how Palley once said that nude beaches were the city's surest cure for urban decay. Another time, they remembered, he staged a life-sized Monopoly game, replacing the usual thimble and race-car pieces with female undergraduates in bikinis.[4] When the dice directed the women to jail, actors dressed as Keystone Kops sprinted out and put them behind bars. Everyone's favorite Reese Palley story was the one about his fiftieth birthday. To mark the occasion, the shop owner chartered two Boeing 747 jets, each with a cartoon image of his face plastered to the fuselage, to take 700 "furred women" and other overdressed customers to Paris. On the way there, he treated his guests to champagne, filet mignon, cake, and a screening of *The French Connection*. Once they arrived, he put them up at the four-star Inter-Continental Hotel and took them to Maxim's. Although Palley spent $200,000 on the celebration, the trip was hardly free for the participants. One hundred and forty guests bought $750 Salvador Dali lithographs, and several purchased $10,000 Boehm birds from their host while overseas. Palley made a $50,000 profit on his birthday, only enhancing his reputation as the merchant to the rich.[5]

With stories of porcelain knickknacks and jet-setting birthday bashes filling their notepads, reporters walked into Palley's store. A man slightly over six feet tall who appeared a few inches shorter because of a "vulturish slouch" greeted the journalists. Invariably Palley had on his uniform, a jet-black turtleneck and dark pants. Thick black-framed glasses, the style that army doctors handed out during World War II, covered the top of his roundish face, making him look a little like an owl or maybe Elvis Costello's father. Frizzy patches of salt-and-pepper hair popped out of his head in a sort of free jazz pattern. Long before it was fashionable, he sported a neatly trimmed, more gray than black goatee. Then there were his matching eyes and smile. Both went off like flashbulbs as he talked. And Palley liked to talk and make those lights flash.[6]

Most correspondents started their interviews by asking Palley about his nickname. No, he would say, he wasn't the merchant to the rich, he was more like a "peddler with a fancy pushcart."[7] "I perform the social service," he once said, "of giving people something to spend money on." "I like newly rich people," he told the same reporter. "They're more honest. They're open, hungry, receptive. . . . What I'm doing is putting fine things into the hands of people who are so unsure of themselves that they have to come to me."[8] Once he'd established himself as a shrewd, iconoclastic, and unsentimental businessman, even a pop psychologist, Palley turned to the subject of gambling. His answers on this front were jarring yet well rehearsed.

Palley told television producer Albert Rose in 1978, "[T]his is the beginning of a kind of ultimate illusion."[9] "Thousands of new jobs are on the way," he said to a pair of *New York* magazine reporters a year earlier. Atlantic City would, he believed, once again become "a safe space . . . for people who have the money and would like to have the privilege [to spend it]."[10] Palley told another newsman that once gambling came, "[E]veryone will be here motivated by their fantasies." While in town, he wanted visitors to feel "a little taller, a little prettier, a little sexier."[11]

If Palley's new Atlantic City would share the power of personal transformation through consumption with the lost city, it would share almost nothing else with the physical city of his youth. Asked in 1978 what the city needed, Palley responded, "[A] bulldozer eight blocks long." "No one should live here," he continued. "There is no logic for residential housing in Atlantic City." The only reason that the elderly, African American and Puerto Rican families, and gay tourists were in Atlantic City in the first place, he insisted, was "because it was cheap." But that was sure to change with gambling. Along the Boardwalk, he envisioned "thousands of first class hotel rooms," "[f]irst-rate rides cheek to jowl with Gucci," and "[l]ots of good restaurants and bars." From Pacific Avenue to the bay, he pictured nothing but parking lots. "Black[s] and old people would be moved out of Atlantic City," he explained. "Why?" he asked rhetorically and then answered, "Land is expensive."[12]

"Do the people who operate Disneyland live in Disneyland?" Palley pressed the reporters.[13] The answer was "no." Palley imagined the new gambling city as a safe place for recreation and that's all. The city as a place to live and work would be replaced by walled-off fantasylands ringed by parking lots. Most people laughed when they heard the merchant's remarks, although some city residents cringed, thinking that they would be the ones standing in the way of the eight-block-wide bulldozers. "They want to push us out," an older man shuddered. "Don't want no poor people. Reese said that. No more poor people in Atlantic City; push them all out."[14]

Reese Palley turned out to be something of a prophet, although his vision was not completely accurate. He knew that gambling was a "devil's bargain" and that, like tourist development everywhere, it would exact a tremendous toll on Atlantic City. Those bulldozers he envisioned did come, and they plowed down much of the city and much of its past along the way. But the power machines didn't, as the art dealer predicted, get rid of all the poor families and people of color. And for those still living in the city there was more crime and congestion and less of just about everything else that makes day-to-day life livable.

The bulldozers didn't, however, remake the city's essential character; they didn't destroy the power of race to etch lines onto the city's map. Class, too, that close cousin of race in post–civil rights America, continued to matter, perhaps more than ever. In their roles as urban planners, casino companies didn't discriminate like the Boardwalk entrepreneurs of old. They unleashed the bulldozers with the same ferocious force in African American and Puerto Rican neighborhoods as they did in blue-collar white ones. The battle that unfolded was in many ways, as Hal Rothman notes, a contest between "locals of all colors" against "outsiders of all colors."[15]

THE CAMPAIGN FOR CASINOS

It is hard to know exactly when the campaign for gambling began in Atlantic City. Locals like to talk about how the city has always had gambling, and they are, of course, right. Almost every corner store sold a chance at the daily number, and dozens of clubs, including the 500 Club, Babette's, and the Bath and Turf Club, operated illegal casinos. But legalized gambling was another matter.[16]

In the late 1950s, Meredith Fox of the women's division of the Atlantic City Chamber of Commerce spoke out in favor of Las Vegas–style gambling. She predicted that slot machines and roulette wheels would increase employment and raise tax revenues. She asked the chamber's male directors to endorse the idea. Knowing the stigma at that time against legalized gambling, the men brushed aside the idea. As one chamber member said, "It's a very controversial issue and will bring sharp reactions." That's where the proposal died. For the next decade, no one talked much about legalized gambling in public. When the idea came up again, much had changed, for the worse, in Atlantic City and across the state.[17]

By 1970, the campaign that would bring casinos to town had started in earnest. That year, Atlantic County's political boss, Hap Farley, by then on his last legs, tried to sneak a gambling bill through the back door of the legislature, but he couldn't do it. Local leaders, however, remained transfixed by Las Vegas and were convinced that only casinos could save their sad city in ruins. This conviction grew as the Warner closed, the Ritz Carlton slipped into bankruptcy, and the Uptown urban renewal site turned from a promised land into an open prairie. Yet before blackjack tables could operate on the Boardwalk and perform their economic magic, gambling advocates had to first get lawmakers and then state voters to sign off on the idea.

The prospect of casinos along the Boardwalk brought together people who didn't usually agree. Obviously Atlantic City hotel and restaurant owners, Boardwalk merchants and rolling-chair operators backed the measure. They spoke about gambling as a panacea. No matter the problem—unemployment, urban decay, or race relations—casinos, they said, would fix it. Organized labor, particularly the construction unions, supported Atlantic City gambling as well. But the key to getting legislation passed, as everyone knew, was gaining the backing of voters north of the Pinelands, people not often concerned with South Jersey. "For generations Atlantic City was known as the World's Playground," explained a North Jersey gambling booster. "It is my desire that this proposal will signal an economic rebirth that will return the city to its image as a resort of world prominence." But even more seductively, he talked of gaming as a magic bullet, as something for nothing. As "desirable" as rebuilding Atlantic City might be, this man continued, "this . . . is not the principal aim of the proposal. The ultimate goal is the benefits that will accrue to the state as a whole."[18]

By the mid-1970s, New Jersey, like many states across the country, stood on the brink of fiscal disaster. Over the previous decade, state spending grew faster than revenues. Some thought the state had no choice but to raise property and income taxes. Yet at the same time, lawmakers confronted the first tremors of a tax revolt that would culminate in California voters approving Proposition 13, a ballot initiative capping property taxes and slashing funds for local governments. From Maine to Oregon in the early 1970s, home owners balked at paying additional levies and so did consumers. As complaints about taxes rose, states turned to games of chance to address the shortfall. In the 1960s, New Hampshire, for instance, started a lottery, while New York officials approved off-track betting on horses. Sensing the changes in the fiscal and moral climate, casino backers from North and South Jersey promised that gambling offered a "painless" alternative to cuts in social services and increased taxes.[19]

Atlantic City gaming proponents gained a powerful ally in Brendan Byrne. Running for governor in 1973, the North Jersey Democrat pledged his support to gambling in Atlantic City if the idea won approval in state and local referendums and if the state ran the tables and machines. After winning the election, Byrne reiterated his support for gambling in Atlantic City and only there. Worried about the appearance of regional favoritism, lawmakers passed a bill calling for statewide gaming, subject to local approval. Atlantic City would get the first crack at government-operated casinos, but after a few years any community could vote in slot machines and blackjack tables. Reluctantly, Byrne signed the measure. Now it was up to the electorate to decide the matter.[20]

New Jersey poll watchers predicted an easy passage for the referendum. Not wanting to take a chance, the bill's backers raised several hundred thousand dollars to trumpet gambling's virtues. They hailed the measure as Atlantic City's economic savior, saying that the casinos would cut welfare rolls and create thousands of good jobs in the hotels and related industries. "We see," remarked a pro-gambling Atlantic City hotel owner, "people leaving New Jersey to travel all over the world for vacations and conventions. . . . We'd like them to remain in New Jersey and the catalyst to draw them would be a casino." The casinos he dreamed about would resemble swank European emporiums "with elegance and class, and . . . dress codes . . . [to] maintain a modest decorum." Atlantic City mayor Joseph Bradway, Jr., hit every corner of the state telling civic groups that he saw casino gambling as the only way to save his city. For workers, he said, the casinos would create year-round employment, not just summer jobs. To voters indifferent to Atlantic City's plight, both the mayor and the hotel owner stressed that the casinos would solve the state's tax problems as well.[21]

A loose coalition of religious leaders and law enforcement officials calling themselves No Dice formed to block the referendum's passage. Despite raising less than $50,000, they still managed to get their message out. Members argued that gambling would bring only an "insignificant amount of money" into state coffers, not the windfall that boosters promised. Others predicted that casinos would not return Atlantic City to its glory days, but would make the town into a thin strip of "gaudy honky-tonk[s]." Above all, No Dice latched onto the issue of organized crime. They denounced gambling as "irresponsible and immoral," charging that it would bring truckloads of "pimps, loan sharks, and prostitutes" into the state. Atlantic City's long history of boss rule and public corruption made it, they said, an easy target for mobsters looking to get into the casino racket. On the Sunday before the referendum vote, No Dice played its strongest hand. Three thousand members of the clergy preached that morning on the evils of gambling.[22]

Two days later, the referendum went down to defeat by a 3–2 margin. The opposition was staunchest in North Jersey suburbs where people feared a rise in crime and worried about slot machines in the gas stations and pharmacies near their homes. Atlantic City business leaders woke up the day after the vote in a collective funk. Many grimly joked about the whole town sinking into the ocean and about the lights going out for good.[23] But after hanging their heads for a week, casino boosters got back to work. They remained convinced that gambling was the only remedy for their city's problems. The question, then, was how to convince a majority of state voters that this would not harm them in any way and would, in fact, serve their own interests.

As a first step, local leaders started to analyze the returns from the 1974 election. Obviously the religious opposition and talk of whores and mob hitmen hurt the cause, so they had to make gambling appear less ominous. They also learned that the idea of slot machines anywhere in the state turned people against the referendum. Mostly they found that they hadn't given enough people enough reasons to vote in favor of casinos. In order to get voters to pull the yes lever, gaming proponents had to offer something more than the salvation of a single worn-out city and vague promises of painless tax relief. They concluded, moreover, that an off-year election exaggerated the opposition's power. Making the vote coincide with a presidential election, they believed, would help their cause. Opinion polls told them that African Americans in particular and working-class voters in general supported gambling more than other groups and that they were more likely to show up at the ballot box when the White House was at stake.[24]

In 1976, New Jersey citizens once again voted on gambling. The referendum's wording reflected the lessons learned from the earlier defeat. The second time around, the measure called for privately owned casinos in Atlantic City only. Taking the state out of the equation opened up wide fundraising channels. With private casino companies hungry to break into the huge, untapped East Coast market on their side, the Committee to Rebuild Atlantic City (CRAC), as the pro-casino forces called themselves, raised more than a million dollars, doubling what they had collected two years earlier.[25]

Using its big bank account, CRAC hired the wizard political consultant Sanford Weiner. The California-based media specialist seemed at all times to be in a frenzy, a phone attached to his ear, a burning cigarette dangling from his mouth, and a Styrofoam cup of coffee plastered to his hand. Looks aside, Weiner had an impressive track record. When he arrived in Atlantic City, he had won 90 percent of the campaigns he had orchestrated. Sensing the challenge ahead, he crafted a plan to get the pro-gambling message out beyond South Jersey. During the fall of 1976, he put teams of "regular" Atlantic City folk through crash courses on casino gambling's economic benefits and then sent them across the state to talk at church socials, library lunches, and town hall meetings. When he could, he tried to match the messengers with the audiences. Accountants talked to accountants, teachers talked to teachers, and construction workers spoke with construction workers. As Election Day neared, Weiner bombarded the airwaves with 5,700 advertisements on eighty television and radio stations. Leaving nothing to chance, Weiner spent $170,000 in "street money" in the state's African American neighborhoods to pay for vans, taxis, and baby-sitters in order to get out the vote.[26]

Only Steve Perskie played a larger role than Weiner in the referendum campaign. Brash, young, even cocky, Perskie, the nephew of Marvin Perskie, the dean of Atlantic County Democrats and long-time rival of Hap Farley, had been in the state house for just five years when the gaming proposal came up a second time. But he was already a key player. A fast talker and even quicker study, the Yale-educated Perskie took little time to master the arts of lawmaking and networking.

Almost as soon as he got to Trenton, he moved into Governor Byrne's inner circle. The state's chief executive, in turn, called on Perskie, by then a familiar pro-gambling face in the media with his black wavy hair and thick glasses, to help write the new referendum in 1976.

After poring over returns and grilling political insiders, Perskie concluded, like others had, that there were not enough New Jersey residents who cared solely about Atlantic City's problems to get the bill approved. Attaching a more broadly sympathetic face to gambling, therefore, represented the pro-casino forces' biggest challenge. Under Perskie's new bill, the revenues from gaming would go into a fund earmarked specifically to pay the utility bills and property taxes of the state's elderly and differently abled poor. Now a vote for gambling was a vote for your grandmother or an unfortunate neighbor. A radio spot that ran in the campaign's closing days told the story of a down-on-her-luck seventy-two-year-old woman. "Although old and alone," a kindly voice explained, "she can still be helped if only you vote for casino gambling in Atlantic City."[27]

Perhaps Perskie's shrewdest move took place behind closed doors. During the 1974 campaign, Hap Farley, the one-time "boss of the Boardwalk," who was voted out of office in 1971, stayed at home. Two years later, he returned to the campaign trail, working the back rooms and urging his old political allies to support gambling and get out the vote. After a visit from Hap, Bergen County sheriff Joseph Job, known then as the "Farley of the North," threw his weight—some said that added up to 250,000 votes—behind the measure. The kingpin of Camden, Angelo Errichetti, followed suit, and so did several others.[28]

As night fell over the Boardwalk on Election Day, November 2, 1976, the air got that icy, mean feeling of winter at the shore. Even conventioneers stayed inside on these kinds of nights. By early evening, poll watchers predicted an easy passage for the gambling referendum. All over Atlantic City—on New York Avenue, at Ky. at the Curb, inside the Marlborough-Blenheim's lobby, on the front stoops of Ducktown, and in the cramped apartments around Holy Spirit Church in the South Inlet—people braved the cold and came out for the night. It felt like the height of the summer season in the old days. Shopkeepers and bellhops snake-danced down the Boardwalk. Waitresses and auctioneers sang songs in taverns as bartenders poured free shots of whiskey and glasses of beer. Outside, jitney drivers and shoe salesmen hollered until they couldn't make another sound.[29] Local restaurateur Arnold Orsatti beamed, "I feel beautiful." To Steve Perskie, it seemed like "everyone was coming from the same wedding . . . and shaking hands."[30] The party lasted until dawn when the morning newspaper hit the sidewalks with a headline screaming, "CITY REBORN."[31]

"Everyone," Reese Palley remembered a few years after the street parties, "was a millionaire that night."[32] Still bleary-eyed, Ralph Hill, the Chalfonte-Haddon Hall's superintendent of bellhops and doormen, told a reporter on the day after the referendum passed, "There will be more jobs. Every January and February we have to lay off 90 percent of the help because there is no business. With casinos, the hotels will be full year around, and we can have steady employment."[33] Wasting little time, the owners of Greenwell's, a Northside tavern, started to redecorate that very same day.[34] "When gambling was passed," John Schultz, a New York Avenue businessman, recalled, "everybody told me, 'It's gonna kill gay life in Atlantic City—gays don't gamble. But I got news for you. . . . They do gamble and they love the beach. This place is busting wide open, and the gays are carving up a section for themselves."[35] Curtis Kugel, the owner of Luigi's Restaurant, predicted, "[T]he city will turn around and be what it was in the twenties and thirties." Still, he warned, sounding one of the few sober notes in the months after the vote, the city might experience slow growth at first, but once four or five casinos opened, he expected to see a "tremendous boom."[36]

Hill, Schultz, and Kugel dreamed of a spillover effect, a flood really, from gambling. Everybody used this same run-off metaphor. Atlantic City residents believed that the money from the casinos would mend the cracks in the sidewalks, slice the welfare rolls, reduce crime, and cut unemployment. Mostly they thought gambling dollars would bring back the past. Nearly everyone imagined the casinos turning Atlantic City once again into the Queen of Resorts. Well-dressed crowds, resembling a cross between the handsome Boardwalk throng of the 1940s and the glamorous gamblers in James Bond movies, would walk down the promenade past new gold-trimmed designer shops and top-end restaurants. Along Atlantic Avenue, the plywood would come down off storefronts. Delis and stationery stores, barbers and beauticians would open up again on side streets. The movies would come back and so would the hot dance shows at the Club Harlem. Even the rolling chairs and the pushers would be back. At the same time, people would come back to the neighborhoods, sprucing up abandoned houses with new windows and fresh paint. Once again, there would be couples and families walking down the streets unafraid of muggers and murderers. The world these Atlantic City residents and businesspeople conjured up was a dusted-off image of the past. They didn't think about the corporations or the state or the devil's bargain they had just entered into.

For the moment, however, the battle over Atlantic City's future shifted from the Boardwalk to paneled conference rooms in Trenton. Day after day in the first few months of 1977, lawmakers and state officials hammered out the details of the state's Casino Control Act. They stipulated who could own a casino, who could work there, how big and elaborate the establishments had to be, how long they could stay open, whether or not they could issue credit and give away drinks, and how many bars, lounges, and restaurants each had to have. Several issues, in particular, weighed on officials' minds as they tussled over the law's grammar. First, they wanted to make sure that the mob stayed out of Atlantic City. To keep organized crime away, they barred anyone with a criminal record from working in the casinos. Second, lawmakers worried that gambling would turn Atlantic City into another Las Vegas, that is, the old Las Vegas. While they wanted the crowds, they didn't want twenty-four-hour gambling. They didn't want noisy slot machines in every bar and grocery store; they didn't want to see little casinos on every corner. They didn't want Atlantic City to become a tacky casino city. "The end is not the casino industry," Steve Perskie declared. "The end is the tourism, resort and convention industry in Atlantic City in particular, and [in] the State of New Jersey."[37] In order to kick-start the convention trade, the authors of the law stipulated that betting could take place only in a casino. Each casino, moreover, had to have a minimum of 500 "first-class rooms," defined as rooms with 325 square feet of living space and a separate bathroom. With hotels of this size and quality, it was thought, there would be room enough in town for gamblers who wanted to stay a couple of nights and visit the city as well as the legions of cardiologists and carpenters expected to return to the Boardwalk for their annual meetings. Each casino, furthermore, had to have a handful of restaurants, a few bars, and a lounge offering live music. Again, the idea was that the casinos would be entertainment destinations rather than the get 'em in, take their money fast, older, Las Vegas–style gambling joints.[38]

The law, finally, dealt with casino taxes. Eight percent of revenues would go straight to the state and then to seniors. A "small bone," in the words of a noted New Jersey urban studies professor, was then thrown at the city. Two percent of the gross earnings *after* a casino had paid its entire initial investment went to community development.[39] Following all kinds of accounting shenanigans— Caesar's at one point said that it had paid its tax by building a statute of the Roman ruler in front of the casino—this was later amended so that casinos paid a straight 1.25 percent of revenues to redevelopment projects in Atlantic City and around the state. This would, in the end, generate significant investment funds for the city, although they would eventually be controlled by a public corporation, not the municipal government.[40]

Still, one phrase in the law's opening section, more than all the stipulations about taxes and rooms, felony convictions and lounges, crystallized the measure's intent for Atlantic City locals. Casinos, lawmakers promised, would act as a "unique tool of urban renewal." But the phrase, as important as it was, dangled like a catfish on a line—it was hard to grasp, and even harder to know exactly what it meant. Did it mean that casinos—private corporations—would become urban planners? What sort of city would they build? What role would the state play? For whom would they build the city? What model would they use—the city of the past, the Boardwalk wonderland ringed by vibrant neighborhoods, or Reese Palley's dreamland of glittery casinos, fashionable shops, parking lots, and no residents?

RESORTS INTERNATIONAL COMES TO TOWN

The Chalfonte-Haddon Hall stood almost directly across the Boardwalk from Steel Pier. Betting big on gambling, Resorts International bought the two buildings in 1976. Then the corporation poured money into the casino referendum fight. Once the measure passed, the company spent millions taking down the Chalfonte, painting Haddon Hall bright white, and bringing its rooms and lobby in line with the Casino Control Act's detailed guidelines.[41] But for a while it didn't look like Resorts would ever open.

Under New Jersey law, casino owners had to undergo thorough background checks. The Resorts investigation dragged on for weeks and uncovered a murky corporate past filled with CIA pilots, a Miami-based paint company staffed by Cold War soldiers of fortune, and a Bahamian casino run by one of the Jewish mobster Meyer Lansky's lieutenants.[42] Anxious to get on with its "unique experiment in urban renewal," state officials cut short their inquiry and issued Resorts a temporary license.[43] On May 26, 1978, after a few days of test runs with fake money, the casino opened its doors to the public.[44]

On that Friday of Memorial Day weekend, entertainer Steve Lawrence, with his wife and singing partner, Eydie Gorme, by his side, placed a $10 chip down on a craps table and threw a five to officially start Atlantic City's casino era. Moments later, crowds of gamblers and anxious onlookers swarmed the building, the only legal casino outside of Nevada in the country at the time. By Saturday evening of that first weekend, the lines in front of the casino stretched down the Boardwalk for blocks. Resorts' management put up signs telling people how long they could expect to wait. Rain didn't diminish the crowds. At one point, it took four hours to get into the casino. One couple set up a backgammon table to help pass the time. Inside, men at the slot machines urinated into cups rather than give up their machines. Blackjack players sold their seats to the next person in line for $100. Local legend has it that "Resorts took in so much money that they went to the produce market around the corner to get empty peach buckets to throw the money into . . . [because] they had no other place to hold it." According to another story, at the end of that first weekend of gambling, Steve Wynn, then a young Las Vegas casino owner, called Jack Davis, one of the principals behind Resorts. "How [did] it go?" Wynn asked. "Great," Davis answered. "We can't even count all the money."[45]

▙WAITING TO GAMBLE
A long line of patrons stand on the Boardwalk trying to get into Resorts
International Hotel and Casino on the first weekend of gambling in Atlantic
City. Once inside, these same people had to wait in more lines before being able
to place a bet (Temple University Libraries, Urban Archives, Philadelphia,
Pennsylvania).

Like the men behind Resorts, Maxwell Goldberg and Milton Neustader, the
owners of the New Steel Pier, its official name since the two men bought the
amusement park from George Hamid, Jr., for a measly $1 million in 1973, bet
everything on casino gambling.[46] Along with other Boardwalk merchants, Goldberg and Neustader prayed that the slot machines and blackjack tables would
bring back to town the middle-class masses, the right kind of people, not the kind
they had been getting for the last few years. During the sixteen months between

the referendum's passage and the opening of the first casino, the entrepreneurs, owners of the Howard Johnson's Regency—one of the only new hotels built in the city in the 1970s—fixed up the aging amusement pier by painting the walls, scrubbing the floors, repairing electric signs, and putting in a brand-new Thrill-sphere, "a 180-degree wraparound 'Living' movie screen." Everything was in place that opening night in May 1978. The diving horse was there; the acrobats were there; and Eddie Fisher was there.[47]

Born in Philadelphia, Fisher had a sugary, easily forgettable baritone voice. In the early 1950s, his bland love songs climbed the charts a handful of times. That success and his teen idol good looks translated into an endorsement deal with Coca-Cola and regular gigs at the 500 Club. By the end of the decade, he had married Debbie Reynolds, and then Elizabeth Taylor, and had become even more famous. When the Democratic National Convention came to Atlantic City in 1964, George Hamid booked Fisher into one of Steel Pier's biggest rooms. Fourteen years later, the singer was back. But only a handful of people—literally—watched as a ghostly Fisher, worn out from years of amphetamine and cocaine abuse, croaked out a few old numbers in a cheerless voice.[48]

The stories of Steel Pier and Resorts International, of Eddie Fisher and Steve Lawrence got replayed around town. In the months and weeks leading up to the first day of gambling, business owners had prepared for overflow crowds as if it were Easter Sunday, the Fourth of July, and Labor Day all rolled into one. The head of the state highway patrol worried about a possible Woodstock situation with cars backed up from the Boardwalk to the Pine Barrens.[49] But he was wrong. Traffic wasn't bad. Only gamblers, it turned out, made the trip. Thousands of freshly wallpapered hotel rooms lay empty. Redecorated restaurants threw out tubs of clam chowder and trays of baked ziti. Boardwalk store owners stared at tall, undisturbed stacks of saltwater taffy boxes. Some businesspeople felt like embarrassed party hosts standing by doors waiting for guests who never showed up. The optimists chalked the slow weekend up to the cool, soggy weather. Others figured out that it wasn't just the cloud cover that was against them. Casino gambling—the city's supposed savior—might just be the problem.[50] "Anybody who's inside," a hotel owner remarked, "couldn't care less if it's sunny, raining, blowing or snowing."[51]

Between the lines of the stories of empty hotel rooms and crowded casinos, locals gleaned the first clues about the reality of Atlantic City's devil's bargain of urban renewal through gambling. For the first time in years, there were jobs and there was hope in town. But even before Resorts opened its doors, a vicious land rush broke out. People on the make bought a vacant house here, an empty lot there, quietly assembling blocks of land under false names and dummy companies. Once Resorts reported its first month's earnings—a whopping $18 million—the land rush grew more heated and harried. The speculators arrived in platoons, driving up the prices of everything in sight. Rotting houses, abandoned a year earlier by owners who would rather get rid of their properties than pay $2,000 in back taxes, were suddenly going for $60–80,000. In this real-life game of Monopoly it was property with a footprint big enough for a hotel with 500 rooms—not little green houses or rectangular red hotels—that investors wanted.[52]

Some locals, one novelist has observed, experienced the casino land rush like the Indians did "the coming of the railroads."[53] Just like in the not-so-mythic West, the cavalry of real estate agents drove people of color and those on the economic margins out of town. Robbed of customers, locally owned businesses shut their doors. Within months of Resorts' opening, some neighborhoods got that lonely feeling, like an abandoned town from a Hollywood western with tumbleweeds rolling down the middle of empty streets. Some speculators and landowners were more brutal than others, but everywhere the story of the city's "unique experiment in urban renewal" was the same. Gambling transformed Atlantic City, but it didn't save it, although for a time it did make Reese Palley look clairvoyant.

Nowhere did the Indian analogy work better, or more ruthlessly, than in the South Inlet. Landlords who had milked their drafty, dangerously wired properties for years, squeezing rents out of Puerto Rican families and the elderly, were eager to cash in on their newfound good luck. They started by jacking up the rents, although they weren't necessarily looking for more income. What they wanted were empty lots to sell to speculators. New Jersey law, however, made it difficult to evict tenants. Running around the statutes, landlords ambushed South Inlet residents. Maintenance calls coming into management offices went unanswered. Some landlords illegally cut off tenants' heat, water, and electricity. During the damp winter months of 1978 and 1979, nurses at area schools noticed sharp jumps in absenteeism. They couldn't figure it out at first; then after reading about the "freeze outs" in the South Inlet, one health-care worker put the children's illnesses and unheated apartments together. Other landlords, meanwhile, slipped a little money into the pockets of housing inspectors, who then checked out properties for the first time in years and immediately condemned them.[54]

When the rent increases, blackouts, freeze outs, and official terror failed, the fires began. In the first four months of 1981, 117 fires broke out in the South Inlet. The exhausted fire fighters considered 105 of these blazes to be suspicious. Tipping them off was the fact that most fires started on top floors, making them harder to put out and certain, if not caught right away, to destroy the entire building. After the blazes, it looked like Palley's bulldozers had driven through the South Inlet, leaving scarred lands cleared for speculators.[55]

DETERMINATION IN THE SOUTH INLET
Carmen Santigo and her grandson José Felicano stand in front of the building
where they live at the corner of Oriental and Rhode Island Avenues. Behind
them flies the Puerto Rican flag and a message of defiance. Not long after,
Santigo and Felicano would be gone from the South Inlet (Temple University
Libraries, Urban Archives, Philadelphia, Pennsylvania).

South Inlet Puerto Ricans protested against the removal campaign. Several
times, they marched on city hall. "We're the ones who do the dishes, clean the toilets," one demonstrator told a reporter, "and we need a place to live and we're
going to stay whether you like it or not."[56] Defiance like this rallied the community, but it didn't stop the onslaught. By 1981, the city's Puerto Rican barrio was a
thing of the past. More than 2,000 people had been pushed out of the city, in what
a study conducted by a Temple University law professor called a "systematic effort

by landlords to evict Hispanic, poor and elderly residents from Atlantic City tenements to raze buildings and sell property at rates inflated by the expected arrival of casino gambling."[57]

The South Inlet was not the only place where residents were being pushed out and where different segments of the community locked horns. The land rush jarred relationships everywhere. In 1978, developers bought the Ritz Carlton Apartments—the Boardwalk showplace had stopped being an upscale hotel in the early 1970s—and evicted elderly residents on fixed incomes to make room for luxury condominiums. Many of the exiles moved into the nearby Brighton Towers, only to have the owners of that building push them out three years later to make room for more condos.[58] After the city's first post-gambling master plan marked the North Inlet for casino development, some residents, including the elderly, wanted the area rezoned as residential. That way, they could afford to remain in their homes. Young families, however, wanted to get the cash out of their properties. The two groups argued on street corners and in public meetings, but the results were almost always the same. The city and its residents bent to the will of the speculators and casino owners; then the houses came down; and after that, stores shut, and the gaps in the city's built environment grew wider.[59]

Atlantic City locals divide the city's history into two periods: B.C., before casinos, and A.C., after casinos. Urbanists often say that Italians "stick"—for complicated reasons—longer in old neighborhoods than other ethnic groups.[60] This seems to be true in Atlantic City. Before casinos, Ducktown remained a cohesive, front porch–centered neighborhood. In part, remaining cohesive meant, as a local might whisper, keeping blacks out. Well into the 1970s, Ducktown remained, with the possible exceptions of Chelsea and Chelsea Heights, the city's whitest neighborhood. Yet at the same time, the area was graying. Throughout the postwar period, twenty-something women and men who grew up on Florida and Georgia avenues started to move out of the city; they wanted driveways for their Pontiac station wagons, backyards for swing sets, and schools for their children without too many black students. But their parents stayed behind, in houses paid for long ago.

Gambling unraveled the last threads of community in parts of Ducktown. Most of the casinos that opened up after Resorts—Bally's, Caesar's, Playboy, Claridge, Golden Nugget, Tropicana, and Sands—stood on the edges of Ducktown, especially the areas of the neighborhood south of Atlantic Avenue. None of the gaming halls at first provided parking for average gamblers. Only the high rollers were guaranteed spots for their cars. Parking lots, then, provided a chance for the "little guy" to get in on the gambling windfall. All over Ducktown, locals and their children seized the moment and tore down moldering old buildings. They cleared the land, posted hand-painted signs advertising parking spaces, and they were in business. Not only did the lots generate cash—in a nearly perfectly calibrated market, customers paid anywhere from $5 to $20 depending on the time of day, season of the year, and general traffic flow to store their cars—but they also produced a tax break. Property assessments value improved lots over empty ones. While some people made money on the cleared land, their individual and economically rational decisions cut gaping holes in the urban frontage. As a result, Ducktown and other neighborhoods looked uglier, meaner, and more desolate, not the kinds of places that welcomed foot traffic and front porch sociability.[61]

With its brick row houses covered with aluminum siding, the beach blocks of Bellevue and Texas avenues represented a rather typical slice of Ducktown. Before the referendum passed, the block looked clean, but slightly worn. Shutters dangled from some houses and the trim on most needed touching up. Locals locked their porch furniture to their railings to ward off thieves. The Pussy Cat Lounge, a dingy topless bar, took up one corner at the end of the block.[62] But even with its best days behind it, the two streets remained home to nearly six dozen year-round families. After dinner on warm nights, these men and women sat in front of their houses, chatting, picking up stray cups and hoagie wrappers, and listening to Phillies games on the radio.[63]

Jean Savage didn't care about the social world of the front stoop when she came to Ducktown. What brought this tall, blonde, a bit too tanned, forty-something woman to a rented room on Bellevue Avenue were the reports of Resorts taking in $18 million in its first month in operation. Savage dreamed of getting a piece of the gaming pie. In order to do so, she did what countless other people had done over the years on their way to Atlantic City—she remade herself.

In Atlantic City, Savage wasn't a struggling Brooklyn insurance agent; she was a real estate mogul. She didn't live in a cramped basement apartment in Nutley, New Jersey; she was the president of the Lucky Lady, a company with backers in Miami and Las Vegas and a $60 million plan to turn the beach blocks of Bellevue and Texas avenues into a casino wonderland.[64] If Savage wanted to turn her blueprint into reality, she had to get her hands on a footprint big enough for a 500-room casino hotel. This was no simple matter. Unlike the Las Vegas strip, built on the outskirts of the city and stretching into the seemingly endless desert, Atlantic City sat on an island, an already developed island in 1978 with houses, hotels, motels, ice cream stands, miniature golf courses, and parking lots on every inch of the city. Except for Pauline's Prairie, the barren urban renewal site in the South Inlet, the city was completely built over. One way to get into the casino game—

the one followed by Resorts—was to buy an existing hotel and get the building in line with the law. But the faulty wiring, rusted pipes, and small, quirky rooms in most of the older hotels made these gut and rehabilitation plans expensive and complicated. This didn't stop developers from buying up the city's crumbling Boardwalk towers of excess. But as soon as the companies signed the paperwork, they tore the buildings down. Fixing an old hotel or putting up a new one was obviously expensive, and only corporate giants like Bally's or Caesar's had enough money and access to financing to launch such elaborate projects. Companies like Jean Savage's H.E.J.J. Incorporated—no one knew what the initials stood for—didn't have the bankroll or the clout to build a casino the conventional way, so they had to think of a more daring way to get into the $18 million-a-month casino game.

When Grace Patroni got a letter in the mail from Savage inviting her to a Sunday night meeting in October 1978, she had been living in the same house on Bellevue Avenue for forty years. She showed up at the Salvation Army on time and found most of her neighbors inside drinking coffee and eating cannolis. After a short while, Savage mounted the podium and put her cards on the table. She would pay Patroni and her seventy-one neighbors $100,000 apiece for their houses—houses that they couldn't give away before gambling came to town and that still weren't worth more than $30,000. But there was a catch. Everyone on the block had to sell, or no one got the $100,000.

Within a few days, sixty families signed the options giving Savage the right to buy and sell their houses. John DiGiallorenzo wasn't one of them. He had worked all of his life as a carpenter and always wanted to live at the shore. In the late 1960s, he bought a Texas Avenue row house for $12,000. Over the next decade, he fixed up the place. By the time Savage came around, he and his wife were retired and living year-round in their freshly painted and newly wired and landscaped shore house. At first, the couple told Savage's local real estate agent, Rick Bloom, that they didn't want to sell. They liked their house and loved living near the beach. Later, DiGiallorenzo told Bloom that he would sell, but only if Bloom found him a comparable house on a beach block in a safe, quiet—presumably, white—neighborhood. That kind of property didn't exist in Atlantic City any more.

Soon everyone on the block knew about the DiGiallorenzos' reluctance to sell. The couple received a testy letter from several neighbors accusing them of selfishness. A young married woman from the block told a reporter, "I sympathize with the old people but I got children and I don't want to raise them next door to a casino." The families who didn't sign the option, she believed, "are standing in our way."[65] At the grocery store and on the street, the DiGiallorenzos got the "cold-

BELLEVUE AVENUE, 1978

Emily Gaspero (left) and Josephine Vitelli sit in front of their neat row houses talking. Taken not long after Jean Savage rented a room on the block and offered them $100,000 if everyone on this street and Texas Avenue agreed to sell their properties (Temple University Libraries, Urban Archives, Philadelphia, Pennsylvania).

shoulder treatment." At night, their phone rang and rang. When they picked it up, no one was there. Rattled by the pressure, they signed the option.[66]

By the summer of 1979, Bloom and Savage were down to a handful of holdouts.[67] Several lived in rundown houses on Stanley Court—an alley barely wide enough for a Volkswagen Beetle to drive down—located in the middle of the block with no parking or ocean views. Court residents convinced themselves that they could use their strategic position as leverage to get more money. Harassed and cajoled by neighbors, several caved in and joined the deal, but not everyone.

Time was running out on Bloom and Savage. Other property assemblers started knocking on doors and making bids on the houses. Bloom and Savage tried to hold the deal together, but they couldn't. Savage couldn't find another developer interested in the project, and none of the moneymen from Florida and Las Vegas about whom she had talked emerged to rescue the deal. It was time to fold, and she knew it, so she packed up her stuff and moved to Florida. At least that's where locals think she went.[68]

The headline read, "No Boardwalk Deal." The brief, unsigned *New York Times* article, dated August 14, 1979, explained:

A $100,000 offer for each of 72 houses in a Boardwalk neighborhood has fallen through and the real-estate man who tried to assemble the land says greedy residents scuttled the deal.

Many homeowners on the Boardwalk block between Bellevue and Texas Avenues are bitter.

Peter Gaspero of Bellevue Avenue said: "We went through a year of aggravation on this block. And for what? Nothing. Most of these people haven't gotten a cent."

Sam Plantania, a Texas Avenue resident for 39 years, said, "I'm glad the whole stir is done with."

Richard Bloom, the real estate man who last year offered $100,000 to each homeowner if all agreed to sell, said that many owners "suddenly came back and argued that their land was worth more."[69]

John and Rita DiGiallorenzo's son, Philadelphia dentist John Lorenzo, agrees with Bloom. "A clash of greed," he says, killed the deal. A second group, Lorenzo remembers, came along a few months later and offered everyone on the block $125,000 for their houses, but this deal also fell through. Eventually, in 1981, the DiGiallorenzos sold their house for $85,000 and moved back to northeast Philadelphia.[70]

A few years later, Lorenzo came back to Atlantic City to take a look at the area. There was no casino and all the houses were still there, but the neighborhood he remembered was gone. Most of the Italian families his parents chatted with or talked about had moved away. A Cash for Gold sign hung over the front door of what used to be the corner store. The old-timers who were left had stopped scrubbing the sidewalks and putting money into their houses. Some were afraid to go outside. A drug market had opened at the end of the street. Even block residents who had the money to fix up their properties or the political connections to run out the pushers must have wondered, what was the use? They knew that the condition of their homes and the safety of the area didn't matter any more. The only thing that counted in the game of Monopoly being played in Atlantic City in the 1970s and 1980s was having enough property to make a footprint big enough to build a casino.[71]

What the speculators and parking lot operators started in Ducktown, buses and ideas about racial exclusion finished. As soon as there was more than one place to gamble in Atlantic City, the casino companies initiated a competitive game of paying bus customers to come straight to their buildings. In 1980, a round-trip ticket from Medford, New Jersey, or Pelham, New York, to Resorts or Caesar's cost $13.25. Riders got $10 in quarters, a free pass through the buffet line, and a $5 voucher to the gift shop. Thousands took advantage of the casino give-aways, and the buses rolled day and night, gears grinding, brakes screeching, and exhaust pipes belching out black fumes. Ducktown stood right in the buses' paths. The quickest way to get from the Atlantic City Expressway to the newer casinos—the Golden Nugget and Tropicana—was right through the aging neighborhood.

Ursula Obst, an *Atlantic City Press* reporter, visited Ducktown in 1979 and no-ticed "buses, buses, and more buses." As they rumbled past, she heard a woman sit-ting on a second-floor balcony letting out hacking coughs. For Sale signs dotted the lawns on either side of this woman's house. Some Ducktown residents told Obst that they were throwing in the towel. They couldn't live with the bus fumes and the constant rattling. But the buses weren't the only reason for the For Sale signs.

Formal and informal racial covenants had built the gates around Ducktown. Public officials had led the way. In 1939, the head of the Atlantic City Housing Au-thority told reporters that his agency was about to launch a "new housing project for whites."[72] For the next two and a half decades, Pitney Village, a red brick com-plex just down the street from St. Michael's Church, near the corner of Mississippi and Fairmont avenues, remained all white. Following the government's lead, Duck-town landlords and real estate agents rented and sold area properties to whites only.

Things started to change in the mid-1960s. Faced with the civil rights move-ment, local officials could no longer enforce segregation, and a few African American families started to move into Pitney Village. As they did, whites moved out. By the time the buses started rolling, black families occupied almost every unit in the complex. In response, For Sale signs popped up on front lawns all over the area. As more whites fled the neighborhood, landlords, especially on the fringes of Ducktown, started to follow the law and rent for the first time to the first qualified applicant regardless of race. Ducktown's remaining white residents watched the blurring of the color line with unease.[73]

"Gambling. It's no good. It's no good for anybody," declared John Joseph as he spit out a long stream of tobacco onto the curb in front of his neat North Texas Ave-nue home. The casinos, he grumbled, pushed up land prices and crime rates. But the worst thing they did was force African Americans out of the "ghetto" into Duck-town. "All the coloreds," Joseph said. "We got every kind."[74] Some elderly residents, a group of college professors found out, felt "that their Italian community was being invaded" by African Americans. Others thought that Pitney Village blacks were planning crime raids on the neighborhood. More For Sale signs popped up, and Ducktown stopped being Ducktown—a tight-knit, insular, Italian community.[75]

"Everybody got a little greedy," one New York Avenue guesthouse owner said of the A.C.—after casinos—era. Gay club owners jacked up cover charges and raised drink prices. Nearby "fraternity houses"—gay-friendly rooming houses—joined the gold rush. During the early 1970s, these plain, three-story buildings on New York Avenue and Snake Alley charged as little as $80 to $100 per person for a week-long stay. Cheap rooms made Atlantic City accessible to gay men and lesbians from all walks of life. When the casinos opened, rooming-house operators charged the same rate for one night as they previously had for an entire week. "That's what's destroying the street," one man insisted at the time. "[T]here are no more cheap hotel rooms where people can stay." Other guesthouse owners did not raise their rates, but they let their buildings rot. One man looking for a place to stay thought he could smell one of the older New York Avenue hotels from the street. He ended up in a room a few blocks away. Why fix up a drafty old guesthouse, some owners thought, when a developer was sure to buy it and immediately tear it down? Again, it was land, not houses and hotels, that mattered most in the new, real-life game of Monopoly.[76]

In the late 1970s, New York Avenue property owners were convinced that it was just a matter of time before they would be bought out. So they waited for a man with a checkbook to come around.[77] The developers did come calling with rolled-up architectural designs and detailed scale models. In 1979, Atlantic Land Limited opened an office near New York Avenue and started to map out a booming future for the area. According to its drawings, the company planned to build a $135-175 million, 31-story, 504-room art deco hotel with a 60,000-square-foot casino. The blueprints penciled in space for a 1,000-seat show room, a fifth-floor weight room, a swimming pool, a health club, and rooftop tennis courts. The company also hinted at an eventual expansion of the project to include another 750 rooms and even more casino space. By July 1980, however, a For Rent sign hung in the corner of Atlantic Land Limited's Atlantic City office, and no one answered the telephone.[78]

A few years later, Natco Realty and Development Company of Greenwich, Connecticut, bought up property around New York Avenue and talked about turning several beach blocks into a dazzling hotel and shopping complex for gamblers and their families called Boardwalk Marketplace modeled on New Orleans' French Quarter. In 1986, the project's leading investor, John Peter Galanis, was wanted by the Internal Revenue Service, the U.S. Justice Department, the New Jersey State Police, and the Manhattan District Attorney's Office. The properties he purchased were left abandoned and neglected, more ugly reminders of the feverish race for riches touched off by the gambling gold rush.[79]

As New York Avenue business leaders waited for the big payday, buildings on the street disappeared. By the early 1980s, it was clear that the area had changed. Five or six gay bars and a couple of gay-oriented gift shops—about half of what was there before—remained in business. On weekends, drag queens still roamed the beach in front of the Claridge and they still strutted up and down New York Avenue at night, but the days of the big street parties were clearly in the past.[80]

The movie business suffered the same fate. Several months before Resorts opened, a Long Island developer bought the Hollywood and Center theaters along Atlantic Avenue. He promptly razed the buildings to make room for a gigantic parking lot. There was talk of replacing the crumbling movie houses with a new $100 million "megastructure" complete with a hotel, office building, television production studio, and movie theater, but nothing came of it. The destruction of the Hollywood and Center theaters left the city with only three screens on Atlantic Avenue and three on the Boardwalk.[81]

The night that Resorts opened, the Strand on the Boardwalk played the 1970s classic *Saturday Night Fever*. The Virginia and the Apollo Burlesque theaters were also still open when the dice started to roll. By the time Resorts celebrated its one-year anniversary, however, all of the Boardwalk theaters had closed.[82] The last picture shows along Atlantic Avenue died right along with the Boardwalk showplaces. The Embassy closed in 1978, the Charles sometime in 1979.[83]

That left the Beach as the only theater in town. For years, the movie house, with a liquor store on one side and a check-cashing place on the other, survived—just barely—by showing X-rated films. Then, in November 1983, the building caught fire. "It's a big mess," a fire department official commented the morning after the three-alarm blaze. "[T]he roof collapsed and it is still burning down deep." Some suspected arson.[84] Whatever the cause, the theater owner decided that the building wasn't worth fixing because not enough people were willing to go out at night or leave the casinos for a couple of hours to make a downtown cinema profitable. As a result, beginning in 1983, Atlantic City, home to nine casinos and host to tens of millions of visitors each year, did not—and still does not—have a single movie theater.[85]

Local residents and commentators pointed to the Beach Theater's closing as a symbol of the Disneyland that didn't come.[86] Despite all the jobs and the hundreds of millions of dollars in casino revenues, Atlantic City was, they insisted, in many ways, a worse place to live in 1978 than before. At least before, the city still had some quality stores left on Atlantic and Arctic avenues, dozens of good restaurants on side streets, a few nightclubs, and a handful of movie theaters, albeit aging ones, scattered in between. Five years after Resorts opened, the last pieces of the city's public entertainment industry and the public places around them were disappearing. In those traditional urban neighborhoods, it looked like Palley's bulldozers had plowed through, leaving behind a flat, desolate lunar landscape of streets increasingly empty except for the luckless and dispossessed. In the distance, the casinos stood, ablaze in neon lights, a world apart.[87]

9

Casino
Publics

Eight years after Resorts opened, television reporter Bill Moyers brought a camera crew to Atlantic City.[1] During the intervening years, he found out, ten more casinos had opened, giving the city's 30 million yearly visitors eleven different places to try their luck. By 1986, Moyers marveled, the city had become the single most popular tourist destination in all of America—more popular than Las Vegas or even Florida's Disneyworld. The casinos, the clearly amazed television journalist noted, brought in $5 billion a year and employed 40,500 people. After eight years in business, they accounted for two-thirds of the city's tax revenues and had already poured $1 billion into state coffers to pay the utility bills of the elderly and poor from Cape May to Edison. Millions more were spent on housing and road projects in Atlantic City. These were, Moyers readily acknowledged, impressive numbers. But there were other numbers and other stories that astonished the Texan even more.

Crime, Moyers discovered, had risen by 80 percent since Resorts opened. A third of the city's homes had been destroyed, but the casino gold rush had made land so expensive that most buildings couldn't be replaced. One speculation story astonished him. In 1985, the city needed a new high school, but it couldn't afford a building big enough in town, so local leaders filled in marshland a few miles from the Boardwalk and put the new school there. Land prices weren't the only striking statistics. More than 200 restaurants, Moyers learned, had gone out of business since 1978. Before the casinos, the kitchen at Curt Kugel's Luigi's restaurant had cranked out as many as 1,000 dinners a night when the Miss America Pageant or the AFL-CIO convention came to town. After Resorts opened, Kugel's revenues fell by half. By the time Moyers spoke with him in 1986, his restaurant had been turned into a parking lot.

Not far away from Luigi's, Moyers found Father Dante Girolami at St. Nicholas of Tolentine Roman Catholic Church. At one point, the clergyman told him, his congregation totaled 700 members. Now there were only two families left, and he couldn't think of a single child living in his parish. The only people who came to mass were gamblers, practicing the "virtue of hope."

Trying to understand the stark contrast between the city's startling casino prosperity and its remarkable public poverty, Moyers followed the well-worn journalistic path to Reese Palley's office. Decked out in his trademark black turtleneck with his salt-and-pepper hair pointing toward the sky, the merchant lectured Moyers as they walked down the Boardwalk past tacky T-shirt shops, glass buildings, and gaping holes where stores used to be. "I want you to look at this here," Palley implored his guest. "[T]his is probably the greatest urban tragedy that has happened in this country."

"Urban tragedy," Moyers repeated.

Shaking his head, Palley continued, "A city gets old and ugly and that's no tragedy, but when a city's got everything . . . money and power . . . that's a tragedy."

Moyers talked to a few more locals before he left town. One man told him, "I don't see a single neighborhood that has benefited from casino gambling." Another man said to the television essayist, "People ask me what kind of place Atlantic City is. . . . it's a no place, it's not a real place." Based on the evidence he gathered, Moyers offered his own assessment of the city's future: "It will be casino city, not Atlantic City. The city of the Steel Pier, Miss America, of families strolling on the Boardwalk . . . that Atlantic City is lost forever."

For Moyers, the casinos represented a sharp break with the past. Using wrecking balls and bulldozers, the casino owners had knocked down the city's famed fantasy backdrop, the ashes drifting onto empty lots in disappearing neighborhoods. But Moyers saw only part of the story. In order to stay afloat, mass resorts like Atlantic City must be malleable enough to change to meet the shifting tastes and values of the target audience—in this case, middle-class vacationers and funseekers.[2] The casinos did bring the crowds and with them a slew of jobs and peach basketsful of tourist dollars back to town. The people and the money returned to the Boardwalk because the casino companies, the city's chief urban planners after 1978, manufactured through architecture and urban design an updated version of exclusion. With confidence-building walls and bridges, parking decks, and surveillance cameras, which all told middle-class visitors that they were safe and insulated from the city outside, a new public took shape in the casino wonderlands of the new Atlantic City. This one, as Moyers sensed, borrowed less from the past than it did from Disneyland, the malls, and suburban gated communities.[3]

CASINOLANDS

Later in his program, Bill Moyers cut back to Reese Palley. The Atlantic City tragedy, the art dealer explained, picking up an earlier thread, is not the "loss of paradise; it's the loss of precious, irreplaceable opportunity. [I]t will never come back." For Palley, the fate of William Price's Orientalist dreamland, the Marlborough-Blenheim Hotel, symbolized the city's shortcomings. In the fall of 1978, Palley and local lawyer Martin Blatt acquired an option on the property. While the "birdman" and his partner didn't have the capital to build a casino, they did have a footprint. Their phone rang off the hook. Hotel chains and gaming companies made outrageous offers on the land. Eventually Palley and Blatt struck a multimillion-dollar deal with the Bally Corporation.

Not long after getting its hands on the property, the pinball and slot machine manufacturer announced plans to destroy the old hotel, saying that it could not remake the eighty-year-old, weather-beaten structure into a bright new casino hotel with 500 first-class rooms. Worried that "patch and paint" jobs like the Resorts remodel wouldn't create enough jobs and spending, Governor Brendan Byrne encouraged Bally's and other companies to take down the city's landmarks. A handful of architects and preservationists protested the Blenheim's destruction, even coming up with a detailed, retrofitted model of the old hotel, but the city and the state bowed, as they had before and would do again, to the wishes of the new urban planners—the casino giants—and the building came down in a dark plume of gray dust and debris.[4]

No longer grinning, Palley told Moyers that he regretted what had happened. "We were all innocents," he maintained. "We didn't know what would happen. . . . We were third-rate merchants and politicians." He didn't let himself or others off the hook. He told Moyers, "It was an obligation not to take the money and run, but we did. We took the money and ran. That's a big black mark against us. I'm not ashamed about taking the money. . . . I'm ashamed we let them take that building down . . . ashamed we didn't fight against it." "Tearing the Blenheim down," he lamented, "was the talisman of what would happen. . . . We didn't have to sacrifice everything . . . for a building like this [*pointing to Bally's*] . . . that has no other function but to take thirteen cents on every dollar from old ladies."[5]

Racing to cash in on the gambling windfall started by Resorts, Bally's tore down the ornate hotel in January 1979 and threw up a building that looked like an unimaginative merging of a Days Inn and a K-Mart.[6] It was, in a sense, the anti–Marlborough-Blenheim—a building with so little distinction that it was hard to describe. This sort of colossal and studied blandness became the blueprint for many of Atlantic City's first generation of casinos. Architecturally, these buildings turned their backs on the outdoors and the past, while they embraced, and even celebrated, the principle of exclusion—an exclusion that fit their needs and the needs of the crowd.

Between 1978 and 1985, construction crews knocked down beachfront hotels and nearby apartment buildings and row houses. On the cleared lands, workers with hard hats, logging countless overtime hours, put up a string of towering structures that rose above the ocean. While the new buildings shared spaces on the map with the old Atlantic City, they embraced almost none of its over-the-top spirit nor its relationship to the Boardwalk world of public entertainment and showing off in front of thick crowds of strangers. They were not, moreover, in the business of putting middle-class Americans on display. All of their functions were on the inside. Following the Bally's model, each of the casinos that went up in the late 1970s and early 1980s looked the same; they were monotonous lumps of glass and steel,[7] little more than neon-splashed warehouses built to store bars, slot machines, blackjack tables, and armies of gamblers. With their flat roofs, right angles, blank walls, and dearth of oceanfront shops, these casinos said that the streets, the beach, and the Boardwalk didn't exist. By setting themselves off from their surroundings, the casinos generated an eerie "ageographic," ahistoric feel. They could just as easily have been plopped down at the Dallas/Fort Worth Airport or in downtown Orlando or any other place where developers put up atrium-centered hotels in the 1970s and 1980s as on the Atlantic City Boardwalk.[8] Tracing these popular hotel plans, Bally's architects and their followers deliberately manufactured this sense of placelessness, laying out their buildings to make sure that no one accidentally stumbled across the ocean, a local Italian restaurant, or a city street. At the same time, they tried to keep the city away from the gamblers.[9]

Unlike the Eastern temple and wedding cake–topped showplaces of the old Atlantic City, the casinos did not make a single architectural gesture, not even a nod, to the Boardwalk or the beach. None of the first wave of gaming halls had stores on the Boardwalk side.[10] They wanted customers inside, near the slots and green felt tables. "[O]ne could live for days in most of the casinos," a *Time* reporter cracked in 1981, "and think that the only water around was that coming out of the bathroom faucet."[11] One family checked into a casino hotel in 1980 not to gamble, but to go to the ocean. Yet they kept getting lost on their way to the beach. After several failed attempts to get out of the hotel, the father talked to a security guard. The uniformed official pointed across the casino. As soon as the family started in that direction, he stopped them, telling them that children under the age of twenty-one couldn't walk on the casino floor. When they asked him again how to get to the beach, he shrugged and pointed to a door that opened onto Pacific Avenue.[12]

None of the 1980s-era hotel towers had a place to sit outside in the sun or have a drink. Only one had a top-floor cocktail lounge, now closed, with an ocean view.[13] Each casino, an official admits, was designed to "capture . . . customers . . . [and] not let them go until they were ready to go." Most lobbies were no bigger than suburban living rooms. Even fewer had comfortable chairs or conversation pits. Frank Sinatra, Cher, Sammy Davis, Jr., and other entertainers performed for an hour, an hour and fifteen minutes at the most, no more. Only a couple of casinos had swimming pools. In-room televisions picked up few stations and scarcely any movie channels. The dim lights by the beds made it almost impossible to read. All of this, of course, was part of a well-researched plan to get people out of their rooms and onto the windowless, clockless casino floor, where the lighting and temperature never changed.[14] Leaving nothing to chance, casino operators pumped oxygen-filled air onto the gaming floors at regular intervals to keep bettors awake. The climate-controlled environment was there to shut out everything and to confuse players who might stop dropping quarters into slot machines or tossing chips onto craps tables if they realized the time of day. Casino managers knew that the odds favored the house and that the longer players remained on the floor, the more they would lose. That's why the casinos gave away free food and drinks and closed their buildings off from the outdoors.[15]

In one case, the new architecture proved downright dangerous. Following the Bally's model, Caesar's put up its own slot machine shed a few blocks to the north. Trying to give their building a little exterior flare, the company decorated the bottom floors of the otherwise flat structure with a chilly pattern of large, angular glass triangles. The reflections off the building's sharp edges generated so much heat that it could set fire to cigarette butts and balls of trash stuck between the planks of the Boardwalk.[16]

Even more conspicuous than the glass fronts—and in the end perhaps more dangerous to the city—are the casino parking lots. When the gambling halls first opened, they provided only high rollers with parking. Quarter-slot and $5 blackjack players had to leave their cars in side-street lots, like the ones that popped up in Ducktown, a few blocks from the gaming halls. As players walked to the hotels, they passed boarded-up businesses, seedy guesthouses, and vacant lots. Frightened by the scarred, "Hill Street Blues" landscape, some patrons complained about having to deal with the city. Casino executives detected another problem with this parking situation—they couldn't control the flow of patrons. So up went the colossal cement parking decks.[17]

The Harrah's Corporation started Atlantic City's parking deck building boom. Under the first casino-era master plan, city officials zoned the marina area by the bay, two miles from the Boardwalk on the edge of the Northside and just off the Absecon Boulevard entrance to town, for casino development. In 1979, Harrah's, a subsidiary of Holiday Inn, purchased a footprint in the area and started to build a $120 million, 506-room hotel with 40,000 square feet of gambling space.[18] Quickly the Memphis-based company decided to turn its ex-urban setting into a marketing advantage. Executives named the property Harrah's Marina to emphasize, according to one journalist, "its away-from-the-Boardwalk location" and presumably its distance from the city.[19] Then they turned the casino toward the road. The only way to get to the hotel was by car or bus, so the company set up its property to service drive-up gamblers, the bread and butter of Atlantic City's business. They started with a 2,400-space, eight-level parking structure. Then they fit the casino, a building without a trace of architectural style except for the lettering on the neon sign, around the clean, well-lit, and spacious deck. That's all they put on the property—and that's all they needed. A parking deck, a casino, and a little landscaping, and they were in business. Harrah's customers had no place to walk and no place to look out at the bay, the ocean, or the Atlantic City skyline except from the parking deck's top floor. The deck, however, turned away from the Boardwalk and toward the casino, which emerged as a separate city, or at least as a mall, with slot machines.[20]

Drive-up gambling fit not just Harrah's location, but also the national mood. Across the country, cities and suburbs remade themselves to accommodate the car and its passengers, who saw walking as a mild inconvenience and, even worse, as a potentially risky gamble—riskier even than the craps table. Not surprisingly, Harrah's strategy of designing a contained casino world—a combination of a mall, a gated community, and a private house with the virtual equivalent of an electric garage-door opener—quickly paid off. In 1981, Harrah's Marina earned $142.5 million, the third highest revenue of all Atlantic City casinos despite the fact that it was smaller and more modest than most of the other gaming places.[21]

Over the next five years, just about every casino followed the Harrah's model and refitted their properties for drive-up gambling. With his typical bullishness, Donald Trump tried to get the city to evoke eminent domain and tear down a family-owned Italian restaurant, a moldering forty-room guesthouse, and a cash-for-gold store owned by a family of Russian immigrants to make room for a landscaped limousine-parking area in front of one of his casinos.[22] In 1990, Caesar's Palace built a parking garage nearby with space for 2,500 cars and 24 buses. Announcing the opening, company officials bragged that the hotel-sized concrete deck fronted by a milky white statue of Caesar provided "a unique embellishment to the Atlantic City skyline," adding that the "highly aesthetic" design reflects "an overall Roman stylization."[23]

Each year, the casinos, following the Caesar's model, further embellished the city's skyline with fatter and wider parking decks with bigger and brighter signs. Indeed the signs on these structures draw more attention to the casinos than do the buildings themselves. Stretching two full blocks away from the ocean and creeping ever closer to the Atlantic City Expressway, the main entry point into the city, the sprawling parking decks act like vacuums, swallowing up Camrys, Town Cars, and Explorers as soon as they get to town. Once the cars are sucked into the cement towers, passengers are led through carpeted walkways wired with Muzak versions of "Yesterday" and the amplified sounds of slot machines spitting out jackpots. What the people movers don't do—won't do—is engage with Atlantic City as a place.

Parking is not just about storing gamblers' cars. Reese Palley, remember, predicted that, after the arrival of the casinos, no one would live in Atlantic City, and he was, at least in part, right. Speculation, the closing of movie houses and corner stores, real estate scams, big city traffic, and the relentless blare of car and bus horns drove just about anyone who could leave out of the city. In the twenty-five years since Resorts opened, the city has lost a third of its population and housing stock. Now there are more casino employees than city residents, and most of these people live in the suburbs.

Unlike Atlanta, Phoenix, and other sprawling, car-dependent metropolitan areas, however, the city is not irrelevant in Atlantic City. Many families have fled Ducktown, the South Inlet, and the Northside, but the jobs have remained in the old central city. It would seem, then, that blackjack dealers and housekeepers, even if they lived out of town, would have been potential sources of revenue for local businesses, stopping off on the way home for a beer or to drop off dry cleaning. But few workers—like gamblers—ever stepped foot on Atlantic City streets. Early on, casino managers didn't want their bar maids, pit bosses, and buffet cooks competing with gamblers for parking spaces, so they built intercept lots outside the city and bused their employees directly from their cars to their jobs and back again at the ends of their shifts. As a result, there was little chance for any of the casino riches to trickle down into the city.

Extending the antiurban principles of the parking decks and the intercept lots, the casino companies have constructed a grid of walkways and bridges over the city. The Sands stands only a short block away from the Boardwalk in the heart of the city. Rather than have patrons walk through a once-elegant park from the promenade to the casino, company executives built a themed walkway over the green space. Carried along on a moving sidewalk, guests can look nostalgically at the city's past portrayed in a timeline of black-and-white photographs of the Traymore, Sammy Davis, Jr., at the 500 Club, and the diving horse at the end of Steel Pier.[24]

⮞MAKING THE CASINO PUBLIC

This is the walkway between the Boardwalk and the Sands Casinos over the city. Notice the security guard protecting the enclosed space from outsiders (Atlantic City Free Public Library, Heston Room, Atlantic City, New Jersey).

When the Sands first installed its people mover, Donald Trump owned one casino across from Harrah's on the marina, the Castle, and another on the Boardwalk near the Convention Hall, the Plaza. But the biggest—an essential adjective for Trump—was about to come. In the spring of 1990, the real estate tycoon opened the Taj Mahal on the southern half of Pauline's Prairie, the vacant urban renewal site in the Inlet.[25] Billed as a place "where wonders never cease," the forty-two-story, 1,250-room hotel stood as New Jersey's tallest building. With its four football fields of gaming space and 3,000 slot machines, it was, at the time, the world's largest casino.[26]

Asked if the Taj could save Atlantic City—which just a year and a half earlier *Money* magazine had tagged as the worst place to live in all of America—the building's architect, Francis X. Dumont, talked of the past. Before gambling, he said, the city "survived on flamboyant architecture, luxurious resort hotels, and public spectacles." With seventy turquoise and teal fiberglass minarets and a dozen gold-tinged domes on the outside and wrecking ball–sized chandeliers and cocktail waitresses dressed like "harem girls" on the inside, the Taj stood in sharp contrast to the "airport hotels with casinos" around it. Glittering and whimsical, Dumont's oversized playground splashed color and style onto Atlantic City's

THE TAJ MAHAL
Donald Trump's answer to the Marlborough-Blenheim Hotel just after it
opened in the 1990s (Atlantic City Free Public Library, Heston Room, Atlantic
City, New Jersey).

dreary skyline. But could it save Atlantic City? Dumont never answered that question.[27]

For all of its excess and extravagance, the Taj did not, however, break the mold of the Atlantic City casino. "We want this to be a complete fantasy," the Donald's brother, Robert Trump, declared, "a place where you close the door behind you and are in another world."[28] Giving shape to Trump's hopeful escapism, the building emphasized its exclusive interior as much as its public exterior. Dumont saved his most elaborate and ornate gestures for the hotel's drive-up entrance. Two immense white gates, quoting Disney's own security regime, greeted visitors near Pacific Avenue at the point where the city ended and the casino started. From there, drivers passed three larger-than-life cast-stone elephants, a handful of red and orange lamps, a gushing fountain, and what seemed like enough trees and flowers to cover all of Central Park on their way to the city's largest parking deck—a massive white concrete structure that Trump once claimed beautified the city and entitled him to a tax break. Once they parked their cars, guests walked through enclosed halls and tunnels to the casino, never touching a city street. In a remarkably stark version of the tale of two cities, even for Atlantic City, within a couple of blocks of Trump's billion-dollar wonderland lay what used to be the

South Inlet neighborhood, which was by then, even with all of this investment, a part of town where, borrowing a line from Bruce Springsteen, "when you hit a red light you don't stop."[29]

There are two cities in Las Vegas, but the casino companies there have made stark intersections like those in the Inlet irrelevant by moving away from them. The famed strip sits just on the outskirts of town. Adding another barrier between the gaming halls and the city, the megacasinos of the "neon metropolis" of today insist that the sidewalks in front of their buildings are private property. They reserve the right to remove union picketers or anyone else they don't want as part of the crowd.[30] Unlike their Vegas counterparts or even their Atlantic City predecessors, Donald Trump and other New Jersey casino owners couldn't move from the city or take over the sidewalks, so they built over them and around them. Highlighting the principle of exclusion over inclusion, Trump's Taj Mahal used a series of interior bridges rather than the Boardwalk to link to neighboring casinos. In the mid-1990s, Trump planned to put a high-roller gaming parlor—another form of exclusion—on the site of the old Steel Pier, which he had taken over in 1987 and reconfigured a few years later into a helipad. Rather than let his potential customers—the project never came off because Trump ran into fiscal and regulatory problems—walk forty feet across the Boardwalk, he built a fully enclosed bridge to connect the spaces and cut off his property from the northern end of the Boardwalk and the abandoned Inlet.[31] Again, no company wanted to risk losing a gambler to the city or to take a chance of letting the city into the casino.

Outside the gated casino communities, there is still the Boardwalk, and it remains a public place. On summer weekends, crowds continue to jam the "eighth wonder of the world," and the promenade remains a marvelous transition between the ocean and the skyscrapers. But it is no longer a magical place. Dollar stores and pizza stands fill the spaces between the glass-fronted hotels. Some visitors still stroll the Boardwalk in opera clothes and some even ride the rolling chairs, now powered as often by young Russians as by African Americans. More people use the Boardwalk in the gaming city, however, as a conveyor belt to get from one casino to the next. Along its sides, there are still benches—benches that in the past used to be full of people from morning to night watching the endless parade of fashionable tourists. Now the benches are mostly empty, except in the late afternoons when seniors, their rolls of quarters long gone and their food vouchers already spent on the buffet, wait for the next bus home. Most Atlantic City visitors don't really care about the ocean or the Boardwalk, not when there are jackpots to be won and traffic to beat.[32]

But the real change is that the Boardwalk, while remaining the city's calling card, is not its central boulevard any more. The casinos with their parking decks are oriented toward the highway. The Monopoly streets where people once lived, walked, and shopped are, as historian Eugene Moehring notes, "merely arteries that feed tourists" to the garages and then to the gaming tables. They aren't really even city streets any more. Pacific Avenue, once home to the Carnegie Library, the power company's main office, and a dozen churches and synagogues, is now a place for prostitution, Seven-Elevens, and cash-for-gold stores. But this sidewalk-lined street is, like other sidewalk-lined streets in this town, really a placeless tributary of the Atlantic City Expressway, the city's umbilical cord, which supplies it with what it now must have to survive—a steady infusion of cars and buses. That makes this forty-four-mile-long stretch of blacktop, not the Boardwalk, the city's lifeline and main drag.[33]

Not long after Trump opened the Taj Mahal, Atlantic City faced a new form of competition. In the mid-1990s, Mohegan Sun and Foxwood's, Indian-owned casinos located a few hundred miles north of the Jersey shore, opened. They vied for the same East Coast drive-up gamblers and high rollers that Trump and Bally's did. By then, Atlantic City didn't really compete with Las Vegas. As the nation's most malleable place, the glittery strip had remade itself in the 1990s into a desti-nation resort, not just a place to gamble for a few hours and then go. Both Indian casinos, however, were in the business of local gambling, and both were newer, cleaner, and greener than Atlantic City. Each rose from a field along a major high-way, away from, but not too far from the urban areas of New York, Boston, New Haven, and Hartford. They had, in other words, a control over place that Atlantic City lacked. Trying to solidify Atlantic City's hold over the East Coast market, shore casino managers and local leaders looked to rewrite the city's tourist script by underlining once again the disconnection between the city and the casinos.[34]

Borrowing from the Disney model, they started at the entrance. Eight out of every ten people who came to Atlantic City in 1990 came over the Atlantic City Expressway. Whether they drove their own cars from northeast Philadelphia or from Bayside, Long Island, or rode buses from Chinatown or Cherry Hill, they entered town over this highway.[35] From the end of a bridge over the bay, visitors dipped down into town. Directly in front of them stood a tall chain-link fence en-casing the grimy backside of the city's bus station. To the right was Pitney Village, by then a half-empty and boarded-up housing project inhabited mostly by poor, underemployed African Americans. To the left was the Northside. From the road, passengers couldn't see the neighborhood's hundred-year-old churches with stained-glass windows or the little museum starting up at Ky. at the Curb. But they could see squalid bars, dilapidated buildings, and stray dogs rummaging through trash piles on empty lots. Between Ducktown and the Northside stood Columbus Park. Foot traffic had long ago worn away the grass and local kids had scribbled graffiti on the base of the statue of the Italian seaman. What was left was a dusty lot with a few benches for down-and-out gamblers, junkies, and unemployed locals waiting for their next meal at the community food kitchen.

In 1993, two writers well schooled in the Disney model of controlled spaces complained in a casino industry trade journal that negotiating "passage through a depressed and deteriorated urban war zone" was not conducive to a "memorable entertainment experience." With this in mind, the authors advised Atlantic City officials to "comprehensively redevelop its major access routes, so that visitors will gain a favorable impression on their arrival, and especially on their way to the beach, the Boardwalk, and the casinos."[36] City leaders and gaming representatives took this advice to heart. Over the next four years, the Casino Reinvestment Development Agency (CRDA), the public corporation formed in the 1980s to oversee the reinvestment of casino dollars, spent $88 million, raised from parking fees and the redevelopment tax on gambling revenues, in widening roads, bulldozing the bus station, and tearing down a couple of gloomy bars and dozens of Northside houses and apartment buildings. Irate over CRDA's allocation of resources, a local activist denounced the corridor project, as it came to be called, as a "Negro remover."[37] Others complained that the redevelopment agency took funds intended to improve the quality of life in the city and gave them right back to the casinos.[38] But the grumbling didn't stop the bulldozers, and on the cleared land around Columbus Park, CRDA designed a series of fast-moving one-way streets, erected a lighthouse with laser beams that pointed over the highway not the ocean, and planted 20,000 shrubs, 8,000 flowers, and 1,000 tall trees arranged in two straight lines on either side of the road.

"Instead of seeing dilapidated housing, idling buses, [and] the barren lawn of Columbus Park," John Williams, the mastermind behind what was formally dubbed "The New Grand Boulevard—Gateway to America's Favorite Playground," "visitors . . . see a lush garden setting, culminating in a vertical feature—the lighthouse monument—that uses laser beams, recorded sounds and a waterfall along a concrete jetty to express the themes of the healthy seaside recreation on which the city was founded." "The lighthouse," Williams beamed, "is supposed to be attractive enough to make people want to come back and see it closer, on foot, and thus create a walkable environment where there wasn't much in the way of street life before."[39] But of course, not many people got out of their cars to sit on the benches and look at the lighthouse in its bucolic setting. How could they? There is no lighthouse parking. The real point of all the landscaping, demolition, and road building was to get gamblers to the machines and tables as fast as possible. But even more, the project tried to conceal the city from visitors, making sure they didn't see a single luckless resident on their way to the gaming floor.[40]

As part of the corridor project, CRDA raised funds for a brand-new convention center anchored by a bland, utterly predictable atrium hotel not unlike the Marriotts and Hyatts attached to convention centers in downtown Phoenix, Detroit, and New Orleans. The Atlantic City Sheraton was the first noncasino hotel built in the city since gaming came to town. (The casinos didn't really care about where nongamblers slept.) Located five blocks from the Boardwalk and even farther from the marina, the glassy tower sticks out like a midwestern corn silo on the region's flat lands. There is nothing really around the building. Drivers going by the hotel sometimes see men with name tags pinned to their blue blazers running up Arkansas Avenue or across Grand Boulevard's desolate landscaped centerpiece. The only thing chasing them, it seems, is the city.

City leaders surely know that buildings and roads alone will not keep people, especially New Englanders, away from Mohegan Sun or Foxwood's or lure them away from Las Vegas where, again, visitors increasingly go not just to gamble, but also to eat at Spago and Emeril's, swim in gargantuan pools with ocean-sized waves, visit Paris, Venice, and New York City, catch a glimpse of rare white tigers and sea sharks, and indulge guilty pleasures. Atlantic City needs attractions; it needs something other than the casinos to bring people to town, keep them there for more than six hours—the average length of an Atlantic City visit—and get them out of their cars and other enclosed spaces.[41] In the search for that something new, city leaders and gaming executives have rediscovered something old— the public, urban, outdoor entertainment world of the past. The city's former mayor proposed paying stilt walkers, magicians, and popcorn and cotton candy vendors to amuse Boardwalk strollers.[42] During the summer of 2000, the Atlantic City Hilton put umbrellas on the beach in front of its hotel and encouraged its guests to go outside to swim and sunbathe. Down the boardwalk, Trump's Taj Mahal staged beach parties every weekend under gold-fringed sultan's tents. A few years later, a couple of casinos opened beachfront outdoor bars without a single slot machine. Along the bay, meanwhile, CRDA paid for the Sand Castle, the cozy, 5,900-seat home of the city's minor league baseball team, the Surf. The return to this kind of outdoor public entertainment is probably Atlantic City's last best hope, but it might be too late.[43]

The physical city may now be too decrepit, with too much open space and too many moldering buildings, to attract middle-class crowds for anything but gambling behind closed doors. Put another way, in its decayed state, there is still too much city in Atlantic City for suburbanites used to Disney-like public spaces, and that fact suggests that the city's future will be more of what it is today, a collection of grind gambling joints for slots and poker players from towns and cities within easy driving distance, and little more. Having bet big on gambling, there is no going back. A little like an addict, the city lives off casino taxes and needs to keep that revenue stream coming, so political and business leaders continue to mold, out of necessity, the urban landscape to fit the needs of their cash cow and the people who go there, the casino public.

Behind the gates, walkways, puny lobbies, and clockless, climate-controlled environments, the casinos have, however, done something quite remarkable. Offering that luxury experience at a middle-class price, they have created an updated, suburban-friendly public realm. To be sure, sad, lonely tales get acted out every day between the slot machines and roulette wheels. Blank-eyed "casino zombies" mesmerized by the flashing lights and clanging sound of quarters hitting metal trays will stand, pulling the levers of one-armed bandits like robots, saying nothing for hours at a time.[44] City officials and journalists regularly recount stories of mothers who leave their two-year-olds on the Boardwalk so that they can play video poker and of brilliant mathematicians who try to beat the system and lose and end up sleeping at the local homeless shelter. Shaking his head, a doctor recalled a case of a man who collapsed between two blackjack tables and remained sprawled on the floor for ten minutes as gamblers stepped over him to place their bets. Every day, desperate men put down more than they have, lose, and then rush to get a credit card advance they can't afford, hoping that the very next roll of the dice will mark the start of a winning streak. Others cash their welfare checks as soon as they get them. It is not just the poor who deceive themselves. Conservative cabinet officers, who preach the virtues of family values, wager amounts that approach the yearly food budgets of Caribbean nations without apology. Marriages, businesses, and families get destroyed every day at the tables and slot machines. Yet for better or worse, profit-hungry casinos offer a kind of newfangled version of public space, one of the few that exists outside of the malls and theme parks in the increasingly privatized world of today.[45]

In the late 1990s, Shirley and David Gold, both in their mid-sixties, went to the casinos every Thursday. "We don't feel old here," Shirley said. "It's nicer now, because we see people we've gotten to know." David added, "I don't have anything bad to say [about the casinos]. If we didn't come here, we would probably just sit home and watch television." "It's a place to meet other people," a Brooklyn woman told a reporter.[46] Like shopping malls, Atlantic City casinos attract a cross section of people—a broader and more diverse swath of the country than the segregated Boardwalk crowds of yesteryear. High rollers flown in on helicopters mingle with bus riders in windbreakers with the names of their unions on the back. College professors lured by the bright lights and come-ons of cocktail waitresses in cowboy outfits sit at the blackjack tables with engineers following the rules of basic strategy laid out in how-to books. In buffet lines, housewives from

Queens rub elbows with psychologists from Manhattan. During breaks in the action, waiters from Chinatown talk poker with Main Line doctors. Over at the craps tables, salesmen from the suburbs join retired accountants calling, begging, and praying for the shooter to make the point. Crowds two and three deep stand around the wheel of fortune yelling and groaning in unison, all members for that moment of the collective "us"—gamblers—versus "them," the house. "One forms brief but intense relationships with utter strangers while gambling together," explain Frederick and Steven Barthelme, writers and one-time degenerate blackjack players, "which is as intoxicating and as intimate as drinking together, although usually less messy."[47]

The casinos are clearly dangerous places for some, like the Barthelme brothers, but for others, those who can afford to gamble and lose and those who just like being out, they are, like the lost worlds of the Boardwalk, the rolling chair, and the nightclubs, fantasy zones. In every gaming hall, there are packs of women and men in shapeless shorts and gray T-shirts, but there are also, especially at night, couples in sequined dresses and silk jackets. There are people staying up a little later than usual, feeling, as Reese Palley hoped they would, "a little taller, a little prettier, a little sexier" than usual, eating lavish meals, and talking louder, smiling brighter, and bending their stiff bodies to every turn of the cards and roll of the dice.[48] Swept up by the extraordinary displays of excess, some shed detached poses of distance and isolation. Sunglasses come off, people make eye contact, and some, breaking that most entrenched of modern taboos, even talk in elevators. Away from the floor, lounge singers manufacture another moment of community, getting black and white, Latino and Asian, straight and gay, women and men to do the hustle and to sing along to "My Girl."

Gambling, not Motown, is, of course, the casinos' real intoxicant. Betting on spinning cherries or the roll of the dice is about living by chance rather than by the law of the clock or paycheck. Gambling is, moreover, about beating logic, feeling special, and getting lucky. Even the most hardened realists, their heads full of odds and percentages, think for a moment when they drop a coin in a slot machine or place a chip on a blackjack table that, as the Barthelmes write, "something wonderful might happen, something could change their lives."[49] Winning is, as everyone knows, a huge, exhilarating, and powerful rush. Mario Puzo, the author of *The Godfather*, confessed, "I got more pure happiness winning 20 grand at the casino crap[s] table than when I received a check for many times that amount as the result of honest hard work on my book."[50] Gambling, admitted the legendary Las Vegas casino owner Benny Binion, "is a manufactured thrill—you intensify the anticipation of an event by putting money on it."[51] But in perhaps the ultimate illusion and deception, the casino's public of chance gathers to act as if money doesn't matter in a world where money seems to mean everything and so often weighs on people like a concrete slab.[52]

Adding to the fantasy feel, every casino pampers its high-volume players with suites as big as penthouse apartments, lobster dinners, and cocktail parties with supermodels and retired Hall of Fame baseball players. All of the unnecessary service embarrasses some. Other suck it up like a drug, and it becomes as addictive and destructive as crack cocaine and heroin. But others play along with the deception, with money they can afford to lose. "You're not going to win," Manhattan's Rocco Santarcangelo, a high roller, explains, "but you get all the amenities. Resorts even sends me birthday presents. Everybody here knows me. They yell my name at the craps table when they see me coming. It's show business, but let's face it, it makes you feel good."[53]

Bringing the casino public together requires the deployment of updated confidence builders. The crowd must feel safe. In the past, this meant racial and class segregation. But the casino companies' updated version of exclusion entails the real and performed containment of the city. Harrah's and Bally's no doubt erected all those parking decks and conveyor belts to keep the city—the scary city—away. Inside they have turned surveillance into a public show. All of the casinos employ uniformed security teams the size of a midsized city's police force. Every guest, moreover, knows that the house has installed hundreds of magic eyes in the ceilings to watch everything. Obviously, gambling executives mount and then conceal this hardware to foil card counters, cheats, and thieves. But surveillance serves another function. For visitors already heavily invested in private security—with their punch cards to gated communities, cell phones, automatic garage-door openers, and cars equipped with satellite tracking devices—the cameras are reassuring. They don't create the chilling feeling of an Orwellian *1984*, but rather they tell people who live in economically and racially segregated suburbs, send their kids to segregated schools, and shop at segregated malls, that this space—this seemingly public and integrated space—is safe. If anyone from the mean streets outside slips into the casino and makes a move against them, there is, they know, someone watching, and someone will rush to protect them.[54]

When the guards and cameras aren't enough, the casinos help gamblers, especially wealthy ones, to wall themselves off even further. Every hotel offers qualified players exclusive betting and dining rooms blocked off by dark curtains and protected by teams of security guards. Going one step further, in the late 1980s, Caesar's officials removed female and black dealers from a table at a high roller's request. (State gaming regulators later fined the company $250,000 for the offense.)[55] The Atlantic City casino, then, is another version of Mike Davis's postmodern city—a built environment constructed out of fear, uncertainty, and most important, the unremitting desire for exclusion.[56] Recognizing its audience's unspoken hostility to truly inclusive, unguarded public spaces, casino executives continue to install cameras and to build parking decks, skywalks, and puffed-up Wal-Marts. What this architecture and urban planning are trying to do is make the city irrelevant.

In the early 1990s, just as landscapers put the last touches on Grand Boulevard, local officials tried to lure Las Vegas casino mogul Steve Wynn, who had left the city in a huff in the 1980s, back to town. In the intervening years, he had gone to the desert and created the Mirage Resort—the casino of the future, the place that transformed Las Vegas from a gambling mecca to *the* most important entertainment destination anywhere and, perhaps, into the first city of the twenty-first century. Wynn set a high price tag for his return. He would build a $1.1 billion French garden palace and megaresort on the H-Tract, a 168-acre landfill near the marina, if the city built him what his competitor Donald Trump called a "private driveway."[57] Demanding direct access without stoplights from the Atlantic City Expressway to his Le Jardin Palais, Wynn directed state and city officials to dig a tunnel under the city. Some local residents suspected that the gaming wizard wanted something more than a clear, traffic-free pathway. One resident said of the underground project, "They don't need it. I think they're afraid to come through the black communities." Eventually, government representatives signed off on the idea and mapped a route for the tunnel that cut through the Westside, a small middle-class black enclave of tree-lined streets, freshly painted fences, and well-kept lawns. Nine houses, the engineers said, would have to be destroyed. Six families rose up in opposition. One man whose house stood in the tunnel's way raged against the plan, "Atlantic City residents haven't benefited at all from casino gambling. . . . Unemployment was 15 percent before casinos got here and it's still 15 percent now. . . . I don't think an Atlantic City neighborhood, an African American neighborhood, should be destroyed for rednecks and racists from out of town."[58]

The protests didn't stop the digging. But Wynn never came back to Atlantic City either. In 2000, MGM bought out the financially strapped Wynn and pulled out of Atlantic City just after construction workers finished the underground roadway.[59] After years of delay, a massive casino—the Borgata—finally did open at the end of this "private driveway," but the city was still out there and so were middle-class attitudes about the city. Together, this urban landscape and the fears of places that look like this represent the greatest impediments to Atlantic City's comeback. CRDA and other developers have tried to change the set design again. In May 2002, New Jersey governor James E. McGreevey announced "a major plan" of "neighborhood beautification" for Atlantic City. His proposal called for the destruction of "the five worst blocks near the casinos and corridors." After these buildings are cleared away, the glass towers and parking decks would probably be the only structures left in these neighborhoods.[60] The city would get nothing. And it is this paradox between casino-led economic development and urban stagnation that fascinated Bill Moyers in 1986 and that continues to shape Atlantic City.

Beginning in the late 1980s, author William Goldman learned that the Miss America Pageant started using two sets of judges. One had to remain in Atlantic City for a week, while the other panelists—the celebrities—came only for a day or so. Pageant officials, he writes, found it increasingly difficult to get "anyone you've ever heard of to spend a week in Atlantic City. One day was a lot more likely." A little more than a decade later, Samantha, a character from the HBO hit series "Sex in the City," told her girlfriends that her boyfriend was taking her to Atlantic City for the weekend. Puzzled, they responded by asking her what she did wrong.[61]

Why is Atlantic City a joke? The joke is the city. But the city is also the problem—at least from the audience's perspective. No casino or, for that matter, aquarium, convention center, or retro-looking baseball stadium can save a city. Yet they can't obliterate a city either. Despite decades of bulldozer assaults, Atlantic City is still there and because of that there is too much city left for suburbanites raised on Disney-like notions of gated public spheres to get them out of their cars or the casino cocoons.

If visitors somehow break free or stray from the landscaped corridor and underground tunnel, they find themselves in a city of bleak projects, painted-over storefronts, blocks with more holes than houses, and packs of African American and, increasingly, Asian and Latino teenagers on street corners. Immediately, they think, city, crime, riots, and car jackings, and they hit their automatic lock buttons and reach for their cell phones. Only a few get out of the protected spaces of their cars to see what lies beyond these flashes of urban life. And because so few people get out of their cars and the only business in town is tourism, there really isn't much to do or see any more beyond a great sub shop, a few decent Vietnamese, Italian, and soul food restaurants, a couple of busy bars, a second-generation pawnshop, and hints here and there, usually covered up, of the architectural flourishes of yesterday. But again, there is a paradox here, really a grim irony.

For the thousands of people who still live in Atlantic City—and there still are

"GHOSTS," *overleaf*
Ursula Brady's photograph from 1998 looks away from the Boardwalk down St. James Place toward Pacific Avenue.

thousands left despite aspects of this place that make it seem as desolate and alien as the moon—they are stuck between the worst of two worlds. The casinos aim to erase the city, but they can't. Yet what's left behind for those who still live there—the people who can't be erased—is a rough world with few public amenities. The city parks are desolate patches of crabgrass and rimless basketball courts; the public library and sole supermarket are virtual fortresses protected by metal detectors and private security guards; and the downtown is a motley collection of men's clothing stores offering cabaña wear that looks like it's been in stock since the resort's long-ago glory years, greasy spoons, empty buildings, parking lots, and street vendors selling fragrances and knock-offs of the latest cinema releases—and that's as close as the movies get to town. The old corner stores, friendly taverns, jazz clubs, Jewish delis, fresh fruit stands, and butcher shops for the most part are all gone.

For locals, there isn't much of anything. The city government has little control over what CRDA does, so it has a limited voice in local development and reinvestment. There aren't that many good jobs for city residents either. The casino law that aimed at keeping mobsters away and barred anyone with a felony conviction from working in the casinos has blocked many residents, especially African American men, from breaking into the gaming industry. Thousands of locals were arrested in the years when the city's economy bottomed out, the crack epidemic exploded, and there were few nonwhite police officers on the streets. Barred from unionized, well-paying casino jobs, these men are then thrown into another tier of the local economy. Employers assume that anyone applying for a noncasino job has an arrest record. The only positions offered to these people are minimum-wage jobs, and thanks to the bulldozers and speculators, Atlantic City is not a minimum-wage town.

Unlike the glorious postmodern Las Vegas strip built and rebuilt on the outskirts of town, there was a city in Atlantic City before gambling came, and there is still a city, albeit a fading one. Most middle-class visitors see this city—as they do most real cities without theme park markers—as a place to be avoided at all costs. Not long ago, a travel writer told his readers about a number of murders in the city. "If you hear a pinggg!! pinggg!! pingggggggggg!!!" he instructed, "fling yourself to the ground. It may or may not be gunfire, but why take chances?" A Japanese tourist guide, meanwhile, warned visitors against straying too far from the casinos after midnight, and *Newsday* reported in 1998, "[M]ost people do not feel safe walking the streets at night."[62] Strangely enough, the Atlantic City gaming industry benefits from the perception of urban space as dangerous. Fear of the city keeps gamblers locked inside casino fortresses glued to the blackjack tables and slot machines, feeling safe under the watchful eyes of hundreds of surveillance cameras. And that's just where the casinos want them. They don't want them at the movies—so there aren't any in the city. They don't want guests sitting in the lobbies talking—so none of the hotels have lobbies; they just have high-speed computerized check-in desks. They don't want them eating at a local restaurant, and they don't want them watching the Surf, Atlantic City's minor league baseball team. As a result, there is very little trickle-down from the Boardwalk, marina, and H-Tract gaming palaces to the city. In fact, there is less and less city left each day. But that doesn't mean gambling hasn't had a trickle-down effect; there is no way $5 billion in investment and 50,000 jobs can't make an economic dent—somewhere.

SUBURBAN PUBLICS

Lisa Johnson, a former casino spokesperson and television news anchor, offered a clear-eyed assessment of gambling's contribution to the community. "We now have a cultural infrastructure," Johnson, who was born in Atlantic City, explained in 1998. "When I was growing up here, there were no museums, maybe two movie theaters, no playhouse, and certainly no bookstore. . . . Now we have museums, multi-screen theaters, an Equity playhouse—everything that any major suburban community has, plus a thriving resort." In twenty years, she concluded, "[W]e've gone from a cultural wasteland to an interesting, stimulating great place to live."[63]

Johnson gave her reading of Atlantic City's history from a Starbuck's coffee shop inside a Borders bookstore situated twelve miles west of the city, next to the Macy's department store that anchors the Hamilton Mall. Location is crucial here. The trickle-down from the casinos has bypassed the city and ended up in the suburbs. Gambling set up an economic framework for the creation of these new public worlds, public worlds built along the roads leading out of town and at the malls, not where the old neighborhoods used to be.

Like the new Las Vegas, the new Atlantic City economy is a bit like the old Detroit.[64] Backed by the strong arms of Local 54 of the Hotel Employees and Restaurant Employees International Union (HEREIU), casino workers make a decent living. With two people on the job, families can buy a new 2,000-square-foot house and a piece of the American Dream. But their dreams usually drift to suburban enclaves with pastoral names like Blue Herron Pines and LaTonka Lakes. While Atlantic City itself has rotted from neglect, losing thousands of residents and hundreds of shops and restaurants, these car-friendly, parking lot–centered worlds with new houses on half-acre lots fronted by garages have multiplied. Between 1980 and 1998, the populations of Galloway, Hamilton, and Egg Harbor townships, the fastest growing communities in the area, increased by 132 percent, 92 percent, and 43 percent, respectively. It is in these new suburban places as well as in older suburbs like Northfield, Linwood, and Somers Point that the casino-generated growth has made the greatest impact.[65]

Today, while Atlantic City remains without a single cinema, there are nine screens across a busy four-lane road from the Kensington furniture store, now the size of an entire strip mall. Outside of Sears Town, now the Shore Mall, a fourteen-screen theater stands in a massive parking lot. About ten miles away in Somers Point, the Village Cinema presents four movies nightly. Down the street from the Hamilton Mall and Borders bookstore, a new theater complex with stadium seating and another huge parking lot just opened. While suburban movie houses premiere the newest releases every Friday, plans for an Atlantic City movie theater have repeatedly fallen apart. No investor or casino, in this grind gambling town, seems willing to build a theater that will take people away from the gaming floor for two hours at a time. They are betting instead on video poker machines—which one industry analyst has called the crack cocaine of gambling.[66]

Casino operators' desire to keep poker players glued to Joker's Wild machines does not fully explain the limits of Atlantic City's casino-driven reindustrialization. While the city's reign as the Queen of Resorts ended with the collapse of segregation, its rebirth has been shaped by the refusal of most people—especially white Americans—to live in and vacation in inclusive spaces. In an all-too-familiar story, scores of white residents, followed by black residents, bolted to the suburbs the moment civil rights activists desegregated city hotels and theaters. White tourists, meanwhile, stayed at home or headed elsewhere, in some cases to the essentially segregated shore towns south of Atlantic City, like Avalon and Stone Harbor, both of which have small, but still working, downtowns with picture shows. The casino owners have tried to erect Disney-style theme parks with gates and security guards, like the Taj Mahal and later Bally's Wild, Wild West Casino, on top of a city that once had showy department stores, crowded downtown sidewalks, neighborhood hangouts, and several American Legion chapters. They argue that more hotels, a bigger convention center, taller parking decks, and larger, more intricately themed casinos—essentially, unfettered consumer capitalism—can cure the city's ills. According to this increasingly popular model of urban renewal, suburbanites will heal the cities by traveling downtown not to live, but to visit for an afternoon or a weekend. The money they leave behind is supposed to trickle down to the poor. But having private casino corporations rebuild urban spaces has not worked in Atlantic City or anywhere else it has been tried. At the end of the day, they are not the best urban planners.[67]

Epilogue

I t is hard to know exactly where to end this story about Atlantic City and the people who lived there and went there. The city is, after all, still there on the northern end of Absecon Island. Every day, local residents wait at bus stops, go to work, visit doctors' offices, and stop off on the way home to pick up a video, fill a prescription, and buy a lottery ticket. Cars roll off the Atlantic City Expressway in steady streams from dawn to dusk. Each morning, cooks prepare slices of pepperoni and broccoli pizza and mounds of grilled peppers, onions, and sausage for sale at Boardwalk food stands. In the casinos, bus riders cash in their vouchers, high rollers check into seven-room suites with gold-tinged wallpaper, and slot players stand wide-eyed before machines that light up and blare carnival sounds to announce another lucky winner.

In March 2003, Bruce Springsteen walked onto the stage of the newly refurbished Boardwalk Hall—the repairs paid for by CRDA with casino dollars—grinning as a recording of Bert Parks singing "There she is, Miss America" played in the background. "Real old school," the New Jersey–born singer said as he strapped on his scratched-up Telecaster and launched into a ferocious rendition of "Atlantic City." When he got to the chorus, roadies turned on the bright house lights, and the crowd sang along:

> Everything dies baby that's a fact
> But maybe everything that dies someday comes back
> Put your makeup on fix your hair up pretty and
> Meet me tonight in Atlantic City[1]

Maybe Springsteen and his fans were right. Maybe they were there on the Boardwalk that night, their hair fixed up pretty, to bear witness to yet another of Atlantic City's rebirths. Many were probably convinced that the city will, someday, come back. Some surely think that time is now. As concert goers drove into town that night, they passed the skeleton of a new $60 million upscale shopping complex and outlet mall going up on cleared land near the corridor's laser beam lighthouse. On the Boardwalk, cranes had just made space for Siganos Plaza, a block of new, high-end retail shops. No T-shirt stores or pizza parlors allowed. Across from the Boardwalk Hall, construction crews were on their way home after spending another day gutting the Ocean One Mall, once Million Dollar Pier, in preparation for its transformation into Park Place on the Boardwalk, a Monopoly-themed, $80 million shopping, dining, and entertainment center.[2] Tropicana officials, meanwhile, were in the middle of building the Quarter, a $245 million hotel and casino expansion project. When finished, it will, company representatives promise, "evoke images of Old Havana, Cuba."[3] And Springsteen fans, waiting on the Boardwalk for the show to start that night, couldn't help but notice the shimmering, copper-colored, tube-shaped, forty-story tower rising from the swamps near the marina. That is the Borgata Hotel, Casino, and Spa—the first new resort hotel to open in the city since Donald Trump's Taj Mahal opened its gates in 1990.

Financial analysts, local politicians, and regular visitors see the Borgata, taller than the Taj, with twice as much parking and casino space, as the city's future—a future as bright as the building itself. Civic leaders eagerly await an anticipated $10 million yearly tax windfall, and store owners all over the area are already counting on the 2,600 new employees to fill their shops and boost their revenues. Businesspeople expect to see a tidal wave of new investment in town as the older casinos try to keep up with the new kid on the block.[4] Some believe the Borgata represents, finally, the start of the city's latest comeback. From the Inlet to Ducktown, over at the Hamilton Mall, and along Wall Street, people are predicting that the new resort hotel will do for Atlantic City what Steve Wynn's Mirage did for Las Vegas—remake the town from a drive-up, grind gambling center to a destination resort, from a place where people come for less time than it takes to finish a shift on the assembly line to one where they stay for days at a time, and from a dying resort with eleven neon-lit, slot warehouses to a burgeoning city with its own cultural and social infrastructure. The fact that Springsteen was in town, playing at the Boardwalk Hall, not at a casino, was evidence to some that this transition was already on its way.

"We didn't sign up to change Atlantic City," says the Borgata's executive vice president, Larry Mullin.[5] Yet the firm's press agents did fuel expectations that the hotel's opening would mark the start of something truly significant in the city's history. "We will build a new environment," boasted one company official, "in which people will have a sense that something has changed in Atlantic City."[6] "Every Night," the casino's Web page says, "Magic Happens."[7] Press releases describe the $1.2 billion development, a joint venture between Las Vegas companies Boyd Enterprises, owner of Circus, Circus, and MGM, as "upscale, not uptight" and as a "place to interact, play, indulge, and escape."[8] Another company official calls the sprawling resort "fun, upscale, sensual, and international."[9]

Everyone associated with the Borgata insists that it is, above all, different from the city's other gaming halls. In many ways, it is. There are no Bibles in Borgata rooms, but there are Internet access, showers for two, and "sexy" pillows that say "Tonight" on one side and "Not Tonight" on the other. Its 3,600 slot machines have plush cushioned chairs in front and footrests underneath, and they are all cashless, running on the casino's version of the Kinko's copy card, not rolls of quarters. "Say buh-by to heavy slot cups and long lines," company publicists write. "Oh yes. Don't forget clean hands, too."[10] Barely covered cocktail waitresses will deliver drinks on the casino floor, at the pool, and even, one would think, in the hotel's twenty-two Botox treatment rooms. Borgata executives promise "entertainment for grown-ups": a luxurious spa, private rooms for "players" in the nightclub, stand-up comedy from Carrot Top and Dennis Miller, and classic rock from Crosby, Stills, and Nash and Meatloaf. With the words to "Bat Out of Hell" still ringing in their ears, guests can, the morning after the show, get a double cappuccino with skim milk from Starbuck's, shop at boutiques in the "retail piazza" with "classic Italian architecture" showing off designer wares from DKNY, Prada, Cartier, Versace, and Dolce and Gabbana, and choose among eleven "unique" restaurants.[11]

But for all of its trend-setting "firsts" and its "unique" and "upscale" attractions, the Borgata isn't really that different from Atlantic City's other casinos. Company press agents stress not only the hotel's grown-up, sexy pleasures but also its distance from the city and urban residents. A billboard announcing the casino's arrival pictures a man staring up at the immense copper tower. He is utterly alone in a wide-open field of knee-high green grass, his back, literally and metaphorically, to the city. Even the casino's name highlights its antiurban, bucolic character. Borgata means "little village" in Italian, and that, or an oversized mall, is what the forty-three-acre complex with its landscaped gardens and a pool the size of a motel is trying to become.[12] Built on the H-Tract at the end of the tunnel under the city, the same place Steve Wynn imagined as the site of his Le Jardin Palais, the casino, hotel, and spa is meant to be its own, self-contained world. And that's what all of the city's casinos want to be: self-contained worlds shut off from the everyday worries of work and family, crime and city streets. The Borgata will simply do this better than its competitors. Offering greater distance from urban decay, more opportunities for self-indulgence and gourmet food, thicker clumps of exotic plants, and less emphasis on gambling will allow the casino to present a better articulated, more exclusive version of the casino public spaces operating all over town.

Once the people with "aspirations," "looking to trade up"—the Borgata's target audience, according to a company executive—check into the hotel, bellhops, dealers, cocktail waitresses, and personal trainers—cast members—will do everything they can to keep them there. With more eateries than most small towns, the casino wants to offer something for every mood and every time of day. Guests rushing to the tables can get a "quick hit" lunch at the Gypsy Bar and later settle in for a sumptuous dinner at New York's Old Homestead Steak House. Or maybe they will want to explore the Asian-fusion menu at acclaimed Philadelphia chef Susana Foo's brand-new Suilan. Where the Borgata doesn't want its social-climbing guests to go is Atlantic City, to Scannochio's or Angelo's, the Knife and Fork or the White House Sub Shop. The casino's Web page, in fact, says almost nothing about Atlantic City, its history or its present, the beach or the Boardwalk. All it tells people is how to find the tunnel and go under the city to the Borgata. Like the other casinos, this new one, built as much for entertainment as for gambling, is designed as a world apart from the city. Today's upscale fantasies, and the playacting they require, can only be produced behind closed doors, in exclusive, walled-off, or in this case, tunneled-off settings. The Borgata is, then, at best, a fifty-fifty bet to remake the city. There is no guarantee that its white-collar swingers and Generations X and Y visitors will ever see the city or that its new employees will spend any of their earnings along Atlantic Avenue.

The irony is that the city is being remade every day. But not many people seem to recognize where this rebuilding is happening.

Four years ago, I met the then-mayor of the city, James Whelan, over steamed clams and lobster at a dinner hosted by the Visitors and Convention Bureau on Garden Pier. I told him I was writing a book about Atlantic City. He looked down at me—Whelan is as tall as a basketball forward—and scoffed, "Will this be another tale of two cities?"

"No, no," I said.

Apparently I didn't convince him because Whelan advised, "Go visit the North Inlet before you write anything." Then he walked away.

I took his advice, and at lunchtime the next day, I drove from the public library downtown through the wide-open spaces of the South Inlet and then over to the North Inlet, the one-time Jewish neighborhood, then African American neighborhood, then abandoned land on the northern tip of the island and the end of the Boardwalk. By the late 1990s, this area had become the showcase for CRDA's plans to rehabilitate the city's housing stock and neighborhood life. As I made a left turn onto Maine Avenue, I saw a line of attractive, two-story, beige row houses. I slowed down to get a closer look. All I could think about was James Howard Kunstler, Andres Duany, and other new urbanist designers. They would, I thought, like what was there. Built close together and near the sidewalks—yes, there were sidewalks—with easy-to-find front doors, the homes had elegant vertical windows, comfortable front porches, and four-step stoops. Parking was available on the street and in the back in garages on narrow alleyways.

But there was something strange about the area. There was no one there. No one was walking on the sidewalks or sitting on their porches or eating at the deli anchoring the little shopping center. A few cars went by, but I didn't see anyone else. It felt as lonely and desolate as a suburban cul de sac in the middle of a weekday afternoon. I went back to the North Inlet a few more times at different times of the day, and it was always the same—empty. Everyone was either at work or inside behind covered windows. But there are a lot of police cars around. Several years ago, CRDA put in place a program aimed at stabilizing city neighborhoods, like the North Inlet, making them "more economically viable and safer for the citizens who work and live there." Under the plan, the redevelopment agency subsidized mortgages for city police officers and gave them marked patrol cars to take home and drive during off-duty hours.[13]

On my way home to Ventnor one day, I drove along Atlantic Avenue through Chelsea, on the city's southern end. I had traveled this route hundreds of times before, but I hadn't really paid much attention to the surroundings. But that day, I pulled over and watched what was happening. The street was alive with activity. There were families and couples, single men and teenagers moving in and out of corner stores, restaurants, bakeries, ice cream stands, bars, law and dental offices, and a branch of the Atlantic City Free Public Library.

Over time, I learned that most of the people on the street were Vietnamese and Salvadoran, Chinese and Mexican. They lived in Chelsea and walked or took the jitney to their jobs in the casinos. They were remaking the city from the bottom up. But the grassroots city building they were doing seemed to be going on under the radar screen. I never heard anyone really say much about the area, except to tell me what it used to be like or recommend one of its newer ethnic eateries. "They're cheap and real authentic," people would tell me, and they were right on both counts.

Over the next few years, as I watched the dance of people on Chelsea's streets more closely, I started to wonder what would happen if the city ever zoned this area for casino redevelopment or needed to put a new road there or maybe a bus parking lot. What if middle-class people did come back to the city? Would they take over Chelsea again, making it too expensive for its current flock of working-class residents? How long, I wondered, would it be until the bulldozers came and plowed down this beachfront neighborhood in the making, possibly the city's most deeply rooted piece of its future? Maybe I'm wrong, and maybe Chelsea will thrive for a long time as a multiethnic neighborhood. Maybe the past won't be prologue and the city will come to value this nonwhite, not-so-exclusive space, and it, not the rather sterile North Inlet, will become the blueprint for the city that, someday, might come back.

Not long ago I asked Reese Palley about the city and what he saw in its future. He didn't mention Chelsea, but he did, as always, have something interesting to say. Although he splits his time now between South Florida and downtown Philadelphia, the one-time peddler with a fancy cart still thinks about his home-town and its "unique experiment with urban renewal." Now, however, he doesn't think so much about bulldozers and Disneyland; he thinks instead about the Pequot casino in Connecticut and other Indian-owned casinos. "What might have been enormously interesting (but certainly too radical)," he says, "would have been to tribalize all of the residents so that ownership of the casinos, à la the Indian casinos, would have devolved upon all."[14] But this massive redistribution of wealth didn't happen, and, of course, it won't happen. That leaves Atlantic City pretty much as it is, a stark, vacant, poor city with a beach, the Boardwalk, and, now that the Borgata has opened, twelve separate, inward-looking casino villages that leave only crumbs on the Monopoly streets around them.

NOTES

INTRODUCTION (pages 3–18)

1. Interview with Jordan E. Sayles by Cynthia Ringe, April 24, 1978, Atlantic City Living History, Heston Room, Atlantic City Free Public Library (hereafter, ACFPL).

2. Bill Kent, *Down by the Sea* (New York: St. Martin's, 1993), 130.

3. On resorts as fantasy spots, see Susan Fainstein and David Gladstone, "Evaluating Urban Tourism," in *The Tourist City*, ed. Dennis R. Judd and Susan F. Fainstein (New Haven, Conn.: Yale University Press, 1999), 21; and John Hannigan, *Fantasy City: Pleasure and Profit in the Postmodern Metropolis* (London: Routledge, 1998), 7.

4. Charles E. Funnell, *By the Beautiful Sea: The Rise and High Times of That Great American Resort, Atlantic City* (New York: Knopf, 1975), 37; and Jonathan Van Meter, *The Last Good Time: Skinny D'Amato, the Notorious 500 Club, and the Rise and Fall of Atlantic City* (New York: Crown, 2003), 23.

5. Robert Kotlowitz, *The Boardwalk* (New York: Knopf, 1977), 185, 186. On the "bewitching" quality of the rolling chairs, see Vicki Gold Levi, "Rolling Chairs: The Sex Symbol of 1905," *Philadelphia Bulletin*, January 10, 1981.

6. Van Meter, *The Last Good Time*, 26.

7. Harrison Rhodes, *In Vacation America* (New York: Harper and Brothers, 1915), 7.

8. Funnell, *By the Beautiful Sea*, inside cover. On Roosevelt's (and Atlantic City's) complicated politics, see Gary Gerstle, *American Crucible: Race and Nation in the Twentieth Century* (Princeton, N.J.: Princeton University Press, 2001).

9. David Halberstam, *The Fifties* (New York: Ballantine, 1994), x. For more on the formation of this middle class, see Loren Baritz, *The Good Life: The Meaning of Success for the American Middle Class* (New York: Knopf), 56–165; and Sherry B. Ortner, *New Jersey Dreaming: Capital, Culture, and the Class of '58* (Durham, N.C.: Duke University Press, 2003).

10. Philip Roth, *American Pastoral* (New York: Random House, 1997), 69.

11. On this notion of the national community, see Baritz, *The Good Life*, 83.

12. Cindy S. Aron, *Working at Play: A History of Vacations in the United States* (New York: Oxford University Press, 1999), 206–7.

13. Ibid.

14. I have adopted a rather broad definition of *public space* for this project, because I think the people who went to Atlantic City had an equally broad definition of public space. For them and for me, public space is any place where access is an issue. That distinguishes public space then from, for example, the home and country clubs. But it does include parks and playgrounds and, even more important, for Atlantic City and most of twentieth-century America, sites of consumption like amusement parks, malls, theaters, nightclubs, sidewalks, and neighborhood taverns.

15. Robert Zausner, "Atlantic City's Most Unwanted," *Philadelphia Inquirer*, May 25, 2003.

16. Donald Wittkowski, "A.C. Residents Hope Program Gets Thriftway to Remove Bars," *Atlantic City Press*, April 28, 2003.

17. Baritz, *The Good Life*, 148.

18. "A Dowager's Decline," *Newsweek* (June 8, 1970), 86.

19. Quoted in Gaeton Fonzi and Bernard McCormick, "Bust-Out Town," *Philadelphia Magazine* (August 1970), 58.

20. Zausner, "Atlantic City's Most Unwanted," 20.

21. There are a number of important and interesting studies of Atlantic City as a gambling town; see, for instance, George Sternlieb and James W. Hughes, *The Atlantic City Gamble* (Cambridge, Mass.: Harvard University Press, 1983); Michael Pollack, *Hostage to Fortune: Atlantic City and Casino Gambling* (Princeton, N.J.: Center for Analysis of Public Issues, 1987); Gigi Mahan, *The Company That Bought the Boardwalk: A Reporter's Story of Resorts International* (New York: Random House, 1981); Ovid Demaris, *The Boardwalk Jungle* (New York: Doubleday, 1986); Paul Teske and Bela Sur, "Winners and Losers: Politics, Casino Gambling, and Development in Atlantic City," *Policy Studies Review* 10 (Spring/Summer 1991), 130–37; David Johnson, *Temples of Chance* (New York: Doubleday, 1992); and for a particularly scathing attack, Robert Goodman, *The Luck Business: The Devastating Consequences and Broken Promises of America's Gambling Explosion* (New York: Free Press, 1995).

22. For an interesting commentary on the hold of the declension narrative over urban studies, see Max Page, "Crucibles of Culture: Telling Stories of Urban Vitality amidst a Narrative of Decline" (unpublished paper delivered at the Urban History Association Meeting, Pittsburgh, Pa., September 2002).

23. James Howard Kunstler, *The Geography of Nowhere: The Rise and Decline of America's Man-Made Landscape* (New York: Simon and Schuster, 1993), 228.

24. George Sternlieb, "The City as Sandbox," *Public Interest* 25 (Fall 1971): 14–21.

25. Andres Duany, Elizabeth Plater-Zyberk, and Jeff Speck, *Suburban Nation: The Rise of Sprawl and the Decline of the American Dream* (New York: North Point, 2000); Michael Sorkin, ed., *Variations on a Theme Park: The New American City and the End of Public Space* (New York: Hill and Wang, 1992); and Ray Suarez, *The Old Neighborhood: What We Lost in the Great Suburban Migration, 1966–1999* (New York: Free Press, 1999). See also Jane Jacobs, *The Death and Life of Great American Cities* (New York: Random House, 1961).

26. Interview with James Usry by author, September 30, 1999.
27. For the best book exploring exclusion in the old city, see David Nasaw, *Going Out: The Rise and Fall of Public Amusements* (New York: Basic, 1993).
28. On Disney and urban tourism, see essays by Margaret Crawford, "The World in a Shopping Mall"; M. Christine Boyer, "Cities for Sale: Merchandising History at South Street Seaport"; and Michael Sorkin, "See You in Disneyland," all in Sorkin, ed., *Variations on a Theme Park*, 3–30, 181–204, 205–32.
29. For a smart, perceptive treatment of the making of the newest public spaces, see Hal Rothman, *Neon Metropolis: How Las Vegas Started the Twenty-First Century* (New York: Routledge, 2002), esp. 117–18.
30. Paul Goldberger, "The Rise of the Private City," in *Breaking Away: The Future of Cities: Essays in Memory of Robert F. Wagner, Jr.*, ed. Julia Vitullo Martin (New York: Twentieth Century Fund, 1996), 135–47; Kenneth Jackson, "All the World's a Mall," *American Historical Review* 101 (October 1996): 1111–21; Robert Putnam, *Bowling Alone: The Collapse and Revival of American Community* (New York: Simon and Schuster, 2000); and Goodman, *The Luck Business*.
31. Web postings, Nick Geiger, October 13, 2001, and Tom Chambers, February 14, 2001, Atlantic City Memory Lane, available: www.iloveac.com/memory.
32. Web posting, Chris Meyers, June 14, 2001, Atlantic City Memory Lane, available: www.iloveac.com/memory.

CHAPTER 1 (pages 19–44)

1. Bruce Bliven, "The American Utopia: Atlantic City," *New Republic* (December 29, 1920), 126–27.
2. For more on this version of the American Dream, see Jim Cullen, *The American Dream: The History of an Idea That Shaped a Nation* (New York: Oxford University Press, 2003), 59–102.
3. Martin Paulsson, *The Social Anxieties of Progressive Reform: Atlantic City, 1854–1920* (New York: New York University Press, 1994), 14.
4. On some of the city's first businesses and other institutions, see Reese Smith, "Smoother Motoring in Atlantic City," *New York Times*, June 24, 1956; and Vicki Gold Levi and Lee Eisenberg, *Atlantic City: 125 Years of Ocean Madness* (Berkeley, Calif.: Ten Speed, 1979), 1–9.
5. Paulsson, *Social Anxieties of Progressive Reform*, 21.
6. Levi and Eisenberg, *Atlantic City*, 17–25; Jonathan Van Meter, *The Last Good Time: Skinny D'Amato, the Notorious 500 Club, and the Rise and Fall of Atlantic City* (New York: Crown, 2003), 23; Mark Tyrrell, "The Boardwalk," *Atlantic City Magazine* (June 1992), 94–95. For more on the history of the Boardwalk, see Frank M. Butler, *The Book of the Boardwalk* (Atlantic City: The 1954 Association, 1952), 1–14; Frank Ward O'Malley, "The Board-Walkers," *Everybody's Magazine* (August 1908), 233–43; Sam Baol, "Eighty Years of 'the Eighth Wonder,'" *New York Times Magazine*, June 25, 1960, 16; and G. Patrick Pawling, "Boardwalk: The People's Park Place," *American Legion Magazine* (August 1998), 27–28.
7. Earle L. Ovington, "The City of Robust Health," n.d., Vertical Files: History of AC:

Early History 1800s, Heston Room, ACFPL; Levi and Eisenberg, *Atlantic City*, 8; Gay J. Talese, "Famous Rolling Chairs beside the Sea," *New York Times*, February 21, 1954; and Cindy S. Aron, *Working at Play: A History of Vacations in the United States* (New York: Oxford University Press, 1999), 15–44.

8. Ovington, "The City of Robust Health."

9. Quoted in Glen Duffy, "She 'Did Her Part' for the Blenheim," *Atlantic City Press*, August 20, 1978.

10. On the history of the rolling chair, see Butler, *Book of the Boardwalk*, 35; William McMahon, *So Young . . . So Gay* (Atlantic City: Press Publishing, 1970), 100–101; Talese, "Famous Rolling Chairs"; A. E. Seidel, "100 Years of Boardwalk Rolling Chairs: 1884 to 1984," Vertical Files: Historical File: Atlantic City Boardwalk, ACFPL; and *The WPA Guide to 1930s New Jersey* (1939; reprint, New Brunswick, N.J.: Rutgers University Press, 1986), 192.

11. Interestingly, the city banned the rolling chairs in 1905, but tourists complained, and the next year the chairs were back on the Boardwalk. McMahon, *So Young . . . So Gay*, 101.

12. Conan Doyle's account of the Boardwalk is reprinted in *Shore Chronicles: Diaries and Travelers' Tales from the Jersey Shore*, ed. Margaret Thomas Buchholz (Harvey Cedars, N.J.: Down the Shore Publishing, 1999), 267–68. See also *Atlantic City Press*, May 30, 1939, Vertical Files: Rolling Chairs, ACFPL; Talese, "Famous Rolling Chairs"; and Seidel, "100 Years of Boardwalk Rolling Chairs."

13. For the description of the sound of the rolling chairs, see Despina Messinesi, "Atlantic City: The Big Gamble—Sun and Sea, All-Night Life," *Vogue* (April 1980), 182. Also see "Ocean Unlocked," "Moaning Isn't the Surf, It's the Hotelmen with Vacation Bonanza Headaches," *Philadelphia Bulletin*, May 30, 1941; July 28, 1944.

14. Talese, "Famous Rolling Chairs."

15. James Huneker, *New Cosmopolis: A Book of Images* (New York: Scribner's, 1915), 312.

16. George A. Birmingham, *From Dublin to Chicago: Some Notes on a Tour in America* (New York: Doran, 1914), 97, 110–12.

17. Martin Waldron, "AC's Grand Hotel," *New York Times*, August 7, 1977.

18. Quoted in George E. Thomas, *William L. Price: Arts and Crafts to Modern Design* (New York: Princeton Architectural Press, 2000), 135, 340.

19. Huneker, *New Cosmopolis*, 328.

20. Bill Kent with Robert Ruffolo and Lauralee Dobbins, *Atlantic City: America's Playground* (Encinitas, Calif.: Heritage Media, 1998), 194.

21. Jim Waltzer, "The Marlborough Blenheim," *Atlantic City* (April 1995), 83–84; and Thomas Hine, "Report from Atlantic City," *Progressive Architect* 58 (March 1977): 25.

22. On Orientalist themes, see, of course, Edward Said's classic study, *Orientalism* (New York: Random House, 1978). See also the insightful reading of Orientalist themes in the resort buildings of Coney Island in Woody Register, *The Kid of Coney Island: Fred Thompson and the Rise of American Amusements* (New York: Oxford University Press, 2000), 98–99, 113–21. See also Matthew Bernstein and Gaylyn Stadler, eds., *Visions of the East: Orientalism in Film* (New Brunswick, N.J.: Rutgers University Press, 1997), 3.

23. Thomas, *William L. Price*, 134–35, 164; and William L. Price, "The Price of Early Modernism," *Interiors* (December 2000): 29–30.

24. See the phrase *architecture of fantasy* in John F. Kasson, *Amusing the Millions: Coney Island at the Turn of the Century* (New York: Hill and Wang, 1978), 63; and David Naylor, *American Picture Palaces: The Architecture of Fantasy* (New York: Prentice Hall, 1981).

25. Huneker, *New Cosmopolis*, 325.

26. Jim Quinn, "Slouching towards Brigantine," *Philadelphia Magazine* (June 1978), 257.

27. Robert Kotlowitz, *The Boardwalk* (New York: Knopf, 1977), 42; and Butler, *Book of the Boardwalk*, 12.

28. Jacquelin Robertson coined this phrase, which is quoted by Andrew Ross, *Celebration Chronicles: Life, Liberty, and the Pursuit of Property Value in Disney's New Town* (New York: Ballantine, 1999), 15.

29. On lights and fantasy, see David Nasaw, *Going Out: The Rise and Fall of Public Amusements* (New York: Basic, 1993); Register, *The Kid of Coney Island*; and David E. Nye, *Electrifying America: Social Meanings of New Technology, 1880–1940* (Cambridge, Mass.: MIT Press, 1990). On Atlantic City, see Jim Waltzer and Tom Willis, *Tales of South Jersey: Profiles and Personalities* (New Brunswick, N.J.: Rutgers University Press, 2001), 94–98; and Elaine Finn, "Fire Destroys Steeplechase Pier," unidentified clipping, December 11, 1988, Vertical Files: Atlantic City Boardwalk, Piers #1, Atlantic County Historical Society, Somers Point, New Jersey.

30. Witold Rybczynski, *City Life* (New York: Touchstone, 1995), 154–55.

31. Atlantic City historian Charles Funnell is quoted in Gay Talese, "One More Spin of the Wheel for Atlantic City," *New York Times*, September 8, 1996.

32. Birmingham, *From Dublin to Chicago*, 106–7. For more on the Boardwalk barkers, see "Atlantic City," *Holiday Magazine*, n.d., Scrapbook 1959–1960–1961, Greater Atlantic City Chamber of Commerce (hereafter GACCC), Atlantic City, New Jersey.

33. Charles E. Funnell, *By the Beautiful Sea: The Rise and High Times of That Great American Resort, Atlantic City* (New York: Knopf, 1975), 137–41. See also John A. Jakle, *The Tourist: Travel in Twentieth-Century North America* (Lincoln and London: University of Nebraska Press, 1985), 57–58.

34. Michael Maattala, "What a People-Watcher Saw at Atlantic City," *Philadelphia Bulletin*, June 1, 1975.

35. "Learning from Las Vegas: Thomas Hine interviews Robert Venturi and Steven Izenour," *AIA Journal* 71 (November 1982): 45. See a similar observation in O'Malley, "The Board-Walkers," 238.

36. Dorothee Polson, "Romantic, Enchanted AC," *Arizona Republic*, May 28, 1969, G. Lody's Book, Heston Room, ACFPL.

37. Kotlowitz, *The Boardwalk*, 187.

38. Jim Waltzer, "The Marlborough Blenheim," *Atlantic City* (April 1995), 84; and "Talk of the Town," *New Yorker*, October 31, 1988.

39. Kotlowitz, *The Boardwalk*, 48, 197; George Anastasia, "Blenheim Hotel Demolished for Casino," *Philadelphia Inquirer*, November 10, 1978; Louis D. Hertz, "Marlborough Memories," unpublished typescript, n.d., Vertical Files: Hotel Index, Heston Room, ACFPL. See also interview with Marlene Faust by author, August 30, 1999.

See furthermore how the lobbies functioned in Thomas Hine, "Atlantic City," *AIA Journal* 71 (November 1982): 38.

40. Paul Goldberger, "The Secret Life of Lobbies," *Gourmet* (May 2000), 187–88.

41. *Polk's Atlantic City Directory* (Philadelphia, Pa.: Polk, 1945, 1948, 1955), Heston Room, ACFPL. On the fur shops, see interview with Murray Raphel by author, September 8, 1999; and on the Needlecraft, see Van Meter, *The Last Good Time*, 134.

42. *The WPA Guide to 1930s New Jersey*, 192; *Polk's Atlantic City Directory* (Philadelphia, Pa.: Polk, 1955), Heston Room, ACFPL. For an example of one such postcard, see Gertrude and Jim (last name unknown) to John W. McKay, November 11, 1948, 647.94 Cha 107, Postcard Collection, Heston Room, ACFPL.

43. For a list of Boardwalk stores, see *Polk's Atlantic City Directory* (Philadelphia, Pa.: Polk, 1944 and 1954), Heston Room, ACFPL.

44. Lewis A. Erenberg observed a very similar trend in New York at the same time; see his book *Steppin' Out: New York Nightlife and the Transformation of American Culture, 1890–1930* (Chicago: University of Chicago Press, 1981), 10, 17.

45. Russel B. Nye, "Eight Ways of Looking at an Amusement Park," *Journal of Popular Culture* 15 (Summer 1981): 65–66. See also Nasaw, *Going Out.*

46. Steven V. Cronin, "100 Years of Magic," *Atlantic City Press*, June 18, 1998.

47. On the attractions of the pier, see, for example, *Steel Pier Program and Guide Book, 1947*, Allen "Boo" Pergament Private Collection, Margate, New Jersey; and George A. Hamid, *Circus* (New York: Sterling, 1950).

48. Kent et al., *Atlantic City*, 210; and "Bridge to the Old World," *Time* (June 7, 1961), 53–54.

49. "Hamid Recalls Greats," n.d. (after 1964), Vertical Files: Steel Pier, Heston Room, ACFPL; and Stephanie Zatwaska, "Pier Was Nation's Premier Showplace," *Atlantic City Press*, December 11, 1982.

50. Quotes from Laura Italiano, "Diving Bell Offered Patrons Undersea Adventure—Of a Sort," *Atlantic City Press*, n.d., Vertical Files: Amusements, Atlantic County Historical Society, Somers Point, New Jersey. See also "Bridge to the Old World," 53–54; Web post, Rick Ackerman, April 30, 2000, Atlantic City Memory Lane, available: www.iloveac.com/memory; and Ed Davis, *Atlantic City Diary: A Century of Memories, 1880–1985* (McKee City, N.J.: Atlantic City Sunrise Publishing, 1986), 100–101.

51. Quotes from Linda Oatman High and Ted Lewin, *The Girl on the High Diving Horse* (New York: Philomel, 2003). For several good accounts of the diving horse, see "The Girl of the Diving Horse," *Family Weekly*, July 10, 1966; Laura Italiano, "Atop Horse, They Dived to Glory," *Atlantic City Press*, September 13, 1988; and Bill Kent, "The Horse Was in Charge," *New York Times*, May 4, 1997. A movie was made about Sonora Webster Carver, the woman blinded in a diving accident, entitled *Wild Hearts Can't Be Broken* (Disney, 1991). See also Mark Tyler, "A.C.'s First Diving Horse Rider, 99, Dies," *Atlantic City Press*, September 23, 2003.

52. On the idea of an outdoor picnic, see Nye, "Eight Ways of Looking at an Amusement Park," 65–66. On Steel Pier, see Cronin, "100 Years of Magic."

53. *Steel Pier Program and Guide Book, 1947*, inside back page, Allen "Boo" Pergament Private Collection, Margate, New Jersey.

54. Huneker, *New Cosmopolis*, 312.

55. See this estimate in *The WPA Guide to 1930s New Jersey*, 190.

56. On Coney Island, see Kasson, *Amusing the Millions*; Register, *The Kid of Coney Island*; and Michael Immerso, *Coney Island: The People's Playground* (New Brunswick, N.J.: Rutgers University Press, 2002).

57. Bruce Bliven, "Coney Island for Battered Souls," *New Republic* (November 23, 1921), 372–74.

58. This phrase about Coney Island is from John M. Findlay, *Magic Lands: Western Cityscapes and American Culture after 1940* (Berkeley: University of California Press, 1992), 86–87.

59. Hal Rothman, "A Hard Look at Las Vegas," *Las Vegas Review-Journal*, April 22, 2001. See also Rothman's books, *Devil's Bargains: Tourism in the Twentieth-Century American West* (Lawrence: University Press of Kansas, 1998), 287–90, and *Neon Metropolis: How Las Vegas Started the Twenty-First Century* (London: Routledge, 2002). Additionally see David G. Schwartz, *Suburban Xanadu: The Casino Resort on the Las Vegas Strip and Beyond* (New York and London: Routledge, 2003).

60. Ray Suarez, *The Old Neighborhood: What We Lost in the Great Suburban Migration, 1966–1999* (New York: Free Press, 1999), 59.

61. Huneker, *New Cosmopolis*, 315, 326. For more background on urban tourism, see Catherine Cocks, *Doing the Town: The Rise of Urban Tourism in the United States, 1850–1915* (Berkeley: University of California Press, 2001).

62. See a similar observation in Ross, *Celebration Chronicles*, 225.

63. On the idea of "riskless risk," see John Hannigan, *Fantasy City: Pleasure and Profit in the Postmodern Metropolis* (London: Routledge, 1998), 192–93; and Nye, "Eight Ways of Looking at an Amusement Park," 65–66.

64. Nasaw, *Going Out*, 8.

65. On the laws, see Butler, *Book of the Boardwalk*, 23; Funnell, *By the Beautiful Sea*, 146–47; Vicki Gold Levi, "Down to the Sea in Woolen Bathing Suits," *Philadelphia Bulletin*, n.d., Bulletin Collection, Envelope: Atlantic City—Atlantic City: History and Development, Urban Archives, Temple University, Philadelphia, Pa.; and "Bermuda Gets Advice," *New York Times*, August 3, 1951.

66. Harrison Rhodes, *In Vacation America* (New York: Harper and Brothers, 1915), 5. See a similar account in Edward S. Morgan, "New Freedoms and the Girls," *Harper's* (August 1926), 391.

67. Letter from Lois Wallen to author, February 16, 1999.

68. Interviews with Mrs. Herman Silverman, Frank Havens, and Frank Schwickerath, Jr., by Cynthia Ringe, May 2, 12, 15, 1978, Atlantic City Living History, Heston Room, ACFPL. See also Atlantic City High School, "Atlantic City Remembers," pp. 29–31, 39, Heston Room, ACFPL.

69. "Bareback Bathing Ban Off," and "Atlantic City Keeps Ban on Shirtless Bathing Suit," *New York Times*, March 30 and May 20, 1937; and Regular Meeting, Board of Directors, Atlantic City Chamber of Commerce, July 10, 1945, GACCC.

70. "Friendly Suggestions from a Friend," *Atlantic City Press*, August 7, 1946.

71. "Special Squad Will Enforce 'Walk Rules," *Atlantic City Press*, July 3, 1952.

72. Ibid.

73. Untitled article, *Atlantic City Press*, July 17, 1948, Vertical Files: Rolling Chairs, Heston Room, ACFPL.

74. "Group Cites 'Eyesore,'" *Atlantic City Press*, April 14, 1950.

75. Bob Queen, "Stormy Was the Road We Trod," *Perspectives* (January–February 1992): 37, Sid Trusty Library, Atlantic City.

76. Commissioner William S. Cuthbert to Mayor A. M. Ruffu, Jr., August 16, 1928, and Hotel Traymore Company to Mayor Ruffu, August 15, 1928, Pierre Hollingsworth Papers (private collection), Absecon, New Jersey, copies in author's possession.

77. "Recreation," Box 3, Folder 33, Record Group: Works Progress Administration, Subgroup: New Jersey Writers' Project, New Jersey State Archives, Trenton.

78. Gregory Howard Williams, *Life on the Color Line: The True Story of a White Boy Who Discovered He Was Black* (New York: Plume, 1995), 95–96.

79. Baldwin quoted in Alexander Wolff, *Big Game, Small World: A Basketball Adventure* (New York: Warner, 2002), 56.

80. On the enforcement of segregation, see interviews by author with James Usry, September 30, 1999; Pierre Hollingsworth, August 19, 1999; Sid Trusty, April 16, 1999; and Reverend Boozie, May 18, 1999. On Chicken Bone Beach, see Levi and Eisenberg, *Atlantic City*; and Chicken Bone Beach, available: www.chickenbone beach.com. See also Isaac N. Nutter to William Cuthbert, the city's police commissioner, July 25, 1931, Hollingsworth Papers. Nutter complains about the police policy of ejecting African Americans from the beaches. Also see Bill Kent, "Sid Trusty, Museum Advocate," February 27, 2003, available: www.ACWeekly.com. Allen "Boo" Pergament does remember black couples participating in dance contests like the jitterbug on the pier in the 1950s. E-mail from Pergament to author, February 19, 2004.

81. E-mail from Terri McNichol to author, May 9, 2003.

82. Robin D. G. Kelley, *Race Rebels: Culture, Politics, and the Black Working Class* (New York: Free Press, 1994), 177.

83. On the idea of cultural pluralism, see Gary Gerstle, "Liberty, Coercion, and the Making of Americans," *Journal of American History* 84 (September 1997): 524–58; Gerstle, *American Crucible: Race and Nation in the Twentieth Century* (Princeton, N.J.: Princeton University Press, 2001); Thomas J. Sugrue, "Crab-Grass Politics: Race, Rights, and Reaction against Liberalism in the Urban North," *Journal of American History* 82 (September 1995): 551–78; Lizabeth Cohen, *Making a New Deal: Industrial Workers in Chicago, 1919–1939* (New York: Cambridge University Press, 1992); Roland Marchand, "Visions of Classlessness, Quests for Domination: American Popular Culture, 1945–1960," in *Reshaping America: Society and Institutions, 1945–1960*, ed. Robert H. Bremner and Gary W. Reichard (Columbus: Ohio State University Press, 1982), 163–190; Sarah Banet-Weiser, *The Most Beautiful Girl in the World: Beauty Pageants and National Identity* (Berkeley: University of California Press, 1999), 162; and Andrew Hurley, *Diners, Bowling Alleys, and Trailer Parks: Chasing the American Dream in the Postwar Consumer Culture* (New York: Basic, 2001). For an overview of the politics of assimilation, see Russell A. Kazal, "Revisiting Assimilation: The Rise, Fall, and Reappraisal of a Concept of American Ethnic History," *American Historical Review* 100 (April 1995): 437–71. For an Atlantic City story, see Martin Sherman, *Rose* (London: Methuen, 1999).

84. Lewis A. Erenberg, "Swing Goes to War: Glenn Miller and the Popular Music of World War II," in *The War in American Culture: Society and Consciousness during World War II*, ed. Lewis A. Erenberg and Susan E. Hirsch (Chicago: University of Chicago Press, 1996), 148–50. On films, see Larry May, "Making the American Consensus: The Narrative of Conversion and Subversion in World War II Films," in ibid., 71–103; and Gary Gerstle, "The Working Class Goes to War," *Mid-America* 75 (October 1993): 313–18. For a fictional version, see Philip Roth, *American Pastoral* (New York: Random House, 1997), 212–13.

85. Tocqueville quoted in Jim Cullen, *The American Dream: The History of an Idea That Shaped a Nation* (New York: Oxford University Press, 2003), 113.

86. Song sheet, "On the Boardwalk," Heston Room, Vertical Files: Songs, ACFPL.

87. "Survey of Negro Life in New Jersey: Making a Home," from the Interracial Committee, Department of Institutions and Agencies, New Jersey Conference of Social Work, July 1932, Vertical Files: WPA Papers, Negroes, Atlantic County Historical Society, Somers Point, New Jersey.

CHAPTER 2 (pages 45–62)

1. Interview with Jordan E. Sayles by Cynthia Ringe, April 24, 1978, Atlantic City Living History, Heston Room, ACFPL.

2. *Good Morning Blues: The Autobiography of Count Basie*, as told to Albert Murray (New York: Random House, 1985), 275–76. On the Basie band, see Geoffrey C. Ward and Ken Burns, *Jazz: A History of America's Music* (New York: Knopf), 247–49. Columbo quoted in Vicki Gold Levi and Lee Eisenberg, *Atlantic City: 125 Years of Ocean Madness* (Berkeley, Calif.: Ten Speed, 1979), 143; for more on Paradise performers, see 135–36.

3. For several readings on the meaning of the World's Columbian Exposition, see Robert W. Rydell, *All the World's a Fair: Visions of Empire at American International Expositions, 1876–1916* (Chicago: University of Chicago Press, 1984), 38–71; John Kasson, *Amusing the Millions: Coney Island at the Turn of the Century* (New York: Hill and Wang, 1978); William Cronon, *Nature's Metropolis: Chicago and the Great West* (New York: Norton, 1991), 341–69; James Gilbert, *Perfect Cities: Chicago's Utopias of 1893* (Chicago: University of Chicago Press, 1991), 75–130; and Gail Bederman, *Manliness and Civilization: A Cultural History of Gender and Race in the United States, 1880–1917* (Chicago: University of Chicago Press, 1995), 31–41 (quote on 31). In a rather interesting coincidence, part of the original Midway was brought to Atlantic City in 1893. The Japanese Tea Garden, selling Japanese goods and offering a Japanese theater with Japanese actors, operated on the Boardwalk until 1900. See Frank Butler, "'Walk Once Had Jap Tea Garden," *Atlantic City Press*, July 7, 1957.

4. Mumford quoted in Gilbert, *Perfect Cities*, 45.

5. On managed eroticism, see Henry A. Giroux, *The Mouse That Roared: Disney and the End of Innocence* (Lanham, Md.: Rowman and Littlefield, 1999), 41, and on soft primitivism, see Jane C. Desmond, *Staging Tourism: Bodies on Display from Waikiki to Sea World* (Chicago: University of Chicago Press, 1999).

6. Cindy Aron talks about how vacationers get turned into tourists; see Aron, *Working*

at Play: A History of Vacations in the United States (New York: Oxford University Press, 1999), 152–53.

7. E-mail from Allen M. Pergament to author, September 5, 12, 2001; and interview with Frank Havens by Cynthia Ringe, May 12, 1978, Atlantic City Living History, Heston Room, ACFPL. On the cultural interest in Hawaiians, see Lewis A. Erenberg, *Steppin' Out: New York Nightlife and the Transformation of American Culture, 1890–1930* (Chicago: University of Chicago Press, 1981), 224–26; and Desmond, *Staging Tourism*. Also see John Jakle, *The Tourist: Travel in Twentieth-Century North America* (Lincoln: University of Nebraska Press, 1985), 260–62.

8. Charles E. Funnell, *By the Beautiful Sea: The Rise and High Times of That Great American Resort, Atlantic City* (New York: Knopf, 1975), 154–55; and on Million Dollar Pier, see *Philadelphia Bulletin*, September 14, 1981. See also interview with George Kato by author, September 15, 1999.

9. These kinds of nights were a long-standing Atlantic City tradition. As early as 1921, the Ambassador Hotel featured Egyptian, Hawaiian, and Venetian nights. See Ed Davis, *Atlantic City Diary: A Century of Memories, 1880–1985* (McKee City, N.J.: Atlantic City Sunrise Publishing, 1986), 59.

10. The Chalfonte-Haddon Hall began holding these parties just after the war; see Vicki Gold Levi, "On the Site of Resorts, a Wood-Frame Hotel," *Atlantic City Press*, March 21, 1981. For more on the events, see "Talk from the Captain's Walk at Chalfonte-Haddon Hall," January 1959, Vertical Files: Hotels: Chalfonte-Haddon, Heston Room, ACFPL; brochure for Three Winter Weekend Parties, n.d., Box: Hotels (Pamphlets and Brochures), Folder: Chalfonte-Haddon Hall Polynesian Feast, Menu, Feb. 8, 1957, Chalfonte-Haddon Hall, Box 33, Menus, Heston Room, ACFPL.

11. "Roving Reporter," *Atlantic City Press*, December 19, 1943; Ed Hitzel, "The Piers: From 1880 to Now," *Atlantic City Press*, October 18, 1970. Hitzel notes that the Steel Pier minstrel shows ended in 1945 as a result of "the public's lack of interest."

12. Davis, *Atlantic City Diary*, 99–100; and Program for BPOE [Elks] Minstrel Show to Benefit the Welfare Fund, April 15, 1956, Ed Davis Papers, Folder: Davis Programs, Heston Room, ACFPL.

13. On the minstrel show in general, see Eric Lott, *Love and Theft: Blackface Minstrelsy and the American Working Class* (New York: Oxford University Press, 1993); Grace Elizabeth Hale, *Making Whiteness: The Culture of Segregation in the South, 1890–1940* (New York: Pantheon, 1998), 151–57; and Michael Rogin, *Blackface, White Noise: Jewish Immigrants in the Hollywood Melting Pot* (Berkeley: University of California Press, 1993).

14. For more on this, see Susan J. Douglas, *Where the Girls Are: Growing Up Female with the Mass Media* (New York: Times Books, 1994), 139, 157–61 (quote on 158); and Robin Morgan, ed., *Sisterhood Is Powerful: An Anthology of Writings from the Women's Liberation Movement* (New York: Vintage, 1970), 584–88. For a history of the pageant, see Frank Deford, *There She Is: The Life and Times of Miss America* (New York: Viking, 1971); and for a feminist reading, see Sarah Banet-Weiser, *The Most Beautiful Girl in the World: Beauty Pageants and National Identity* (Berkeley: University of California Press, 1999).

15. Columbo quoted in Misty Kammerman, "This Side of Paradise," *Atlantic City Press*, June 12, 1977; and interview with Sayles. For a similar observation about the clubs,

see Mrs. Margaret Caution to Miss Lucille Black, August 16, 1956, NAACP Papers, Group 3, Box C83, Folder: Branch Department, Atlantic City, 1956–57, Library of Congress, Washington, D.C.

16. On the scene, see "The City That Never Sleeps," *Ebony* (October 1952): 25; flyer, "Kentucky Avenue Renaissance Festival," June 27–28, 1992, Sid Trusty Library, Atlantic City; and Karen E. Ouinones Miller, "Those Jammin' Days," *Philadelphia Inquirer Magazine*, February 10, 2001.

17. Arlen quote is from Jervis Anderson, *This Is Harlem: A Cultural Portrait, 1900–1950* (New York: Farrar, Straus, and Giroux, 1981), 174.

18. On the Club Harlem, see Jim Waltzer and Tom Wilk, *Tales of South Jersey: Profiles and Personalities* (New Brunswick, N.J.: Rutgers University Press, 2001), 16–19; notes written by Marie Boyd, July 30, 1991, Vertical Files: Club Harlem, Heston Room, ACFPL; "Kentucky Avenue Museum," pamphlet, Vertical Files—Kentucky Avenue Museum, Heston Room, ACFPL; Billy Kelly, "Harlem Club Decades," *Atlantic City Monthly* (November 1989), 21–22; interview with Chris Columbo by Cynthia Ringe, May 4, 1978, Atlantic City Living History, Heston Room, ACFPL.

19. Horne quoted in Anderson, *This Is Harlem*, 175.

20. For descriptions of "jungle music," see Mark Turner and Duke Ellington, eds., *The Duke Ellington Reader* (New York: Oxford University Press, 1993), 29–32, 304, 396, 404; and Philip Roth, *American Pastoral* (New York: Random House, 1997), 48. For a description from Atlantic City, see Joseph T. Wilkins, *The Skin Game and Other Atlantic City Capers* (Xlibris, 2002), 12. See also George S. Schuyler, *Black No More* (1931; reprint, New York: Random House, 1999), 7.

21. Flyer, "Kentucky Avenue Renaissance Festival"; interview with Columbo; and Schuyler, *Black No More*, 7.

22. Barbara J. Kukla, *Swing City: Newark Nightlife, 1925–1950* (Philadelphia, Pa.: Temple University Press), 67–71, 75–77.

23. Ann Douglas calls these types of excursions "emotional holidays." See Douglas, *Terrible Honesty: Mongrel Manhattan in the 1920s* (New York: Farrar, Straus, and Giroux, 1995), 74.

24. Jonathan Van Meter, *The Last Good Time: Skinny D'Amato, the Notorious 500 Club, and the Rise and Fall of Atlantic City* (New York: Crown, 2003), 74.

25. Van Meter, *The Last Good Time*; and Grace D'Amato, *Chance of a Lifetime: Nucky Johnson, Skinny D'Amato, and How Atlantic City Became the Naughty Queen of Resorts* (Harvey Cedars, N.J.: Down the Shore, 2001), 111.

26. David Spatz, "Davis Key Part of A.C. Entertainment History," *Atlantic City Press*, May 17, 1990.

27. Van Meter, *The Last Good Time*, 83.

28. Descriptions of Skinny come from Van Meter, *The Last Good Time*; D'Amato, *Chance of a Lifetime*, 112; and Nelson Johnson, *Boardwalk Empire: The Birth, High Times, and Corruption of Atlantic City* (Medford, N.J.: Plexus, 2002), 175.

29. On Skinny, his past, and his mob connections, see Ovid Demaris, *The Boardwalk Jungle* (Toronto: Bantam, 1986), 32–33; Van Meter, *The Last Good Time*, 39–88; Richard Ben Cramer, *Joe DiMaggio: A Hero's Life* (New York: Simon and Schuster, 2000), 377, 381–83; and "The Rat Pack" (A&E Entertainment, 2001). See also Archie

Black, "The 500 Club," parts 2–3, *Atlantic City Newsletter* (March 2000), available: www.chequers.com/black.shtml.

30. Interview with Mrs. Herman Silverman by Cynthia Ringe, May 2, 1978, Atlantic City Living History, Heston Room, ACFPL; and George Anastasia, "He Remembers Back-Room Bets of Another Era," *Philadelphia Inquirer,* May 28, 1978.

31. On clothing and the public marking of sexual desire, see George Chauncey, *Gay New York: Gender, Urban Culture and the Making of the Gay Male World, 1890–1940* (New York: Basic, 1994), 3, 4, 52.

32. Debbie Doyle, "'The Salt Water Washes Away All Impropriety': The Middle-Class Body on the Beach and Mass Culture in Turn-of-the-Century Atlantic City" (unpublished article in author's possession); and "El Paso Hands It to Atlantic City," *New York Times,* May 17, 1925. Debbie Doyle graciously provided me with both of these citations from her own research on Atlantic City.

33. On the importance of gay clubs being inconspicuous and out of the way, see Jeffrey Escoffier, *American Homo: Community and Perversity* (Berkeley: University of California Press, 1998), 72–73.

34. Elaine Rose, "Atlantic City of Yesteryear: Gone and All but Forgotten," *Atlantic City Press,* April 27, 1997.

35. Glen Duffy, "Goodbye to Gay Street," *Atlantic City* (November 1986), 55.

36. Bill Kent, "The Queen of New York Avenue," *Atlantic City* (August 1984), 99; and Ann Kolson, "Faded," *Philadelphia Inquirer,* November 10, 1982. See also interview with Herb Tapper by author, February 26, 2000.

37. For descriptions of the club, see interview with Tapper and interview with Mike Mann—his name has been changed—by author, February 22, 2000. On Mack's behavior, see interview with Betty McGlynn Walls by author, January 18, 2001.

38. On the closing of Louise Mack's by the city, see Minutes of Commissioners, November 10, 1955, p. 1168, City Clerk's Office, Atlantic City.

39. On the geography of gay space, see Kent, "The Queen of New York Avenue," 99. On the world of gay house parties, see Daniel Burning, *Lesbian and Gay Memphis: Building Communities behind the Magnolia Curtain* (New York: Garland, 1997), 33; and John Howard, "Place and Movement in Gay American History," in *Creating a Place for Ourselves: Lesbian, Gay, and Bisexual Community Histories,* ed. Brett Beemyn (London: Routledge Kegan Paul, 1997), 213.

40. See a specific reference to Atlantic City in Chauncey, *Gay New York,* 321. For more on these bars, see "Atlantic City Clubs All Dark: Mayor Bans Pansies," *Variety,* January 17, 1933, 55; Gary Giddins, *Bing Crosby: A Pocketful of Dreams: The Early Years, 1903–1940* (New York: Little, Brown, 2001), 83.

41. D'Amato, *Chance of a Lifetime,* 91; "Night Clubs Penalized," "Club in Atlantic City Is Ordered Closed until Oct. 4," *Philadelphia Bulletin,* September 17, 1943, and May 2, 1963; and Brochure, "Amusements: Where to Go and What to See: Atlantic City," June 20, 1942, Heston Room, ACFPL.

42. John Howard tells the story of an Alabama merchant who regularly came to Atlantic City for business meetings and conventions and "developed satisfying, if fleeting, sexual relationships." See Howard, "Place and Movement in Gay American History," 212, 219.

43. For more on prostitution, see interview with Chester (no last name) by Cynthia Ringe, May 23, 1978, Atlantic City Living History, Heston Room, ACFPL; Robert Kotlowitz, *The Boardwalk* (New York: Knopf, 1977), 23, 38; and Bert Wilson, "The Atlantic City Trivia Quiz: And the Answers," *Atlantic City Press*, January 29, 1984. On New York Avenue and Snake Alley, see Rick Murray, "Cab Driver Tells Where Action Was around Town," *Atlantic City Press*, May 8, 1987.

44. Steffens quoted in Buzz Bissinger, *A Prayer for the City* (New York: Random House, 1997), 3.

45. Johnson, *Boardwalk Empire*, vii; and Joseph Tanfani, "The History of Resort Politics: Unending Tale of Corruption," *Atlantic City Press*, July 28, 1989. For more on the old regime, see D'Amato, *Chance of a Lifetime*, 8–108; and interview with Steven Perskie by author, April 17, 1999.

46. "Atlantic City Seen as a Hub of Crime," *New York Times*, July 8, 1951.

47. Ethel Waters and Hattie Hite, another singer, used this expression to describe the city. Waters is quoted in Kukla, *Swing City*, 56. See also D'Amato, *Chance of a Lifetime*. Others used the very same term; see, for instance, "Two Detectives Cleared," February 19, 1952; "Rackets Charged in Atlantic City," April 12; and "Jury Clears Police in Shore Gambling," August 30, 1956, *New York Times*.

48. For a similar observation, see interview with James Usry by author, September 30, 1999.

49. Jack Alexander, "That's How They Got Nucky Johnson," *Readers' Digest* (May 1942), 80.

50. For the best description of the machine, see Johnson, *Boardwalk Empire*, and interviews with Perskie. See also interview with Usry; George Sternlieb and James W. Hughes, *The Atlantic City Gamble* (Cambridge, Mass.: Harvard University Press, 1983), 31–38; interview with Leslie Kammerman by Cynthia Ringe, n.d., Atlantic City Living History, Oral History Project, Heston Room, ACFPL; Jack Alexander, "Boss on the Spot: The Case History of Nucky Johnson," *Saturday Evening Post*, August 26, 1939.

51. Reese Palley, "How It Happened (Approximately)," typescript in author's possession.

52. On Farley, see untitled typescript, Vertical Files: Biography, Frank S. Farley, Heston Room, ACFPL; Sternlieb and Hughes, *The Atlantic City Gamble*, 35–37; Constance Learn, "Farley Has Had Unique Impact in 32 Years as N.J. Lawmaker," *Catholic Star Herald*, January 1, 1969; Greg Walter, "The Only Game in Town," *Philadelphia Magazine* (August 1971), 55; and "Conversations with a Politician: Interview with Hap Farley," Robert Hughey and Herbert Simmens, Video Collection, Stockton College, Pomona, New Jersey.

53. Alan Ehrenhalt, *The Lost City: The Forgotten Virtues of Community in America* (New York: Basic, 1995), 16.

54. Ellison, quoted by Giddins, *Bing Crosby*, 79.

CHAPTER 3 (pages 63–82)

1. Rick Murray, "Cab Driver Tells Where Action Was around Town," *Atlantic City Press*, May 8, 1987.

2. James Howard Kunstler, *Home from Nowhere: Remaking Our Everyday World for the Twenty-First Century* (New York: Simon and Schuster, 1996), 110 (first quote); Kunstler, *The Geography of Nowhere: The Rise and Decline of America's Man-Made Landscape* (New York: Simon and Schuster, 1993), 127 (second quote).

3. Kunstler, *The Geography of Nowhere*, 228.

4. On the sound of heels and more generally on downtown's formality, see Michael Johns, *Moment of Grace: The American City in the 1950s* (Berkeley: University of California Press, 2003), 9.

5. Jack Thomas of the *Boston Globe* quoted in Robert M. Fogelson, *Downtown: Its Rise and Fall, 1880–1950* (New Haven, Conn.: Yale University Press, 2001), 2. On the downtown experience in Atlantic City, see Paul Carr, Web post, November 23, 1998, Atlantic City Memory Lane, available: www.iloveac.com/memory.

6. See, for example, "Creative Description of the Northside," Box 3, Folder 33, Record Group: Works Progress Administration, Subgroup: New Jersey Writers' Project, N.J. State Archives, Trenton; and Brad Bennett, "Civil Rights Movement Has Long History in A.C.," *Atlantic City Press*, February 21, 1993.

7. On housing, see Charles E. Funnell, *By the Beautiful Sea: The Rise and High Times of That Great American Resort, Atlantic City* (New York: Knopf, 1975), 143; and Charles Stansfield, "Atlantic City and the Resort Cycle: Background to the Legalization of Gambling," *Annals of Tourism Research* 5 (April–June 1978): 240.

8. E. B. White's template for looking at neighborhoods can be found in Johns, *Moment of Grace*, 3. On the city as a walking city, see interview with Allen "Boo" Pergament by author, March 3, 1999; and Robert Nigro, "Where Were You in '62?" *Atlantic County Journal*, April 16, 1992, Vertical Files: Folder: Atlantic City General #9, Atlantic County Historical Society, Somers Point, New Jersey. See other descriptions of walking neighborhoods in Kunstler, *The Geography of Nowhere*, 127; and Kunstler, *Home from Nowhere*, 125–27.

9. Interview with Pergament.

10. Quoted in "In Search of Atlantic City," May 22, 1990, WHYY Television Station, Heston Room, ACFPL.

11. On mothers, storekeepers, and policing, see Jane Jacobs, *The Death and Life of Great American Cities* (New York: Random House, 1961); and Johns, *Moment of Grace*, 52, 58–59.

12. Lisa Belkin, *Show Me a Hero: A Tale of Murder, Suicide, Race, and Redemption* (Boston: Little, Brown, 1999), 15.

13. Richlyn F. Goddard, " 'Three Months of Hurry and Nine Months to Worry': Resort Life for African Americans in Atlantic City, N.J. (1850–1940)" (Ph.D. diss., Howard University, 2001).

14. Quoted in Herbert James Foster, "The Urban Experience of Blacks in Atlantic City, 1850–1915" (Ph.D. diss., Rutgers University, 1981), 41.

15. Bennett, "Civil Rights Movement Has Long History in AC"; interview with James Usry by author, September 30, 1999; and *Maguerite Edwards, Plaintiff, v. the Board of Education, City of Atlantic City* [May 16, 1928], NAACP Papers, Box 44, Group 1, D, Folder: Cases Supported, AC School Segregation, Library of Congress; Nelson Johnson, *Boardwalk Empire: The Birth, High Times, and Corruption of Atlantic City* (Med-

ford, N.J.: Plexus, 2002), 35–53; interview with Steve Perskie by author, April 17, 1999.

16. On the naming patterns, see interview with Usry, and interview with Pierre Hollingsworth by author, August 19, 1999.

17. Martin Paulsson, *The Social Anxieties of Progressive Reform: Atlantic City, 1854–1920* (New York: New York University Press, 1994), 40. On the later observation, see Foster, "The Urban Experience of Blacks," 45–46.

18. Interview with Ruth S. Hinton by Cynthia Ringe, n.d., Atlantic City Living History, Heston Room, ACFPL.

19. James Brock, "In Being Together There Was Strength," n.d., Scrapbook 1, Sid Trusty Collection.

20. See, for example, Minutes of Commissioners, February 21, 1952, City Clerk's Office, Atlantic City.

21. Interview with Ruth S. Hinton by Cynthia Ringe, n.d., Atlantic City Living History, Heston Room, ACFPL; Interview with Usry; "Survey of Negro Life in New Jersey," from the Interracial Committee, Department of Institutions and Agencies, New Jersey Conference of Social Work, July 1932, Vertical Files: WPA Papers, Negroes, Atlantic County Historical Society, Somers Point, New Jersey; and "Education of Negroes in Atlantic City," Box 3, Folder 29, Record Group: Works Progress Administration, Subgroup: New Jersey Writers' Project, New Jersey State Archive, Trenton.

22. Interview with Milton Greenburg, president of AC Jitneymen's Assoc., by Cynthia Ringe, n.d., Atlantic City Living History, Heston Room, ACFPL.

23. Interview with Usry; Bett Norcross McCoy, "Woman of Substance: A.C. Entrepreneur Washington among Inductees into County's Women's Hall of Fame," *Atlantic City Press*, n.d., Vertical Files: Sara Spencer Washington, Atlantic County Historical Society, Somers Point, New Jersey; and Vicki Gold Levi and Lee Eisenberg, *Atlantic City: 125 Years of Ocean Madness* (Berkeley, Calif.: Ten Speed, 1979), 88–89.

24. Introduction to a history of St. Augustine's Church, in author's possession.

25. "Creative Description of the Northside," Box 3, Folder 33, Record Group: Works Progress Administration, Subgroup: New Jersey Writers' Project, New Jersey State Archives, Trenton. On black commerce in another city, see Alan Ehrenhalt, *The Lost City: The Forgotten Virtues of Community in America* (New York: Basic, 1995), 195.

26. The *New Jersey Afro American*—the Newark edition of the Baltimore paper—regularly listed where Atlantic City guests lived.

27. Chana Kai Lee, *For Freedom's Sake: The Life of Fannie Lou Hamer* (Urbana: University of Illinois Press, 1999), 86.

28. *New Jersey Afro American*, August 4, 1956. For some historic background, see Clifford J. Newsome, "General History of the Atlantic City Board of Trade," *Negro History Bulletin* 16 (November 1952): 27–30; "Black Businesses, Trade Associations," *Atlantic City Press*, February 1, 1988.

29. For a wonderful description of postwar Arctic Avenue, see "The City That Never Sleeps," *Ebony*, October 1952, 25.

30. Mary "Kate" Dunwoody, "Atlantic City Movie Theaters," unpublished paper (May 14,

1991), p. 8, Vertical Files: Art and Cultural Events, Theaters, Heston Room, ACFPL; "Recreation," Box 3, Folder 33, Record Group: Works Progress Administration, Subgroup: New Jersey Writers' Project, New Jersey State Archives, Trenton; and see *Atlantic City Press*, July 1, 1937, for an announcement of its opening. According to William F. Parker, "Theaters of Atlantic City, NJ" (1982), Heston Room, the Alan closed in 1956. According to James Usry, the Fitzgerald Auditorium on Kentucky Avenue showed matinees for Northside audiences in the 1930s, perhaps before the Alan opened. Interview with Usry.

31. On Mabley, see "Moms Mabley," available: Home.earthlink.net/~dinaksa/mabley. htm; and Nadine Cohodas, *Spinning Blues into Gold: The Chess Brothers and the Legendary Chess Records* (New York: St. Martin's, 2000), 195–96, 205.

32. Flyer, "Kentucky Avenue Renaissance Festival," June 27–28, 1992, Sid Trusty Library, Atlantic City; Misty Kammerman, "This Side of Paradise," *Atlantic City Press*, June 12, 1977; and Bill Kent, *Down by the Sea* (New York: St. Martin's, 1993), 104–5.

33. Thomas Oommen, "Downtown Area Generally Slum-Free," *Atlantic City Press*, December 14, 1966; and "Housing Issue," *Atlantic City Press*, August 30, 1956. See also Ray Suarez, *The Old Neighborhood: What We Lost in the Great Suburban Migration, 1966–1999* (New York: Free Press, 1999), 143.

34. "Atlantic City Remembers: Illustrious Alumni for the 100th Reunion of the First Graduating Class of the Atlantic City High School," Vertical Files: Schools, Atlantic City, #1, Atlantic County Historical Society, Somers Point, New Jersey.

35. "Housing Project Nearly Complete," *New York Times*, February 21, 1937.

36. Ehrenhalt, *The Lost City*, 29–30.

37. "Northside News," *Atlantic City Press*, June 11, 1955.

38. "Master List of Predominantly Negro Organizations Contacted," City of Atlantic City, Application to the Department of Housing and Urban Development for a Grant Plan, A Plan for a Comprehensive City Demonstration Program, Part One, Model A, 1968, RG 207, Model Cities Reports, Box 139, National Archives, College Park, Maryland. For more on the club scene, see *The WPA Guide to 1930s New Jersey* (1939; reprint, New Brunswick, N.J.: Rutgers University Press, 1986), 193–94.

39. "Recreation," Box 3, Folder 33, Record Group: Works Progress Administration, Subgroup: New Jersey Writers' Project, New Jersey State Archives, Trenton.

40. "Also Disgusted," *Atlantic City Press*, n.d. [Spring 1955?], Heston Room, Atlantic City Housing Authority Press Clippings, Scrapbook 4, ACFPL. One of the first warnings was Carlo M. Sardella, "Unsightly Approaches to City Could Be Remedied if Effort Is Made," *Atlantic City Press*, September 20, 1951.

41. "Reclaim by 'Baltimore Plan,'" *Atlantic City Press*, January 23, 1950; "Northside Redevelopment Hearing Slated Tonight," and "Urban Redevelopment Plans Seen Designed to 'Decorate' Boulevard," *Atlantic City Press*, June 23, 24, 1959; Greater Atlantic City Chamber of Commerce, *Action*, June 1957, GACCC, Atlantic City.

42. On the strike, see Paulsson, *The Social Anxieties of Progressive Reform*, 34; "Labor," Box 3, Folder 28, Record Group: Works Progress Administration, Subgroup, New Jersey Writers' Project, New Jersey State Archives, Trenton.

43. Ducktown Revitalization Association, "The Shops of St. Michael's: Atlantic City's Italian Village," Heston Room, Vertical Files: Ducktown, ACFPL.

44. Web postings from Tony Munafo, November 1, 2000, and Philip Sereni, December 21, 2000, Atlantic City Memory Lane, available: www.iloveac.com/memory.

45. Photo caption, "Thousands of Faithful Gather," August 16, 1979; photo caption, "Picture of the Wedding of the Sea," August 13, 1981, *Philadelphis Bulletin.*

46. On Italy Terrace, see Bill Tonelli, "How Are Things on Italy Terrace," *Atlantic City* (June 1983), 77.

47. Interview with Rose Fedelli by author, September 21, 1999.

48. Quoted in Ellen Karasik, "All-or-None Offer Splits Residents," *Philadelphia Inquirer,* December 3, 1978.

49. Glen Duffy, "Neighbors: Caught in $100,000 Vise," *Atlantic City Press,* October 26, 1978.

50. *Atlantic City: The Queen Takes a Chance,* produced and directed by Albert Rose, tape, 90-41B, September 19, 1978, Heston Room, ACFPL; and Web posting from Susie Geissinger, August 28, 2002, Atlantic City Memory Lane, available: www.iloveac. com/memory.

51. Interview with Pat Smith by author, October 11, 1999. On Japanese families, see interview with George Kato by author, September 15, 1999.

52. Buzz Bissinger talks about the neighborhoods in pre–World War II Philadelphia in a similar way. See Bissinger, *A Prayer for the City* (New York: Random House, 1997), 71.

53. Web posting by Connie Turton Degrassi, April 12, 2000, Atlantic City Memory Lane, available: www.iloveac.com.

54. Web posting by Jennette Patterson Adams, February 27, 2000, Atlantic City Memory Lane, available: www.iloveac.com/memory.

55. For the quote on the definition of "uptown" spaces, see Fogelson, *Downtown,* 3.

56. Interview with Leslie Kammerman by Cynthia Ringe, n.d. [1978?], Atlantic City Living History, Heston Room, ACFPL. For more on the physical look of the neighborhood, see Michael Prichard, "Diamonds Didn't Always Shine on Atlantic City Urban Tract," *Atlantic City Press,* August 1, 1994.

57. Nigro, "Where Were You in '62?"; and interview with Paul Carr by author, September 30, 1999.

58. Interview by author with Paul Carr.

59. Interview with Theodore (Teddy) Leonard by Cynthia Ringe, April 25, 1978, Atlantic City Living History, Heston Room, ACFPL.

60. McPhee, "The Search for Marvin Gardens," in *The John McPhee Reader,* ed. William L. Howarth (New York: Farrar, Straus, and Giroux, 1976), 82 (first quote); 85–86 (second quote); 81 (third quote).

61. For information on the history of the game, see Richard's Monopoly Page, available: http://richard_wilding.tripod.com/history.htm. Some, by the way, have argued that Darrow did not invent the game but rather it was invented by a turn-of-the-century radical, Lizzie J. Magie. On this, see Burton H. Wolfe, "The Monopolization of Monopoly: The $500 Buyout," *San Francisco Bay Guardian* (1976), available: www. adena.com/adena/mo/mo13.htm.

62. McPhee, "The Search for Marvin Gardens," 85 (first quote), 81 (second and third quotes).

63. Ibid., 88–89.

64. Ibid.

65. On one form of memory in the African-American community, see Chicken Bone Beach, Inc., available: www.chickenbonebeach.org.

66. Ehrenhalt, *The Lost City*, 16, 21, 265–66.

67. Jonathan Rieder, *Canarsie: The Jews and Italians of Brooklyn against Liberalism* (Cambridge, Mass.: Harvard University Press, 1985), 71.

CHAPTER 4 (pages 83–102)

1. This opening story is based on an interview with the Frosts—their names have been changed—by the author, August 31, 1999. All direct quotations throughout this section are from this interview.

2. Martin Sherman, *Rose* (London: Methuen, 1999), 24.

3. See this description in Gillian Roberts, *How I Spent My Summer Vacation* (New York: Ballantine, 1994), 15.

4. Details filled in from Mark R. Perlgut, "Auctions Hustle Gems," *Atlantic City Press*, January 10, 1967. This was one installment of a four-part informative series Perlgut wrote on the city's auction houses.

5. On movie going, see Robert Butsch, "American Movie Audiences in the 1930s," *International Labor and Working-Class History* 59 (Spring 2001): 107.

6. Quoted in Mary "Kate" Dunwoody, "Atlantic City Movie Theaters," unpublished paper (May 14, 1991), p. 8; and "The Warner Theater—Inaugural Program," both in Vertical Files: Art and Cultural Events, Theaters, Heston Room, ACFPL. See also pictures of the Warner in the Irving Glazer Theater Collection, Folder: Atlantic City, Warner, Athenaeum, Philadelphia, Pa. More generally on the architecture of theaters, see Ben M. Hall, *The Best Remaining Seats: The Golden Age of the Movie Palace* (1975; reprint, New York: Da Capo, 1987); David Naylor, *American Picture Palaces: The Architecture of Fantasy* (New York: Prentice Hall, 1981); and Karen J. Safer, "The Functions of Decoration in the American Movie Palace," *Marquee* 14 (Second Quarter 1982), 3.

7. On the fantasies of the movie house, see Karal Ann Marling, "Fantasies in Dark Places: The Cultural Geography of the American Movie Palace," in *Textures of Place: Exploring Humanist Geographies*, ed. Paul C. Adams, Steven Hoelscher, and Karen E. Till (Minneapolis: University of Minnesota, 2001), 8–23.

8. Josef Israels II, "The Movie Usher and How He Got That Way," *Liberty* (April 28, 1929), 76.

9. David Nasaw, *Going Out: The Rise and Fall of Public Amusements* (New York: Basic, 1993); Israels, "The Movie Usher," 75–79; Douglas Gormery, "The Movies Become Big Business: Publix Theatres and the Chain Store Strategy," *Cinema Journal* 1 (Fall 1978): 28. For the recollections of ushers, see e-mail of Stanley Slome to author, August 6, 2002; and interview with Frank Schwickerath, Jr., by Cynthia Ringe, May 15, 1978, Atlantic City Living History, Heston Room, ACFPL.

10. *Atlantic City* (Republic Films, 1944).

11. On this challenge, see Lizabeth Cohen, *A Consumer's Republic: The Politics of Mass Consumption in Postwar America* (New York: Knopf, 2003), 175. For an example of confronting segregation at the movies, see Anne Moody, *Coming of Age in Mississippi* (New York: Dell, 1968), 38–39.

12. Interview with Chris Columbo by Cynthia Ringe, May 4, 1978, Atlantic City Living History, Oral History Project, Heston Room, ACFPL. See also interview with Jordan E. Sayles by Cynthia Ringe, April 24, 1978, Atlantic City Living History, Heston Room, ACFPL; and Yvette Craig, "Ex-AC Mayor Remembers the Pains of Segregation," *Atlantic City Press*, February 19, 1991. When I talked with James Usry, the city's first African-American mayor, and he spoke of segregation in town, the first thing he mentioned was the movie theaters. See interview with Usry by author, September 30, 1999.

13. I have borrowed this phrase from Hal Rothman's *Neon Metropolis: How Las Vegas Started the Twenty-First Century* (London: Routledge, 2002), xiii.

14. For a comment on the city's style, see Thomas Hine, "Atlantic City," *AIA Journal* 71 (November 1982): 38.

15. "The Warner Theater—15 Black and White Photos by John Herr—Interior Pre-Demolition," Vertical Files: Art and Cultural Events, Theaters, Heston Room, ACFPL; photocopy of postcard, Irving Glazer Theater Collection, File: Atlantic City, Photos, Athenaeum, Philadelphia, Pa.

16. *Atlantic City Host*, August 25, 1956, Bunny Josephson Collection, Folder: Collection [of] Various Organizational Events' Books, Heston Room, ACFPL.

17. Dunwoody, "Atlantic City Movie Theaters."

18. Butsch, "American Movie Audiences in the 1930s"; and Lary May with the assistance of Stephen Lassonde, "Making the American Way: Moderne Theatres, Audiences, and the Film Industry," *Prospects* 12 (1987): 89–124.

19. For a description of this sandwich, see John L. Boucher, "Famed Kornblau's Is Closing," *Atlantic City Press*, October 12, 1968. On going to Penn Atlantic Hotel after the movies, see letter from Lois Wallen to author, February 16, 1999.

20. Interview with Buddy and Stanley Grossman by author, April 8, 1999; and interview with Marty Wood by author, February 11, 1999.

21. *Steel Pier Souvenir Program and Guide Book, 1954*, Vertical Files: Atlantic City Piers, #2, Atlantic County Historical Society, Somers Point, New Jersey.

22. *Atlantic City Host*, August 25, 1956, Bunny Josephson Collection, Folder: Collection [of] Various Organizational Events' Books, Heston Room, ACFPL.

23. *Steel Pier Souvenir Program and Guide Book, 1954*.

24. "Rebirth of Interest in City Swings Sale," *Atlantic City Press*, February 28, 1955.

25. *Atlantic City Press*, November 20, 1956; Ed Davis, *Atlantic City Diary: A Century of Memories, 1880–1985* (McKee City, N.J.: Atlantic City Sunrise Publishing, 1986), 114.

26. *New York Times*, March 27, 1958; and Bill Kent, "Fighting Off the Final Curtain," *New York Times*, January 21, 1996.

27. "The Warner Is Coming Down," unidentified clipping, November 8, 1960, Irving Glazer Theater Collection, Folder: Atlantic City, Warner, Athenaeum, Philadelphia, Pa.

28. Mark E. Heisler, "Warren Maybe Victim of Changing Era," *Atlantic City Press*, No-

vember 20, 1960; Irving R. Glazer, "The Atlantic City Story," *Marquee* 1 (First and Second Quarter 1980): 6; Naylor, *American Picture Palaces*, 207–8; and Kent, "Fighting Off the Final Curtain."

29. Gary Morris, "Beyond the Beach," AIP's Beach Party Movies, available: www.bright lightsfilms.com.

30. See a picture of the opening of the Boardwalk Bowl in Vicki Gold Levi and Lee Eisenberg, *Atlantic City: 125 Years of Ocean Madness* (Berkeley, Calif.: Ten Speed, 1979), 146.

31. "Famous Playhouse Begins New," *Atlantic City Press*, March 10, 1934; e-mail from Anthony Kutschera to author, October 16, 2000; and William F. Parker, "Theatres of Atlantic City" (1982), Vertical Files: Art and Cultural Events, Theaters, Heston Room, ACFPL.

32. James C. Young, "Burlesque Makes Comeback and a Bid for Respectability," *Philadelphia Inquirer*, July 31, 1966; Ed Appel, "Burlesque Returns to Atlantic City's Boardwalk Next Week," *Philadelphia Bulletin*, June 13, 1974; Larry Light, "Jersey's Summer Fiasco," *Philadelphia Bulletin*, August 15, 1976; and *Atlantic City: The Queen Takes a Chance*, produced and directed by Albert Rose, tape, 90-41B, September 19, 1978, Heston Room, ACFPL.

33. "If Hairy Shirts Tickle You," *Philadelphia Bulletin*, May 5, 1974.

34. Ed McMahon as told to Carroll Caroll, *Here's Ed; or, How to Be a Second Banana . . . or, From Midway to Midnight* (New York: Putnam's, 1976), 188–92.

35. Wade Greene, "On the Boardwalk: What a Difference a Century Makes," *New York Times*, July 12, 1970.

36. Typescript on movies, Vertical Files: Art and Cultural Events, Theaters, Heston Room, ACFPL; and Charles Librizzi, "Few Theaters Are Left for Atlantic City Vacationers," *Philadelphia Bulletin*, June 25, 1974.

37. On the Embassy, see Librizzi, "Few Theaters Are Left for Atlantic City Vacationers."

38. On Starr's performance, see Davis, *Atlantic City Diary*, 127. For the more general scene, see "Children Win Fight in Atlantic City," *Philadelphia Bulletin*, November 23, 1969.

39. Mark E. Heisler, "Family Movies Due," *Atlantic City Press*, November 22, 1969, Vertical Files: Art and Cultural Events, Theaters, Heston Room, ACFPL. On the kinds of films shown and middle-class perceptions, see Jon C. Teaford, *The Rough Road to Renaissance: Urban Revitalization in America, 1940–1985* (Baltimore, Md.: Johns Hopkins University Press, 1990), 208–9; and Andrew Hurley, *Diners, Bowling Alleys, and Trailer Parks: Chasing the American Dream in the Postwar Consumer Culture* (New York: Basic, 2001), 314.

40. Eliot Michael Friedland, "Death of the 'World's Playground': An Examination of the Decline and Fall of Atlantic City, New Jersey" (M.A. thesis, Glassboro State College, 1972), 95–97; "Plan to Fill Empty Stores Outlined," *Atlantic City Press*, March 19, 1963; interview with Marty Woods by author, February 11, 1999; and interview with Larry Miller by author, February 11, 1999.

41. See Jane Jacobs, *The Death and Life of Great American Cities* (New York: Random House, 1961). In his book on cities and decline, Ray Suarez makes a similar point about stores closing early and emptiness; see *The Old Neighborhood: What We Lost in*

the Great Suburban Migration, 1966–1999 (New York: Free Press, 1999), 20, 82–83, 87. On the problem of high vacancy rates in downtown areas, see Witold Rybcynski and Peter D. Lineman, "How to Save Our Shrinking Cities," *Public Interest* 135 (Spring 1999): 30–44.

42. Mark E. Heisler, "Four Men Held after Burglary at Atlantic Avenue Men's Store," "Storeman Robbed, Hit," and "Men Beat, Rob A.C. Merchants," *Atlantic City Press*, February 1; August 17, 1968; and November 23, 1975. On these crimes, see also interview with Murray Raphel by author, September 8, 1999.

43. "Atlantic City Theater Robbed of $760," *Philadelphia Bulletin*, October 28, 1971.

44. Mark Heisler, "4 Youth Held in Walk Assault," *Atlantic City Press*, July 4, 1968.

45. "Boardwalk Strollers Hit, Robbed," *Atlantic City Press*, August 11, 1971.

46. "Traymore Demolishers Burglarized," *Atlantic City Press*, February 3, 1972.

47. Levi and Eisenberg, *Atlantic City*, 205.

48. Friedland, "Death of the 'World's Playground' "; and Frank Lowe, "The Boardwalk: Great Place to Walk, but Few Realize That Danger Exists," *Philadelphia Inquirer*, November 14, 1971.

49. Alex Stern and Barry Koltnow, "26 Wounded at Club Harlem," *Atlantic City Press*, Vertical Files, File: Club Harlem, Heston Room, ACFPL; Charles Librizzi and S. William White, "4 Killed, 10 Shot in Shore Club," *Philadelphia Bulletin*, April 13, 1972.

50. Among those who discuss the decline of the downtown spaces, see John Hannigan, *Fantasy City: Pleasure and Profit in the Postmodern Metropolis* (London: Routledge, 1998), 43; and Robert M. Fogelson, *Downtown: Its Rise and Fall, 1880–1950* (New Haven, Conn.: Yale University Press, 2001), 317–80.

51. In terms of numbers of conventioneers, the figures remained pretty steady through the 1960s and early 1970s. For these data, see Atlantic City Housing Authority and Urban Redevelopment Agency, "Market Research for Specialty Shopping Center, Uptown Renewal Site, Atlantic City, New Jersey" (April 1974), 10–11, Heston Room, ACFPL.

52. "A Dowager's Decline," *Newsweek* (June 8, 1970), 86; Michael Pollack, "The City in Shock," *Atlantic City Press*, March 28, 1982; and G. G. LaBelle, "Veneer Wears Thin in Atlantic City," *Trenton Times Advertiser*, April 16, 1972.

53. John Roak, "Inspector Calls 'Walk Upgrading Everybody's Job," *Atlantic City Press*, August 1, 1972.

54. "Cross Incident Brings Warning," *Atlantic City Press*, April 30, 1955; and Minutes of Commissioners, July 21, 1955, p. 491, City Clerk's Office, Atlantic City. On the shifts in the neighborhood, see *Polk's Atlantic City Directory* (Philadelphia: Polk, 1955, 1956, 1957), Heston Room, ACFPL. As early as 1951, a North Inlet group was formed to keep African Americans out of the area. See "Inlet Group Seeks to Block Sale of House to Negro," *Atlantic City Press*, June 16, 1951.

55. Dunwoody, "Atlantic City Movie Theaters." On drive-ins, see Hurley, *Diners, Bowling Alleys, and Trailer Parks*, 298–99.

56. Interview with Buddy and Stanley Grossman by author, April 8, 1999; and Newsletter of the Greater Atlantic City Chamber of Commerce, May 1970, Heston Room, ACFPL. For more on the relocation of businesses and institutions, see Friedland, "Death of the 'World's Playground,' " 95–96.

57. Atlantic City Housing Authority and Urban Redevelopment Agency, "Market Support for Specialty Shopping Center, Uptown Renewal Site, Atlantic City, New Jersey" (April 1974), pp. 10–11, Heston Room, ACFPL.

58. For a brilliant discussion of the dispersal of urban life and the part played by government tax policies, see Thomas W. Hanchett, "U.S. Tax Policy and the Shopping-Center Boom of the 1950s and 1960s," *American Historical Review* 101 (October 1996): 1082–1110. See also Kenneth T. Jackson, *Crabgrass Frontier: The Suburbanization of the United States* (New York: Oxford University Press, 1985).

59. U.S. Bureau of the Census, *Sixteenth Census of the United States: Population*, vol. 2, 851; U.S. Bureau of the Census, *Nineteenth Census of the United States: 1970 Census of Population and Housing, Atlantic City, N.J.*, 1.

60. In 1974, Atlantic City had the highest general tax rate in Atlantic County. See "Atlantic County and Atlantic City Tax Figures (1978)," Vertical Files: Taxes, Heston Room, ACFPL.

61. For more on this, see Fogelson, *Downtown*; and Teaford, *The Rough Road to Renaissance*, 18–25, 27, 95, 97–98, 105.

62. "The Town of Bethany Beach—The Quiet Resorts," available: www.townofbethany beach.com.

63. E-mail to author from Lois Wallen, April 11, 2002. See also Larry McMurtry, *The Last Picture Show* (New York: Simon and Schuster, 1966). For a similar discussion of McMurtry's book, and the movie of the same name, see Marling, "Fantasies in Dark Places."

CHAPTER 5 (pages 103–131)

1. See Maria San Filippo's insightful essay "Boardwalk Xanadu: Time and Place in *The King of Marvin Gardens* and *Atlantic City*," available: www.rottentomatoes.com/ click/movie-1045645/reviews.php?critic.

2. According to the former curator of the Atlantic City collection at the public library, the Traymore came down in three blasts in the spring of 1972. See Marie E. Boyd to Ann Marie Cunniffe, September 20, 1989, Vertical Files: Hotels: Traymore, ACFPL.

3. Gay Talese, "One More Spin of the Wheel for Atlantic City," *New York Times*, September 8, 1996. See also interview with Murray Raphel by author, September 8, 1999; Daniel Heneghan, "Casinos' Beginning Rooted in AC Decay," *Atlantic City Press*, November 12, 1986; Charles E. Funnell, *By the Beautiful Sea: The Rise and High Times of That Great American Resort, Atlantic City* (New York: Knopf, 1975), 153; James Howard Kunstler, *The Geography of Nowhere: The Rise and Decline of America's Man-Made Landscape* (New York: Simon and Schuster, 1993), 228–30; and interview with Dian Spintler by author, January 27, 1999.

4. "More Hotels Taken Over by Army in A.C.," *Variety*, July 8, 1942, 45; "4 More Hotels to Army in A.C.," *Variety*, July 15, 1942, 46; "20 More Hotels in A.C. Taken by Army," *Variety*, August 12, 1942; and brochure: "Camp Boardwalk Revisited: AC Remembers Its Part in World War II, November 2–4, 1986," Vertical Files: Atlantic City, General #5, Atlantic County Historical Society, Somers Point, New Jersey.

5. Theodore White, *The Making of the President, 1964* (New York: Atheneum, 1965),

274–75. See also Michael Pollack, *Hostage to Fortune: Atlantic City and Casino Gambling* (Princeton, N.J.: Center for Analysis of Public Issues, 1987), 21–23; Joseph F. Sullivan, "AC: Images of '64 Made Blurry," *New York Times*, August 16, 1981; and interview with Allen "Boo" Pergament by author, March 3, 1999. In a Web posting on Atlantic City Memory Lane, Jim Bloom writes, "The Atlantic City of the 1920s through the 1950s died after the Democratic Convention of 1964 and all the bad publicity. But the ghosts are still all around." Bloom, October 27, 2000, Atlantic City Memory Lane, available: www.iloveac.com/memory.

6. Joseph T. Wilkins, *The Skin Game and Other Atlantic City Capers* (Xlibris, 2002), 43.

7. Interview with Jordan E. Sayles by Cynthia Ringe, April 24, 1978, Atlantic City Living History, Heston Room, ACFPL; and Greater Atlantic City Chamber of Commerce, *Action*, September 1964, GACCC, Atlantic City.

8. Quotes from Warren B. Murphy and Frank Stevens, *Atlantic City* (Los Angeles, Calif.: Pinnacle, 1979), 221–22; and "A Dowager's Decline," *Newsweek* (June 8, 1970), 86. On air travel and the decline of Atlantic City, there are a host of sources; see, for example, Frank J. Prendergast, "Resort Hotels' Outlook, Operations Changing," *Atlantic City Press*, September 21, 1968; Bruce Boyle, "Technology, Racism, and Rolling Chairs May Revive Us Yet," *Philadelphia Bulletin*, September 23, 1981; Michael Pollack, "The City in Shock," *Atlantic City Press*, March 28, 1982; Daniel Heneghan, "Casinos' Beginning Rooted in AC Decay," *Atlantic City Press*, November 12, 1986; Funnell, *By the Beautiful Sea*, 154, 156; and Wilkins, *The Skin Game*, 43. For the larger trend of middle- and working-class people taking flight, see Ray Suarez, *The Old Neighborhood: What We Lost in the Great Suburban Migration, 1966–1999* (New York: Free Press, 1999), 106–7; and Alan Ehrenhalt, *The Lost City: The Forgotten Virtues of Community in America* (New York: Basic, 1995), 67.

9. Funnell, *By the Beautiful Sea*, 153–54.

10. First quote from William Mandel, "Shore Lures Stars," *Philadelphia Bulletin*, June 13, 1971; second quote from Susan Vandongen, "Nostalgic View of AC," *Atlantic City Press*, n.d., Vertical Files: Hotel Chalfonte-Haddon, Atlantic County Historical Society, Somers Point, New Jersey.

11. On the importance of air conditioning and swimming pools to Atlantic City's decline, see Peter B. Brophy, "A People Which No Longer Remembers Has Lost Its History and Soul," *Atlantic City Press*, June 25, 1978. On air conditioning and the retreat to the private, see Ehrenhalt, *The Lost City*, 94–95. On pools, see also John Hannigan, *Fantasy City: Pleasure and Profit in the Postmodern Metropolis* (London: Routledge, 1998), 35. For a couple of fascinating social histories of air conditioning, see Gail Cooper, *Air-Conditioning America: Engineers and the Controlled Environment, 1900–1960* (Baltimore, Md.: Johns Hopkins University Press, 1998); and Marsha E. Ackerman, *Cool Comfort: America's Romance with Air-Conditioning* (Washington, D.C.: Smithsonian Institution, 2002).

12. Web post, Stanley Slome, August 22, 2002, Atlantic City Memory Lane, available: www.iloveac.com; and Michael Johns, *Moment of Grace: The American City in the 1950s* (Berkeley: University of California Press, 2003), 57–58.

13. Interview with Anthony Kutschera by author, August 13, 1999; and Anthony J. Kutschera, "Atlantic City—A Victim of Technology?" Atlantic City Historical Mu-

seum, Annual Report 1986, Vertical Files: Atlantic City General, #8, Atlantic County Historical Society, Somers Point, New Jersey. On these kinds of advertisements, see Roland Marchand, *Creating the Corporate Soul: The Rise of Public Relations and Corporate Imagery in American Big Business* (Berkeley: University of California Press, 1998). For more on television and the retreat to the private, see Robert Putnam, *Bowling Alone: The Collapse and Revival of American Community* (New York: Simon and Schuster, 2000). On the retreat to the private and vacations with reference to Atlantic City, see Kunstler, *The Geography of Nowhere,* 229. See also David Nasaw, *Going Out: The Rise and Fall of Public Amusements* (New York: Basic, 1993); and Cindy S. Aron, *Working at Play: A History of Vacations in the United States* (New York: Oxford University Press, 1999).

14. James N. Riggio, "Convention Priority Resented by Small Businesses," *Philadelphia Inquirer,* June 3, 1970.

15. "Atlantic City Seen as a Hub of Crime," *New York Times,* July 8, 1951.

16. On Pollack and D'Amato, see Jonathan Van Meter, *The Last Good Time: Skinny D'Amato, the Notorious 500 Club, and the Rise and Fall of Atlantic City* (New York: Crown, 2003), 130.

17. On the older tradition, see interview with Jordan E. Sayles by Cynthia Ringe, April 24, 1978, Atlantic City Living History, Heston Room, ACFPL. On women at work, see Alice Kessler-Harris, *Out to Work: A History of Wage-Earning Women in the United States* (New York: Oxford University Press, 1982). On changing vacation habits, see Juliet Schor, *The Overworked American: The Unexpected Decline of Leisure* (New York: Basic, 1991).

18. On the longer vacation theory and Atlantic City, see interview with Reese Palley by author, September 23, 1999.

19. Quote from Letter to the Editor, *Atlantic City Press,* June 29, 1963. See also Greater Atlantic City Chamber of Commerce, *Action,* January 1966, March 1972, Heston Room, ACFPL. Robert Kanigel noticed a similar environmental degradation in Nice; see Kanigel, *High Season: How One French Riviera Town Has Seduced Travelers for Two Thousand Years* (New York: Viking, 2002), 236–37.

20. Interview with Pergament. For a similar view, see Lois Wallen to author, February 16, 1999. On the storm, see "Heinz Pier: The Great Pickle Promotion," *Atlantic City Press,* May 16, 1976; and Jim Waltzer and Tom Wilk, *Tales of South Jersey: Profiles and Personalities* (New Brunswick, N.J.: Rutgers University Press, 2001), 82–86.

21. On both 1960s storms, see Ed Davis, *Atlantic City Diary: A Century of Memories, 1880–1985* (McKee City, N.J.: Atlantic City Sunrise Publishing, 1986), 121–22, 130–31; Editorial, "The Indestructible Pier," *Atlantic City Press,* December 31, 1969; and Ed Hitzel, "The Piers: From 1880 to Now," *Atlantic City Press,* October 18, 1970.

22. Allen quoted by Peter A. Coclanis, "Urbs in Horto," *Reviews in American History* 20 (September 1992): 16. See also John A. Jakle, *The Tourist: Travel in Twentieth-Century North America* (Lincoln: University of Nebraska Press, 1985), 64. In a wonderful phrase, Jakle writes that people looked for nature in Atlantic City in "extreme moderation."

23. Jennifer Price, *Flight Maps: Adventures with Nature in Modern America* (New York: Basic, 1999), 178, 195.

24. On changing ideas about vacations with reference to Atlantic City, see Kunstler, *The Geography of Nowhere*, 229. For an interesting comparison with vacationing in the West, see Hal Rothman, *Devil's Bargains: Tourism in the Twentieth-Century American West* (Lawrence: University Press of Kansas, 1998).

25. Greater Atlantic City Chamber of Commerce, *Action*, April 1971, Heston Room, ACFPL.

26. "Plastic Canopy Urged for Resort Boardwalk," *Philadelphia Bulletin*, October 27, 1963; Ellen Karasik, "A Stroll under Glass, by the Sea," *Atlantic City Press*, January 13, 1979; and Carlo M. Sardella, "How about a Boardwalk Mall," *New York Times*, July 27, 1980.

27. Newsletter, "Talk from the Captain's Walk at Chalfonte-Haddon Hall," May 1959, Vertical Files: Hotels—Chalfonte-Haddon, Herton Room, ACFPL; Brochure, "Millions for Progress," January 16, 1959, Bulletin Collection, Envelope—City Improvement, Urban Archives, Temple University, Philadelphia, Pa.; "Atlantic City Building Boom Tops $100 Million for Decade," *Atlantic City Press*, June 23, 1966.

28. Bruce Springsteen, "Independence Day," *The River* (Columbia, 1980).

29. Gaeton Fonzi and Bernard McCormick, "Bust-Out Town," *Philadelphia Magazine* (August 1970), 58.

30. Line from the song "Aquarius," from the musical *Hair* (RCA, 1968).

31. On the culture of teenagers, see Johns, *Moments of Grace*, 55–62.

32. "Second Honeymoon," episode 73 of "All in the Family"; see episode guide, available: www.allinthefamilysit.com.

33. Paul Learn, "Open Arms to GIs Urged," *Atlantic City Press*, March 13, 1966; and Minutes of the Board of Directors of the Greater Atlantic City Chamber of Commerce, April 25, 1966, GACCC Files, Atlantic City.

34. For reports of dress, see press accounts of the Atlantic City Pop Festival, *Atlantic City Press*, August 2, 3, 4, 1969.

35. "Resort to End Motel Ban," *New York Times*, November 29, 1952; "Altman Says City Modernized by Luxury Tax and Motel Law," *Atlantic City Press*, October 27, 1957; and Glen Duffy, "The Secret Shore," *Philadelphia Magazine* (June 1982), 99, 114.

36. S. William White, "Landlords Share Blame for Riots, Police Aide Says," *Philadelphia Bulletin*, September 6, 1966; and Richard Stern, "City Hall Parking Reviewed," *Atlantic City Press*, April 19, 1966.

37. Untitled, *Atlantic City Press*, August 4, 1969, Vertical File: Atlantic City Pop Festival, Heston Room, ACFPL.

38. Morgan, quoted by Susan Douglas, *Where the Girls Are: Growing Up Female with the Mass Media* (New York: Times, 1994), 139–40; and Charlotte Curtis, "Miss America Pageant Is Picketed by 100 Women," *New York Times*, September 8, 1968.

39. Curtis, "Miss America Pageant."

40. See quote, but even more generally on the subject of tension between the middle class and the counterculture, see Kenneth Cmiel, "The Politics of Civility," in *The Sixties: From Memory to History*, ed. David Farber (Chapel Hill: University of North Carolina Press, 1994), 271.

41. Interview with Rachel Frost (name changed by author), August 31, 1999; and John Calpin, "Quiet at the Shore," *Philadelphia Inquirer*, July 10, 1968.

42. For a brief discussion of the crowd and burlesque houses, see Andrew Hurley, *Diners, Bowling Alleys, and Trailer Parks: Chasing the American Dream in the Postwar Consumer Culture* (New York: Basic, 2001), 314.

43. Quoted in Mark N. Finston, "Shore Gurgles over the Wave of Prosperity," *Atlantic City Press*, September 15, 1964.

44. Interview with Pierre Hollingsworth by author, August 19, 1999; Wade Green, "On the Boardwalk: What a Difference a Century Makes," *New York Times*, July 12, 1970; and Funnell, *By the Beautiful Sea*, 157–58.

45. Interview with Hollingsworth; interview with James Usry, by author, September 20, 1999; and Brad Bennett, "Civil Rights Movement Has Long History in A.C.," *Atlantic City Press*, February 21, 1993.

46. "Protesters Holding Signs at Woolworth's," March 19, 1960, photograph no. BE047081, available: www.corbis.com.

47. Memo from Mr. Gloster Current to Henry Moon, September 1, 1966, NAACP Papers, Group III, Box C21, Folder: Atlantic City, N.J., 1966–67; and telegram from NAACP National Office to Branches, September 1, 1966, NAACP Papers, Group VI, Box C114, Folder: Branch Department, N.J., AC Branch, 1965–1967, Library of Congress.

48. "Pageant Leader Mum on Charge by NAACP Aide," *Philadelphia Bulletin*, September 11, 1967.

49. Thomas A. Johnson, " 'Keep Pressure On,' Negroes Are Urged in AC Talk," *New York Times*, August 28, 1967; and Thomas A. Johnson, "Negro Policeman Bars AC Promotion," *New York Times*, September 2, 1967.

50. Maxine Leeds Craig, *Ain't I a Beauty Queen: Black Women, Beauty, and the Politics of Race* (New York: Oxford University Press, 2002), 3, 70–71; "Blacks to Stage Rival 'Miss America' Contest," "Sandrua Williams of Philly Winner," *New Jersey Afro American*, September 7, 14, 1968.

51. On efforts to find jobs, see interview with Hollingsworth; S. William White, "Bias Charged in Atlantic City Store Hiring" and "Atlantic City Negroes Seek White Collar Jobs in Hotels," *Philadelphia Bulletin*, March 13, February 24, 1964; Louis Emanuel, "CORE Breaks Off Hotel Job Talks," *Atlantic City Press*, March 11, 1966; "NAACP Newsletter," signed by Mr. Lloyd Holland, VP [March 3, 1966], NAACP Papers, Group IV, Box J7, Folder: Printed Matter, NAACP by State, New Jersey, 1966–1970, Library of Congress; Greater Atlantic City Chamber of Commerce, *Action*, August 1967, GACCC, Atlantic City; and Bennett, "Civil Rights Movement Has Long History in A.C."

52. Interview with Hollingsworth; and interview with Lois Wallen by author, October 11, 1999. For background, see Robert E. Weems, Jr., *Desegregating the Dollar: African-American Consumption in the Twentieth Century* (New York: New York University Press, 1998), 80–99; and Lizabeth Cohen, *A Consumer's Republic: The Politics of Mass Consumption in Postwar America* (New York: Knopf, 2003).

53. "Altman Says Season Is Resort's Greatest," *Philadelphia Bulletin*, July 29, 1966; "Inaugural Address by Mayor William T. Somers," November 12, 1969, Minutes of Commissioners, City Clerk's Office, Atlantic City.

54. Joseph Di Neo, "NAACP Threatens to Isolate Island," *Atlantic City Press*, n.d., NAACP Papers, Group VI, Box C114, Folder, Branch Department, NJ, AC Branch, 1970–1976, Library of Congress. Note that this article was misfiled and is from 1966.

55. Walter H. Waggoner, "Atlantic City Moves to Ease Tensions over Civil Rights," *New York Times*, April 10, 1966; Thomas Oommen, "Walk Scene of Protest," *Atlantic City Press*, May 22, 1966.

56. "2 Restaurants Face Civil Rights Pickets," "Restaurant Pickets Due after 'Sudden Protests,'" "NAACP Wins Row at Starns," *Atlantic City Press*, May 24, 25, 29, 1966; and Henry Spier, "NAACP Criticizes 2 Shore Restaurants," "Truck Hurts Shore Picket at Restaurant," *Philadelphia Bulletin*, May 20, 28, 1966.

57. Jacqueline McBride-Jones, "Continuing Racism Shows Need to Teach Black History," *Atlantic City Press*, n.d., Sid Trusty Library, Current Events Scrapbook, Atlantic City.

58. "Resort Forms Task Force to Curb Juveniles," "Crowd of Teen-Agers Dispersed at Shore," and "Two Boys Hurt in Teen Fracas at Atlantic City," *Philadelphia Bulletin*, June 4, 1966, September 9, 10, 1967.

59. Interview with Pat Smith by author, October 19, 1999; and interview with David Spatz by author, January 29, 1999.

60. "Detective Panel Patrol Urged for Boardwalk Stores," and S. William White, "TV, Dogs Sought to Fight Crime on Boardwalk," *Philadelphia Bulletin*, December 1 and 22, 1968.

61. Alfred Washington, "A Black 'Militant' Speaks," and Maceo Turner, "White People Don't Know Our Problems," both from *Atlantic City Press*, n.d. [1968?], Vertical Files: Black Bios/Profiles/Personality, Heston Room, ACFPL.

62. "Youth Damage Shore Theater in Rampage," *Philadelphia Bulletin*, May 3, 1970. For a synopsis of the film, see E! online, available: www.eonline.com/facts/movies/0.60.58806.00.html.

63. See references to conditions in "Critic Is Refuted on Garbage Pickup," unidentified clipping [1968?], Scrapbook 2, Sid Trusty Library, Atlantic City; Walter Waggoner, "Atlantic City: A Tourist Playground, Negro Battlefield," *New York Times*, December 22, 1967; and Minutes of Commissioners, March 31, 1965, City Clerk's Office, Atlantic City.

64. Martin Sherman, *Rose* (London: Methuen, 1999), 22–33.

65. Bruce Boyle, "Of the Inlet Irish: It Was Summertime and the Card Fell Right," and "Technology, Racism, and Rolling Chairs May Revive Us Yet," *Philadelphia Bulletin*, December 22, 1980, and September 23, 1981.

66. Fonzi and McCormick, "Bust-Out Town," 122–23. Murray Raphel and his wife, Ruthie, also talked about white fears as a factor behind the city's decline. See interview with Raphel.

67. Interview with Leslie Kammerman by Cynthia Ringe, n.d., Atlantic City Living History, Heston Room, ACFPL.

68. Letter from Boreman (his name has been changed) to author, July 10, 1999; and interview with Boreman by author, August 31, 1999.

69. Interview with Theodore (Teddy) Leonard by Cynthia Ringe, April 25, 1978, Atlantic City Living History, Heston Room, ACFPL.

70. See similar reactions in Carlo Rotella, *Good with Their Hands: Boxers, Bluesmen, and Other Characters from the Rust Belt* (Berkeley: University of California Press, 2002), 121–22, 159.

71. Quoted in Friedland, "Death of the 'World's Playground,'" 75–76, 81. See also, on crime and retailing, interview with Raphel.

72. On the idea of tipping points, see Malcolm Gladwell, *The Tipping Point: How Little Things Can Make a Big Difference* (New York: Little, Brown, 2000).

73. Buzz Bissinger, *A Prayer for the City* (New York: Random House, 1997), 84.

74. Rotella, *Good with Their Hands*, 48.

75. Friedland, "Death of the 'World's Playground,'" 79. See also "Crime Here Rose 20% during 1966," *Atlantic City Press*, January 25, 1967; Mark E. Heisler, "Resort Crime Rose 13.5% over 1968," *Atlantic City Press*, April 1, 1969; and Editorial, "The Crime Situation," *Atlantic City Press*, July 15, 1970.

76. Friedland, "Death of the 'World's Playground,'" 78.

77. Quoted in Friedland, "Death of the 'World's Playground,'" 79.

78. Sherry B. Ortner, *New Jersey Dreaming: Capital, Culture, and the Class of '58* (Durham: Duke University Press, 2003), 61.

79. Warren B. Murphy and Frank Stevens, *Atlantic City* (Los Angeles, Calif.: Pinnacle, 1979), 23.

80. James F. Clarity, "Atlantic City's Better Half Is All Most Tourists See," *New York Times*, August 4, 1971.

81. E-mail from Lois Wallen to author, August 30, 2000, and conversation with Ursula Brady, November 20, 2003.

82. For more on Disney architecture, see Paul Goldberger, "Mickey Mouse Teaches the Architects," *New York Times Magazine*, October 22, 1972; and Karal Marling, ed., *Designing Disney's Theme Parks: The Architecture of Reassurance* (Paris: Flammarion, 1997).

83. Disney, John Kasson and John Findlay explain, studied Coney Island closely and tried to create a better model than the older resort space. See John F. Kasson, *Amusing the Millions: Coney Island at the Turn of the Century* (New York: Hill and Wang, 1978), 106; and John M. Findlay, *Magic Lands: Western Cityscapes and American Culture after 1940* (Berkeley: University of California Press, 1992), 65–66.

84. On Main Street, in particular, see Kunstler, *Geography of Nowhere*, 220–21. For other useful sources in reading the park, see Hannigan, *Fantasy City*, 41; Michael Sorkin, "See You in Disneyland," in *Variations on a Theme Park: The New American City and the End of Public Space*, ed. Michael Sorkin (New York: Hill and Wang, 1992), 205–32; George Lipsitz, "The Making of Disneyland," in *True Stories from the American Past*, vol. 2: *Since 1865*, ed. William Graebner (New York: McGraw-Hill, 2000), 209–24; Goldberger, "Mickey Mouse Teaches the Architects," 95.

85. Findlay, *Magic Lands*, 82–83.

86. Lipsitz, "The Making of Disneyland," 215.

87. Findlay, *Magic Lands*, 81. See also Charles W. Moore, "You Have to Pay for the Public Life," *Perspecta, the Yale Architectural Journal* 9–10 (1965): 57–65.

88. Findlay, *Magic Lands*, 81–82.

89. Lipsitz, "The Making of Disneyland," 224.

90. Quoted in Sorkin, "See You in Disneyland," 206.

91. On race and Disneyland, see Lipsitz, "The Making of Disneyland," 222–24, and Findlay, *Magic Lands*, 94.

92. Quote from Kevin Wallace, "Onward and Upward with the Arts," *New Yorker*, September 7, 1963, 204. See how the clean streets impressed one of Richard Russo's fictional characters in his novel *Nobody's Fool* (1993; reprint, New York: Vintage, 1994), 343.

93. Richard V. Francaviglia, "Main Street U.S.A.: A Comparison/Contrast of Streetscapes in Disneyland and Walt Disney World," *Journal of Popular Culture* 15 (Summer 1981): 141–56; and Kunstler, *Geography of Nowhere*, 220–21.

94. Quoted in Josephine A. Kapus, "The Tailor's Story," *Sandpiper*, August 5, 1988.

CHAPTER 6 (pages 132–152)

1. Woody Allen, *Annie Hall* (United Artists, 1977).

2. On the city's promotional efforts, see "Times Square Signs," *Atlantic City Press*, March 31, 1957; "Canadian Week Plans Are Set," Greater Atlantic City Chamber of Commerce, *Action*, June 1966, GACCC, Atlantic City; "Seaquarium Project Set for Atlantic City Awash in Red Tape," *Atlantic City Press*, November 2, 1967, Vertical Files: Amusements, Boardwalk Rides, etc., Heston Room, ACFPL; Urban Renewal Citizens Committee, "Newsletter," March 8, 1969, Box 4, UR 115, Folder, Hamid, Atlantic City Housing Authority, Atlantic City, New Jersey; "Traymore Plan Aired," *Atlantic City Press*, February 3, 1972; S. William White, "A Look at Shore Economy: Sick and Getting Worse," and White, "Bradway Lists Projects to 'Fight for City,'" *Philadelphia Bulletin*, November 3, 1975, January 16, 1976; and "Stressing the Positive: No 'Partly Cloudy' Skies in Resort, It's 'Partly Sunny' from Today On," *Atlantic City Press*, January 24, 1962.

3. On this idea of different markets, see Lizabeth Cohen, *A Consumer's Republic: The Politics of Mass Consumption in Postwar America* (New York: Knopf, 2003), 296–344.

4. *Steel Pier Souvenir Program and Guide Book, 1949*, Allen "Boo" Pergament Private Collection, Margate, New Jersey. See also George A. Hamid's autobiography, *Circus* (New York: Sterling, 1950).

5. On the early part of Hamid's life, see "Bridge to the Old World," *Time* (June 7, 1961), 53–54; and "George Hamid Dies at 75," *New York Times*, June 14, 1971.

6. *New York Times*, May 8 and 18, 1945; and untitled article, *Atlantic City Press*, January 6, 1980, Vertical Files: People, Businessmen, Atlantic County Historical Society, Somers Point, New Jersey.

7. "Bridge to the Old World," 53.

8. "All Roads Lead to Atlantic City," *Atlantic City Press*, May 26, 1963.

9. Steven V. Cronin, "100 Years of Magic," *Atlantic City Press*, June 18, 1998; "Hamid Recalls Greats," n.d., Vertical Files: Steel Pier, Heston Room, ACFPL.

10. Michael Checchio, "Campers Backed by Hamid," *Atlantic City Press*, March 2, 1975 (first quote); and Memo, February 28, 1975, File: Trav-L-Park, Feb. 28, 1975, Box: Proposed Developers, R-115: Marketing Campaign, Atlantic City Housing Authority, Atlantic City, New Jersey; and in blue-collar types, see "Bridge to the Old World," 53.

11. "Women Push for Legal Gambling," *Atlantic City Press*, March 17, 1959.

12. "Merchants Complain about Encroachment along the Boardwalk," *Philadelphia Inquirer*, August 24, 1968.

13. "City Adopts 'Walk Tone Ordinance," *Atlantic City Press*, June 16, 1967.

14. Frank J. Prendergast, "Improved 'Walk Tone Is Sought," *Atlantic City Press*, August 24, 1968.

15. Greater Atlantic City Chamber of Commerce, "Annual Report," *Action*, July 1958, GACCC, Atlantic City.

16. S. William White, "TV, Dogs Sought to Fight Crime on Boardwalk," *Philadelphia Bulletin*, December 22, 1968. See also Minutes of the Board of Directors of the Greater Atlantic City Chamber of Commerce, January 25, 1965, GACCC, Atlantic City.

17. "Hearing Re: Use of Police Dogs by A.C. Police Dep't," January 2, 1969, Minutes of Commissioners, Atlantic City, New Jersey, Atlantic City City Hall. See also "Statement to the Board by Gregg Wells," June 5, 1969, and "Statements regarding the Establishment of a K-9 Corps," December, 18, 1969, Minutes of Commissioners, Atlantic City City Hall, Atlantic City, New Jersey.

18. For an assessment of the convention's impact, see Greater Atlantic City Chamber of Commerce, "Demo Convention Meets Mixed Reactions," *Action*, September 1964, GACCC, Atlantic City.

19. Murray Raphel, "The Democratic National Convention . . . Who Needs It? Atlantic City, Maybe?" *Atlantic City Press*, July 9, 1972.

20. Tom Seppy, untitled article, *Atlantic City Press*, February 2, 1964, Vertical Files: History of Atlantic City Publicity and Promotional Materials, Heston Room, ACFPL; Greater Atlantic City Chamber of Commerce, "Annual Report," *Action*, November 1957, March 1964, GACCC, Atlantic City; "Recommendation for Greater Courtesy, R/UDAT"—American Institute of Architects, Regional/Urban Design Assistance Team, Atlantic City, November 1975, pp. 5–6, 10, Heston Room, ACFPL.

21. Untitled article, *Atlantic City Press*, October 9, 1969, Vertical Files: Steel Pier, Heston Room, ACFPL.

22. *The New Steel Pier Official Bicentennial Souvenir Program, 1976*, Allen "Boo" Pergament Private Collection, Margate, New Jersey.

23. Untitled article, *Atlantic City Press*, May 16, 1968, Vertical Files: Steel Pier, Heston Room, ACFPL.

24. Susan Davis, *Spectacular Nature: Corporate Culture and the Sea World Experience* (Berkeley: University of California Press, 1997), 28–36; and Jennifer Price, *Flight Maps: Adventures with Nature in Modern America* (New York: Basic, 1999), 178.

25. Paul Learn, "They Sing Praises of AC—But in Miami," *Atlantic City Press*, February 20, 1966.

26. Interview with Mildred Fox by Cynthia Ringe, April 28, 1978, Atlantic City Living History, Heston Room, ACFPL; Greater Atlantic City Chamber of Commerce, *Action*, June 1967, GACCC, Atlantic City; "Special Rates for Honeymooners," "Atlantic City Honeymoon Plan Is Economy Deal [for] Newlyweds," and "Cut-Rate Honeymooners," *Philadelphia Bulletin*, April 16, 1960; May 23, 1965; May 15, 1969.

27. James N. Riggio, "Convention Priority Resented by Small Businesses," *Philadelphia Inquirer*, June 3, 1970.

28. Riggio, "Convention Priority Resented by Small Businesses"; " 'Walk Commission to Aid City Salons in Maintaining Tone," *Atlantic City Press*, June 7, 1962; Henry Spier, "Advertising Campaign in Canada Pays Off in Dollars for Atlantic City," *Philadelphia Bulletin*, August 15, 1965; Greater Atlantic City Chamber of Commerce, *Action*, June 1966, GACCC, Atlantic City.

29. Frank Prendergast, "Merchant Says 'Walk a Disgrace," *Atlantic City Press*, August 28, 1971.

30. Quoted in Jim Waltzer and Tom Wilk, *Tales of South Jersey: Profiles and Personalities* (New Brunswick, N.J.: Rutgers University Press, 2001), 38.

31. "Atlantic City Maps Tight Crackdown on Rowdy Teens," *Philadelphia Inquirer*, June 18, 1967.

32. Application of the Psychedelic Fun House, July 15, 1971; August 26, 1971; September, 23, 1971, Minutes of Commissioners, City Clerk's Office, Atlantic City.

33. For a funny, tongue-in-cheek article on shoobies, see "Delights of the Shoobie, or Atlantic City, on 15¢ a Day," *Philadelphia Inquirer*, June 9, 1968; and Michael Pollack, *Hostage to Fortune: Atlantic City and Casino Gambling* (Princeton, N.J.: Center for Analysis of Public Issues, 1987), 32–33.

34. "Merchants Complain about Encroachment along the Boardwalk," *Philadelphia Inquirer*, August 24, 1968. Some African Americans saw the campaign for a beach fee as discriminatory; see "Beach Fee Considered in Atlantic City," *Philadelphia Bulletin*, September 21, 1971.

35. Frank J. Prendergast, "Improved 'Walk Tone Is Sought," *Atlantic City Press*, August 24, 1968. Years earlier, Hamid opposed such a measure, calling it a "roadblock." Dennis M. Higgins, "O'Connell's Tax Plan Given Chilly Reception," *Atlantic City Press*, December 24, 1962.

36. James N. Riggio, "Boardwalk a Symbol of Black Frustration," *Philadelphia Inquirer*, June 2, 1970.

37. Gaeton Fonzi and Bernard McCormick, "Bust-Out Town," *Philadelphia Magazine* (August 1970), 58.

38. "Crowd of Teen-Agers Dispersed at Shore," "Two Boys Hurt in Teen Fracas at Atlantic City," *Philadelphia Bulletin*, September 9, 10, 1967; and Charles E. Funnell, *By the Beautiful Sea: The Rise and High Times of That Great American Resort, Atlantic City* (New York: Knopf, 1975), 157–58.

39. Riggio, "Boardwalk a Symbol of Black Frustration." Businesspeople in Coney Island echoed this assessment, blaming the decline of their resort town on desegregation. See Harold M. Scheck, Jr., "Coney Island Slump Grows Worse," *New York Times*, July 2, 1964.

40. Letter to the Editor, *Atlantic City Press*, June 5, 1969. See also First Reading, Ordinance 13, April 13, 1969, Minutes of Commissioners, City Clerk's Office, Atlantic City.

41. Quoted in James Henrietta et al., *America: A Concise History* (Boston: Bedford/St. Martin's, 1999), 840. In his book on Chicago, Alan Ehrenhalt talks about the middle class's faith in the modern and all things new; see *The Lost City: The Forgotten Virtues of Community in America* (New York: Basic, 1995), 54–55.

42. Sonny Schwartz, "From Hill to Tall Casinos," *Atlantic City Press*, May 19, 1990; and Greg Walter, "The Only Game in Town," *Philadelphia Magazine* (August 1971), 55.

43. Robert Goldman, *After the Planners* (New York: Simon and Schuster, 1971), 59. On urban renewal more generally, see Martin Anderson, *The Federal Bulldozer: A Critical Analysis of Urban Renewal, 1949–1962* (Cambridge, Mass.: MIT Press, 1964); Scott Greer, *Urban Renewal and American Cities: The Dilemma of Democratic Intervention* (Indianapolis, Ind.: Bobbs-Merrill, 1966); Herbert J. Gans, "The Failure of Urban Renewal: A Critique and Some Proposals," *Commentary* 39 (April 1965), 29–37; and Jon C. Teaford, *The Rough Road to Renaissance: Urban Revitalization in America, 1940–1985* (Baltimore, Md.: Johns Hopkins University Press, 1990).

44. Goldman, *After the Planners*, 67; and "Mayors Endorse Rights Program," *New York Times*, June 13, 1963.

45. "The Urban Renewal Program," RG 207, Urban Renewal Subject Files, Box 752, Folder: Reports and Statistics, April–May 1962, National Archives, College Park, Maryland.

46. Roberta Brandes Gratz with Norman Mintz, *Cities Back from the Edge: New Life for Downtown* (New York: Preservation Press, 1998), 49.

47. Memo from Timothy J. Reardon, Jr., special assistant to president, Weekly Report, October 2, 1962, RG 207, Urban Renewal Subject Files, Box 752, Folder: Reports and Statistics, October thru [*sic*] Present, 1962, National Archives, College Park, Maryland.

48. On the transformation of the ghetto, see Arnold Hirsh, *Making the Second Ghetto: Race and Housing in Chicago, 1940–1960* (New York: Cambridge University Press, 1983).

49. For suggestions on Hill's thinking, see Atlantic County CORE to National CORE, May 25, 1966, CORE Papers, Reel 16, Addendum, 1944–1968, Frames 774–75, University Microfilms; and Ray Suarez, *The Old Neighborhood: What We Lost in the Great Suburban Migration, 1966–1999* (New York: Free Press, 1999), 16.

50. Robert Nigro, "Where Were You in '62?" *Atlantic County Journal*, April 16, 1992, Vertical Files: Atlantic City, General #9, Atlantic County Historical Society, Somers Point, New Jersey.

51. Prior to 1952, the city's hotel owners, perhaps the single most powerful force in the city, successfully kept motels out of the city. See "Resort to End Motel Ban," *New York Times*, November 29, 1952. On the city's first motel, John's Motel, see Glenn Duffy, "The Secret Shore," *Philadelphia Magazine* (June 1982), 99, 114; and interview with Frances Ginnetti by Cynthia Ringe, n.d., Atlantic City Living History, Heston Room, ACFPL.

52. "Urban Renewal Seen as Chance to Revitalize City," *Atlantic City Press*, July 9, 1963.

53. For the phrase *demolition fever*, see Gratz, *Cities Back from the Edge*, 49.

54. "Urban Renewal Seen as Chance to Revitalize City," *Atlantic City Press*, July 9, 1963.

55. Richard Stern, "Sound Chance with Renewals, Mrs. Hill Says," *Atlantic City Press*, July 21, 1966.

56. Ian Stenhouse, "Mrs. Hill Can See a Reborn Midtown," *Atlantic City Press*, October 2, 1966.

57. "Urban Renewal Program Seen as Cure for Social Ills," *Atlantic City Press*,

May 4, 1961; and "Speculators Seen Busy in Housing," *Atlantic City Press*, August 4, 1966.

58. Pauline Hill, "Statement of Blight: The Urban Renewal Plan, and the Relocation Plan," May 5, 1965, Records of the Atlantic City Housing Authority and Urban Redevelopment, Atlantic City, New Jersey.

59. Allyn H. Jones, "Renewal Will Mean Tax Slack, but Mrs. Hill Forecasts Cure," *Atlantic City Press*, December 12, 1966.

60. "Unit Told Benefits of Urban Renewal," *Atlantic City Press*, October 10, 1962.

61. Daniel Hilliard, "Renewal to Stimulate $70m Growth," *Atlantic City Press*, April 28, 1967.

62. For an example of Hill's views, see Richard Stern, "City Hall Parking Reviewed," *Atlantic City Press*, April 19, 1966.

63. Quoted in Hillard, "Renewal to Stimulate $70m Growth."

64. Quoted in "Urban Renewal Program Seen as Cure for Social Ills," *Atlantic City Press*, May 4, 1967.

65. For opposition to Hill's plans, see James Cooper, "The Urban Renewal Plan, and the Relocation Plan," May 5, 1965, Records of the Atlantic City Housing Authority and Urban Redevelopment, Atlantic City, New Jersey. In other cities, urban renewal sparked protests; for example, see J. Clarence Davies III, *Neighborhood Groups and Urban Renewal* (New York: Columbia University Press, 1966); and Adam Cohen and Elizabeth Taylor, *American Pharaoh: Mayor Richard J. Daley: His Battle for Chicago and the Nation* (New York: Little, Brown, 2000), 208–11, 228–29.

66. Richard Stern, "City Hall Parking Reviewed," *Atlantic City Press*, April 19, 1966 (first quote); Laura Italiano, "Remembrance of Hill and Prairie," *Atlantic City Press*, March 14, 1992.

67. Quotes, in order, are from "Uptowners Cautioned to Avoid New Building," n.d., *Atlantic City Press*, Box 6, File: Clippings, UR-115, Records of the Atlantic City Housing Authority; Ian Stenhouse, "Mrs. Hill Can See a Reborn Midtown," *Atlantic City Press*, October 2, 1966.

68. On the homes and businesses destroyed, see UR-115 Spread Sheet, UR-115, Records of the Atlantic City Housing Authority.

69. Quoted in Walter, "The Only Game in Town."

70. See, for example, Housing Authority drawings in Local Project Approval Data, Part 1, Uptown Project, November 12, 1964, Records of the Atlantic City Housing Authority; and Richard Stern, "Sound Chance with Renewals, Mrs. Hill Says," *Atlantic City Press*, July 21, 1966.

71. Gustave Amsterdam to Charles Jeffries, January 27, 1972, Box 2, File: Barco, UR-115, Records of the Atlantic City Housing Authority.

72. Michael Prichard, "Diamonds Didn't Always Shine on Atlantic City Urban Tract," *Atlantic City Press*, August 1, 1994; and interview with Fred Klein by author, June 22, 2000.

73. Atlantic County CORE to National CORE, May 25, 1966, CORE Papers, Reel 16, Addendum, 1944–1968, Frames 774–75, University Microfilms.

74. Mark Heisler, "Hamid Unit Asks for Showdown in Lagging Renewal Area," *Atlantic City Press*, October 21, 1969.

75. See comments about Hill after her death: Letter to the Editor, *Atlantic City Press*, June 11, 1990.

76. Catherine Maack and Barry Koltnow, "Mrs. Hill Plays It Cool on Bumper Stickers Critical of Her," *Atlantic City Press*, January 27, 1971; Sonny Schwartz, "Pauline Sees Little Peril," *Atlantic City Press*, February 3, 1971; and Frank Lowe, "Renewal Chief Unruffled by Barbs in Atlantic City," and John Holland, "Ouster of Renewal Chief Demanded in Atlantic City," *Philadelphia Inquirer*, January 31 and March 4, 1971.

77. Letter to the Editor from Seth Grossman, *Atlantic City Press*, February 4, 1971.

78. Alex Stern, "Chelsea Heights Group Fights Reassessment," and "Mrs. Hill Says Reassessment Not Her Doing," *Atlantic City Press*, July 2, 3, 1970.

79. Quotes, in order, Urban Renewal Citizens Committee, "Newsletter," March 8, 1969, Box 4, UR-115, File, Hamid, Atlantic City Housing Authority; caption to photograph, "Vast Wasteland," *Atlantic City Press*, August 3, 1968; and "Hamid Rips Renewal Agency, Brace Corp. for City Tax Ills," *Atlantic City Press*, July 5, 1970.

80. Heisler, "Hamid Unit Asks for Showdown in Lagging Renewal Area."

81. Interviews with Les Kammerman, n.d., and Leon Binder, n.d., by Cynthia Ringe, Atlantic City Living History, Heston Room, ACFPL.

82. Jon Katz, "Mrs. Hill Calls Census Claim 'Grossly Inaccurate,'" *Atlantic City Press*, August 25, 1970.

83. Quotes from interview with Binder. Beth Israel Temple, to look at one religious institution, slowly retreated from the neighborhood in the wake of urban renewal. First it moved its offices, then its religious schools, and eventually it completely relocated to suburban Northfield. See Minutes of Board of Trustees of Congregation Beth Israel, Congregation Records, Northfield, N.J.; and Kevin Shelly, "Houses of Worship Leave Resort in Modern-Day Exodus," *Atlantic City Press*, September 1, 1985. On business closings as a result of urban renewal around the country, see Richard B. McMillian to Urban Renewal Director, June 11, 1962; attached is an editorial from the Anderson (Ind.) *Herald*, June 7, 1962, RG 207, Urban Renewal Subject Files, Box 751, Folder: Public Relations, June, July, August 1962, National Archives; and Ben A. Franklin, "Inequities Seen in Slum Renewal," *New York Times*, April 27, 1965.

84. Jane Jacobs, *The Death and Life of Great American Cities* (New York: Random House, 1961). See also Suarez, *The Old Neighborhood*, 82–83, 87. For a recent study of the importance of the "social capital" gained through these kinds of everyday encounters, see Robert Putnam, *Bowling Alone: The Collapse and Revival of American Community* (New York: Simon and Schuster, 2000).

85. Interview with Paul Carr by author, September 30, 1999.

86. Patrick Jenkins, "Citizens Help Police Nab Purse Snatcher," "Commission Hit on Inlet Crime," *Atlantic City Press*, March 2, 1974; July 25, 1975. For more on Inlet crime, see "2 Atlantic City Sites Get Foot Patrolmen," *New York Times*, April 2, 1974.

87. Alex Stern, "Fear, Crime Stalk Resort Inlet Streets," *Atlantic City Press*, December 23, 1972.

88. Katz, "Mrs. Hill Calls Census Claim 'Grossly Inaccurate'"; and Maack and Koltnow, "Mrs. Hill Plays It Cool on Bumper Stickers Critical of Her."

89. Prichard, "Diamonds Didn't Always Shine on Atlantic City Urban Tract."

90. William Downey to C. E. Snow, May 3, 1973, Box 3, File: Developers, Canadian Hotelmen, UR-115, Atlantic City Housing Authority. At one point in 1973, it looked like the Hilton chain might open a hotel in the area, but this plan fell through. See Donald Janson, "3 Atlantic City Officials Testify in Bribery Study," *New York Times*, August 17, 1973.

91. On the amusement parks, see Memo from Bill Rafferty to File, November 20, 1973; Rafferty to Downey, November 22, 1973, both in Box: Proposed Developers/Marketing Campaign, File: Theme Park, Atlantic City Housing Authority. On the RV park, see Michael Checchio, "Campers Backed by Hamid," *Atlantic City Press*, March 2, 1975; and Memo, February 28, 1975, Box: Proposed Developers/Marketing Campaign, File: Trav-L-Park, Atlantic City Housing Authority.

92. Videotape, Atlantic City Housing Authority, *Atlantic City: Cleared for Take-Off*, 1984, Heston Room, ACFPL.

93. All quotations in the following paragraphs are from John Wideman, "Fear in the Streets," *Philadelphia Bulletin*, February 20, 1972.

CHAPTER 7 (pages 153–170)

1. Joseph T. Wilkins, *The Skin Game and Other Atlantic City Capers* (Xlibris, 2002), 9.

2. Gail Wilson, "101 Women Honors [*sic*] Black Merchants," *Atlantic City Press*, April 13, 1989.

3. Alex Stern, "Misery Tries Inlet Tenants," *Atlantic City Press*, February 25, 1974.

4. For an overview of Puerto Rico and Puerto Rican communities in the United States, see Kal Wagenheim, *The Puerto Ricans: A Documentary History* (Garden City, N.Y.: Anchor, 1973); Joseph P. Fitzpatrick, *Puerto Rican Americans: The Meaning of Migration to the Mainland* (Englewood Cliffs, N.J.: 1971); Fitzpatrick, "Puerto Ricans," in *Harvard Encyclopedia of American Ethnic Groups*, ed. Stephan Thernstrom (Cambridge, Mass.: Harvard University Press, 1980), 858–67; James L. Dietz, *Economic History of Puerto Rico: Institutional Change and Capitalist Development* (Princeton, N.J.: Princeton University Press, 1986), 240–310; and Nicholas Lemann, "The Other Underclass," *Atlantic Monthly* (December 1991), 96–110.

5. Maria E. Perez y Gonzalez, *Puerto Ricans in the United States* (Westport, Conn.: Greenwood, 2000).

6. Quoted in Glen Duffy, "Follow the Yellow Brick Road," *Atlantic City Press*, July 15, 1979.

7. Kal Wagenheim, *A Survey of Puerto Ricans on the U.S. Mainland in the 1970s* (New York: Praeger, 1975), 120–21.

8. Ana Arana, "Gambling on the Future of Atlantic City," *Encore American and Worldwide News*, March 20, 1978, 10–13.

9. Jimmy Breslin, "There Is No Room for the Poor in Atlantic City," unidentified clipping [*Philadelphia Inquirer*?], June 4, 1978, Vertical Files: Development of Atlantic City, 1970s, Heston Room, ACFPL.

10. Donna Rood, "Greed Routs Hispanics from Decaying Homes," *Atlantic City Press*, November 14, 1978.

11. Wagenheim, *A Survey of Puerto Ricans*; and Rood, "Greed Routs Hispanics."

12. From the Good and Welfare section, July 13, 1972, Minutes of Commissioners, City Clerk's Office, Atlantic City.

13. Samuel Boreman to author, July 10, 1999; and interview with Boreman by author, August 31, 1999.

14. Quoted in Ursula Obst, "The Myth, Realities," *Atlantic City Press*, June 9, 1981.

15. From the Good and Welfare section, July 13, 1972, Minutes of Commissioners, City Clerk's Office, Atlantic City.

16. Thomas Peele, "South Inlet Awaits Casinos as Past Fades in Empty Lots," *Atlantic City Press*, July 7, 2000. On food, see "Cultural Diversity: Eating in America, Puerto Rican," available: www.ohioline.osu.edu/hyg-fact/5000/5257.html. On bodegas as community institutions, see Terry Agins, "Latin Oases," *Wall Street Journal*, March 15, 1985; and Joseph P. Fitzpatrick, *Puerto Rican Americans: The Meaning of Migration to the Mainland* (Englewood Cliffs, N.J.: Prentice Hall, 1987), 49–50.

17. Obst, "The Myth, Realities"; Donald Janson, "AC's Clerics Say Casinos Hurt Churches," *New York Times*, September 2, 1979; *Atlantic City: The Queen Takes a Chance*, produced and directed by Albert Rose, tape, 90-41B, September 19, 1978, Heston Room, ACFPL; Patrick Jenkins, "Hispanic Self-Help Office Opens," *Atlantic City Press*, May 4, 1976; and interview with Robert Beakley by author, August 16, 1999.

18. Jenkins, "Hispanic Self-Help Office Opens."

19. "On Villa Santa Rosa, Displaced Cry," *Atlantic City Press*, October 3, 1978; Harry Gold, "Inlet Poor Fear Casino Pressure," *Philadelphia Inquirer*, April 23, 1978; Glen Duffy, "Follow the Yellow Brick Road," *Atlantic City Press*, July 15, 1979; and Ursula Obst, "The Slum Hispanics Call Home," *Atlantic City Press*, June 8, 1981.

20. Sonny Schwartz, "Jews Don't Seek Kibbutz," *Atlantic City Press*, March 15, 1978.

21. Interview with Mike Mann by author, February 28, 2000.

22. Gaeton Fonzi and Bernard McCormick, "Bust-Out Town," *Philadelphia Magazine* (August 1970), 118–19; Bill Kent, "The Queen of New York Avenue," *Atlantic City* (August 1984), 99; and interview by author with Reese Palley, September 12, 1999. See also the local gay newsletter, the *Seagull*, Memorial Day, 1977, and "For Our Visiting Friends," *Seagull*, August 11, 1978, Vertical File: Gay and Lesbian Community, Heston Room, ACFPL.

23. Allan Berube, *Coming Out under Fire: The History of Gay Men and Women in World War II* (New York: Free Press, 1990). On Atlantic City, see "Camp Boardwalk Revisited: Atlantic City Remembers Its Part in World War II, November 2–4, 1986," Vertical Files: Atlantic City, General #5, Atlantic County Historical Society, Somers Point, New Jersey; and Bill Kent with Robert Ruffolo and Lauralee Dobbins, *Atlantic City: America's Playground* (Encinitas, Calif.: Heritage Media, 1998), 144–55.

24. Berube, *Coming Out under Fire*, 256; John D'Emilio and Estelle B. Freedman, *Intimate Matters: A History of Sexuality in America* (Chicago: University of Chicago Press, 1997), 260–61, 288–89; and Jeffrey Escoffier, *American Homo: Community and Perversity* (Berkeley: University of California Press, 1998), 75–77.

25. Berube, *Coming Out under Fire*, 123; Kent, "The Queen of New York Avenue," 99; "A.C. Niteries Get Further Orders to Tone Down: More Hotels to Army," *Variety*, July 29, 1942, 44; and interview with John Schultz by author, September 24, 1999.

26. On the increased visibility of gay life in the postwar period, see the comparable scene in Flint, Michigan, in Tim Retzloff, "Cars and Bars: Assembling Gay Men in Postwar Flint, Michigan," in *Creating a Place for Ourselves: Lesbian, Gay, and Bisexual Community Histories*, ed. Brett Beemyn (New York and London: Routledge, 1997), 231.

27. For a survey of postwar gay life, see Jerry "Jai" Moore, "The Lady Jai['s] Recommended List," c. 1954, in author's possession. (Tim Retzloff graciously provided me with a copy of this list.) According to this simple, mimeographed list, Louisa's was the only "all the way" gay bar in town. For the location of the clubs, see *Atlantic City Directory* (Philadelphia: Polk, 1956).

28. On Snug Harbor, see interview with Herb Tapper by author, February 26, 2000.

29. Berube, *Coming Out under Fire*, 258–59; George Chauncey, "The Postwar Sex Crime Panic," in *True Stories from the American Past*, ed. William Graebner (New York: McGraw Hill, 1997), 160–78; and Jonathan Katz, *Gay American History: Lesbians and Gay Men in the U.S.A.* (New York: Crowell, 1976), 109.

30. Minutes of Commissioners, June 22, 1951, pp. 590–91, City Clerk's Office, Atlantic City.

31. Minutes of Commissioners, February 19, 1953, p. 127, City Clerk's Office, Atlantic City.

32. "Rockets Charged in AC," *New York Times*, April 12, 1956.

33. Interview with Don Pigolet by author, February 13, 2000.

34. Interview with Schultz. For more on harassment, see Martin Duberman, *Stonewall* (New York: Dutton, 1993).

35. *One Eleven Wines and Liquors, Inc. v. Division of Alcoholic Beverage Control*, 50 N.J., 329, 330, A.2d, 12, p. 2.

36. "Bars Challenge State Ruling on Homosexuals," *Philadelphia Bulletin*, September 3, 1967. For more on the general national legal trends and on New Jersey law, see William N. Eskridge, Jr., "Challenging the Apartheid of the Closet: Establishing Conditions for Lesbian and Gay Intimacy, *Nomos*, and Citizenship, 1961–1981," *Hofstra Law Review* 25 (1997): 872; and Eskridge, *Gaylaw: Challenging the Apartheid of the Closet* (Cambridge, Mass.: Harvard University Press, 1999), 46.

37. For more on early ABC raids, see *One Eleven Wines and Liquors*, pp. 2–3. On the closing of Louisa's by the city, see Minutes of Commissioners, November 10, 1955, p. 1168, City Clerk's Office, Atlantic City. See also "Club Is Closed for 240 Days at Atlantic City," *Philadelphia Bulletin*, May 3, 1963.

38. For a survey of Atlantic City gay bars, see *International Guild Guide* (Washington, D.C.: Guild Press, 1966), 85; *International Guild Guide* (Washington, D.C.: Guild Press, 1967), 87–88; *The Lavender Baedecker '66* (San Francisco: Stairt and Associates, 1966), 15, all from Special Collections, University of Chicago.

39. Descriptions of Val's have come from interviews by author with Mann; and Don Pigolet, February 13, 2000.

40. *One Eleven Wines and Liquors*, p. 3.

41. On the lead-up to the Val's case, see *One Eleven Wines and Liquors*; Marc Stein, *City of Sisterly and Brotherly Loves: Lesbian and Gay Philadelphia, 1945–1972* (Chicago: University of Chicago Press, 2000), 282; and Eskridge, *Gaylaw*, 112. For more on the statewide crackdown, see *Drum*, April 1966, October 1967, Gay, Lesbian, Bisexual,

and Transgendered Archives of Philadelphia, William Way Community Center, Philadelphia, Pa.

42. *One Eleven Wines and Liquors*, p. 8; "N.J. Court Permits Homosexuals in Bars," *Philadelphia Bulletin*, November 6, 1967; "Ruling Affects Homosexuals," *Philadelphia Inquirer*, November 7, 1967; "High Court of NJ Overturns a Ban on Homosexuality," *New York Times*, November 7, 1967. See also Stein, *City of Sisterly and Brotherly Loves*, 283, 423–33.

43. On the impact of Val's challenge to the ABC, see interview with Mann; and Ann Kolson, "Faded," *Philadelphia Inquirer*, November 10, 1982. One guide published in 1967 noted that Val's was "very popular." See *Bob Damron's Address Book 1968* (San Francisco: Pan-Graphic, 1967), 56, Special Collections, University of Chicago.

44. Interview with Mann; *Seagull*, Memorial Day, 1977, Vertical Files, File: Gay and Lesbian Community, Heston Room, ACFPL; and Kolson, "Faded." According to available guides, the Fort Pitts had been a gay bar in the early 1960s, and then, it seems, it switched to being a straight bar, maybe when Stockton College came to Atlantic City. Then, it switched back again to being a gay bar after Val's won its court case. In the 1964 and 1966 *Guild Guides*, the Fort Pitts is listed as a gay bar. It is omitted from the 1967 guide, and then in 1971, it is again listed as a gay bar. This seems to confirm Mann's story about the bar. See *International Guild Guide* (Washington, D.C.: Guild Press, 1964), 54; *International Guild Guide* (Washington, D.C.: Guild Press, 1966), 85; *International Guild Guide* (Washington, D.C.: Guild Press, 1967); and *International Guild Guide* (Washington, D.C.: Guild Press, 1971), 66—this also has information on the rooming houses—Special Collections, University of Chicago. For Freeman's remarks, see "Liquor Hearing Re: Chez Paree," July 15, 1971, Minutes of Commissioners, City Clerk's Office, Atlantic City.

45. Kolson, "Faded." On Cape May and Rehoboth, see *Drum*, August 1965, September 1965, Gay, Lesbian, Bisexual, and Transgendered Archives of Philadelphia, William Way Community Center, Philadelphia, Pa. For an example from the antigay campaign in New York City, see "2 Clubs Catering to Homosexuals Closed by Police," *New York Times*, November 26, 1967.

46. On emptiness and gay space, see John Petsinger to author, February 17, 2000; interview with Tapper; and interview with Beakley. For some details about the scene at the start of the 1970s, see Fonzi and McCormick, "Bust-Out Town," 118–19.

47. Escoffier, *American Homo*, 72–73. On harassment, see interview with Schultz; and e-mail from Petsinger to author, February 17, 2000. On Mafia control of gay bars in New York, see Duberman, *Stonewall*, 115–16.

48. E-mail from Petsinger to author, February 17, 2000; and e-mail from GITANO 1966 to author, February 9, 2000.

49. On the beach scene, see interviews with Schultz and Tapper.

50. Kent, "The Queen of New York Avenue," 99; and Glen Duffy, "Goodbye to Gay Street," *Atlantic City* (November 1986), 55. For a map of the New York Avenue scene, see the local gay newsletter, the *Seagull*, Memorial Day, 1977, and the map "For Our Visiting Friends," *Seagull*, August 11, 1978, Vertical Files, File: Gay and Lesbian Community, Heston Room, ACFPL. See also *Gay Yellow Pages* (New York: Ranaissance House, Spring and Summer 1976), 57; and *Bob Damron's Address Book* (San Fran-

cisco: Bob Damron Enterprises, 1979), 222–24, Gay, Lesbian, Bisexual, and Trans-
gendered Archives of Philadelphia, William Way Community Center, Philadelphia,
Pa. For more, including information on Mama Mott's, see *International Guild Guide*
(Washington, D.C.: Guild Press, 1971), 66, Special Collections, University of
Chicago; and interview with Beakley. On the Metropolitan Community Church, see
Seagull, Memorial Day, 1977, cited above; and *New Wave*, the publication of the Met-
ropolitan Community Church of Atlantic City, July 1981, Vertical Files: Gay, Lesbian,
Bisexual, and Transgendered Archives of Philadelphia, William Way Community
Center, Philadelphia, Pa. (by then, the church had moved to North Indiana Avenue).

51. Quoted in D'Emilio and Freedman, *Intimate Matters*, 355.
52. Quoted in Fonzi and McCormick, "Bust-Out Town," 118–19.
53. Michael Checchio, "Boys for Sale," *Atlantic City Press*, September 1, 1977; Ed Hitzel,
    "A.C.'s Boardwalk: Has It Changed?" *Atlantic City Press*, August 19, 1979; and "Liquor
    Hearing re: Chez Paree," July 15, 1971, Minutes of Commissioners, City Clerk's Of-
    fice, Atlantic City.
54. E-mail from Hal Tarr to author, February 22, 2000; interview with Pigolet; and inter-
    view with Bruce Cahan by author, March 10, 2000.
55. Interviews with Mann and Pigolet; Frank Prendergast, "Merchant Says 'Walk a Dis-
    grace," *Atlantic City Press*, August 28, 1971; and Checchio, "Boys for Sale." Elmore
    Leonard comments on the availability of drugs along New York Avenue in his novel
    Glitz (New York: Arbor House, 1985), 172.
56. Interviews with Mann, Tapper, Beakley, and Palley.

CHAPTER 8 (pages 171–193)

The title of chapter 8 comes from Hal Rothman's *Devil's Bargains: Tourism in the
Twentieth-Century American West* (Lawrence: University Press of Kansas, 1998). There are
several other scholarly assessments of Atlantic City's "gamble," including George Sternlieb
and James W. Hughes, *The Atlantic City Gamble* (Cambridge, Mass.: Harvard University
Press, 1983); Joseph Rubenstein, "Casino Gambling in Atlantic City: Issues of Development and Redevelopment," *Annals of the American Academy of Political and Social Science*
474 (July 1984): 61–71; Richard Ochrym, "Gambling in Atlantic City: The 'Grand Vision'
Blurs," *National Civic Review* 72 (1983): 591–96; and Stephen J. Simurda, "When Gambling
Comes to Town," *Columbia Journalism Review* 32 (January 1994): 36–38. For a more posi-
tive assessment of gambling's impact, see Daniel Heneghan, "Economic Impacts of Casino
Gambling in Atlantic City," in *Legalized Gaming in the United States: The Economic and
Social Impact*, ed. Cathy H. C. Hsu (Binghamton, N.Y.: Haworth Hospitality Press, 1979),
113–33.

1. On Palley's return to the city, see interview with Palley by author, September 23,
   1999; Ed Appel, "Reese Palley: A Maverick on the Boardwalk," *Courier Post*, December 1, 1973; and Stephanie Mansfield, "The Promoter," *Washington Post*, May 29,
   1978.
2. For descriptions of what was in Palley's shop, see "Interview: Reese Palley," unidentified clipping [September 1976?], *Philadelphia Bulletin*, Clipping Collection, File:
   Reese Palley, Urban Archives, Temple University, Philadelphia, Pa.; Sharon Greene

and Ellen Telze, *Atlantic City Tourist's Guide* (Brooklyn, N.Y.: Shopping Experience, 1979), 124–25.

3. The phrase comes from a section of the Kodner Gallery's Web site on Boehm; available: www.kodnergallery.com/Bios/boehmporcelain.htm.

4. Edward Hitzel, "Giant Monopoly Game Promotes 'Our Town,'" *Atlantic City Press*, April 15, 1973.

5. Mansfield, "The Promoter."

6. For descriptions of Palley, see Bill Collins, "It's a Super-Ego Trip," *Philadelphia Inquirer*, February 27, 1972, p. 10; and Mansfield, "The Promoter."

7. Appel, "Reese Palley: A Maverick on Boardwalk."

8. "Interview: Reese Palley."

9. *Atlantic City: The Queen Takes a Chance*, produced and directed by Albert Rose, tape, 90-41B, September 19, 1978, Heston Room, ACFPL.

10. Quoted in Philip Ross and Susan Perkis Haven, "The Little City That Could," *New York*, June 20, 1977.

11 *Atlantic City: The Queen Takes a Chance*.

12. *Atlantic City: Today's Dream Tomorrow's . . .* , 1978, videotape, Peabody Collection, No. 79005, University of Georgia Library, Athens (first quote); Ross and Haven, "The Little City That Could," 36 (second quote); Bill Moyers Reports, "Big Gamble in Atlantic City," CBS, July 28, 1986, Heston Room, ACFPL (third quote). See also interview with Palley; and Reese Palley, "How It Happened (Approximately)" (unpublished essay, in author's possession).

13. *Atlantic City: Today's Dream, Tomorrow's . . .*

14. Marea Teski et al., *A City Revitalized: The Elderly Lose at Monopoly* (Lanham, Md.: University Press of America, 1983), 49.

15. E-mail from Hal Rothman to author, June 15, 2003.

16. On the city's gambling past, see Grace D'Amato, *Chance of a Lifetime: Nucky Johnson, Skinny D'Amato, and How Atlantic City Became the Naughty Queen of Resorts* (Harvey Cedars, N.J.: Down the Shore, 2001); Nelson Johnson, *Boardwalk Empire: The Birth, High Times, and Corruption of Atlantic City* (Medford, N.J.: Plexus, 2002); and Jonathan Van Meter, *The Last Good Time: Skinny D'Amato, the Notorious 500 Club, and the Rise and Fall of Atlantic City* (New York: Crown, 2003).

17. "Women's Unit Favors Atlantic City Gambling," *New York Times*, March 12, 1958; "Women Push for Legal Gambling," *Atlantic City Press*, March 17, 1959; and S. William White, "Woman, 64, Recalls Casino Drive in '58," *Philadelphia Bulletin*, September 29, 1974.

18. Frank Prendergast, "Gambling Given New Hope Here," *Atlantic City Press*, October 22, 1970.

19. Sternlieb and Hughes, *The Atlantic City Gamble*, 1–29; "Casino Gambling at Atlantic City Seen Alternative to Income Tax," unidentified clipping, December 3, 1970, Vertical Files: Casino Gambling, Heston Room, ACFPL.

20. Sternlieb and Hughes, *The Atlantic City Gamble*, 43.

21. Both quoted by Alfonso A. Narvez, "Casinos Become an Emotional Issue," *New York Times*, October 26, 1974. For an overview, see Charles Stansfield, "Atlantic City and

the Legalization of Gambling," *Resort Cycle: Background to the Annals of Tourism Research* 5 (April/June 1978), 238–51.

22. Martin Waldron, "Council of Churches Set for Drive to Bar Casino Gambling in the State," *New York Times*, September 8, 1976; Joan Cook, "Goldstein Broadens Attack on Casinos," *New York Times*, October 15, 1974; Narvez, "Casinos Become an Emotional Issue"; Walter H. Waggoner, "Jersey Group Seeks Voters' Rejection of Casino Gambling," *New York Times*, September 12, 1974; Joseph F. Sullivan, "The Why of 'No' Vote on Casinos," *New York Times*, November 16, 1974; and John Dombrink and William N. Thompson, *The Last Resort: Success and Failure in Campaigns for Casinos* (Reno: University of Nevada Press, 1990), 25–41.

23. Daniel Heneghan, "Casinos' Beginning Rooted in AC Decay," *Atlantic City Press*, November 12, 1986. For more on the mood in the city during those first days after the 1974 referendum's failure, see James F. Sullivan, "Casino Defeat Ends Dreams of Prosperity in AC Realty," *New York Times*, November 7, 1974; and "Outlook Bleak for Atlantic City," *New York Times*, November 10, 1974.

24. Sullivan, "The Why of 'No' Vote on Casinos."

25. "Atlantic City Fund Drive Gains," *New York Times*, September 6, 1976.

26. Van Meter, *The Last Good Time*, 256; Johnson, *Boardwalk Empire*, 194–95; Michael Pollack, *Hostage to Fortune: Atlantic City and Casino Gambling* (Princeton, N.J.: Center for Analysis of Public Issues, 1987), 15–16; and Carlos M. Sardella, "AC Bets on Casinos," *New York Times*, July 18, 1976.

27. Johnson, *Boardwalk Empire*, 194.

28. Sternlieb and Hughes, *The Atlantic City Gamble*, 50; Geoffrey Douglas, "The Selling of Casino Gambling," *New Jersey Monthly* (January 1977): 21–26; Johnson, *Boardwalk Empire*, 190–91; and interview with Steven Perskie by author, April 7, 1999.

29. Alvin Maurer, "The Vote Adds Up to 21, and AC Will Get Casinos," *New York Times*, November 7, 1976.

30. Donald Janson, "Election's Spin of a Wheel Elates Faded Resort of AC," *New York Times*, November 4, 1976.

31. *Atlantic City Press*, November 3, 1976.

32. Bill Moyers, "Big Gamble in Atlantic City." For more on these expectations, see Molly Ivins, "Atlantic City Sees Itself Basking in the Sun Again," *New York Times*, November 7, 1976.

33. Quoted in Janson, "Election's Spin of a Wheel Elates Faded Resort of AC."

34. Harry Gould, "Keeping Fingers Crossed on Kentucky Ave.," *Philadelphia Inquirer*, May 28, 1978.

35. Patrick Pacheo, "Restoration of the Queen of Resorts," *After Dark* (August 1978), 40.

36. *Atlantic City: The Queen Takes a Chance.*

37. Sternlieb and Hughes, *The Atlantic City Gamble*, 59.

38. For more on the comparison between Atlantic City and Las Vegas, see David G. Schwartz, *Suburban Xanadu: The Casino Resort on the Las Vegas Strip and Beyond* (New York and London: Routledge, 2003), 12–13, 178–82.

39. Ibid., 62.

40. Donald Janson, "Jersey Urged to Step Up Casinos' Aid Payments," *New York Times*,

December 3, 1982; Donald Janson, "Agency and Casinos Battle over Urban Aid Funds," *New York Times*, March 27, 1983; Donald Janson, "Casino Investing Weighed," *New York Times*, May 13, 1984; and Kirk Johnson, "With Cash Rolling in, Atlantic City Raises Stakes," *New York Times*, June 24, 1996. On Caesar's, see "Casino Offers a Housing Plan to Meet Redevelopment Rule," *New York Times*, December 2, 1984.

41. Vicki Gold Levi, "On the Site of Resorts," *Atlantic City Press*, March 21, 1981.

42. Gigi Mahon, "Landing on the Boardwalk," *Barron's*, November 20, 1978; Gigi Mahon, *The Company That Bought the Boardwalk: A Reporter's Story of Resorts International* (New York: Random House, 1981); and "The Charges against Resorts," *New York Times*, March 4, 1979.

43. Donald Janson, "Casino Board Gives Go-Ahead to Open First AC Casino," *New York Times*, May 16, 1978.

44. James L. Clarity, "700 Practice Betting at AC Casino," *New York Times*, May 27, 1978.

45. Lee Lescaze, "Eager Gamblers Throng N.J. Casino at Its Opening," *Washington Post*, May 28, 1978; and "Casino Crowds Turned Out for Opening of First Casino," *Trenton Times*, May 5, 2003. On the peach baskets, see interview with Murray Raphel by author, September 8, 1999; and on Wynn and Davis, see Van Meter, *The Last Good Time*, 263–64.

46. Patrick Jenkins and Edward Hitzel, "Pier's New Owners Say Casino Likely," *Atlantic City Press*, January 17, 1973. See Ed Davis, *Atlantic City Diary: A Century of Memories, 1880–1985* (McKee City, N.J.: Atlantic Sunrise Publishing, 1986), 136.

47. On Steel Pier's preparations, see "On the Boardwalk, Steel Pier Sports $2.5 Million New Look," *New York Times*, May 31, 1976; Fred Ferreti, "A Blue Chip Tour of AC," *New York Times*, May 26, 1978; and *Atlantic City Vacationer*, August 13, 1977, Ed Davis Papers, Folder: From Davis, December 4, 1985, Heston Room, ACFPL.

48. On Fisher, see Eddie Fisher and David Fisher, *Been There, Done That: An Autobiography* (New York: St. Martin's, 2000); and Jack Gould, "Television in Review," *New York Times*, June 15, 1953. On that night on the Boardwalk, see James L. Clarity, "Reporter's Notebook: Old Resort, New Era," *New York Times*, May 25, 1978; and interview with David Spatz by author, January 29, 1999.

49. James Clarity, "Dowdy AC Awaiting a Face Lift," *New York Times*, May 26, 1978; Donald Janson, "AC Prepares for 'Worst Ever' Traffic Expected at Casino's First Weekend," *New York Times*, May 23, 1978.

50. James Clarity, "Crowds in Rest of AC Are Sparse, but Casino Is Packed," *New York Times*, May 27, 1978.

51. "Atlantic City: Longest Shot Is Getting into the Casino," *Washington Post*, May 28, 1978.

52. For a very good description of the speculation craze, see Joseph T. Wilkins, *The Skin Game and Other Atlantic City Capers* (Xlibris, 2002), 117, 145, 155. See also George Anastasia's fantastic series on land speculation, "Monopoly: The Resorts Game in Atlantic City," *Philadelphia Inquirer*, June 16–18, 1985.

53. Wilkins, *The Skin Game*, 145.

54. Martin Waldron, "Casinos Bring Atlantic City Woes," *New York Times*, May 8, 1977; Donald Janson, "Curb in Evictions of Poor Is Sought in Atlantic City," *New York*

Times, November 14, 1978; Donna Rood, "Greed Routs Hispanics from Decaying Homes," *Atlantic City Press,* November 14, 1978.

55. Rood, "Greed Routs Hispanics from Decaying Homes"; Ursula Obst, "The Myth, Realities," *Atlantic City Press,* June 9, 1981; Sternlieb and Hughes, *The Atlantic City Gamble,* 116; and interview with Paul Carr, a fire fighter, by author, September 30, 1999.

56. "Ethnic Dream Fades for the South Inlet," *Philadelphia Bulletin,* June 28, 1981.

57. Francisco Troncaso, "Report on the Impact of Casino Gambling on the Welfare of the Poor, the Minorities, and [the] Elderly in the Inlet Section of Atlantic City" (unpublished essay, May 1977, Temple University Library, Philadelphia, Pa.); and Donald Janson, "Effect of Casinos on Housing Scored," *New York Times,* May 24, 1977.

58. Sternlieb and Hughes, *The Atlantic City Gamble,* 118; Letter to the Editor from B. Moyerman, "Plan Carefully," *Atlantic City Press,* September 11, 1978; Donald Janson, "AC Condominiums Bought for Fun and Profit: Luxury High-Rise Units Are Viewed as an Investment," *New York Times,* August 28, 1983; and Janson, "Curb in Evictions of Poor Is Sought in Atlantic City."

59. Patrick Jenkins, "Inlet's Rezoning Urged by Ponzio," *Atlantic City Press* [1980?], Sid Trusty Library, Scrapbook 2, Atlantic City; Donald Janson, "After a Year, AC's Boom Eludes the Poor," *New York Times,* May 28, 1979; Phillip B. Taft, Jr., "A New Night Flock for Boardwalk Minister," *New York Times,* October 28, 1979; and Thomas Turcol, "Vote Sparks A.C. 'State of Siege,'" *Atlantic City Press,* February 5, 1980.

60. For more on this point, see Jonathan Rieder, *Canarsie: The Jews and Italians of Brooklyn against Liberalism* (Cambridge, Mass.: Harvard University Press, 1985), 27; and Gerald Gamm, *Urban Exodus: Why the Jews Left Boston and the Catholics Stayed* (Cambridge, Mass.: Harvard University Press, 1999).

61. Teski et al., *A City Revitalized,* 42.

62. John Fuchs, "Old Homes Worth $100,000," *Philadelphia Bulletin,* October 19, 1978; "Pussy Cat Bar Eyes New Site," *Philadelphia Bulletin,* February 17, 1974.

63. Ellen Karasik, "All-or-None Offer Splits Residents," *Philadelphia Inquirer,* December 3, 1978.

64. On Savage's appearance and rather shadowy background, see John Fuchs, "Are Block-Bidders Straw Group?" *Philadelphia Bulletin,* October 19, 1978; and interview with Rick Bloom by author, October 2, 1999.

65. Quoted in Karasik, "All-or-None Offer Splits Residents."

66. "Atlantic City Homeowners under Pressure to Sell," *New York Times,* December 3, 1978; and interview with John Lorenzo by author, July 15, 1999.

67. "Casinos to Zig-Zag Holdouts," *Atlantic City Press,* April 30, 1979.

68. Interview with Bloom.

69. *New York Times,* August 14, 1979.

70. Interview with Lorenzo.

71. Ibid. See also Daniel Heneghan's examination of potential casino sites in town, "Casino Countdown," *Atlantic City Press,* January 27, 1980. For more on the neighborhood and on drug dealers, see Mark Davis, "In Atlantic City, a Street's Decline Eclipses Its Past," *Philadelphia Inquirer,* January 2, 1989. Interestingly, Davis says nothing in this rather long and in-depth piece about the Jean Savage deal.

72. "Fourth Ward Site Selected for New Housing Project," *Atlantic City Press*, March 24, 1939.

73. Thomas Oommen, "Downtown Area Generally Slum-Free," *Atlantic City Press*, December 14, 1966. For a recent history of the Pitney Village housing project that barely mentions race, see Vernon Ogrodnek, "The Making of a Village," *Atlantic City Press*, October 25, 1998.

74. Quoted in Ursula Obst, "Ducktown," *Atlantic City Press*, November 11, 1979.

75. Teski et al., *A City Revitalized*, 53.

76. Bill Kent, "The Queen of New York Avenue," *Atlantic City* (August 1984), 99; and interview with Herb Tapper by author, February 26, 2000.

77. Kent, "The Queen of New York Avenue," 99; and Kathy Brennan, "The Thrill Is Gone," *Atlantic City Press*, August 10, 1986.

78. On the casino plans for the street, see interview with John Schultz by author, September 24, 1999; Patrick Jenkins, "$135M. Casino Gets Board OK," *Atlantic City Press*, November 22, 1979; and Daniel Heneghan, "Casino Update," *Atlantic City Press*, July 6, 1980.

79. On NATCO, see Donald Janson, "3-Block Rebuilding Due in Atlantic City," *New York Times*, January 12, 1986; Michael Checchio and Joseph Coccaro, "A.C. Boardwalk Project Facing Federal Takeover," *Atlantic City Press*, August 1, 1986; and George Anastasia and Fen Montaigne, "An $82 Million Broken Promise," *Philadelphia Inquirer*, June 15, 1986.

80. Elaine Rose, "Atlantic City of Yesteryear," *Atlantic City Press*, April 27, 1997.

81. Frank J. Prendergast, "Investor to Raze 2 Resort Theaters," *Atlantic City Press*, May 3, 1978.

82. *Atlantic City Press*, May 29, 1978; and undated typescript, Vertical Files: Art and Cultural Events, Theaters, Heston Room, ACFPL. See a picture of the Strand's marquee on the night Resorts opened in Daniel Heneghan, "Still Rolling the Dice," *Atlantic City Press*, May 23, 1993.

83. William F. Parker, "Theatres of Atlantic City" (typescript, 1982), Vertical Files: Art and Cultural Events, Theaters, Heston Room, ACFPL.

84. "Nov. 13 Fire in Atlantic City's Downtown Business District Causes as Much as $1 Million in Damages," *New York Times*, November 15, 1983; and "Arson Suspected in Atlantic City Fire," *Philadelphia Inquirer*, November 14, 1983.

85. For figures on the number of visitors to Atlantic City, see John Contarino, "The Times of Our Life: A Special Look at 15 Years of Casino Gaming," *Atlantic City* (May 1993), 26.

86. Pollack, *Hostage to Fortune*, 17.

87. Donald Janson, "In the Mayor's Race Atlantic City Focuses on Blight," *New York Times*, May 11, 1986.

CHAPTER 9 (pages 194–216)

1. Bill Moyers, "Big Gamble in Atlantic City," CBS News Special Report, July 28, 1986, Heston Room, ACFPL. All quotations in the following paragraphs are from this show.

2. On this crucial point about malleability, see Hal Rothman, *Devil's Bargains: Tourism in the Twentieth-Century American West* (Lawrence: University Press of Kansas, 1998), 313–37.

3. For more on casino spaces and suburban ideals, see David G. Schwartz, *Suburban Xanadu: The Casino Resort on the Las Vegas Strip and Beyond* (New York and London: Routledge, 2003). Some have called the separation of tourists from the city the creation of the "tourist bubble." See Dennis R. Judd, "Constructing the Tourist Bubble," in *The Tourist City*, ed. Dennis R. Judd and Susan S. Fainstein (New Haven, Conn.: Yale University Press, 1999), 35–53; and Harvey K. Newman, "Race and the Tourist Bubble in Downtown Atlanta," *Urban Affairs Review* 37 (January 2002): 301–21.

4. On Byrne, see Jonathan Van Meter, *The Last Good Time: Skinny D'Amato, the Notorious 500 Club, and the Rise and Fall of Atlantic City* (New York: Crown, 2003), 258. On the resistance to the hotel's demolition, see the editorial "Save Marlborough-Blenheim," *Atlantic City Press*, February 27, 1978; James Clarity, "Atlantic City Is Facing the Loss of a Landmark," *New York Times*, July 4, 1978; Ada Louise Huxtable, "Historic vs. New Battle Still Rages On," *Philadelphia Bulletin*, November 19, 1978; Charles Librizzi, "State Joins Fight to Save Old Atlantic City," *Philadelphia Bulletin*, March 6, 1978; and Frank Van Dusen, "National Protest Mounts over Bally's Hotel Plans," *Atlantic City Press*, July 15, 1978. It is worth noting that Bally's at the same time also bought the Dennis. See Donald Janson, "Pinball and Slot-Machine Concern Plans to Purchase Another Hotel for Casino on AC Boardwalk," *New York Times*, August 17, 1977.

5. Bill Moyers, "Big Gamble in Atlantic City"; and interview with Reese Palley by author, September 23, 1999.

6. Martin Waldron, "11-Second Blast Winds Up Razing of the Blenheim," *New York Times*, January 5, 1979.

7. The city's "monotonous lumps of architecture" is a phrase used by Bill Kent in "Park, Lock and Bet," *New York Times*, November 26, 1995.

8. On the architecture of Atlantic City's casinos, see Ursula Obst, "Skyline of Tomorrow: No Hint of Dream World," *Atlantic City Press*, November 11, 1979; Paul Goldberger, "AC Architecture: The Odds Are All against It," *New York Times*, February 17, 1980; Ada Louise Huxtable, "Atlantic City—Analyzing an Urban Phenomenon," *New York Times*, September 21, 1980; Denis P. Rudd, "Social Impacts of Atlantic City Casino Gambling," in *Legalized Casino Gaming in the United States: The Economic and Social Impact*, ed. Cathy H. S. Chu (Binghamton, N.Y.: Haworth Hospitality Press, 1999), 213–14; and especially Thomas Hine, "Atlantic City," *AIA Journal* 71 (November 1982): 34–44, see pp. 36, 39 in particular. On casino architecture in general, see the observations in Andres Martinez, *24/7: Living It Up and Doubling Down in the New Vegas* (New York: Villard, 1999), 13. On the idea of "ageography," see Michael Sorkin, "Introduction: Variations on a Theme Park," in *Variations on a Theme Park: The New American City and the End of Public Space*, ed. Michael Sorkin (New York: Hill and Wang, 1992), xi; and Karl B. Raitz and John Paul Jones III, "The City as Landscape Artifact and Community Symbol," *Journal of Cultural Geography* 9 (Fall–Winter 1998): 32.

9. Hine, "Atlantic City," 36, 39.

10. Ibid.; Patrick Jenkins, "Arts Panel: Retain 'Walk Shop Facade," *Atlantic City Press*, March 23, 1979.

11. Gerald Clarke, "In Atlantic City: The View from the Porch," *Time* (September 7, 1981), 4. See also interview with Murray Raphel by author, September 8, 1999.

12. Shulamite E. Kustanowitz, "Somewhere beyond the Casinos Is the Ocean," *New York Times*, September 28, 1980.

13. Hine, "Atlantic City," 39.

14. Quote from Jackie Spinner, "Atlantic City No Longer Lives by Casinos Alone," *International Herald Tribune*, March 22, 2000; and David Margolick, "Under LV's Neon Beats a Heart of Denim," *New York Times*, February 16, 1984. For more on casino design, see John M. Findlay, *Magic Lands: Western Cityscapes and American Culture after 1940* (Berkeley: University of California Press, 1992), 90; Marc Cooper, "Searching for Sin City and Finding Disney in the Desert," in *Literary Las Vegas: The Best Writing about America's Most Fabulous City*, ed. Mike Tronnes (New York: Holt, 1995), 325–50; and John Hannigan, *Fantasy City: Pleasure and Profit in the Postmodern Metropolis* (London: Routledge, 1998), 161.

15. On this point, see among others, James Howard Kunstler, *The Geography of Nowhere: The Rise and Decline of America's Man-Made Landscape* (New York: Simon and Schuster, 1993), 234; A. Alvarez, *The Biggest Game in Town* (1983; reprint, San Francisco, Calif.: Chronicle, 2002), 23; and Hannigan, *Fantasy City*, 161.

16. See picture in the *Philadelphia Bulletin*, September 28, 1978.

17. On some of the city's early parking problems, see "Beachgoers Will Discover Change in AC," *New York Times*, May 28, 1978.

18. "Harrah's Casino Opens," *New York Times*, November 24, 1980.

19. Bill Kent, "The Casino Name Game," *New York Times*, March 23, 1997.

20. Kent, "Park, Lock and Bet"; and Catherine Slessor, "View from Atlantic City," *Architectural Review* 212 (August 2002): 26–27.

21. "AC's Nine Casinos Won $1.1 Billion in 1981," *New York Times*, January 17, 1982.

22. "Donald Trump's House of Cards," *Economist*, August 30, 1997; Dana Berliner, "Property Taking Favors Big Guy over Little Guy," *USA Today*, May 4, 1998; and Laura Mansnerus, "What Public? Whose Use?" *New York Times*, March 22, 1998.

23. Caesar's Media Information, 1990, Heston Room, Vertical Files: Casinos, Folder: Caesar's, ACFPL.

24. Atlantic City correspondent Bill Kent calls the people mover a "miscellaneous improvement." See Kent, "Just Call SID," *New York Times*, June 11, 1995.

25. The Showboat, which was built to look like a Mississippi riverboat, opened three years earlier, also on the Uptown urban renewal site.

26. John Contarino, "The Times of Our Life: A Special Look at 15 Years of Casino Gaming," *Atlantic City* (May 1993), 55; and Mary Cantwell, "Close to Home," *New York Times*, May 10, 1990.

27. Dumont quoted by Bill Kent, "The Bold Man and the Sea," *Philadelphia Magazine* (May 1990). See also on the Taj Mahal, Paul Goldberger, "It's Themed, It's Kitschy, It's Trump's Taj," *New York Times*, April 6, 1990; and Carole Agus, "Taj Has Lock on Schlock," *Newsday*, June 8, 1990.

28. Advertisement for Taj Mahal, *Philadelphia Daily News*, March 11, 1990.

29. Springsteen, "Johnny 99," *Nebraska* (Columbia, 1982). For these kinds of tales-of-two-cities reports, see Kent, "The Bold Man and the Sea"; Wayne King, "Behind Atlantic City's Glitz Lies Decay," *New York Times*, April 5, 1990; Larry Tye, "Atlantic City: A Tarnished Setting for Trump's Taj," *Boston Globe*, April 8, 1990; and Priscilla Painton, "Boardwalk of Broken Dreams," *Time* (September 25, 1989), 65.

30. Hal Rothman, *Neon Metropolis: How Las Vegas Started the Twenty-First Century* (New York and London: Routledge, 2002), esp. 117–18.

31. On Trump's enclosures, see Craig Whitaker, *Architecture and the American Dream* (New York: Three Rivers, 1996), 155–56.

32. On this point about the unimportance of the ocean to gamblers, see the quiet film, parts of which are set in Atlantic City, *Owning Mahowny* (Columbia Tristar Home, 2003).

33. Quote and the germ of this argument come from Eugene Moehring's wonderfully perceptive comments on my paper "Gambling Alone: Architectural Change and the Public Realm in Atlantic City, New Jersey, 1950–2000," delivered at the Urban History Association Meeting, September 2002, Pittsburgh, Pennsylvania, in author's possession. For more on Pacific Avenue, see Schwartz, *Suburban Xanadu*, 181.

34. John Hiscock, "Wheels of Fortune Turn, Atlantic City to Jettison Its Gambling Reputation," *Daily Telegraph*, May 21, 1994; and Conor O'Clery, "Casino Culture Brings No Wins to Local Business," *Irish Times*, May 11, 1996. For more on Indian-owned gambling, see Jeff Benedict, *Without Reservation: How a Controversial Indian Tribe Rose to Power and Built the World's Largest Casino* (New York: HarperCollins, 2001); Kim Isaac Eisler, *Revenge of the Pequots: How a Small Native American Tribe Created the World's Most Profitable Casino* (New York: Simon and Schuster, 2001); and Donald L. Barlett and James B. Steele, "Wheel of Misfortune," *Time* (December 16, 2002), 44–58.

35. Donald Janson, "Atlantic City Casino Patrons Mostly from 150 Mile Radius," *New York Times*, June 9, 1985.

36. Glenn Fine and J. Mark Reifer, "Two Projects for the Price of Everything," *New Jersey Casino Journal* (April 1993): 8–9, 47.

37. Quote from Lorenzo Langford, who is the city's current mayor, in Bill Kent, "Casinos, Community, and a Mayor in the Middle," *New York Times*, August 25, 1996.

38. Mary Jo Patterson, Robin Gaby Fisher, and Christine Baird, "Atlantic City Shell Game," *Newark Star-Ledger*, May 4, 1997.

39. Quoted in Bill Kent, "To the Lighthouse," *New York Times*, November 16, 1997. Also see brochure: "The New Grand Boulevard: Gateway to America's Favorite Playground," Vertical Files: Corridor Project, Heston Room, ACFPL.

40. Hannigan, *Fantasy City*, 164.

41. Robert Goodman, *The Luck Business: The Devastating Consequences and Broken Promises of America's Gambling Explosion* (New York: Free Press, 1995), 20–21; and Mansnerus, "What Public? Whose Use?" Statistics tell something of the difference between the two cities. Gambling generates 90–94 percent of the casino income in Atlantic City, while in Las Vegas the tables and slots account for less than half of revenues.

42. Mark Tyler, "Atlantic City Tries to Recapture the Feel of the Good Old Days along the Boardwalk," *Atlantic City Press*, July 31, 2000.

43. Jackie Spinner, "Atlantic City No Longer Lives by Casinos Alone," *International Herald Tribune*, March 22, 2000.

44. Some suggest that gambling is an essentially private activity. For instance, James Howard Kunstler writes that gambling "is an intensely private experience. [That] [t]he whole drama is played out in a public space, the casino, is incidental. The private nature of it is essentially the same whether the player is gambling against the machine, or a live human dealer at the blackjack table." This actually is not the way most students of gambling see things. Most would suggest that the slot machines are more private than the tables, but that there is a public, or shared, dimension to the experience. See Kunstler, *The Geography of Nowhere*, 234, 236. See also Igor Kasyszyn, "The Psychology of Gambling," *Annals of the American Academy of Political and Social Sciences* 474 (July 1984): 133–45.

45. Much has been written on the destructive nature of gambling. See, for example, Goodman, *The Luck Business*. For Atlantic City stories, see Eileen Herbert Jordan, "My Affair with the One-Armed Bandit," *Modern Maturity* 38 (July 1995): 37, 86–87; Martin Waldron, "New Jersey Journal," *New York Times*, February 4, 1979; Louise Saul, "3 Gamblers Tell of Life on the Brink," *New York Times*, March 13, 1983; "Compound Casino Risks," *New York Times*, April 3, 1983; Wayne King, "Atlantic City Mission Cares for the Losers," *New York Times*, June 22, 1989; and Gillian Roberts, *How I Spent My Summer Vacation* (New York: Ballantine, 1994), 212.

46. Evelyn Nieves, "Wedded to Casinos, for Richer . . . ," *New York Times*, January 25, 1981; Owen Moritz, "N.J. Casinos: A Big Draw? You Bet!" *New York Daily News*, May 26, 1998; and Carla Cantor, "For Casinos, Players of Every Stripe," *New York Times*, January 6, 1991.

47. Frederick Barthelme and Steven Barthelme, *Double Down: Reflections on Gambling and Loss* (New York: Houghton Mifflin, 1999), 72. See also David Spanier, "The Joy of Gambling," *Wilson Quarterly* 19 (Autumn 1995): 34–40.

48. *Atlantic City: The Queen Takes a Chance*, produced and directed by Albert Rose, tape, 90-41B, September 19, 1978, Heston Room, ACFPL.

49. Barthelme and Barthelme, *Double Down*, 73. On talking in lobbies and elevators, see Martinez, *24/7*, 23, 91.

50. Quoted in Martinez, *24/7*, 254.

51. Quoted in Alvarez, *The Biggest Game in Town*, 128.

52. Donald Janson, "Casino Caters to High Rollers with Free Suites and Tigers," *New York Times*, June 14, 1987. For more on the seduction of the high roller, see Martinez, *24/7*, 59. On some of the meanings of gambling in the past and today, see Jackson Lears, *Something for Nothing: Luck in America* (New York: Viking, 2003), 321–33; and Lewis A. Erenberg, *Steppin' Out: New York Nightlife and the Transformation of American Culture, 1890–1930* (Chicago: University of Chicago Press, 1981), 139.

53. Quoted in Janson, "Casino Caters to High Rollers with Free Suites and Tigers."

54. For a description of this sense of reassurance because of the cameras, see the novel by Roberts, *How I Spent My Summer Vacation*, 212.

55. "Gaming Panel Fines Caesar's, Saying Casino Catered to Bias," *New York Times*, December 7, 1989.

56. Mike Davis, *City of Quartz: Excavating the Future in Los Angeles* (New York: Vintage, 1992); and Davis, "Fortress Los Angeles: The Militarization of Urban Space," in Sorkin, ed., *Variations on a Theme Park*, 154–80.

57. Adam Fine, "The Boardwalk Revolution," *Casino Journal* (August 1996), Vertical Files: Casino/Gaming Industry, Development and Performance, 1980s, Heston Room, ACFPL; David Clay Johnston, "Coming Back to AC," "Wynn Makes His Return to AC," *New York Times*, June 27, 28, 1995; Mark Davis, "Wynn Back in Atlantic City with a $500 Million Plan," *Philadelphia Bulletin*, June 28, 1995; Brett Pulley, "Battle Brews in AC," *New York Times*, January 27, 1996; Kirk Johnson, "With Cash Rolling in, Atlantic City Raises Stakes," *New York Times*, June 24, 1996; and Joe Weinert, "Mirage Shows Off Grandiose Plans for A.C.," *Atlantic City Press*, October 10, 1999. On the phrase "private driveway," see Donald Wittkowski, "State Says Mirage Deal Won't Affect Tunnel Plans," *Atlantic City Press*, March 8, 2000.

58. Mark Tyler, "Marina District Road Plans Get Rough," *Atlantic City Press*, July 6, 1996 (first quote); and Patrick Jenkins, "Casino Tunnel Mines Mixture of Support and Deep Resentment," *Newark Star-Ledger*, February 14, 1997 (second quote). See also Robin Gaby Fisher, "It's Nice, but It's Not Home," *Newark Star-Ledger*, July 25, 1997; and Office of the Governor, "Governor Breaks Ground for Atlantic City Tunnel: Cites Economic Benefits and Traffic Improvements from Project," News Release, November 4, 1998, Vertical Files: Tunnel Project, Heston Room, ACFPL.

59. Terry Pristin, "Talk of a Merger Raises New Concern for Hotel-Hungry Atlantic City," *New York Times*, February 27, 2000; and "Mirage and MGM Make a Bet," March 7, 2000, available: www.cnn.com.

60. "Governor McGreevey Ushers in New Era for Atlantic City," Press Release, May 22, 2002, available: www.state.nj.us/cgi-bin/governor/njnewsline/view_article.pl?id=723

61. William Goldman, *Hype and Glory* (New York: Villard, 1990), 208; and "Luck Be an Old Lady," season 5, episode 3, of "Sex in the City."

62. Michael Thompson-Noel, "A Wintry Fleece in Atlantic City," *Financial Times*, December 9, 2000; *Aruki Kata Guide Book, America and Florida, 1995–1996* (Tokyo: Diamond, 1994), 194 (thanks to Ichiro Miyata for translating this for me); and Olya Thompson, "Atlantic City Leaders Insist the Game's the Thing," *Newsday*, February 1, 1998. On the perception of Atlantic City as crime ridden, see also Ben Mezrich, *Bringing Down the House: The Inside Story of Six M.I.T. Students Who Took Vegas for Millions* (New York: Free Press, 2002), 21.

63. Quoted in Bill Kent, "The Bus Stops Here: Where Do You Have to Go to Get the Story on Gambling," *New York Times*, January 18, 1998.

64. On the idea of Las Vegas as the "new Detroit," see Rothman, *Neon Metropolis*, 63–88.

65. On suburban growth, see Patrick Jenkins, "The Second Wave," *Newark Star-Ledger*, January 30, 2000; Donald Janson, "Casinos Transform AC's Suburbs," *New York Times*, July 11, 1986; Bill Moyers, "Big Gamble in Atlantic City," CBS News Special Report, July 28, 1986, Heston Room, ACFPL; David Vis, "Growth—Atlantic City Explodes and Even More Is on the Way," *Atlantic City Press*, August 22, 1988; and Ted G.

Goertzel and John W. Cosby, "Gambling on Jobs and Welfare in Atlantic City," *Society* 34 (May–June 1997): 62–66.

66. On current movies, see *Atlantic City Press*, August 27, 2000. On plans to build a theater in Atlantic City, see "Cinemas on the Boardwalk? Don't Hold Your Breath," *Variety*, August 9–15, 1989; and W. F. Keough, "Atlantic City Zoning Board Approves Boardwalk Movie Theaters," *Atlantic City Press*, August 13, 1993.

67. For a critique of this form of growth, see Jane Holtz Kay, "Tales of the City," *Nation* 267 (July 6, 1998): 135–38; Marc V. Levine, "Downtown Development as an Urban Growth Strategy: A Critical Appraisal of the Baltimore Renaissance," *Journal of Urban Affairs* 9 (1987): 103–23; M. Christine Boyer, "Cities for Sale: Merchandising History at South Street Seaport," in Sorkin, ed., *Variations on a Theme Park*, 129–48.

EPILOGUE (pages 217–222)

1. Springsteen, "Atlantic City," *Nebraska* (Columbia, 1982). These are my recollections of the concert that night in Atlantic City.

2. Sono Motoyama, "Gambling on a New Atlantic City," *Philadelphia Daily News*, May 23, 2003.

3. Quote from "4 Dead in N.J. Parking Garage Collapse," cnn.com, October 30, 2003, available: www.cnn.com/2003/US/Northeast/10/30/garage.collapse/index.html. As this headline indicates, this project was marred by tragedy. See also Joe Weinert, "Tropicana Project to Open in September," *Atlantic City Press*, February 12, 2004.

4. Laura Mansnerus, "Great Expectations: Money Has Poured into Atlantic City, but a Second Wave, Ever Poised, Still Hasn't Broken," *New York Times*, April 2, 2000.

5. Quoted in Motoyama, "Gambling on a New Atlantic City."

6. Joe Weinert, "Expand Casino Hotel Room Fund, CEO Urges," *Atlantic City Press*, April 26, 2000.

7. See the Borgata's home page, available: www.theborgata.com.

8. Motoyama, "Gambling on a New Atlantic City"; and Catherine Slessor, "View from Atlantic City," *Architectural Review* 212 (August 2002): 26–27.

9. Weinert, "Expand Casino Hotel Room Fund, CEO Urges."

10. See the casino's home page, available: www.theborgata.com.

11. Ibid.

12. On the name and some early planning, see Patrick Jenkins, "Boyd Planning to Bring a Little Italy to Atlantic City," *Newark Star-Ledger*, January 14, 1999.

13. See CRDA's "3-2-1 Program," available: www.njcrda.com/loans-police.html

14. E-mail from Reese Palley to author, February 7, 2003.

INDEX

Italicized page numbers refer to illustrations.